Pastel

10

TOSHIHIKO KOBAYASHI

Translated and adapted by David Ury

Lettered by Foltz Design

D1316404

DEL
REY

BALLANTINE BOOKS • NEW YORK

A Del Rey Manga/Kodansha Trade Paperback Original

Pastel volume 10 copyright © 2005 by Toshihiko Kobayashi
English translation copyright © 2008 by Toshihiko Kobayashi

Published in the United States by Del Rey Books, an imprint of The Random House Publishing Group, a division of Random House, Inc., New York.

DEL REY is a registered trademark and the Del Rey colophon is a trademark of Random House, Inc.

Publication rights arranged through Kodansha Ltd.

First published in Japan in 2005 by Kodansha Ltd., Tokyo

ISBN 978-0-345-49878-6

Printed in the United States of America

www.delreymanga.com

1 2 3 4 5 6 7 8 9

Translator/Adapter—David Ury
Lettering—Foltz Design

CONTENTS

A Note from the Author	iv
Honorifics Explained	v
MIRACLE 62: **THE BEST CHEER EVER**	3
MIRACLE 63: **MANAMI'S LOVE STRATEGY**	51
MIRACLE 64: **OSAKA LOVE QUARREL**	95
MIRACLE 65: **NO ORDINARY DAY**	142
About the Author	190
Translation Notes	191
Preview of Volume 11	196

A Note from the Author

WHENEVER I GO ON A RESEARCH TRIP TO ONOMICHI, I ALWAYS SEE CATS. THIS LITTLE CAT WAS RUNNING AROUND THE TEMPLE GROUNDS. I RAN INTO HIM AGAIN AFTER CLIMBING THE LONG FLIGHT OF STEPS LEADING UP TO THE TEMPLE.

Honorifics Explained

Throughout the Del Rey Manga books, you will find Japanese honorifics left intact in the translations. For those not familiar with how the Japanese use honorifics and, more important, how they differ from American honorifics, we present this brief overview.

Politeness has always been a critical facet of Japanese culture. Ever since the feudal era, when Japan was a highly stratified society, use of honorifics—which can be defined as polite speech that indicates relationship or status—has played an essential role in the Japanese language. When addressing someone in Japanese, an honorific usually takes the form of a suffix attached to one's name (example: "Asuna-san"), is used as a title at the end of one's name, or appears in place of the name itself (example: "Negi-sensei," or simply "Sensei!").

Honorifics can be expressions of respect or endearment. In the context of manga and anime, honorifics give insight into the nature of the relationship between characters. Many English translations leave out these important honorifics and therefore distort the feel of the original Japanese. Because Japanese honorifics contain nuances that English honorifics lack, it is our policy at Del Rey not to translate them. Here, instead, is a guide to some of the honorifics you may encounter in Del Rey Manga.

-san: This is the most common honorific and is equivalent to Mr., Miss, Ms., or Mrs. It is the all-purpose honorific and can be used in any situation where politeness is required.

-sama: This is one level higher than "-san" and is used to confer great respect.

-dono: This comes from the word "tono," which means "lord." It is an even higher level than "-sama" and confers utmost respect.

-kun: This suffix is used at the end of boys' names to express familiarity or endearment. It is also sometimes used by men among friends, or when addressing someone younger or of a lower station.

-chan: This is used to express endearment, mostly toward girls. It is also used for little boys, pets, and even among lovers. It gives a sense of childish cuteness.

Bozu: This is an informal way to refer to a boy, similar to the English terms "kid" and "squirt."

Sempai/

Senpai: This title suggests that the addressee is one's senior in a group or organization. It is most often used in a school setting, where underclassmen refer to their upperclassmen as "sempai." It can also be used in the workplace, such as when a newer employee addresses an employee who has seniority in the company.

Kohai: This is the opposite of "sempai" and is used toward underclassmen in school or newcomers in the workplace. It connotes that the addressee is of a lower station.

Sensei: Literally meaning "one who has come before," this title is used for teachers, doctors, or masters of any profession or art.

-[blank]: This is usually forgotten in these lists, but it is perhaps the most significant difference between Japanese and English. The lack of honorific means that the speaker has permission to address the person in a very intimate way. Usually, only family, spouses, or very close friends have this kind of permission. Known as *yobisute*, it can be gratifying when someone who has earned the intimacy starts to call one by one's name without an honorific. But when that intimacy hasn't been earned, it can be very insulting.

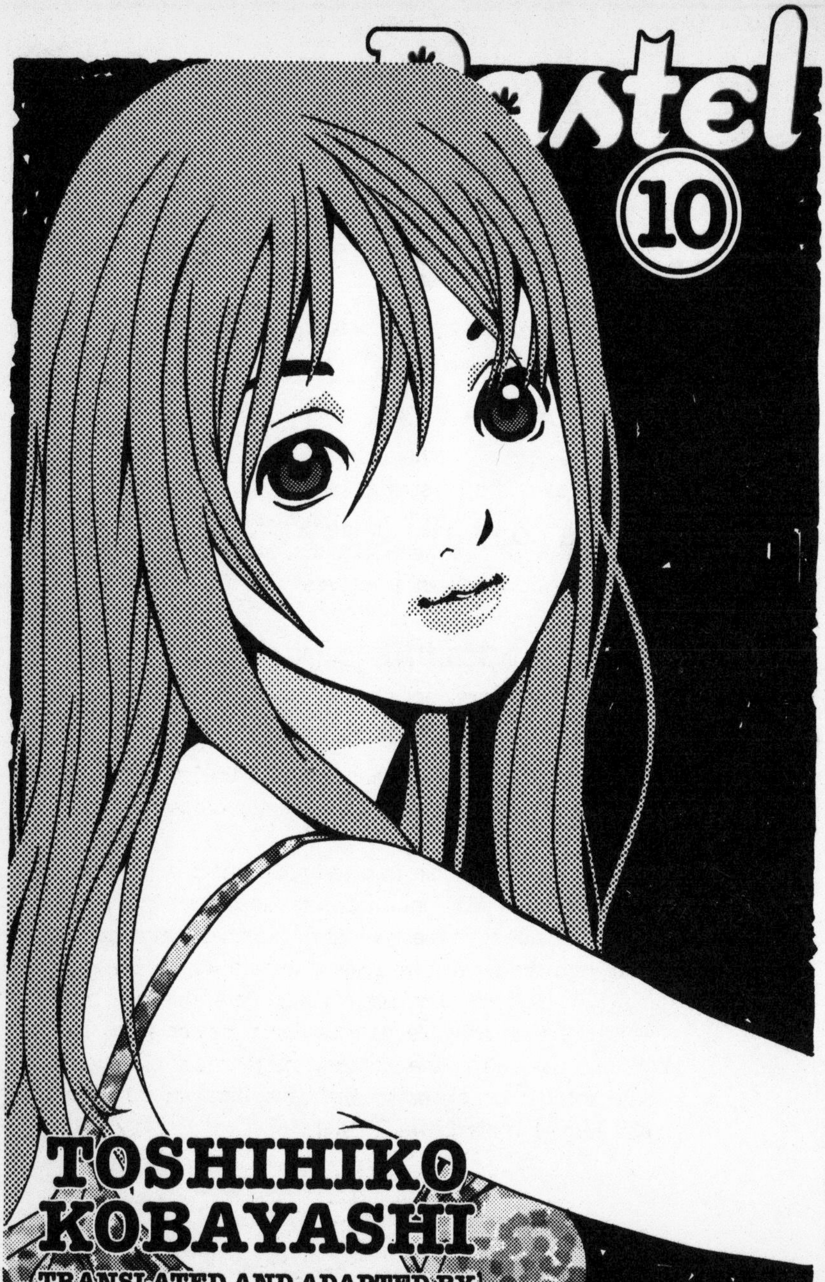
Pastel
10
TOSHIHIKO KOBAYASHI
TRANSLATED AND ADAPTED BY
DAVID URY

LETTERED BY FOLTZ DESIGN

CONTENTS

MIRACLE 62:
 THE BEST CHEER EVER   3

MIRACLE 63:
 MANAMI'S LOVE STRATEGY   51

MIRACLE 64:
 OSAKA LOVE QUARREL   95

MIRACLE 65:
 NO ORDINARY DAY   142

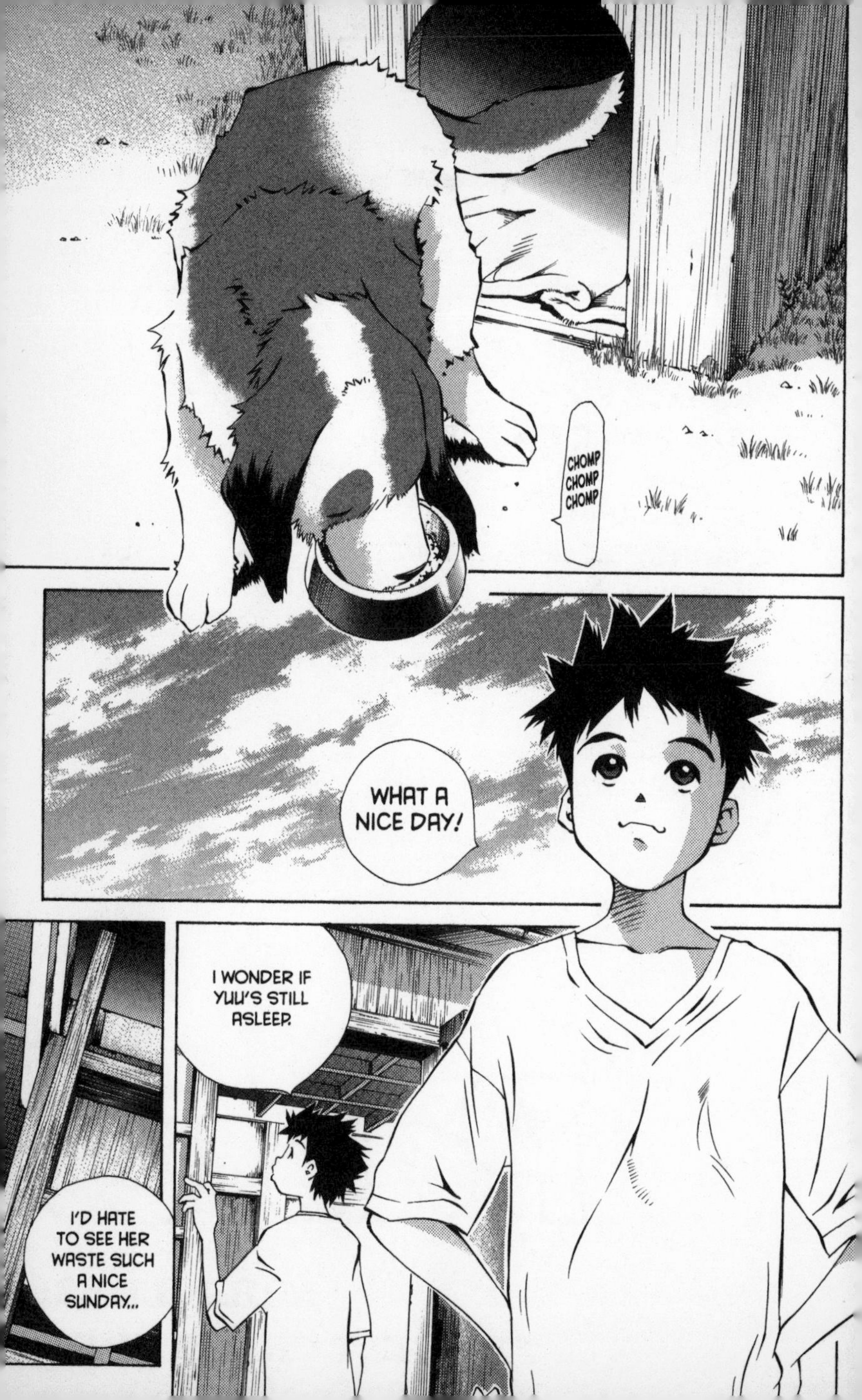
CHOMP CHOMP CHOMP
WHAT A NICE DAY!
I WONDER IF YUU'S STILL ASLEEP.
I'D HATE TO SEE HER WASTE SUCH A NICE SUNDAY...

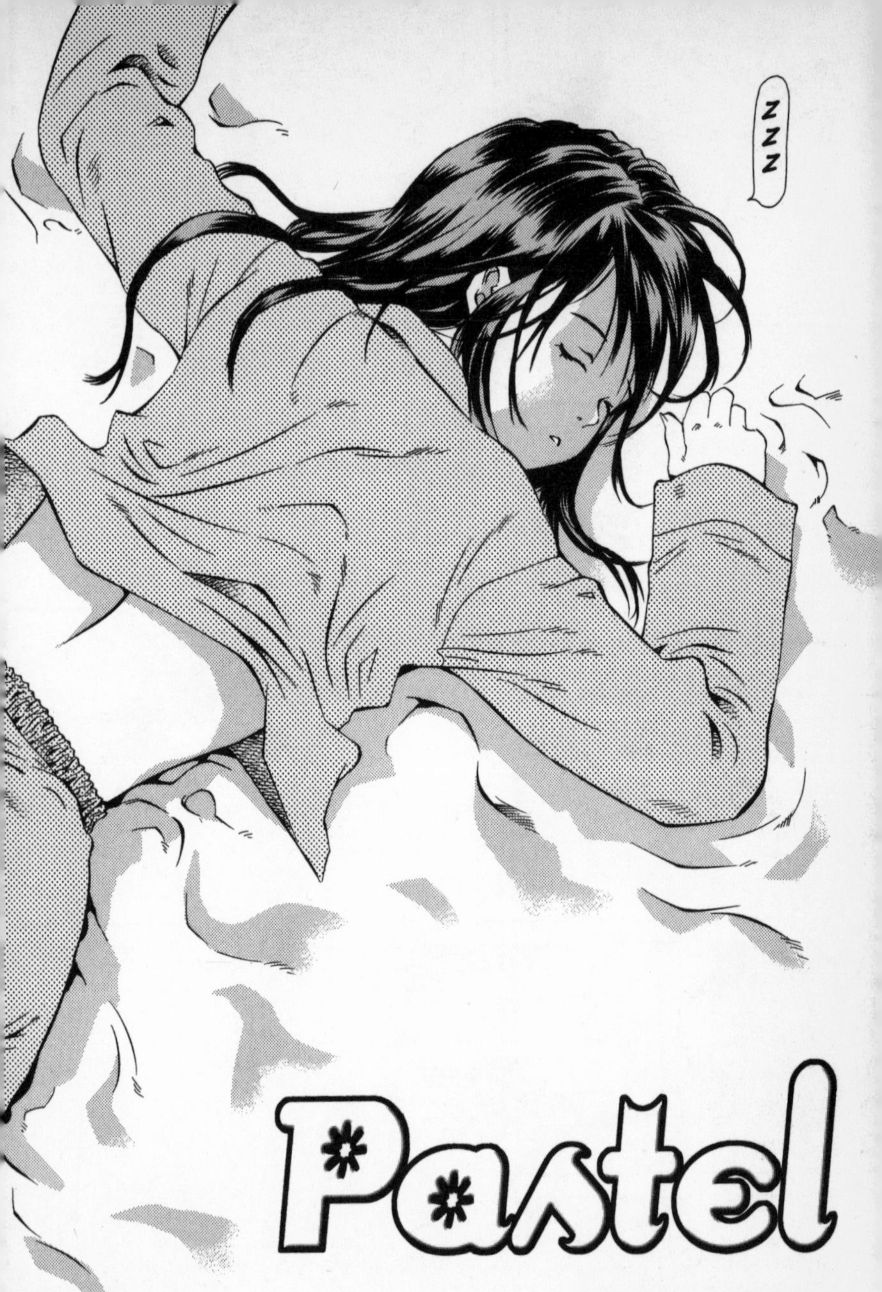
ZZZ
Pastel

MIRACLE 62: THE BEST CHEER EVER

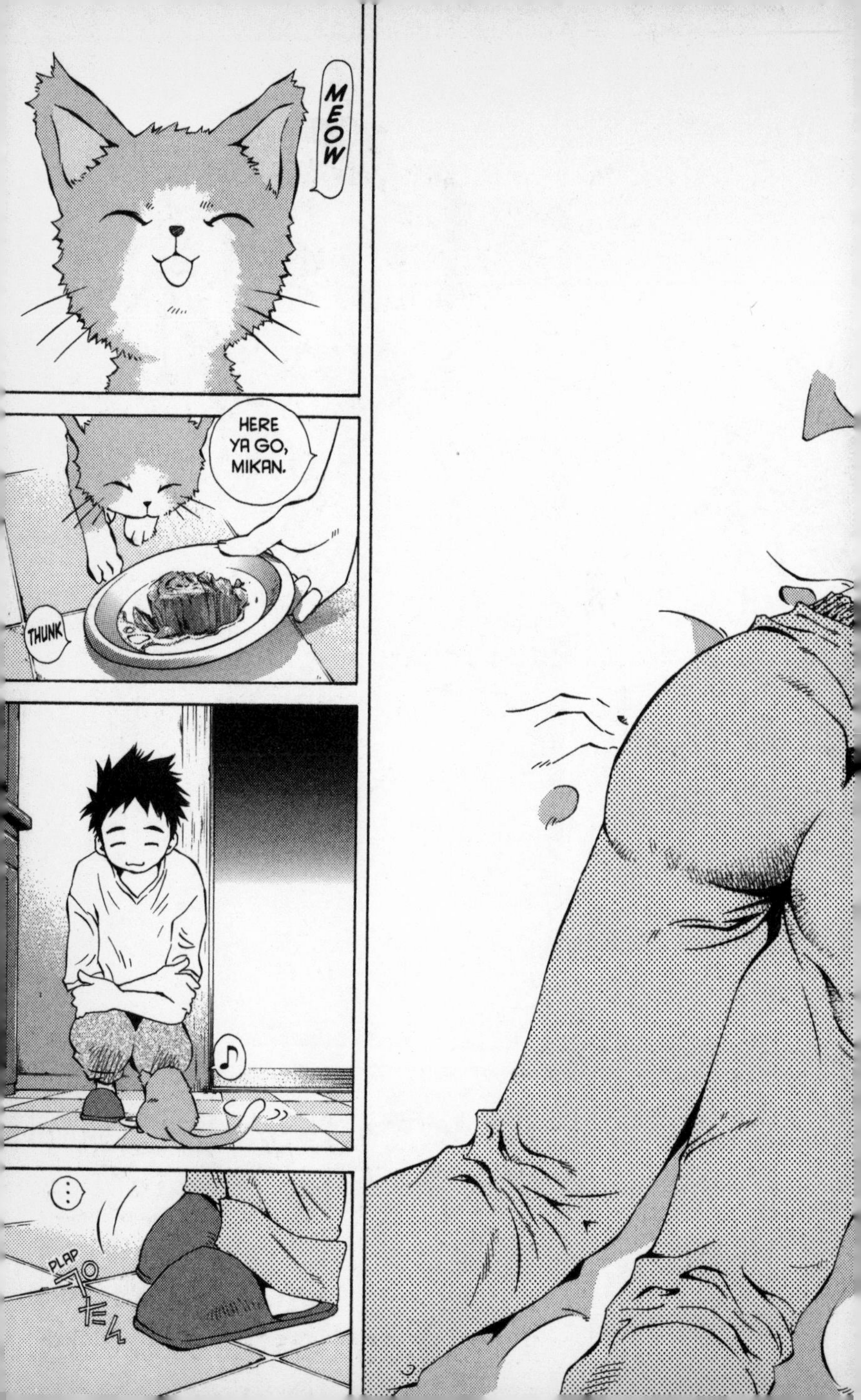
MEOW
HERE YA GO, MIKAN.
THUNK
♪
...
PLAP

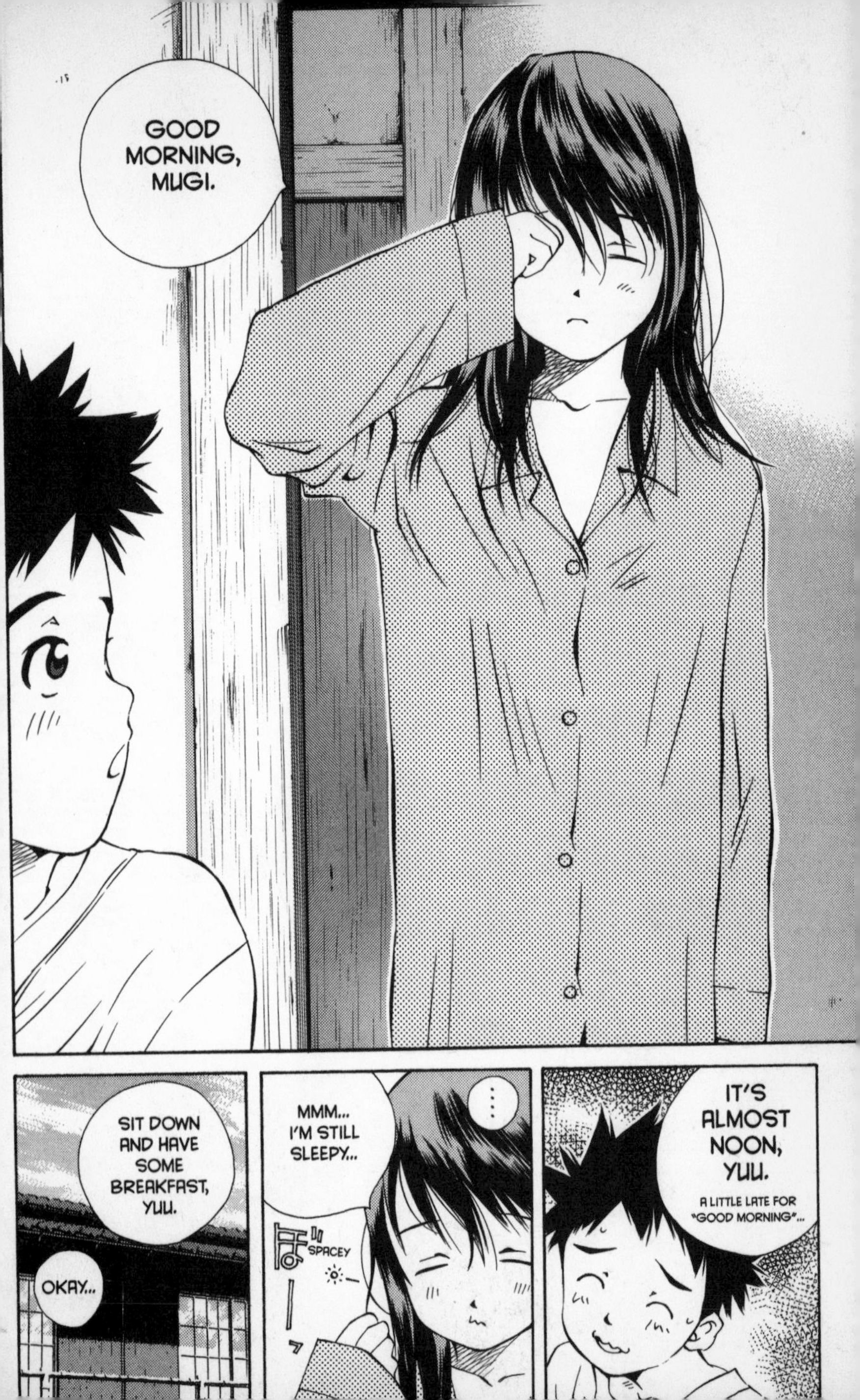
GOOD MORNING, MUGI.
IT'S ALMOST NOON, YUU.
A LITTLE LATE FOR "GOOD MORNING"...
....
MMM... I'M STILL SLEEPY...
SPACEY
SIT DOWN AND HAVE SOME BREAKFAST, YUU.
OKAY...

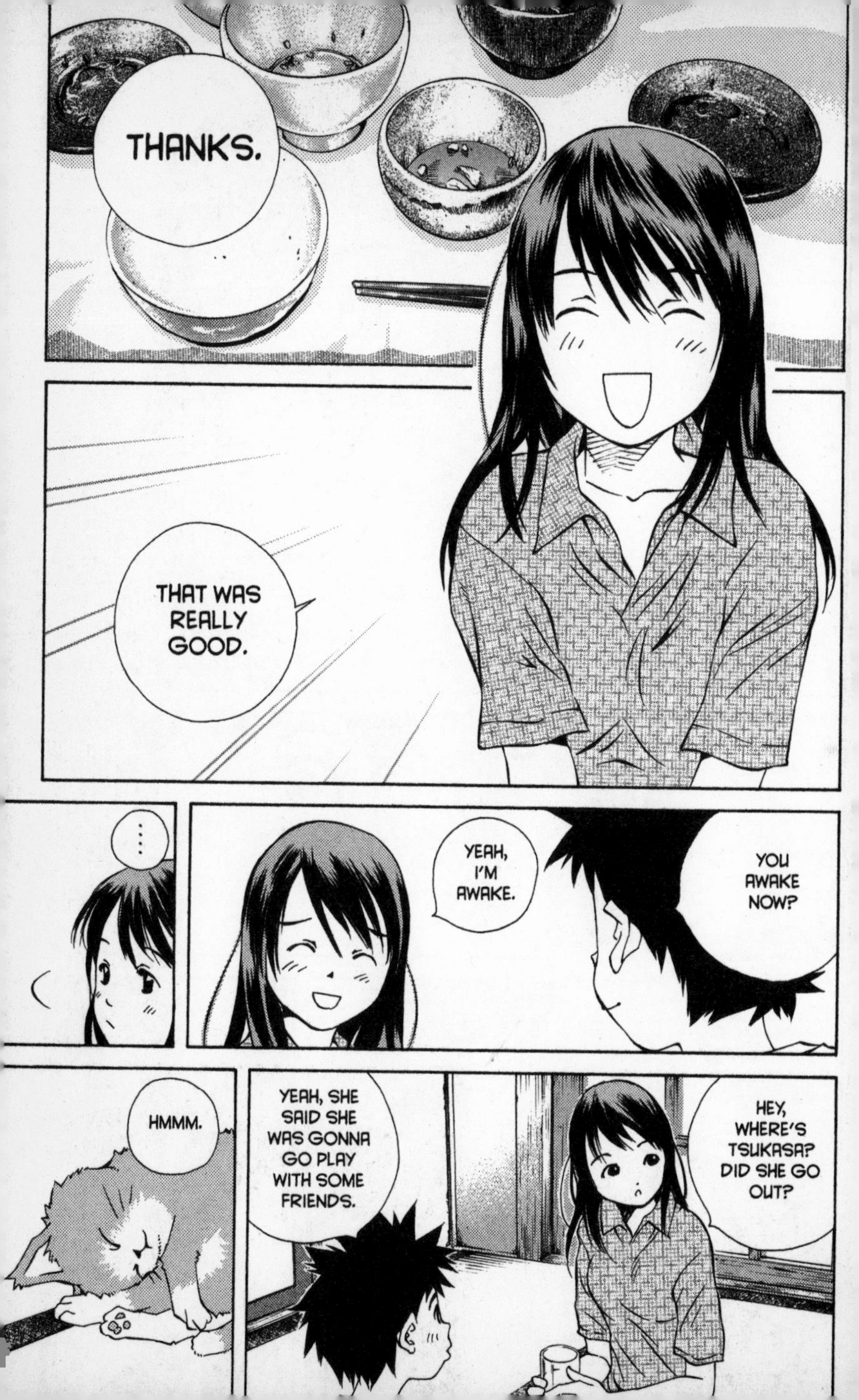
THANKS.
THAT WAS REALLY GOOD.
YOU AWAKE NOW?
YEAH, I'M AWAKE.
....
HEY, WHERE'S TSUKASA? DID SHE GO OUT?
YEAH, SHE SAID SHE WAS GONNA GO PLAY WITH SOME FRIENDS.
HMMM.

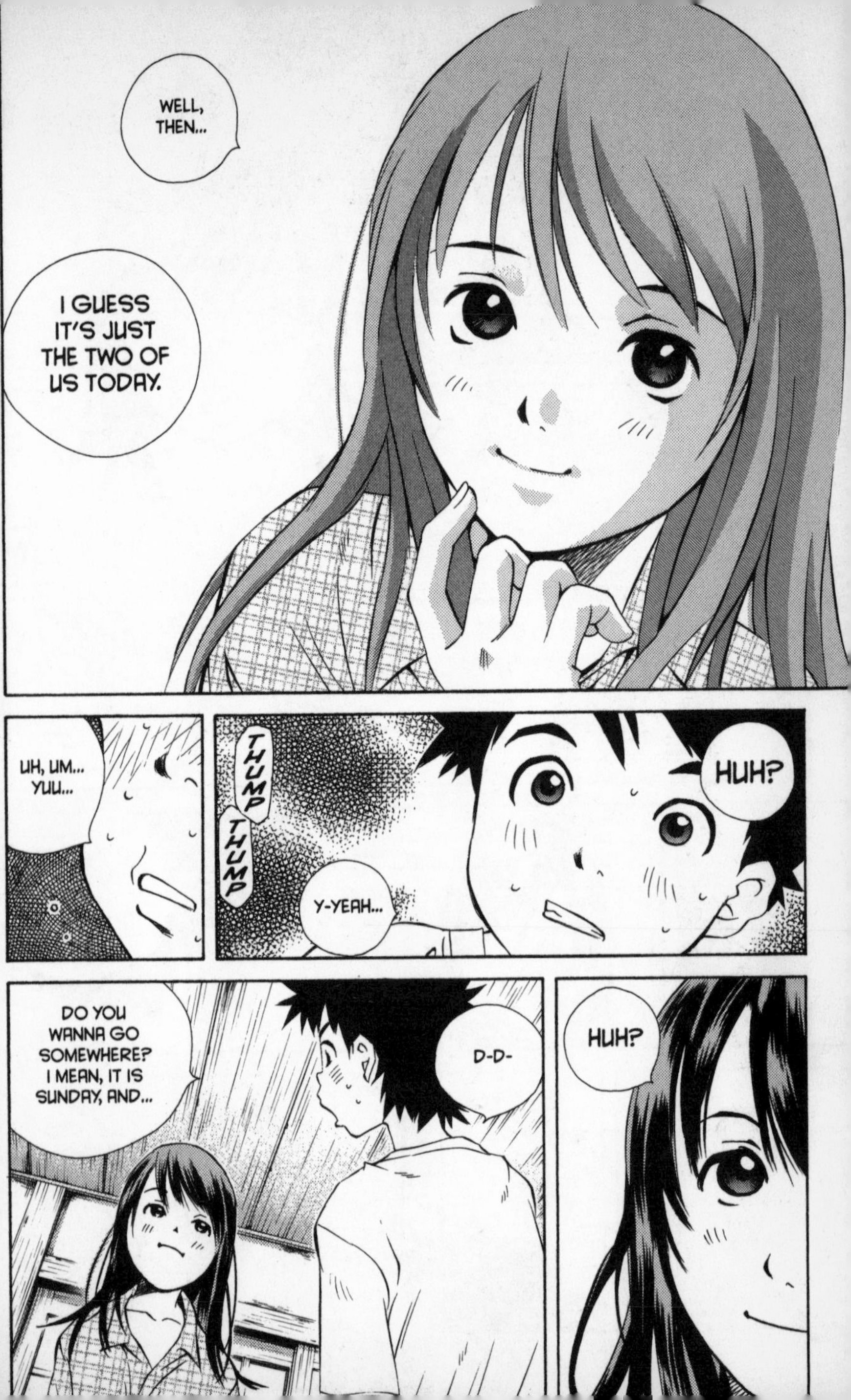
WELL, THEN...
I GUESS IT'S JUST THE TWO OF US TODAY.
HUH?
THUMP THUMP
Y-YEAH...
UH, UM... YUU...
HUH?
D-D-
DO YOU WANNA GO SOMEWHERE? I MEAN, IT IS SUNDAY, AND...

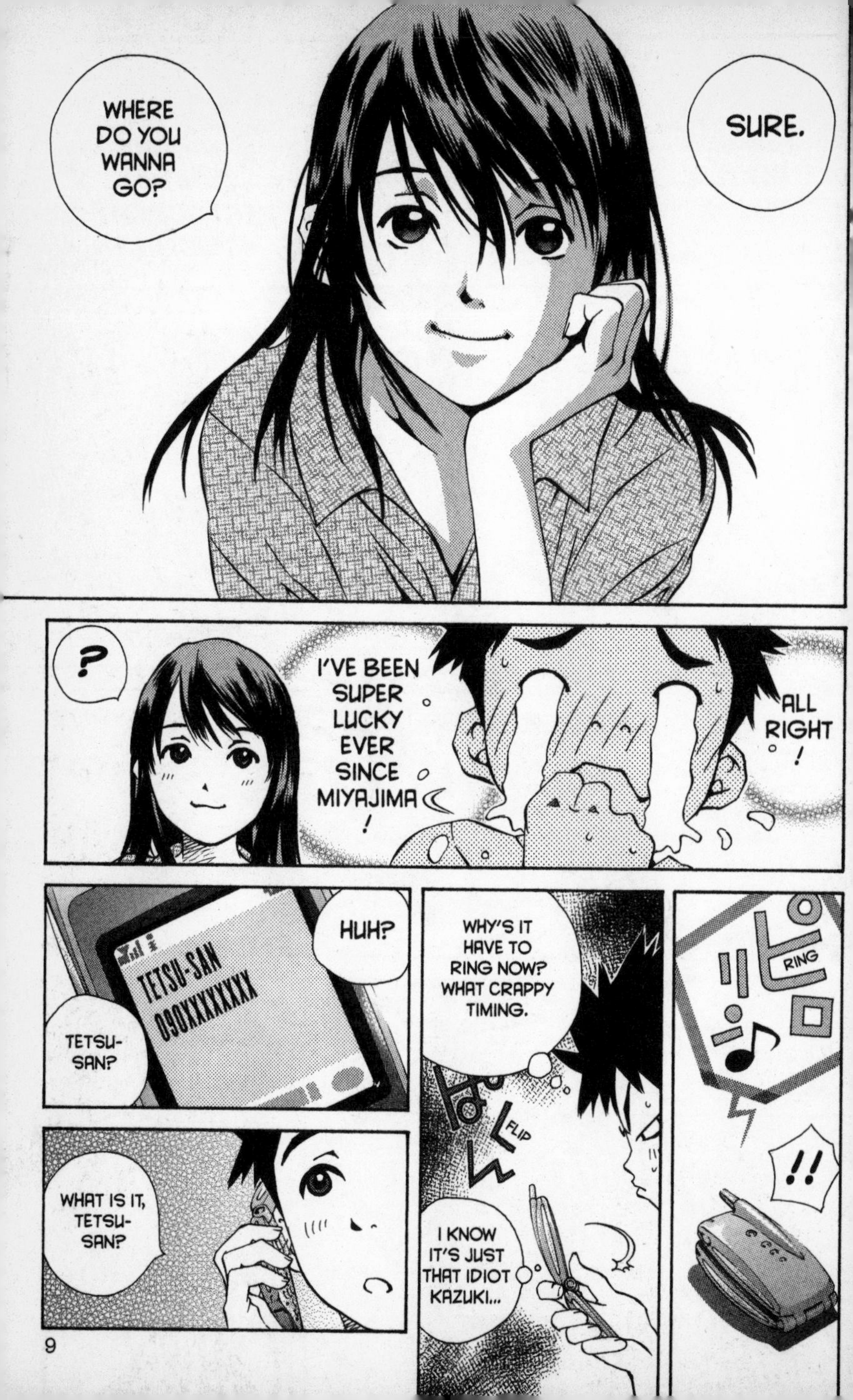
SURE.
WHERE DO YOU WANNA GO?
ALL RIGHT!
I'VE BEEN SUPER LUCKY EVER SINCE MIYAJIMA!
?
RING
!!
WHY'S IT HAVE TO RING NOW? WHAT CRAPPY TIMING.
FLIP
I KNOW IT'S JUST THAT IDIOT KAZUKI...
TETSU-SAN
090XXXXXXX
HUH?
TETSU-SAN?
WHAT IS IT, TETSU-SAN?

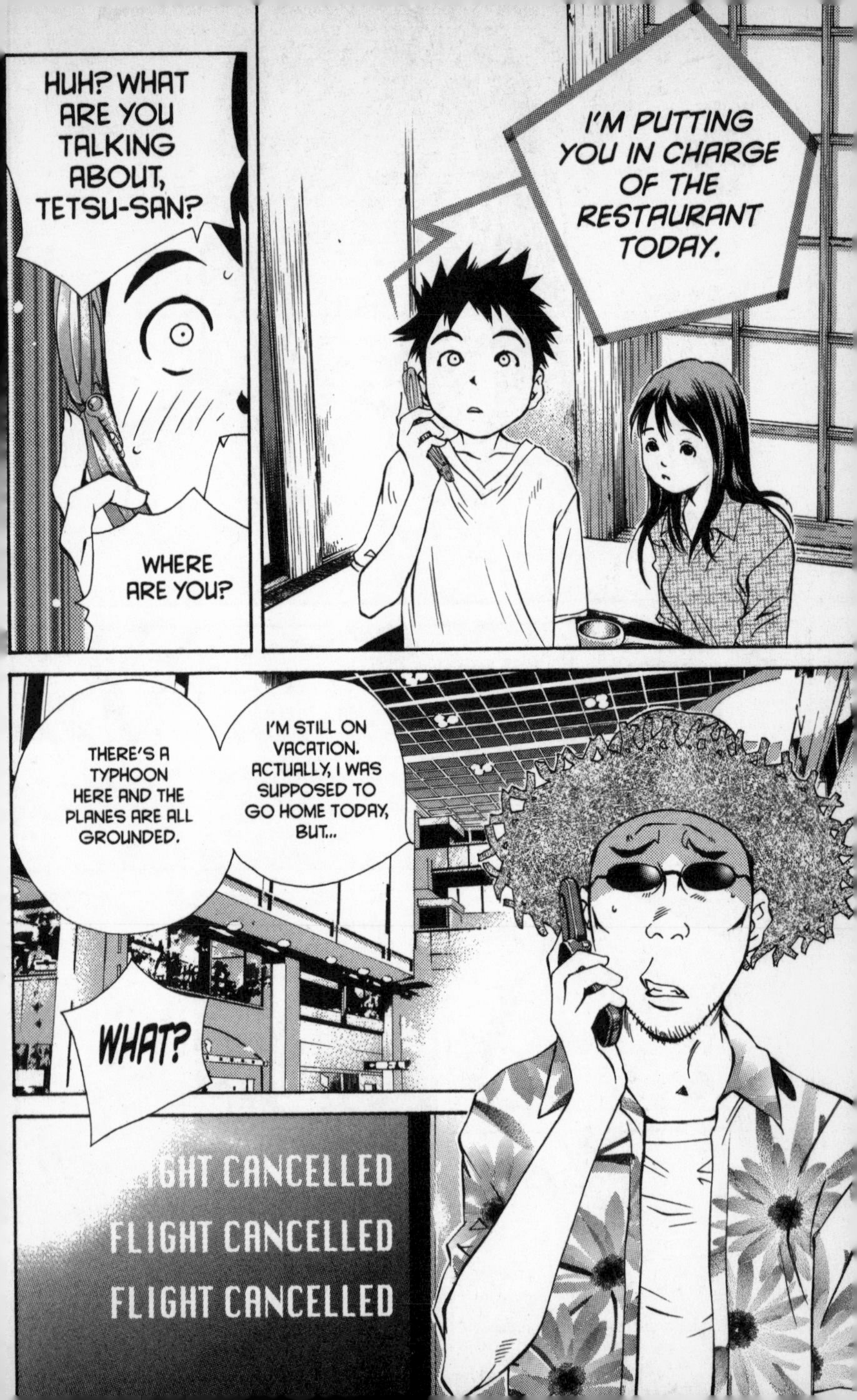
I'M PUTTING YOU IN CHARGE OF THE RESTAURANT TODAY.
HUH? WHAT ARE YOU TALKING ABOUT, TETSU-SAN?
WHERE ARE YOU?
I'M STILL ON VACATION. ACTUALLY, I WAS SUPPOSED TO GO HOME TODAY, BUT...
THERE'S A TYPHOON HERE AND THE PLANES ARE ALL GROUNDED.
WHAT?
GHT CANCELLED
FLIGHT CANCELLED
FLIGHT CANCELLED

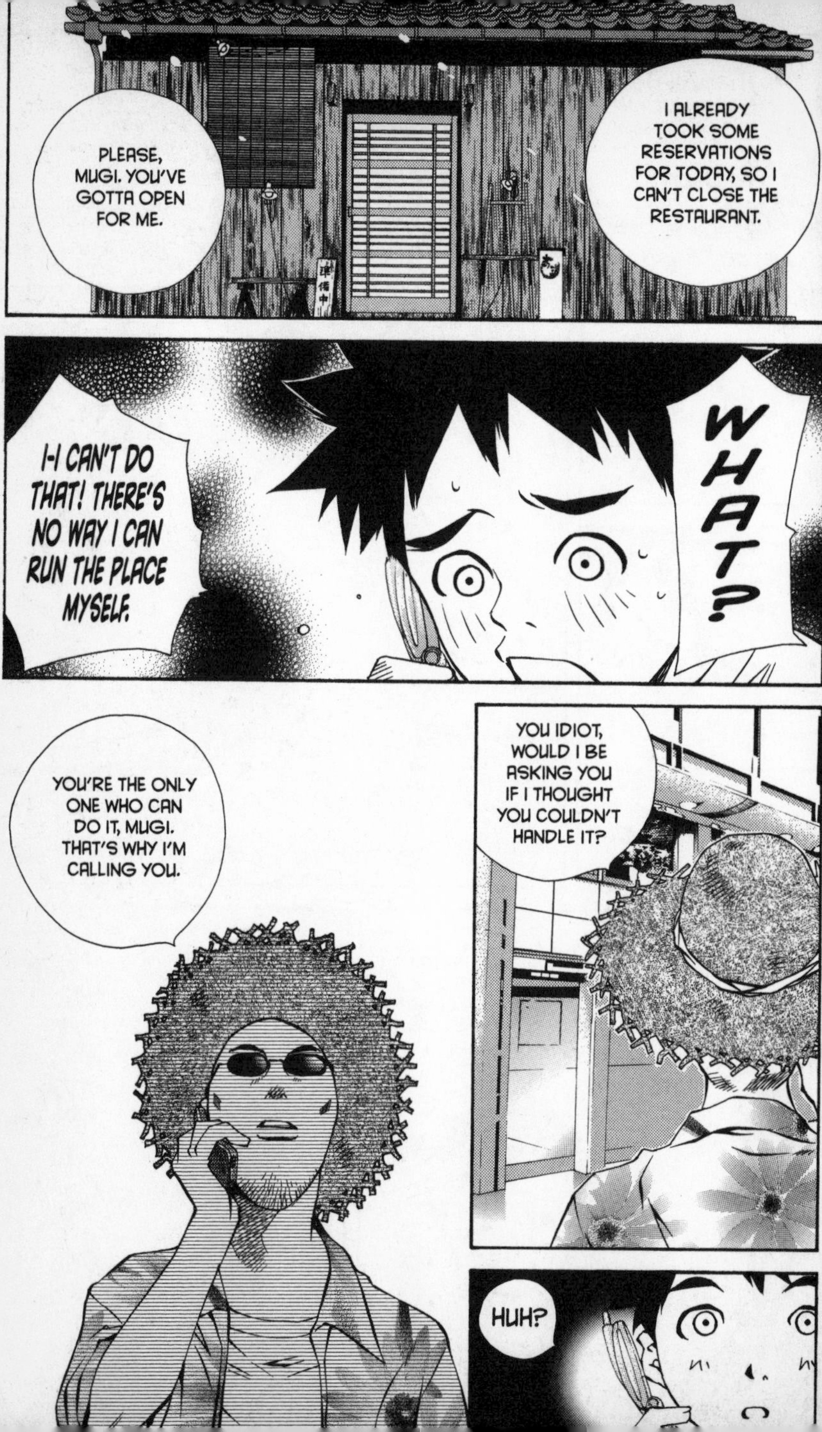
I ALREADY TOOK SOME RESERVATIONS FOR TODAY, SO I CAN'T CLOSE THE RESTAURANT.
PLEASE, MUGI. YOU'VE GOTTA OPEN FOR ME.
WHAT?
I-I CAN'T DO THAT! THERE'S NO WAY I CAN RUN THE PLACE MYSELF.
YOU IDIOT, WOULD I BE ASKING YOU IF I THOUGHT YOU COULDN'T HANDLE IT?
HUH?
YOU'RE THE ONLY ONE WHO CAN DO IT, MUGI. THAT'S WHY I'M CALLING YOU.

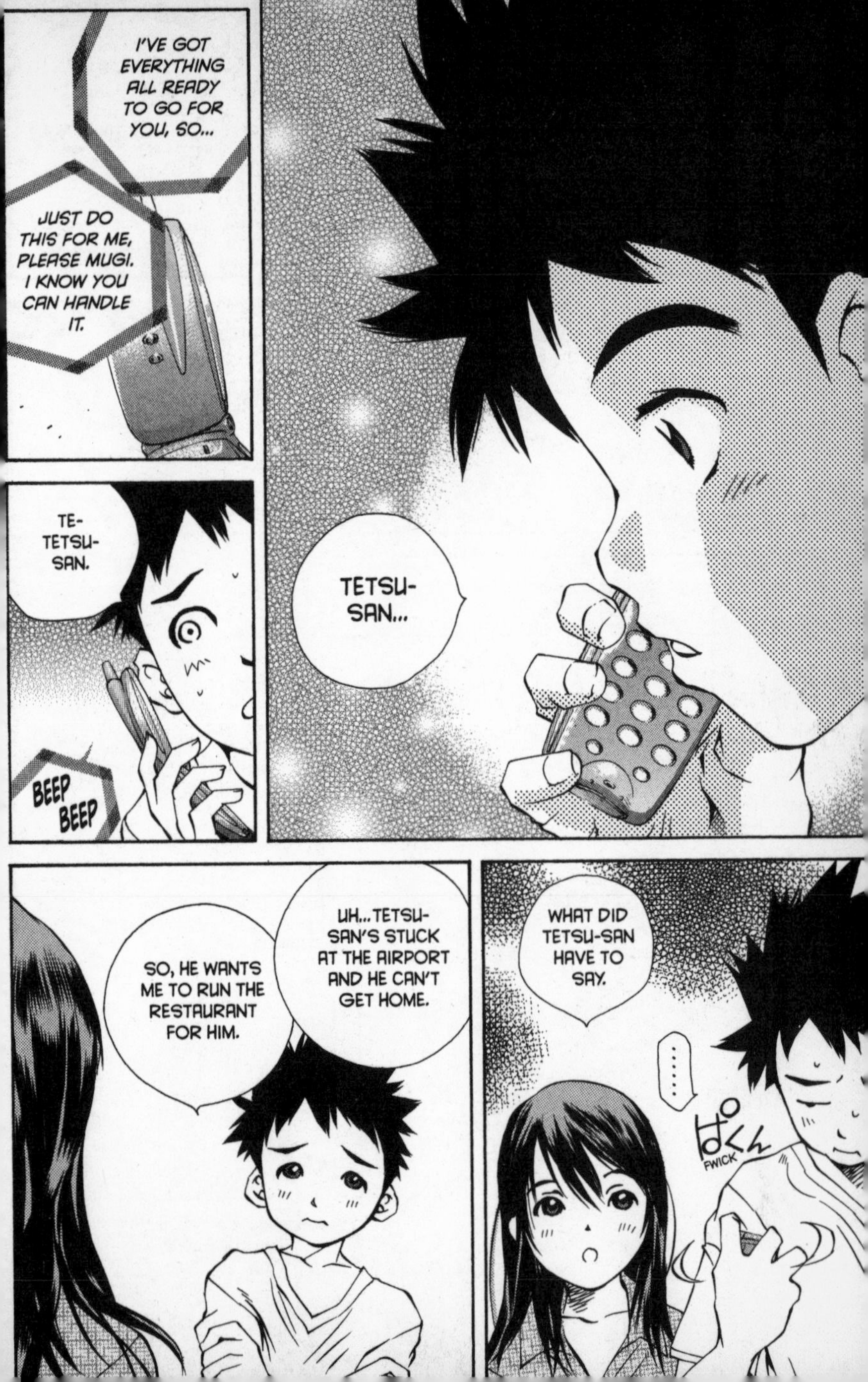
TETSU-SAN...
I'VE GOT EVERYTHING ALL READY TO GO FOR YOU, SO...
JUST DO THIS FOR ME, PLEASE MUGI. I KNOW YOU CAN HANDLE IT.
TE-TETSU-SAN.
BEEP BEEP
WHAT DID TETSU-SAN HAVE TO SAY.
......
FWICK
UH...TETSU-SAN'S STUCK AT THE AIRPORT AND HE CAN'T GET HOME.
SO, HE WANTS ME TO RUN THE RESTAURANT FOR HIM.

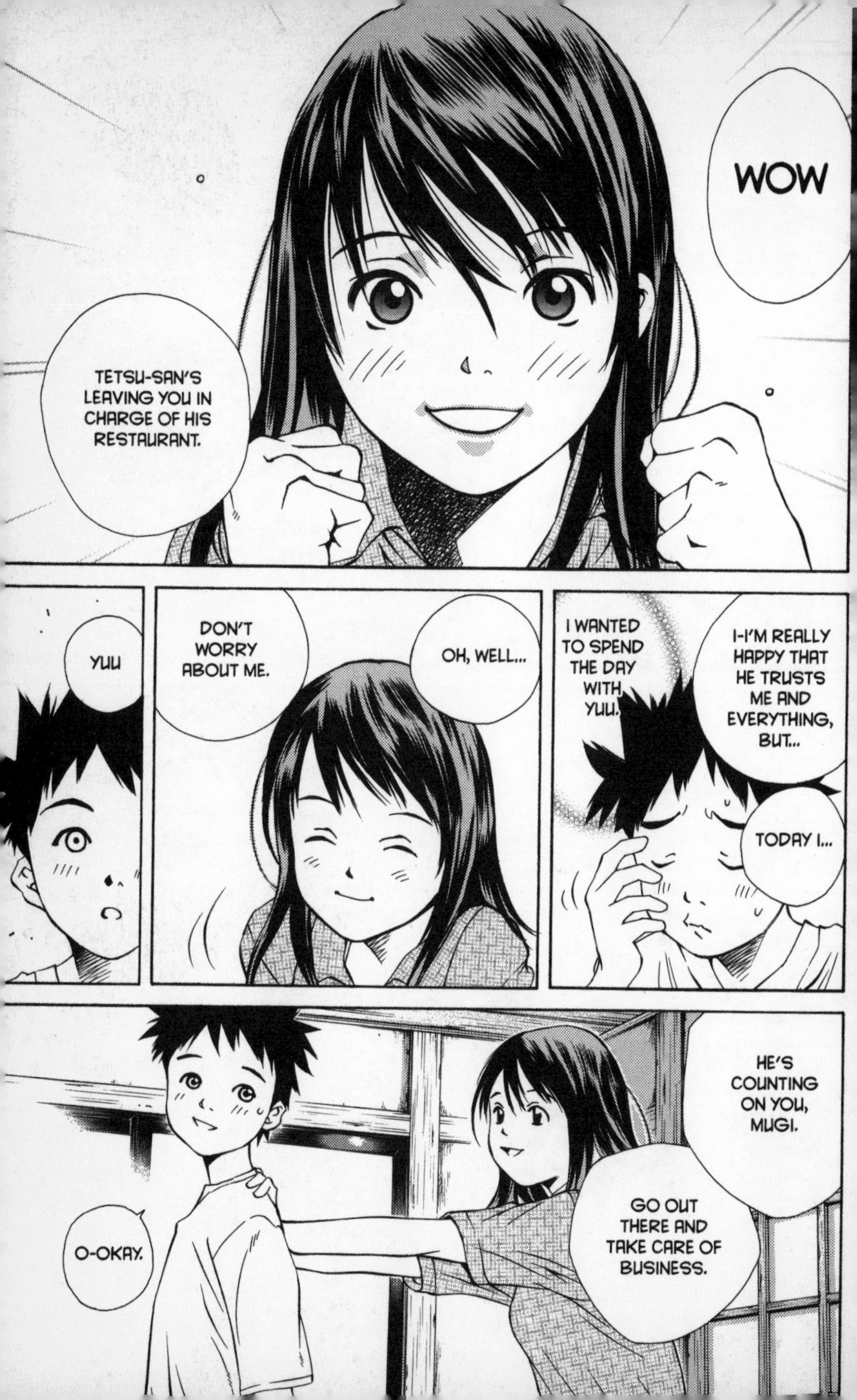
WOW
TETSU-SAN'S LEAVING YOU IN CHARGE OF HIS RESTAURANT.
I-I'M REALLY HAPPY THAT HE TRUSTS ME AND EVERYTHING, BUT...
TODAY I...
I WANTED TO SPEND THE DAY WITH YUU.
OH, WELL...
DON'T WORRY ABOUT ME.
YUU
HE'S COUNTING ON YOU, MUGI.
GO OUT THERE AND TAKE CARE OF BUSINESS.
O-OKAY.

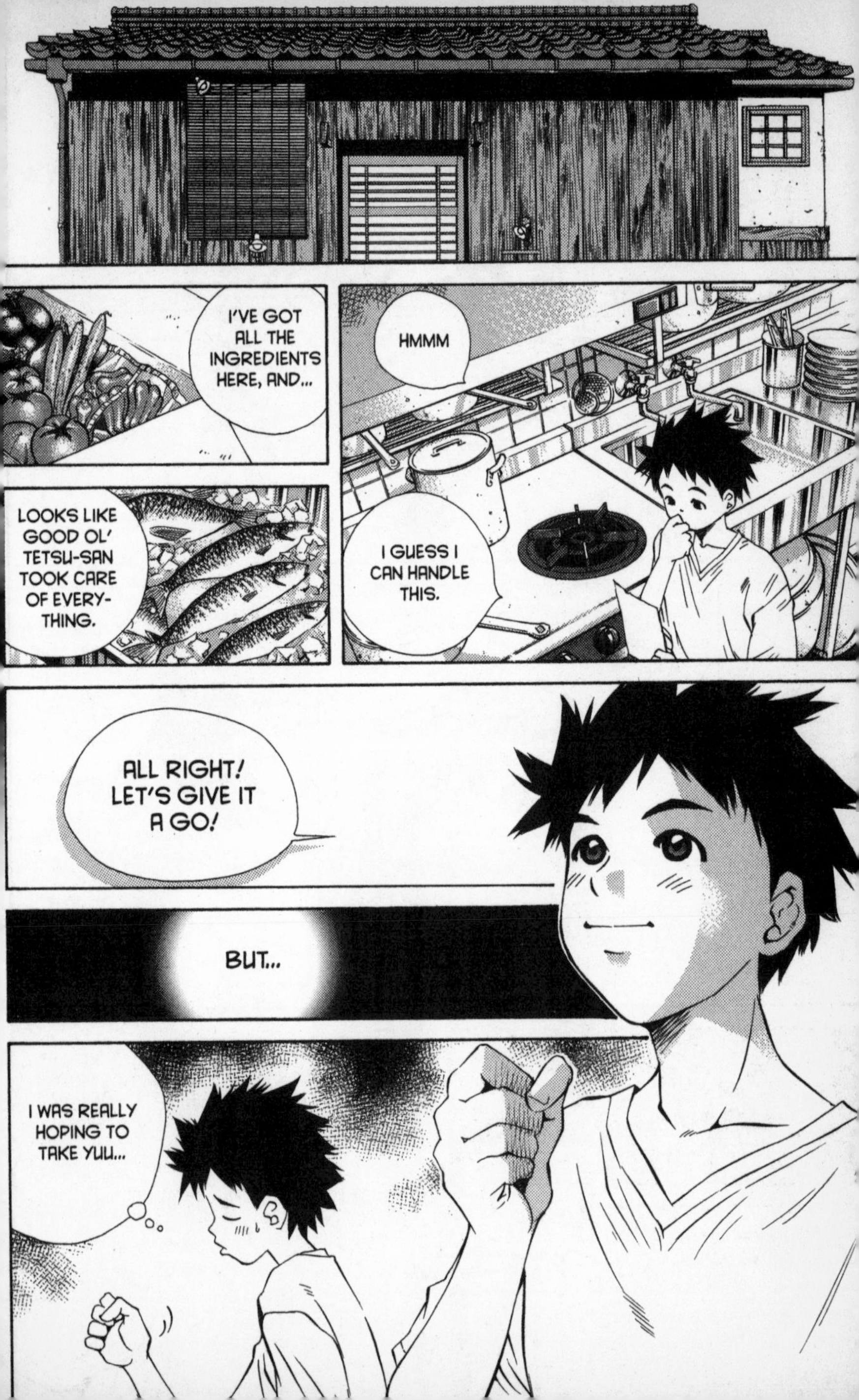
HMMM
I GUESS I CAN HANDLE THIS.
I'VE GOT ALL THE INGREDIENTS HERE, AND...
LOOKS LIKE GOOD OL' TETSU-SAN TOOK CARE OF EVERY-THING.
ALL RIGHT! LET'S GIVE IT A GO!
BUT...
I WAS REALLY HOPING TO TAKE YUU...

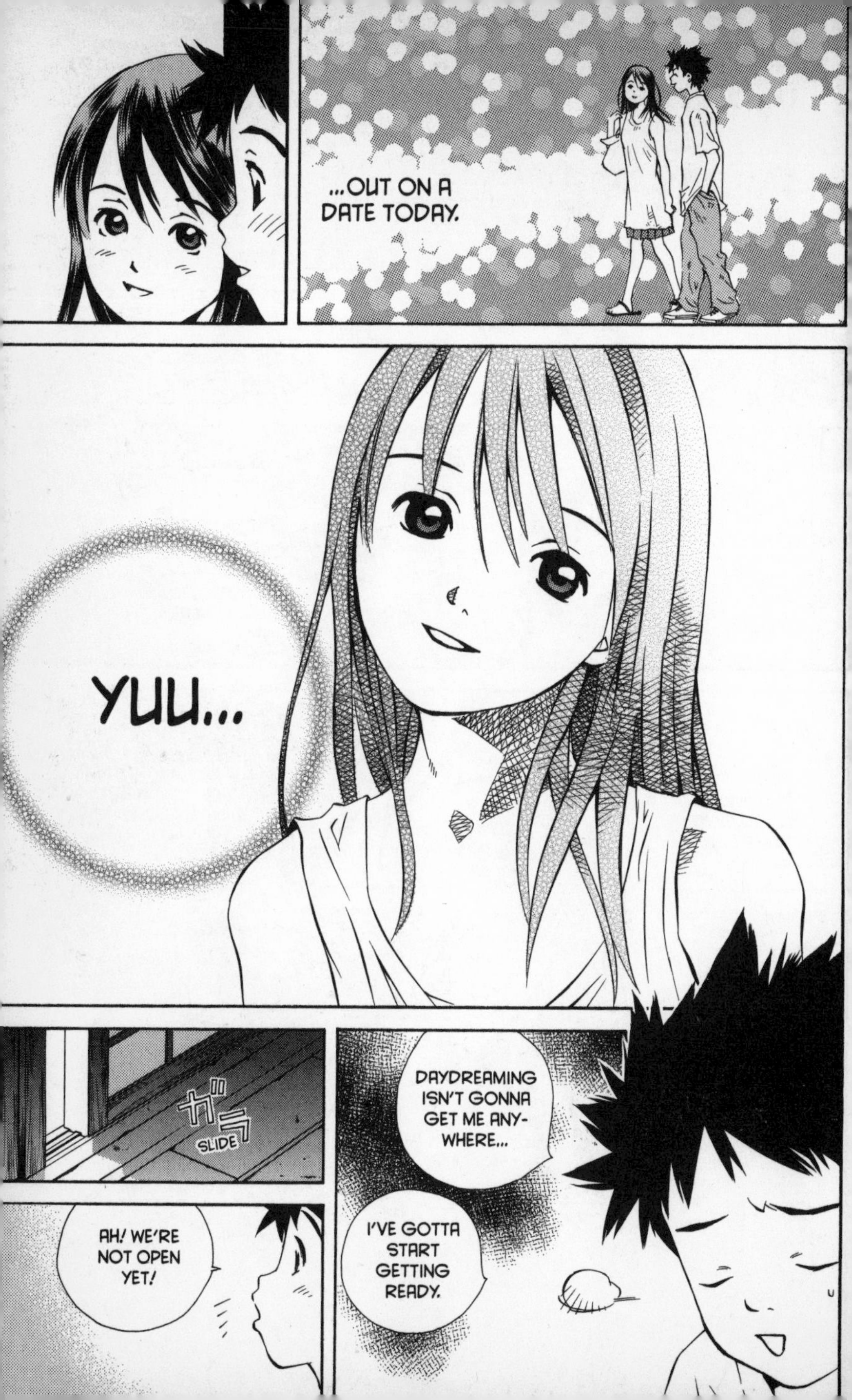
...OUT ON A DATE TODAY.
YUU...
DAYDREAMING ISN'T GONNA GET ME ANY-WHERE...
I'VE GOTTA START GETTING READY.
ガラ
SLIDE
AH! WE'RE NOT OPEN YET!

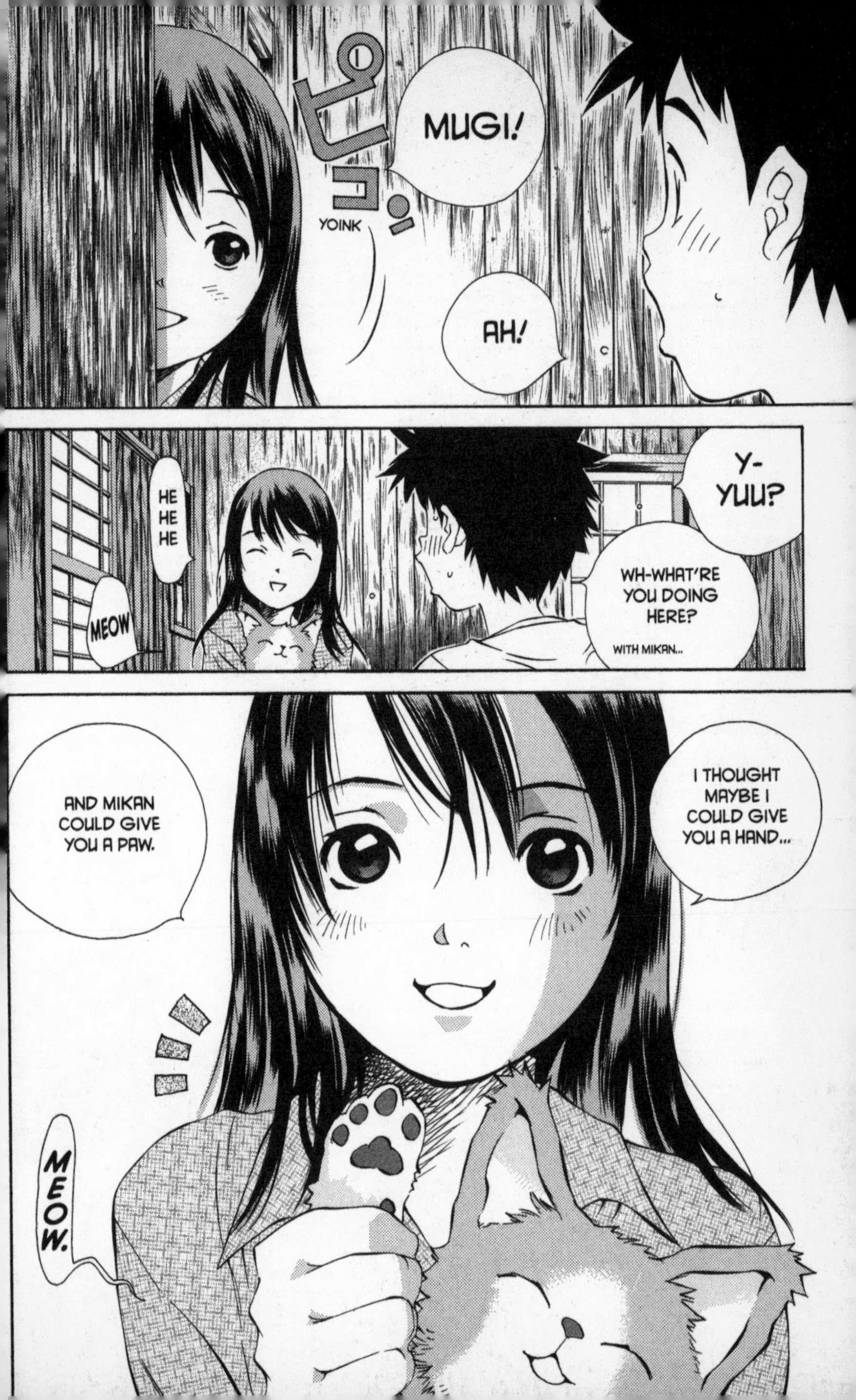
MUGI!
YOINK
AH!
Y-YUU?
WH-WHAT'RE YOU DOING HERE?
WITH MIKAN...
HE HE HE
MEOW
I THOUGHT MAYBE I COULD GIVE YOU A HAND...
AND MIKAN COULD GIVE YOU A PAW.
MEOW.

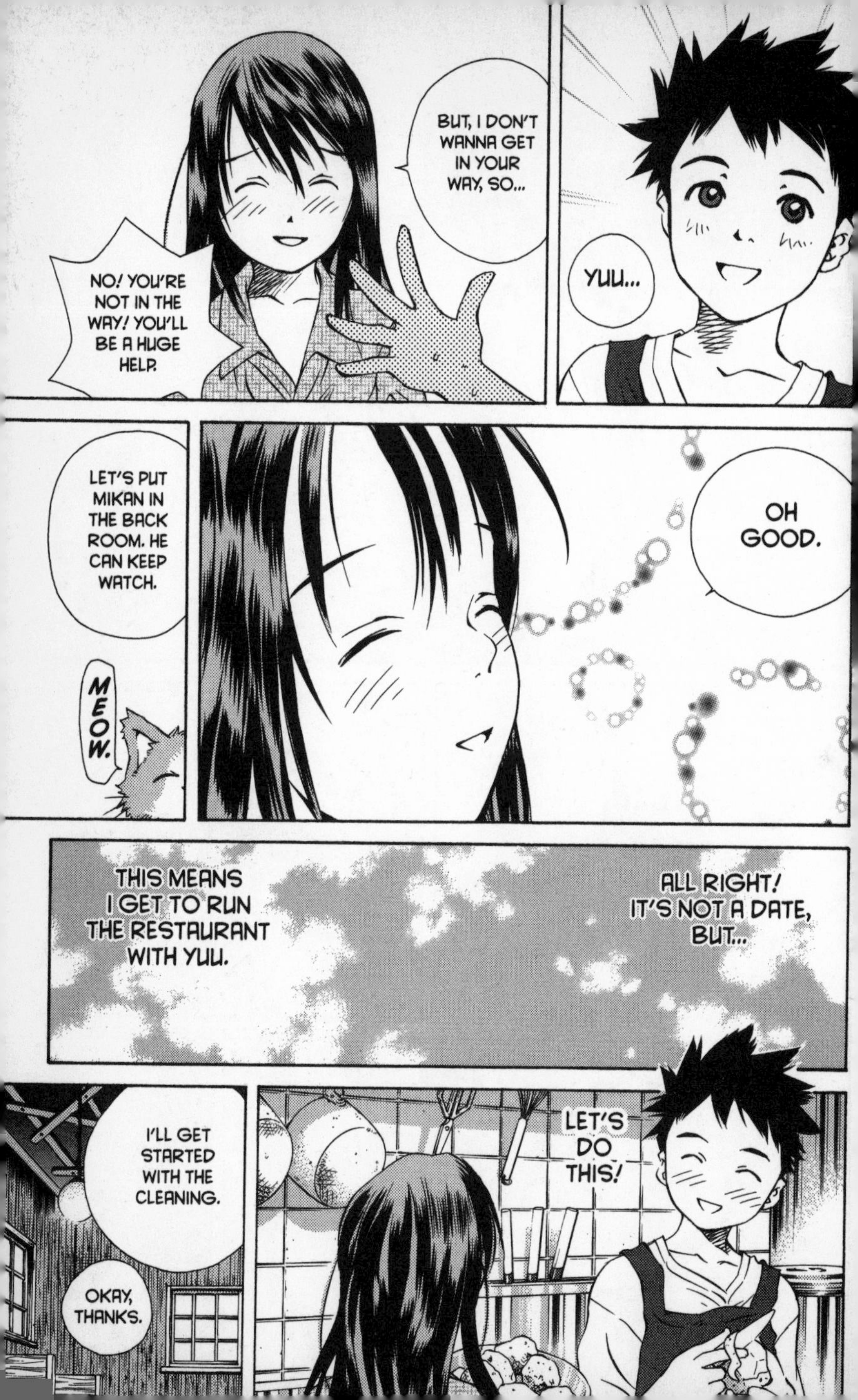
YUU...
BUT, I DON'T WANNA GET IN YOUR WAY, SO...
NO! YOU'RE NOT IN THE WAY! YOU'LL BE A HUGE HELP.
OH GOOD.
LET'S PUT MIKAN IN THE BACK ROOM. HE CAN KEEP WATCH.
MEOW.
ALL RIGHT! IT'S NOT A DATE, BUT...
THIS MEANS I GET TO RUN THE RESTAURANT WITH YUU.
LET'S DO THIS!
I'LL GET STARTED WITH THE CLEANING.
OKAY, THANKS.

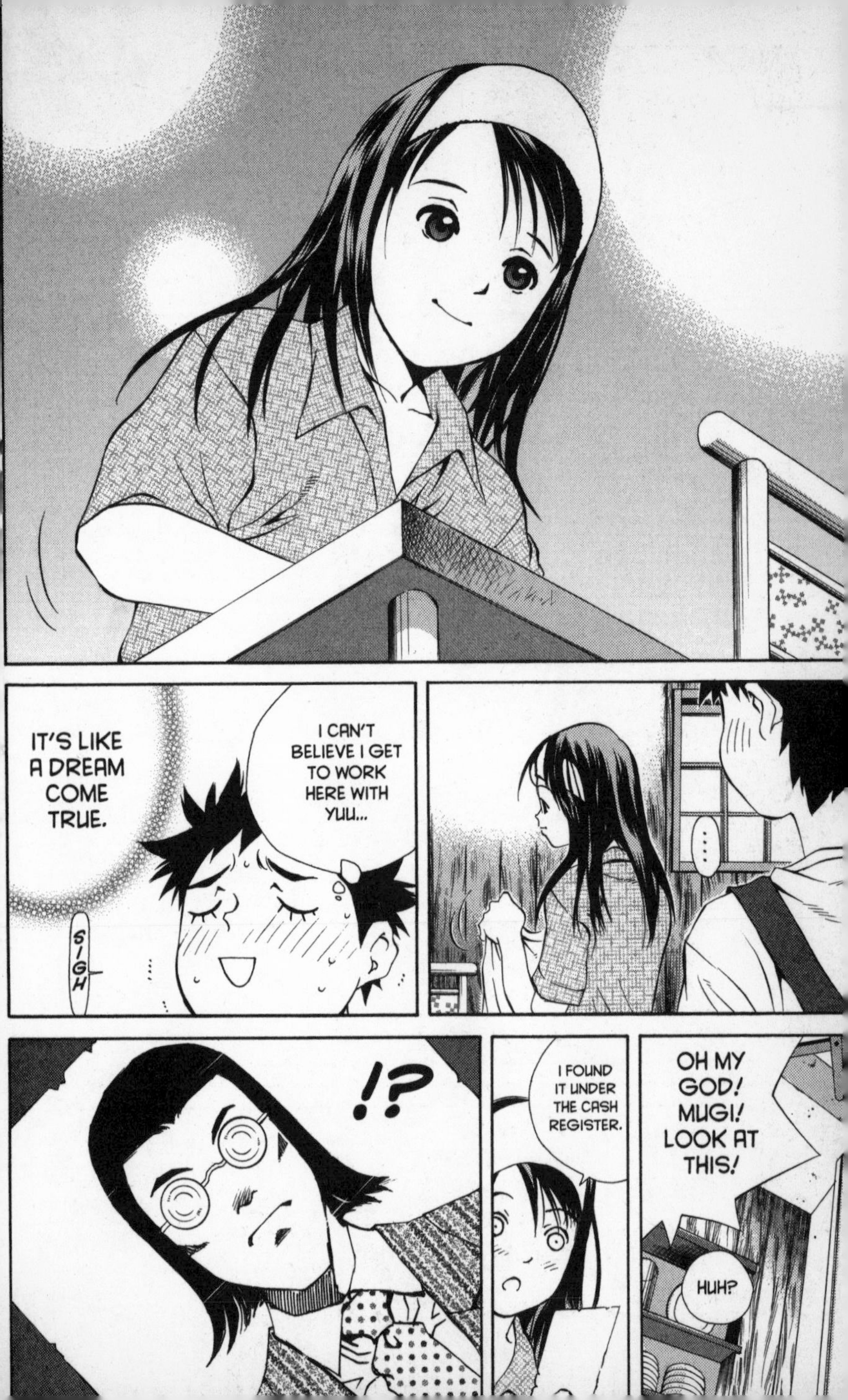
…
I CAN'T BELIEVE I GET TO WORK HERE WITH YUU...
IT'S LIKE A DREAM COME TRUE.
SIGH
OH MY GOD! MUGI! LOOK AT THIS!
HUH?
I FOUND IT UNDER THE CASH REGISTER.
!?

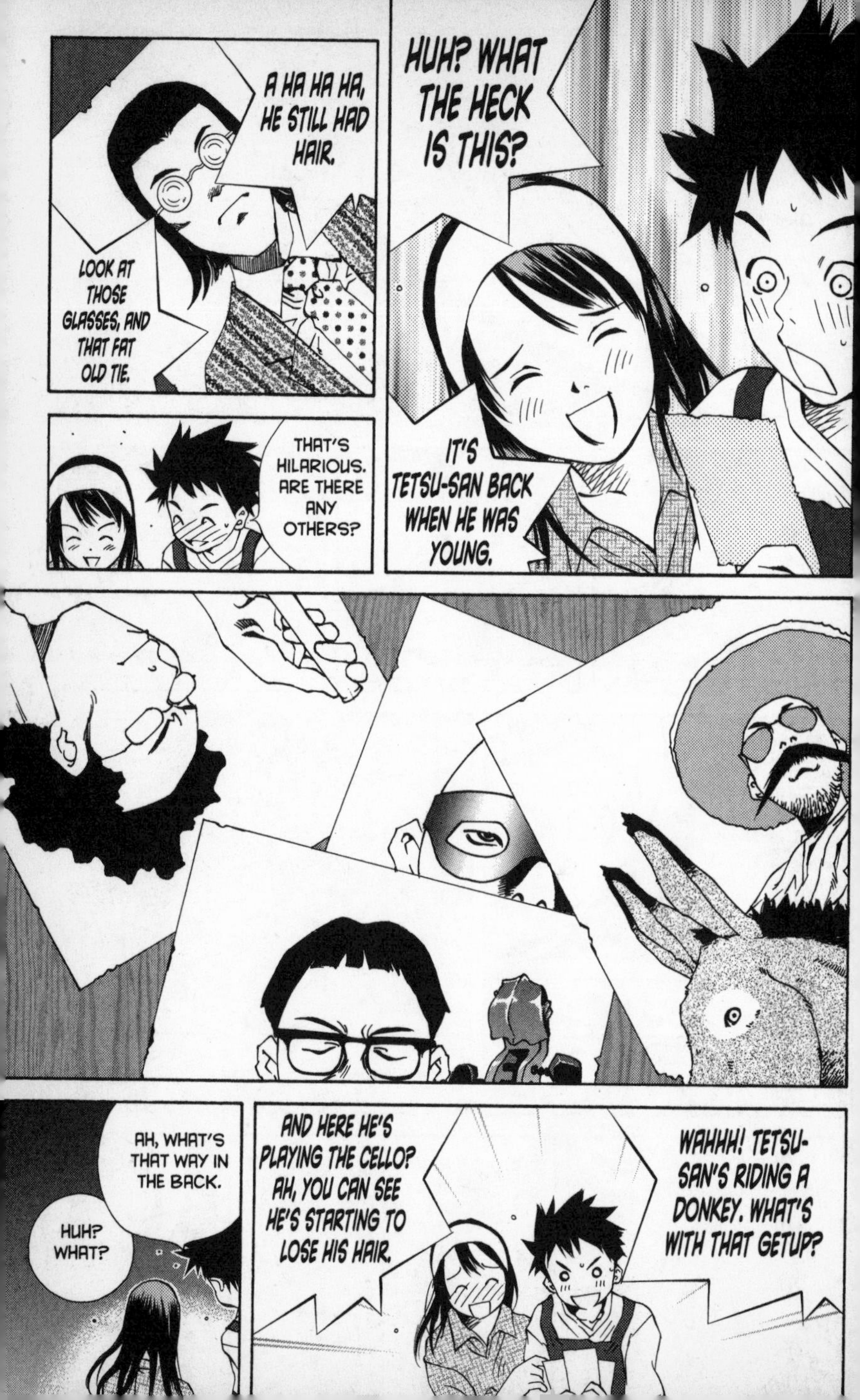
HUH? WHAT THE HECK IS THIS?
IT'S TETSU-SAN BACK WHEN HE WAS YOUNG.
A HA HA HA, HE STILL HAD HAIR.
LOOK AT THOSE GLASSES, AND THAT FAT OLD TIE.
THAT'S HILARIOUS. ARE THERE ANY OTHERS?
WAHHH! TETSU-SAN'S RIDING A DONKEY. WHAT'S WITH THAT GETUP?
AND HERE HE'S PLAYING THE CELLO? AH, YOU CAN SEE HE'S STARTING TO LOSE HIS HAIR.
AH, WHAT'S THAT WAY IN THE BACK.
HUH? WHAT?

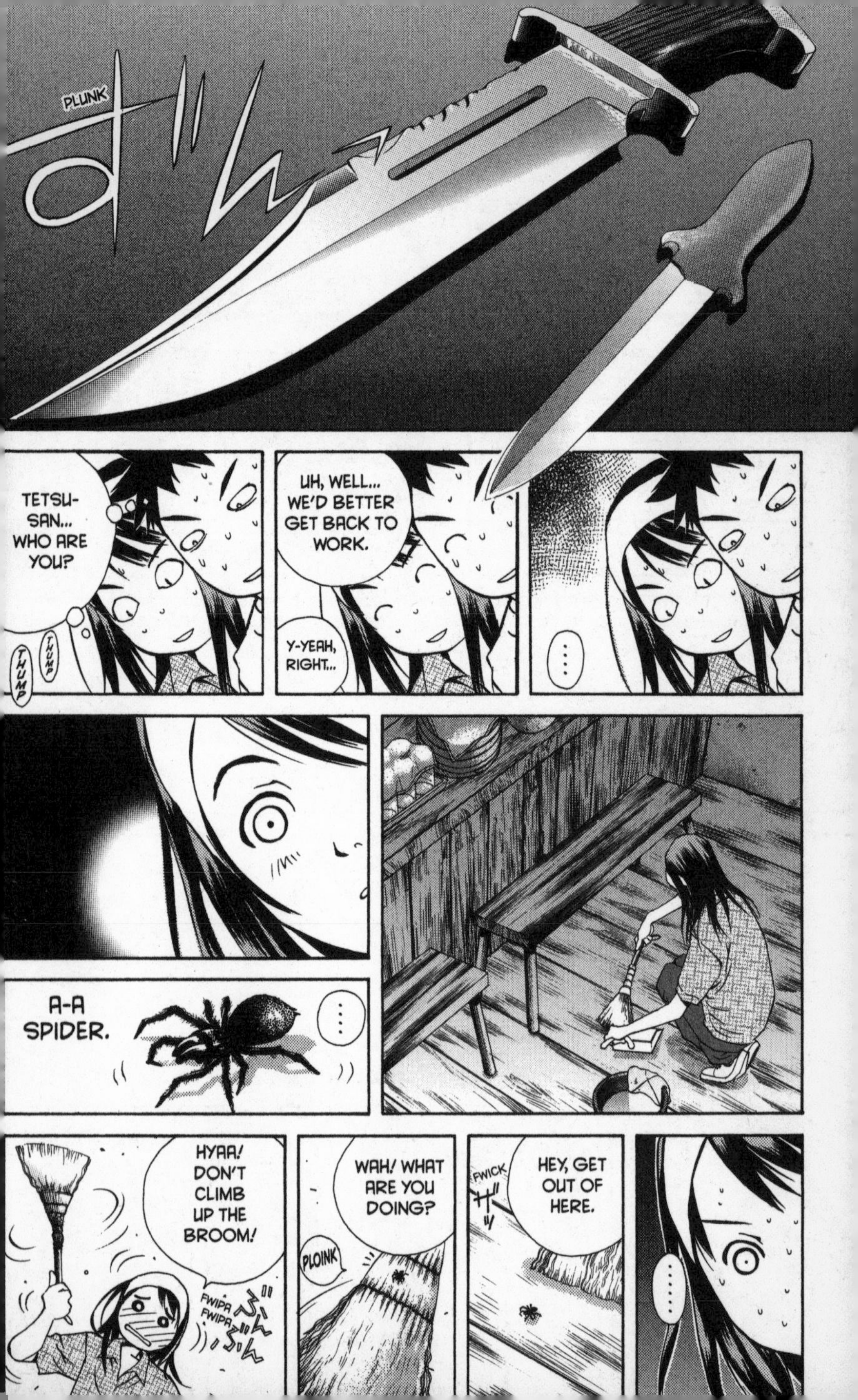
PLUNK
.....
UH, WELL... WE'D BETTER GET BACK TO WORK.
Y-YEAH, RIGHT...
TETSU-SAN... WHO ARE YOU?
THUMP
THUMP
.....
A-A SPIDER.
......
HEY, GET OUT OF HERE.
FWICK
WAH! WHAT ARE YOU DOING?
PLOINK
HYAA! DON'T CLIMB UP THE BROOM!
FWIPA FWIPA

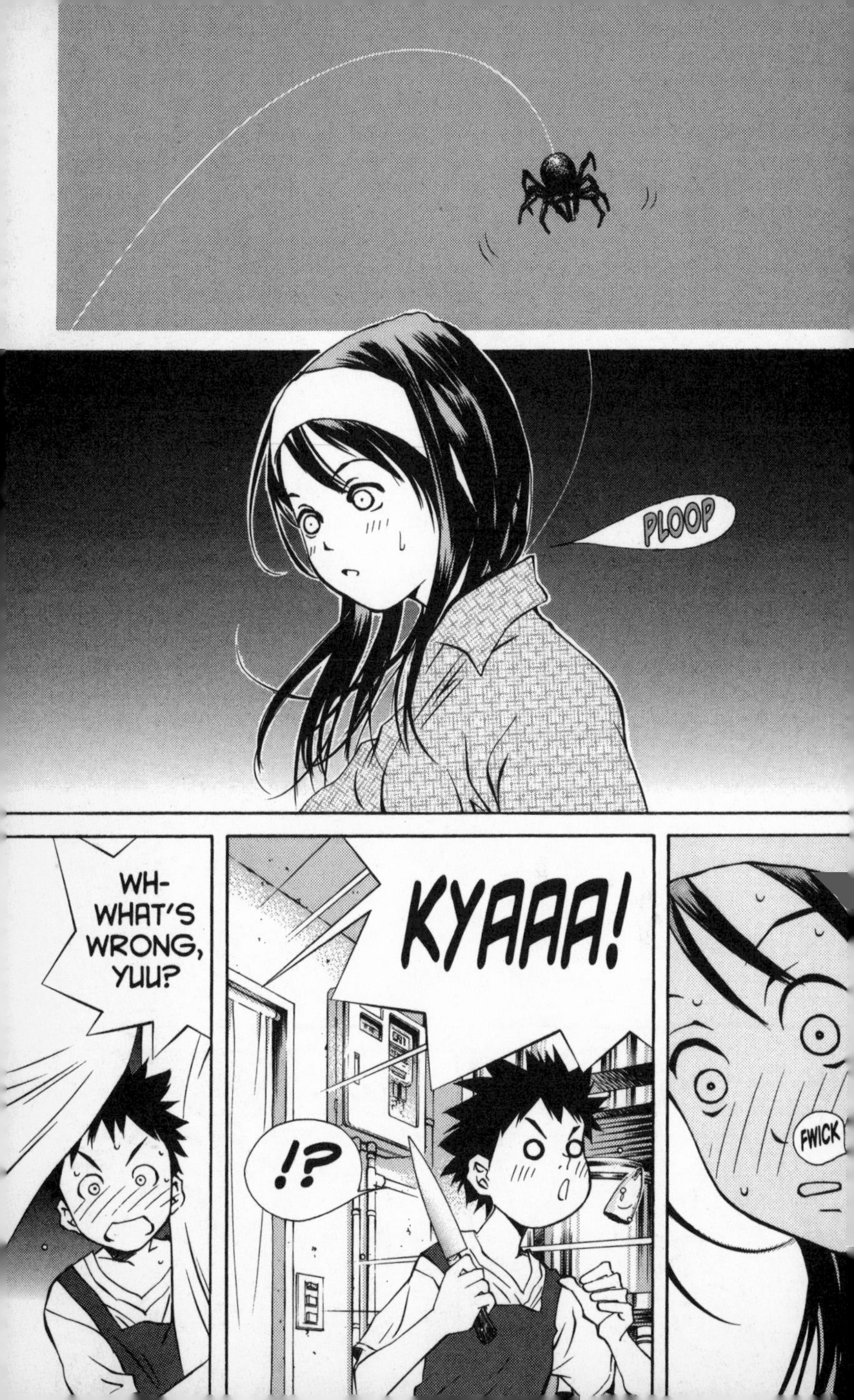
PLOOP
FWICK
KYAAA!
!?
WH-
WHAT'S
WRONG,
YUU?

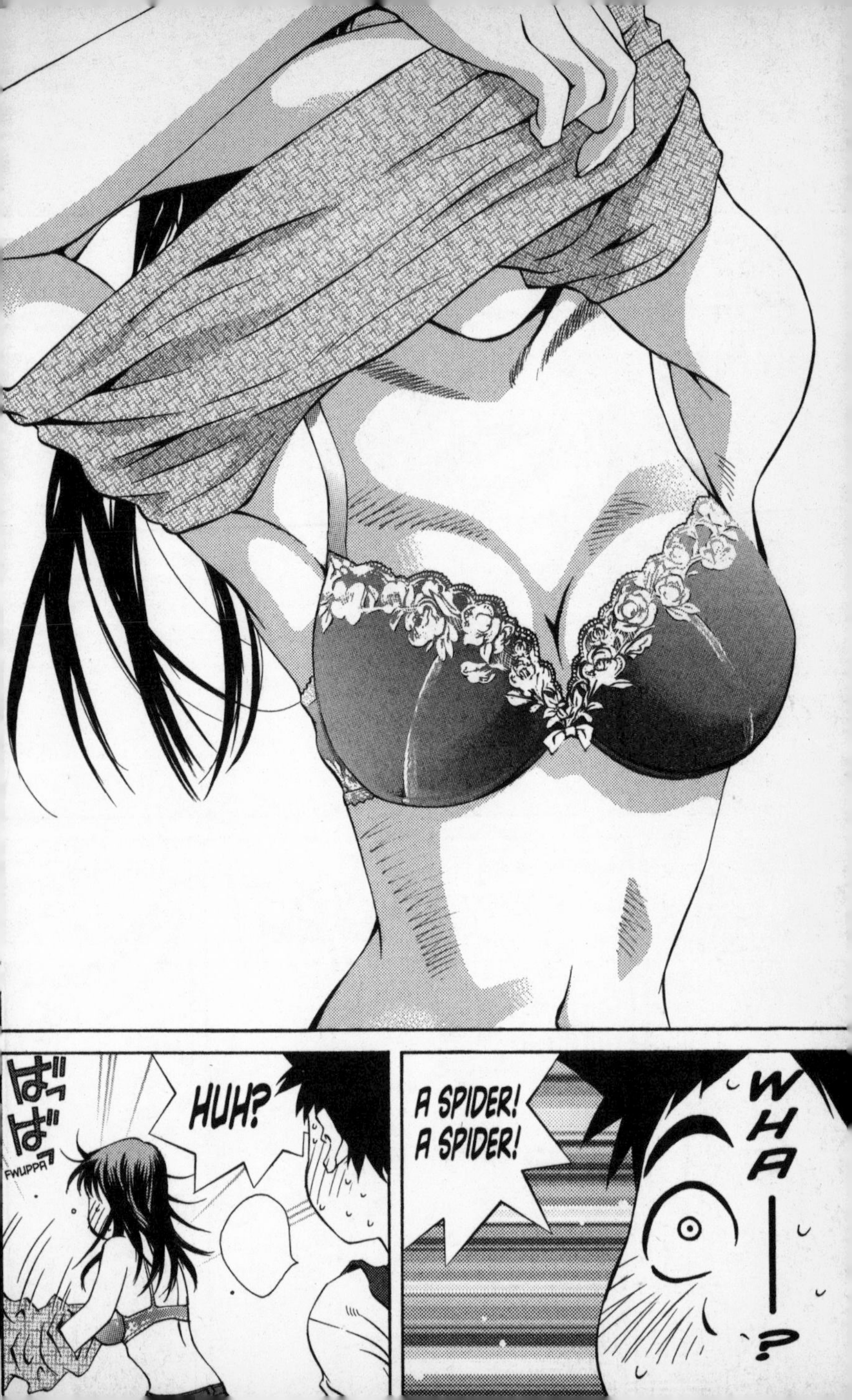
WHA—?
A SPIDER! A SPIDER!
HUH?
ばっばっ
FWUPPA

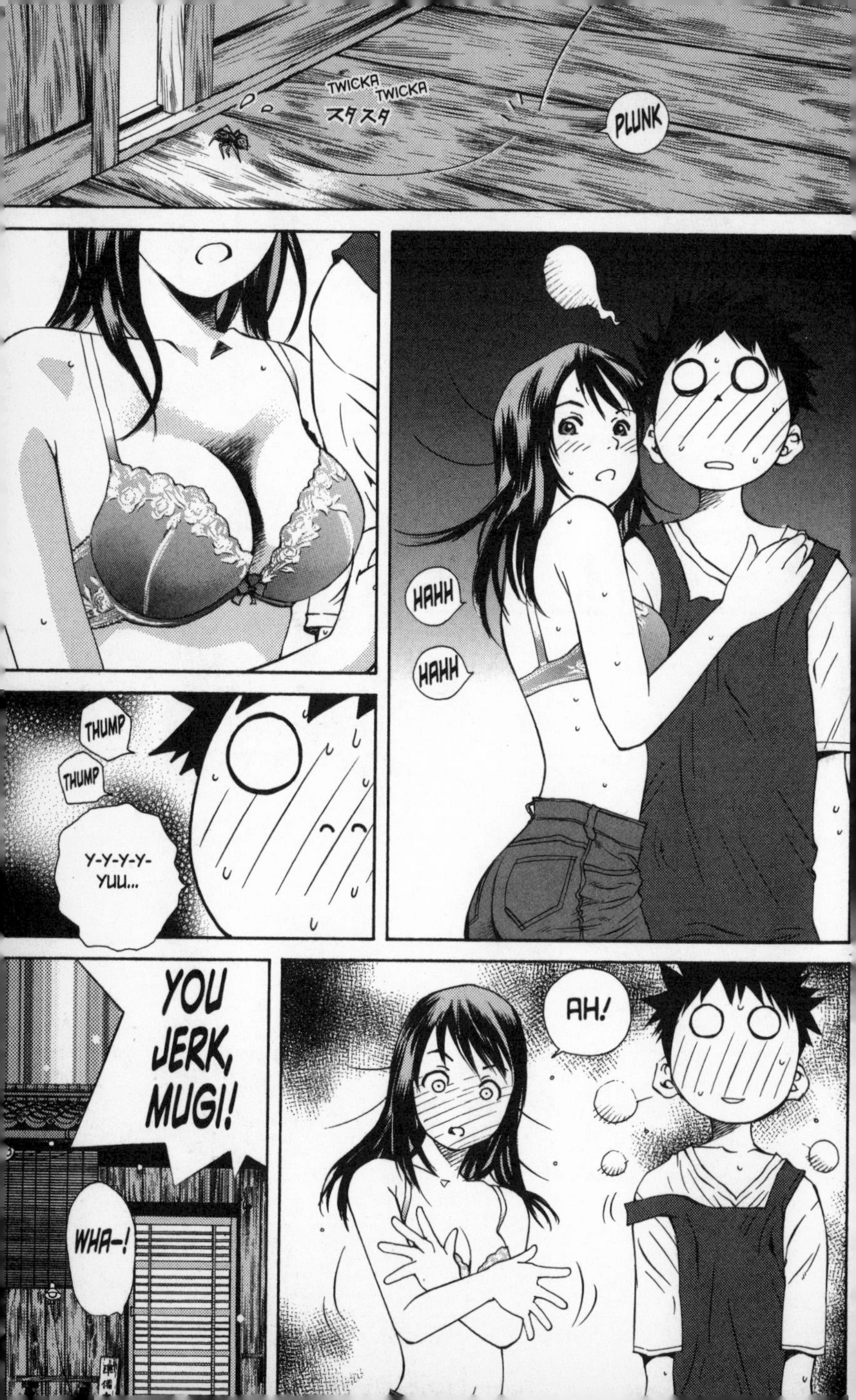
PLUNK
TWICKA TWICKA
スタスタ
HAHH
HAHH
THUMP
THUMP
Y-Y-Y-Y-YUU...
AH!
YOU JERK, MUGI!
WHA-!

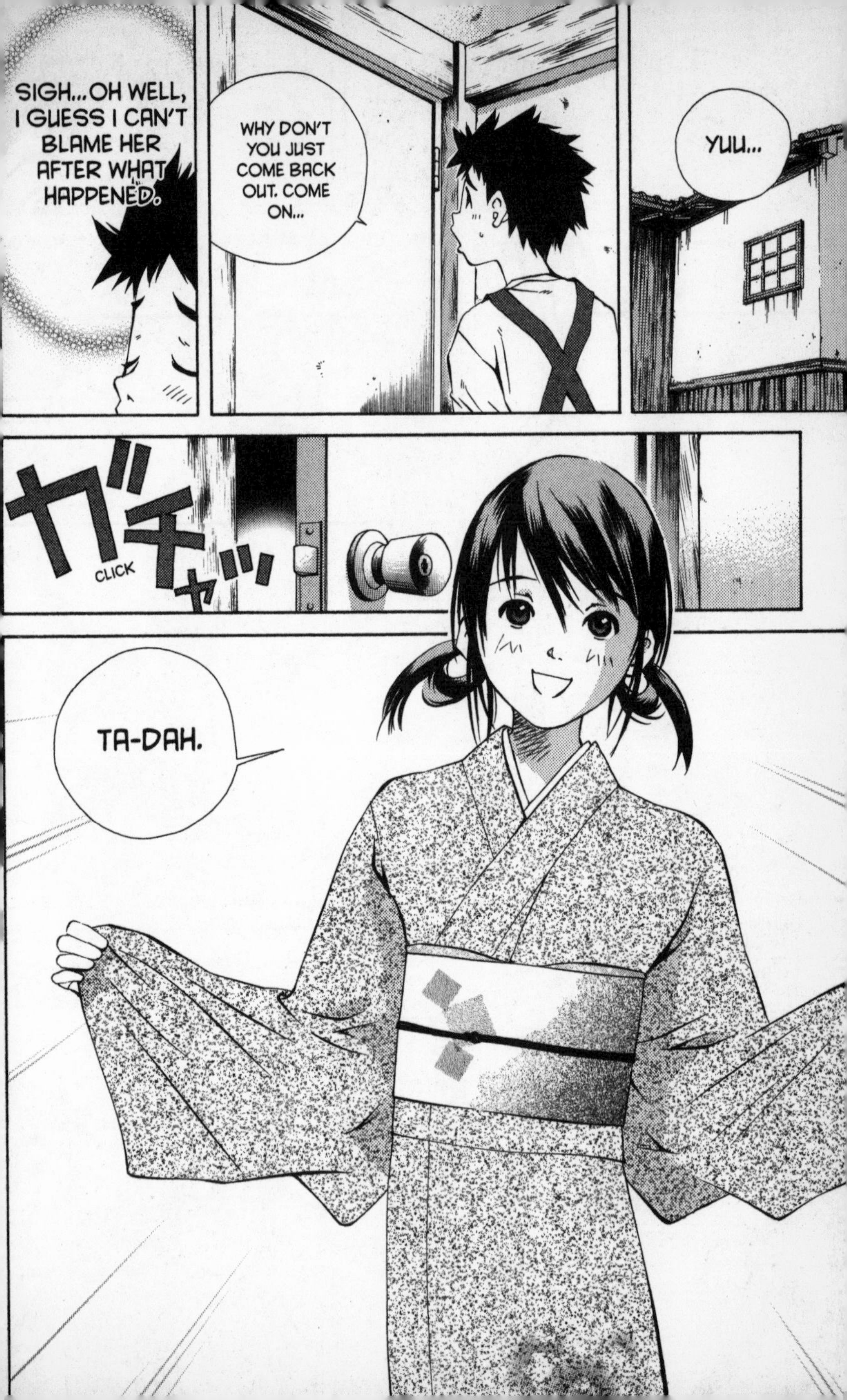
YUU...
WHY DON'T YOU JUST COME BACK OUT. COME ON...
SIGH...OH WELL, I GUESS I CAN'T BLAME HER AFTER WHAT HAPPENED.
ガチャッ
CLICK
TA-DAH.

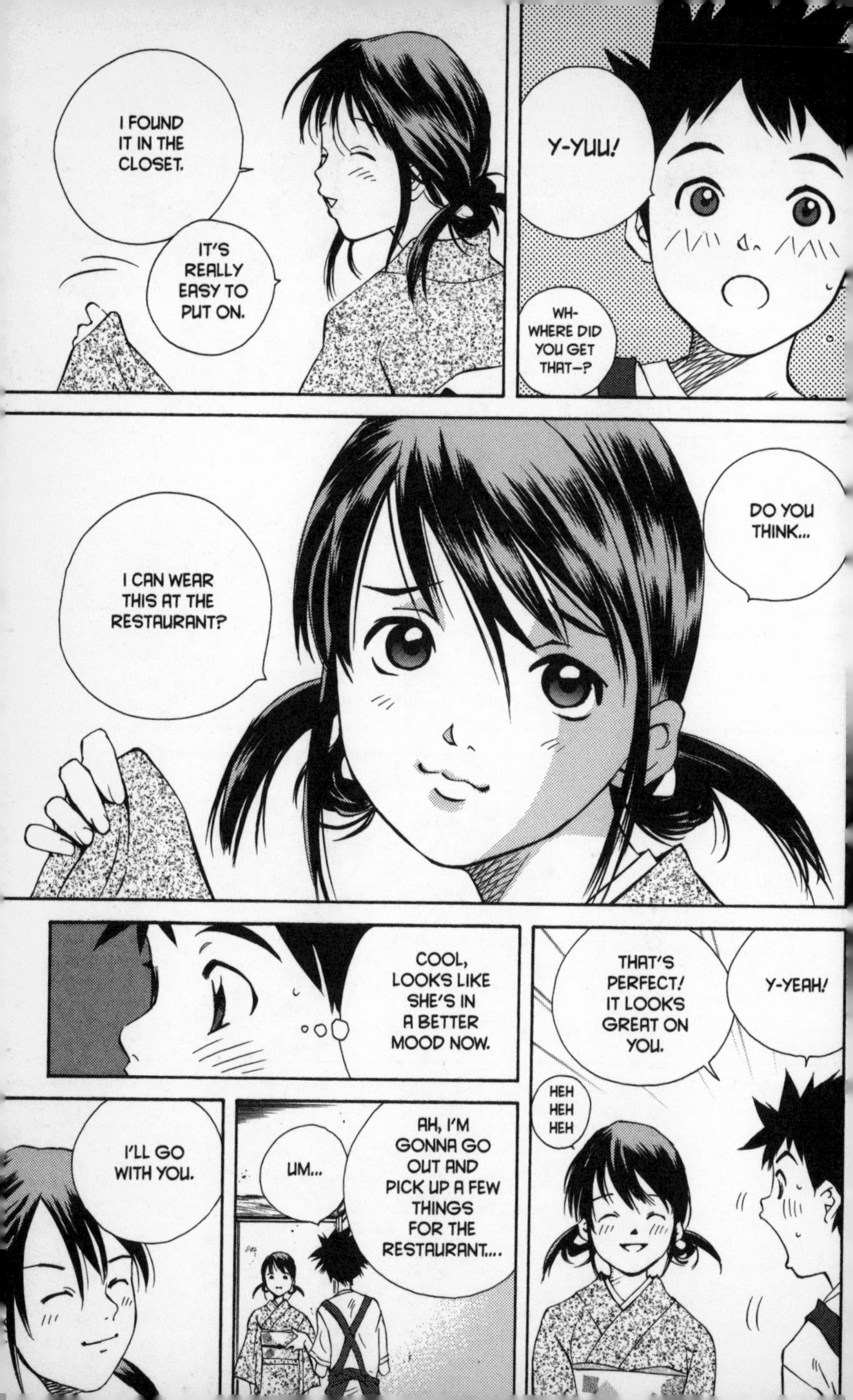
Y-YUU!
WH- WHERE DID YOU GET THAT—?
I FOUND IT IN THE CLOSET.
IT'S REALLY EASY TO PUT ON.
DO YOU THINK...
I CAN WEAR THIS AT THE RESTAURANT?
Y-YEAH!
THAT'S PERFECT! IT LOOKS GREAT ON YOU.
HEH HEH HEH
COOL, LOOKS LIKE SHE'S IN A BETTER MOOD NOW.
AH, I'M GONNA GO OUT AND PICK UP A FEW THINGS FOR THE RESTAURANT....
UM...
I'LL GO WITH YOU.

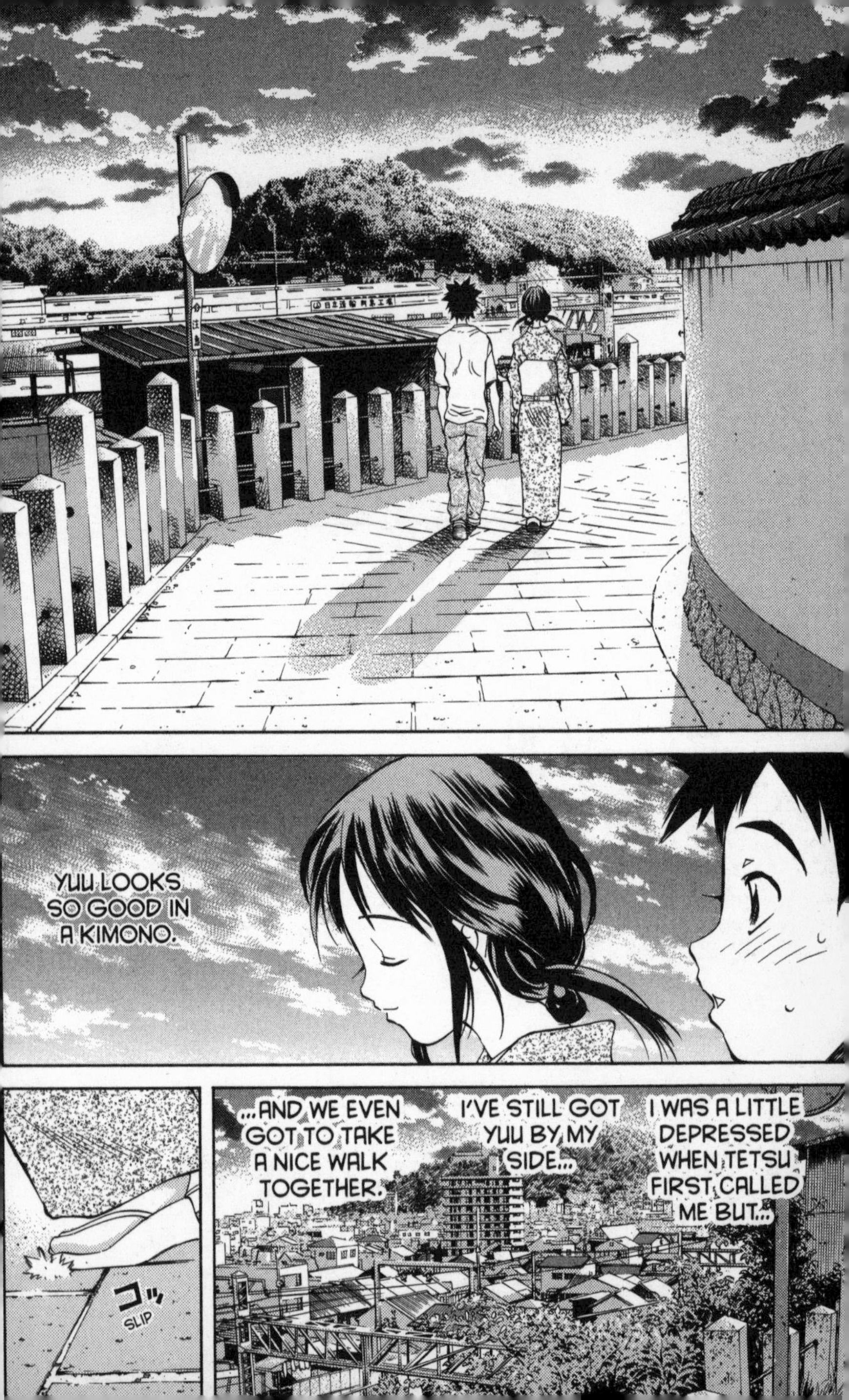
YUU LOOKS SO GOOD IN A KIMONO.
I WAS A LITTLE DEPRESSED WHEN TETSU FIRST CALLED ME BUT...
I'VE STILL GOT YUU BY MY SIDE...
...AND WE EVEN GOT TO TAKE A NICE WALK TOGETHER.
ゴッ
SLIP

I'M SORRY, MUGI.

IT'S HARD TO WALK IN THESE...

KYA!

I AM SO LUCKY!

TH-THAT'S OKAY.

WELL, SHOULD WE OPEN THE RESTAURANT?

YEAH!

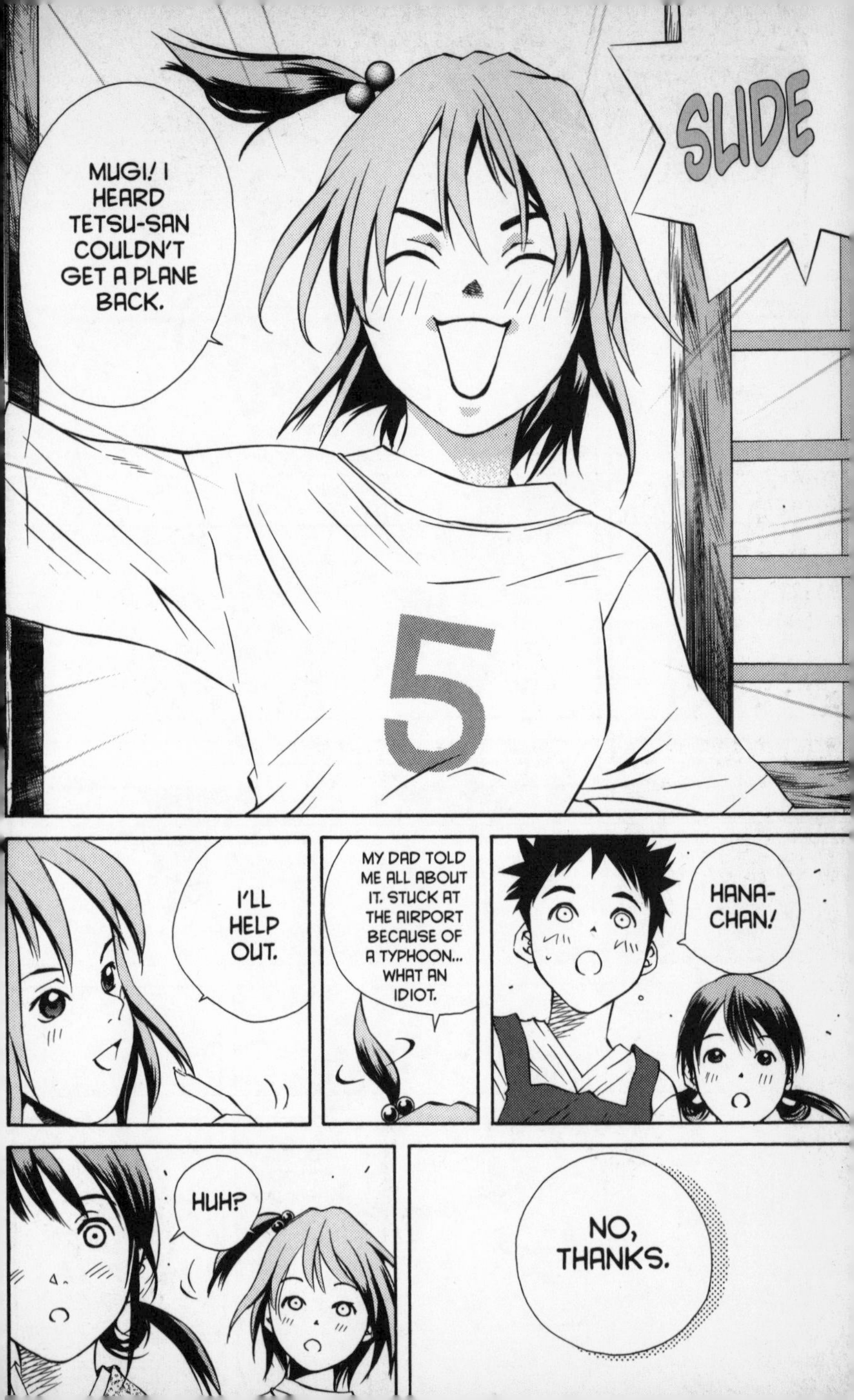
SLIDE
MUGI! I HEARD TETSU-SAN COULDN'T GET A PLANE BACK.
HANA-CHAN!
MY DAD TOLD ME ALL ABOUT IT. STUCK AT THE AIRPORT BECAUSE OF A TYPHOON... WHAT AN IDIOT.
I'LL HELP OUT.
NO, THANKS.
HUH?

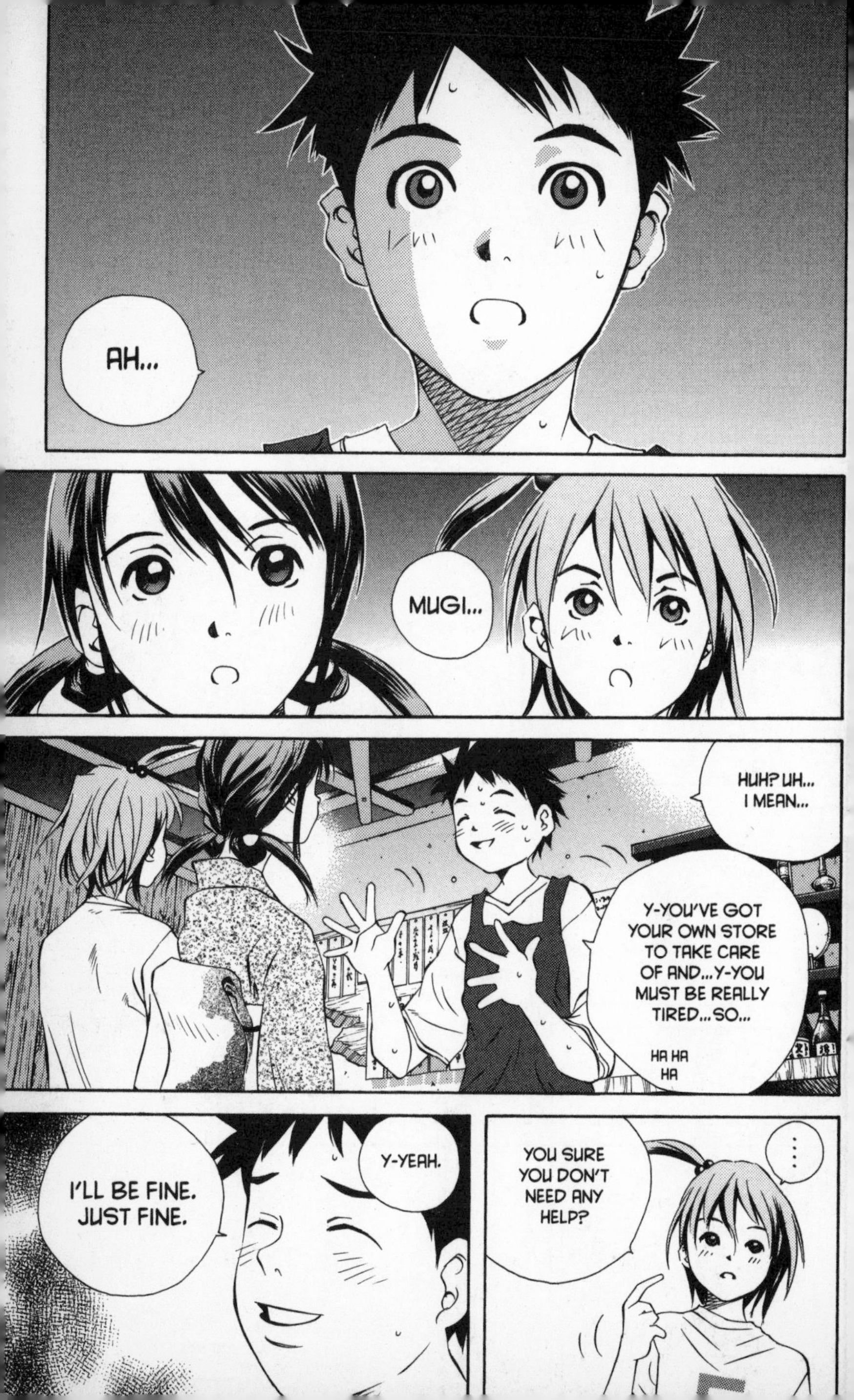
AH...
MUGI...
HUH? UH... I MEAN...
Y-YOU'VE GOT YOUR OWN STORE TO TAKE CARE OF AND... Y-YOU MUST BE REALLY TIRED... SO...
HA HA HA
....
YOU SURE YOU DON'T NEED ANY HELP?
Y-YEAH.
I'LL BE FINE. JUST FINE.

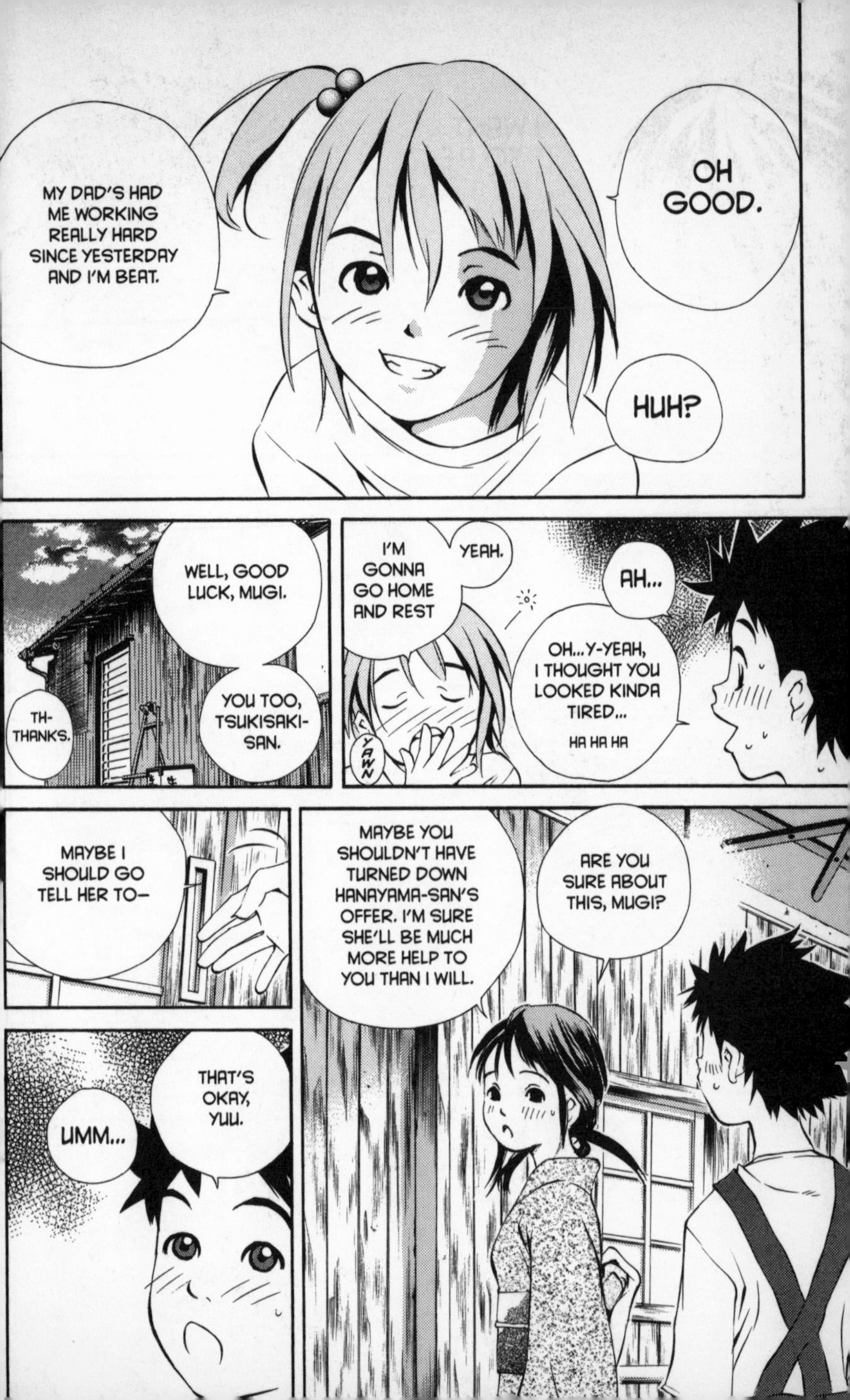
OH GOOD.
MY DAD'S HAD ME WORKING REALLY HARD SINCE YESTERDAY AND I'M BEAT.
HUH?
AH...
YEAH.
I'M GONNA GO HOME AND REST
OH...Y-YEAH, I THOUGHT YOU LOOKED KINDA TIRED...
HA HA HA
YAWN
WELL, GOOD LUCK, MUGI.
YOU TOO, TSUKISAKI-SAN.
TH-THANKS.
ARE YOU SURE ABOUT THIS, MUGI?
MAYBE YOU SHOULDN'T HAVE TURNED DOWN HANAYAMA-SAN'S OFFER. I'M SURE SHE'LL BE MUCH MORE HELP TO YOU THAN I WILL.
MAYBE I SHOULD GO TELL HER TO—
THAT'S OKAY, YUU.
UMM...

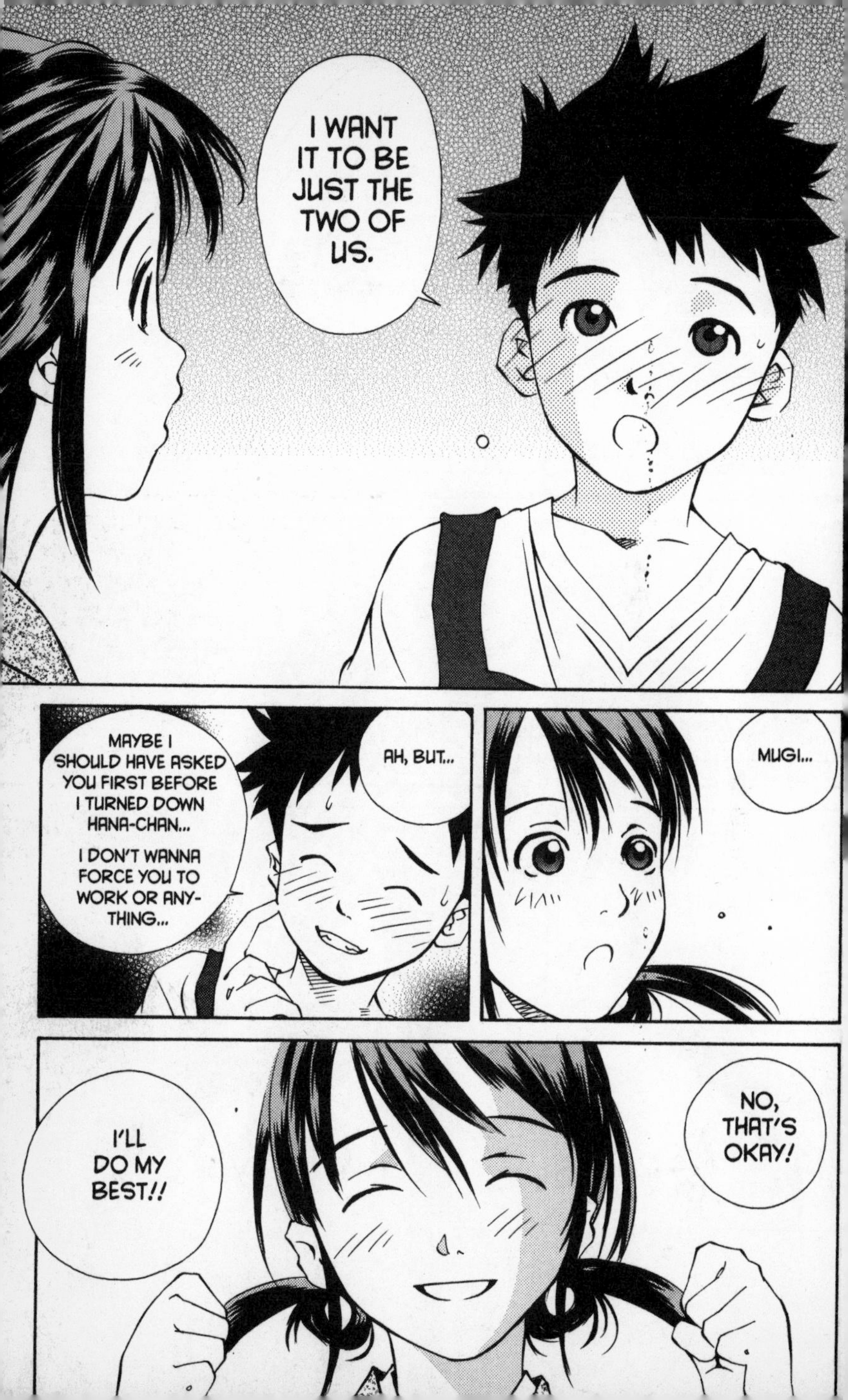
I WANT IT TO BE JUST THE TWO OF US.
MUGI...
AH, BUT...
MAYBE I SHOULD HAVE ASKED YOU FIRST BEFORE I TURNED DOWN HANA-CHAN... I DON'T WANNA FORCE YOU TO WORK OR ANY-THING...
NO, THAT'S OKAY!
I'LL DO MY BEST!!

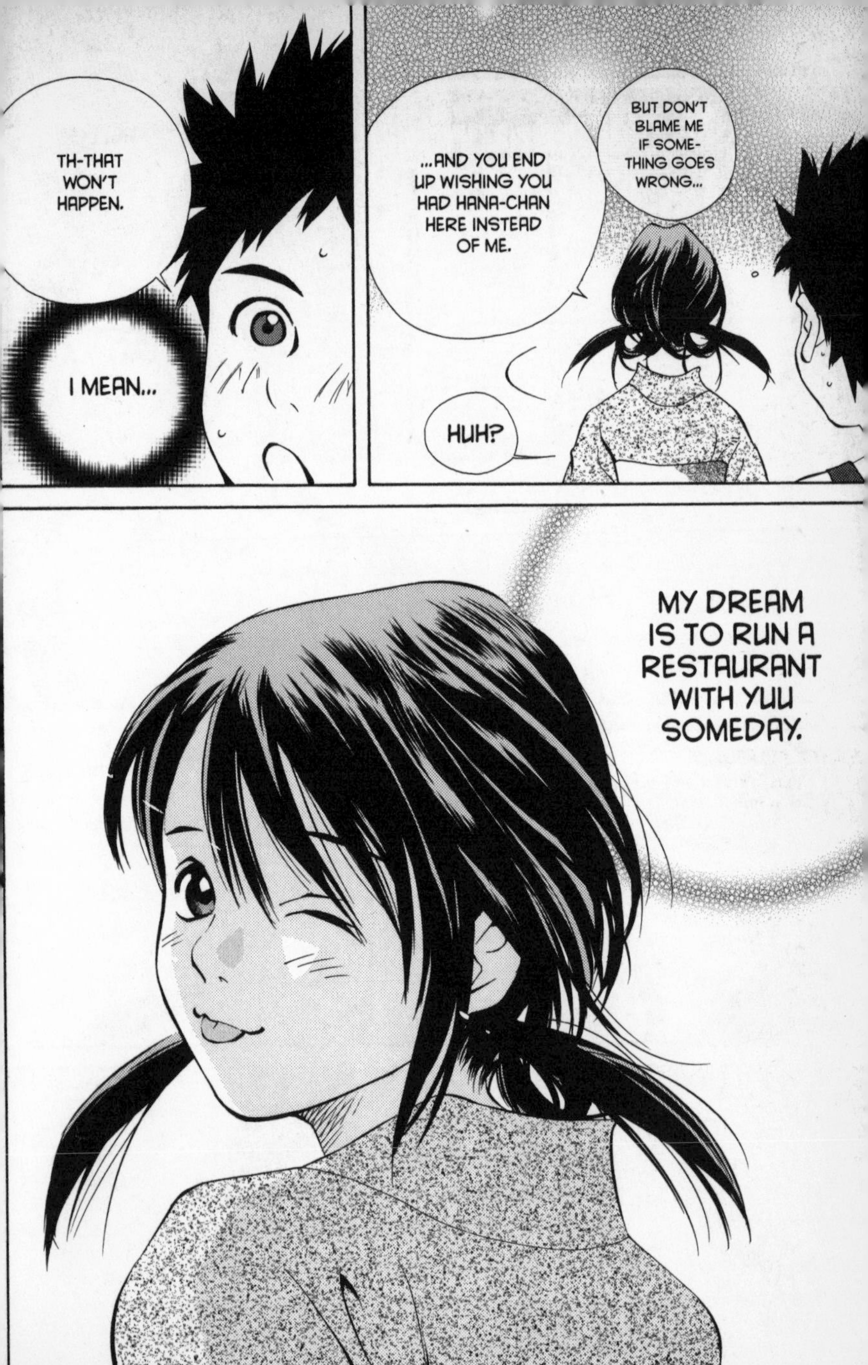
BUT DON'T BLAME ME IF SOME-THING GOES WRONG...
...AND YOU END UP WISHING YOU HAD HANA-CHAN HERE INSTEAD OF ME.
HUH?
TH-THAT WON'T HAPPEN.
I MEAN...
MY DREAM IS TO RUN A RESTAURANT WITH YUU SOMEDAY.

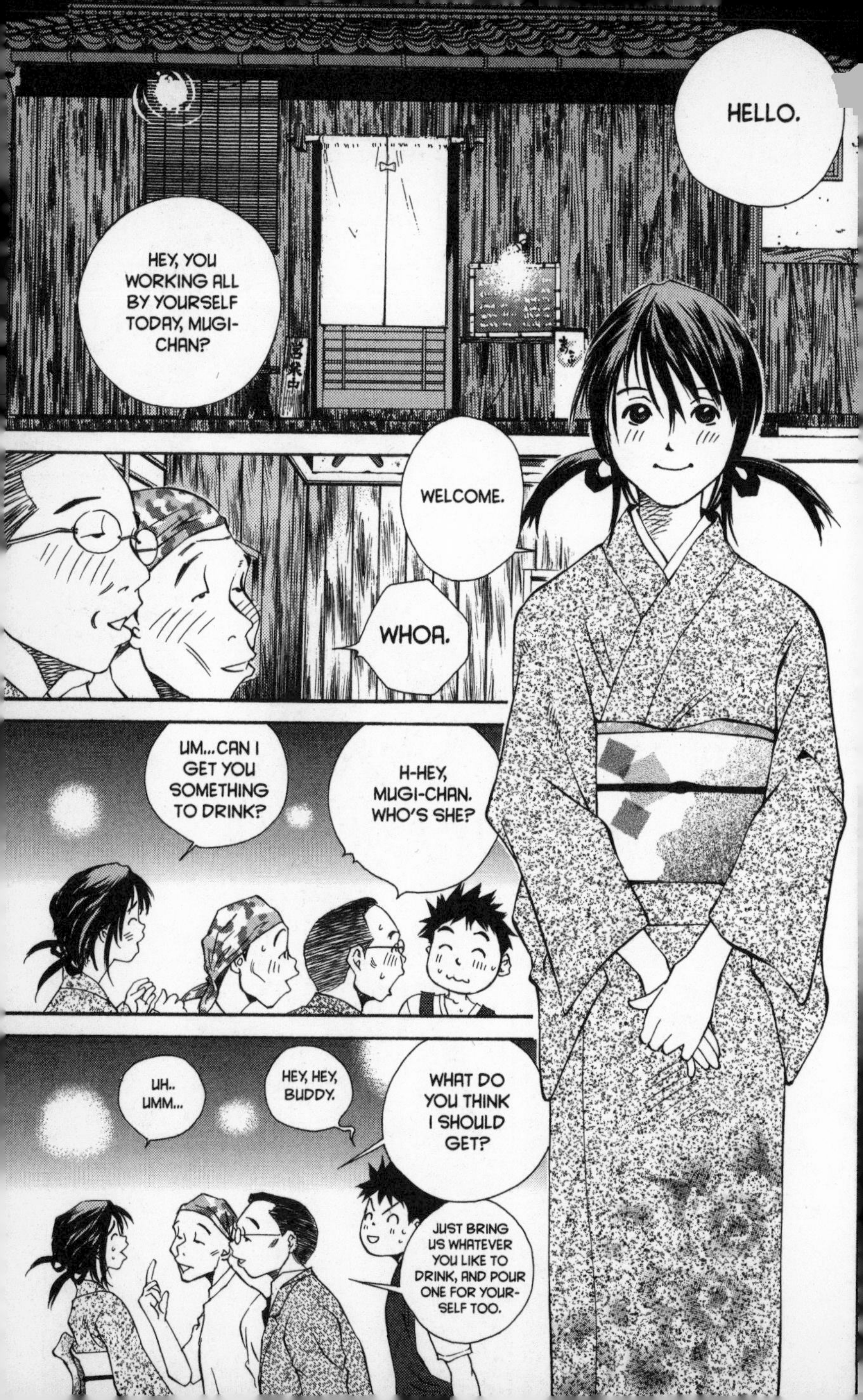
HELLO.
HEY, YOU WORKING ALL BY YOURSELF TODAY, MUGI-CHAN?
WELCOME.
WHOA.
H-HEY, MUGI-CHAN. WHO'S SHE?
UM...CAN I GET YOU SOMETHING TO DRINK?
WHAT DO YOU THINK I SHOULD GET?
HEY, HEY, BUDDY.
UH.. UMM...
JUST BRING US WHATEVER YOU LIKE TO DRINK, AND POUR ONE FOR YOURSELF TOO.

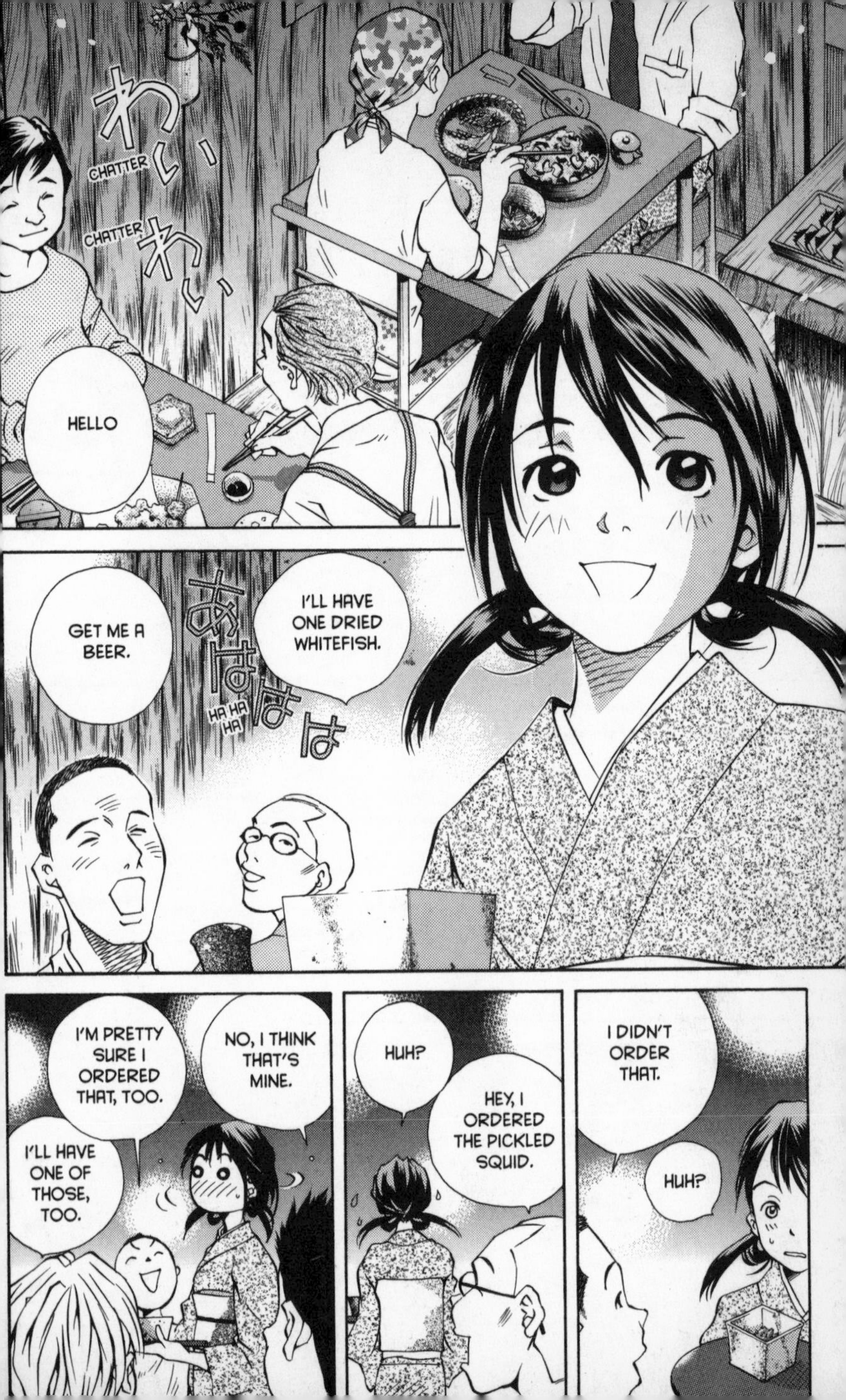
わいわい
CHATTER CHATTER
HELLO
I'LL HAVE ONE DRIED WHITEFISH.
あははは
HA HA HA
GET ME A BEER.
I DIDN'T ORDER THAT.
HUH?
HUH?
HEY, I ORDERED THE PICKLED SQUID.
NO, I THINK THAT'S MINE.
I'M PRETTY SURE I ORDERED THAT, TOO.
I'LL HAVE ONE OF THOSE, TOO.

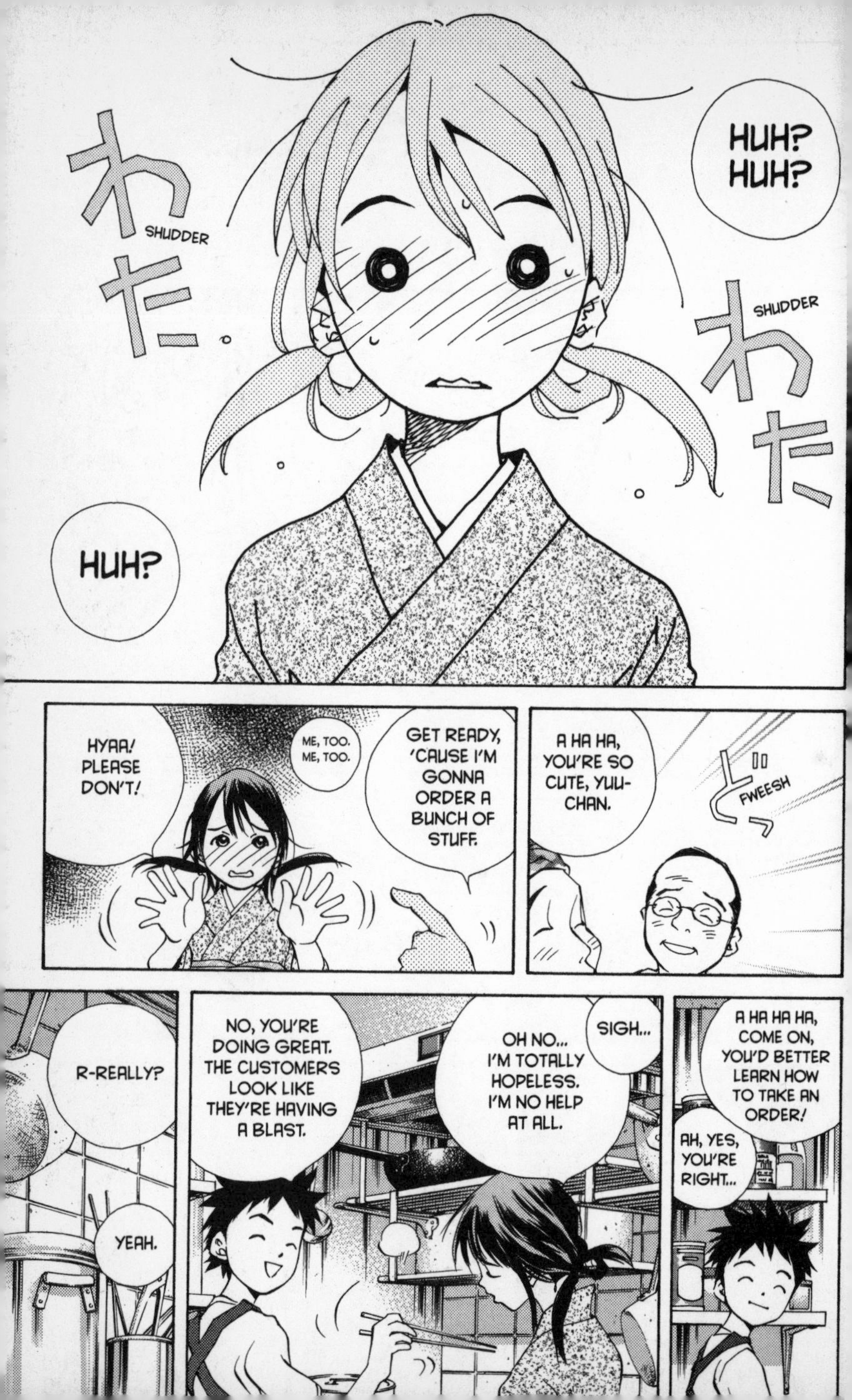
HUH? HUH?
わた
SHUDDER
わた
SHUDDER
HUH?
A HA HA, YOU'RE SO CUTE, YUU-CHAN.
FWEESH
GET READY, 'CAUSE I'M GONNA ORDER A BUNCH OF STUFF.
ME, TOO. ME, TOO.
HYAA! PLEASE DON'T!
A HA HA HA, COME ON, YOU'D BETTER LEARN HOW TO TAKE AN ORDER!
AH, YES, YOU'RE RIGHT...
SIGH...
OH NO... I'M TOTALLY HOPELESS. I'M NO HELP AT ALL.
NO, YOU'RE DOING GREAT. THE CUSTOMERS LOOK LIKE THEY'RE HAVING A BLAST.
R-REALLY?
YEAH.

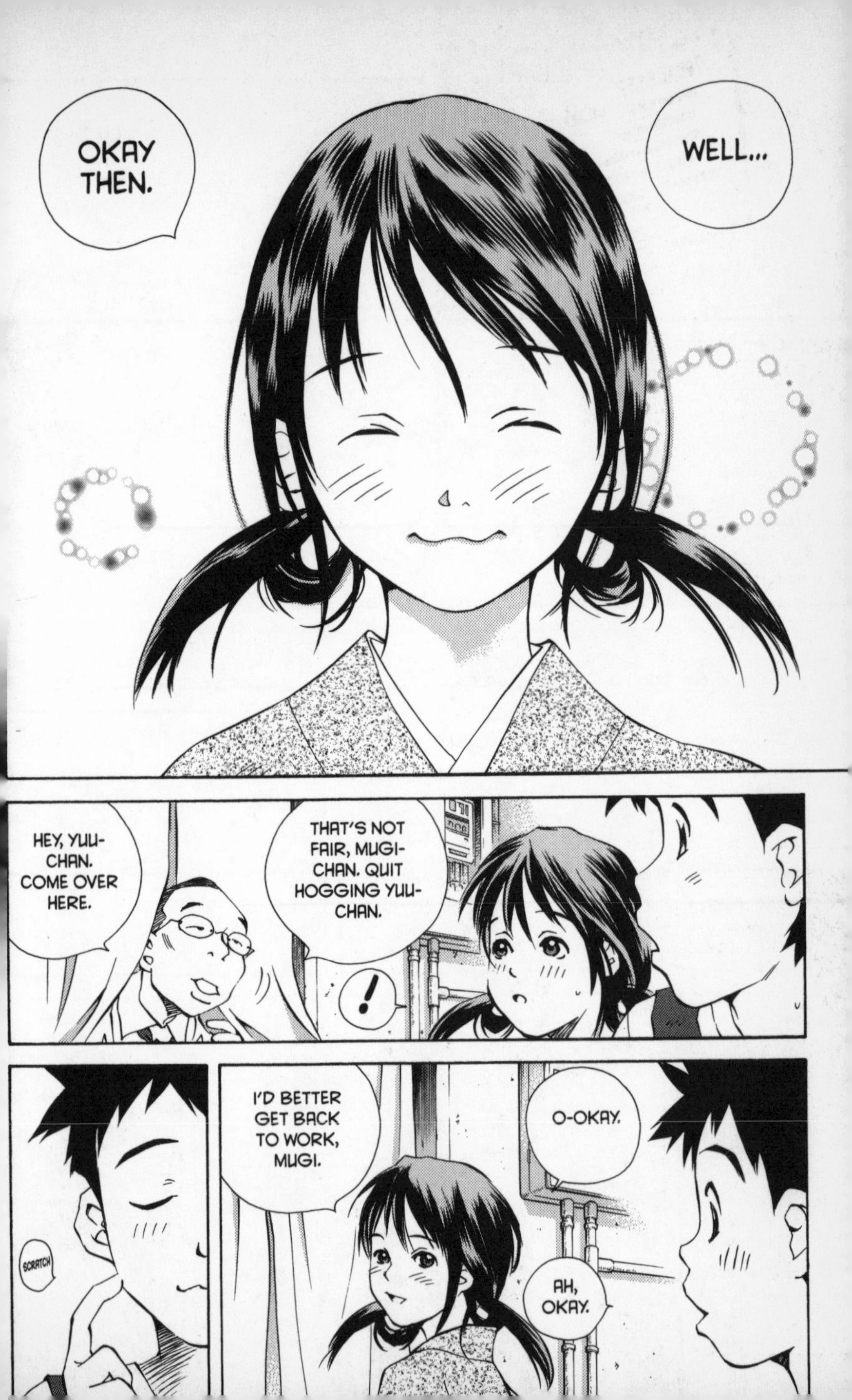
WELL...
OKAY THEN.
THAT'S NOT FAIR, MUGI-CHAN. QUIT HOGGING YUU-CHAN.
!
HEY, YUU-CHAN. COME OVER HERE.
O-OKAY.
I'D BETTER GET BACK TO WORK, MUGI.
AH, OKAY.
SCRATCH

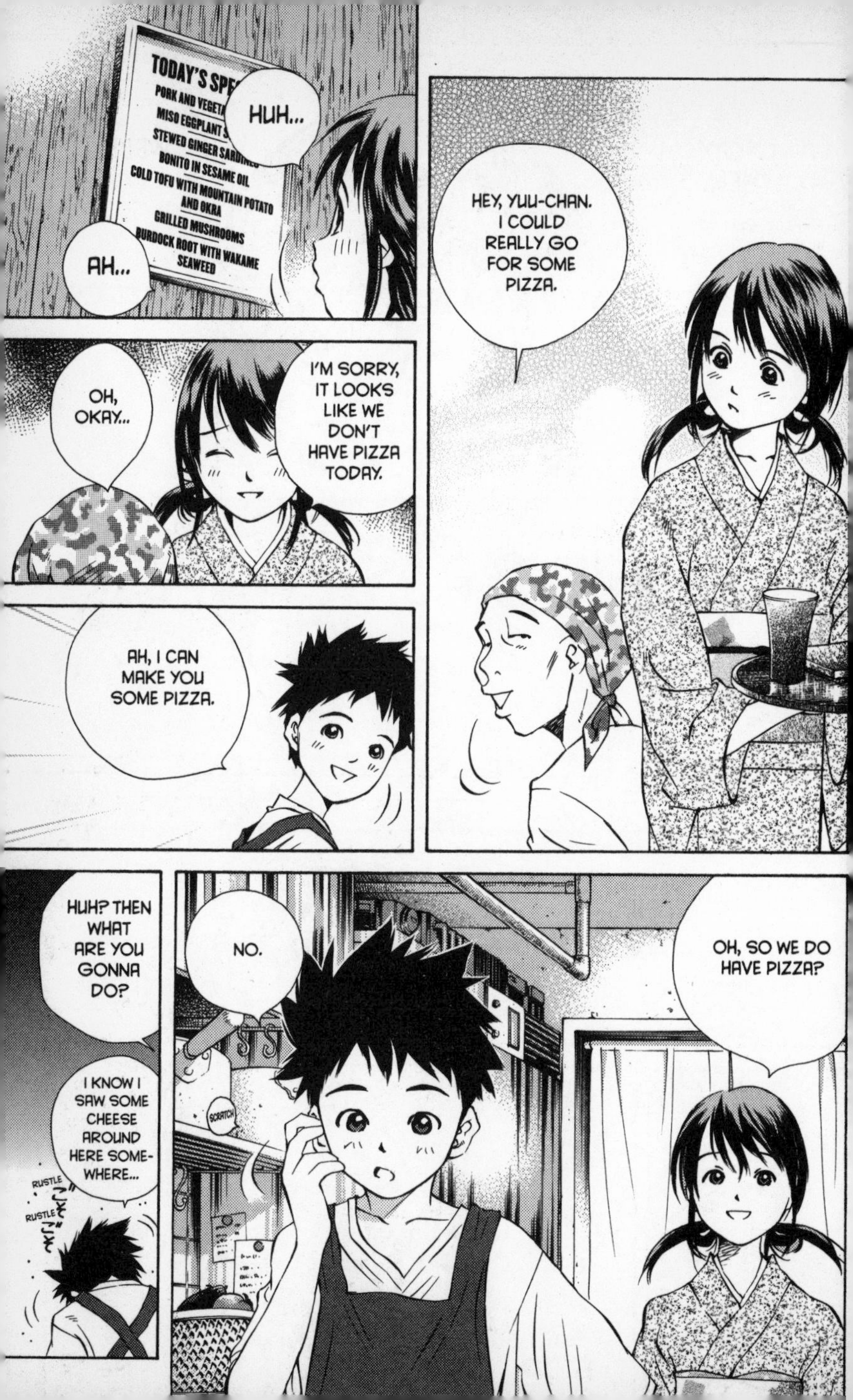
HEY, YUU-CHAN. I COULD REALLY GO FOR SOME PIZZA.
HUH...
BONITO IN SESAME OIL
COLD TOFU WITH MOUNTAIN POTATO AND OKRA
GRILLED MUSHROOMS
BURDOCK ROOT WITH WAKAME SEAWEED
AH...
I'M SORRY, IT LOOKS LIKE WE DON'T HAVE PIZZA TODAY.
OH, OKAY...
AH, I CAN MAKE YOU SOME PIZZA.
OH, SO WE DO HAVE PIZZA?
NO.
SCRATCH
HUH? THEN WHAT ARE YOU GONNA DO?
I KNOW I SAW SOME CHEESE AROUND HERE SOME-WHERE...
RUSTLE
RUSTLE

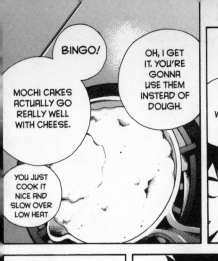

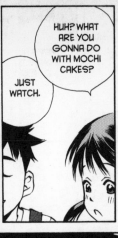

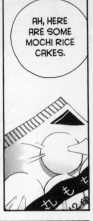

AH, HERE ARE SOME MOCHI RICE CAKES.
HUH? WHAT ARE YOU GONNA DO WITH MOCHI CAKES?
JUST WATCH.
OH, I GET IT. YOU'RE GONNA USE THEM INSTEAD OF DOUGH.
BINGO!
MOCHI CAKES ACTUALLY GO REALLY WELL WITH CHEESE.
YOU JUST COOK IT NICE AND SLOW OVER LOW HEAT
WHEN THE CHEESE IS ALL MELTED, IT'S DONE!
SIZZLE
HERE YOU GO. ONE MOCHI CAKE PIZZA.
WHOA, LOOKS GOOD.

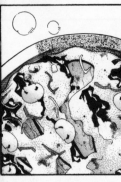

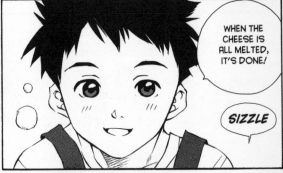

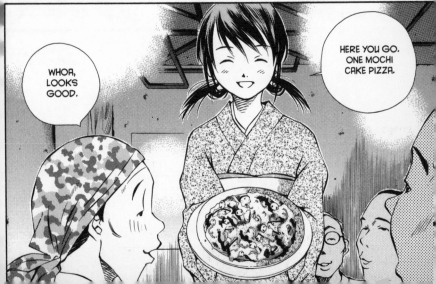

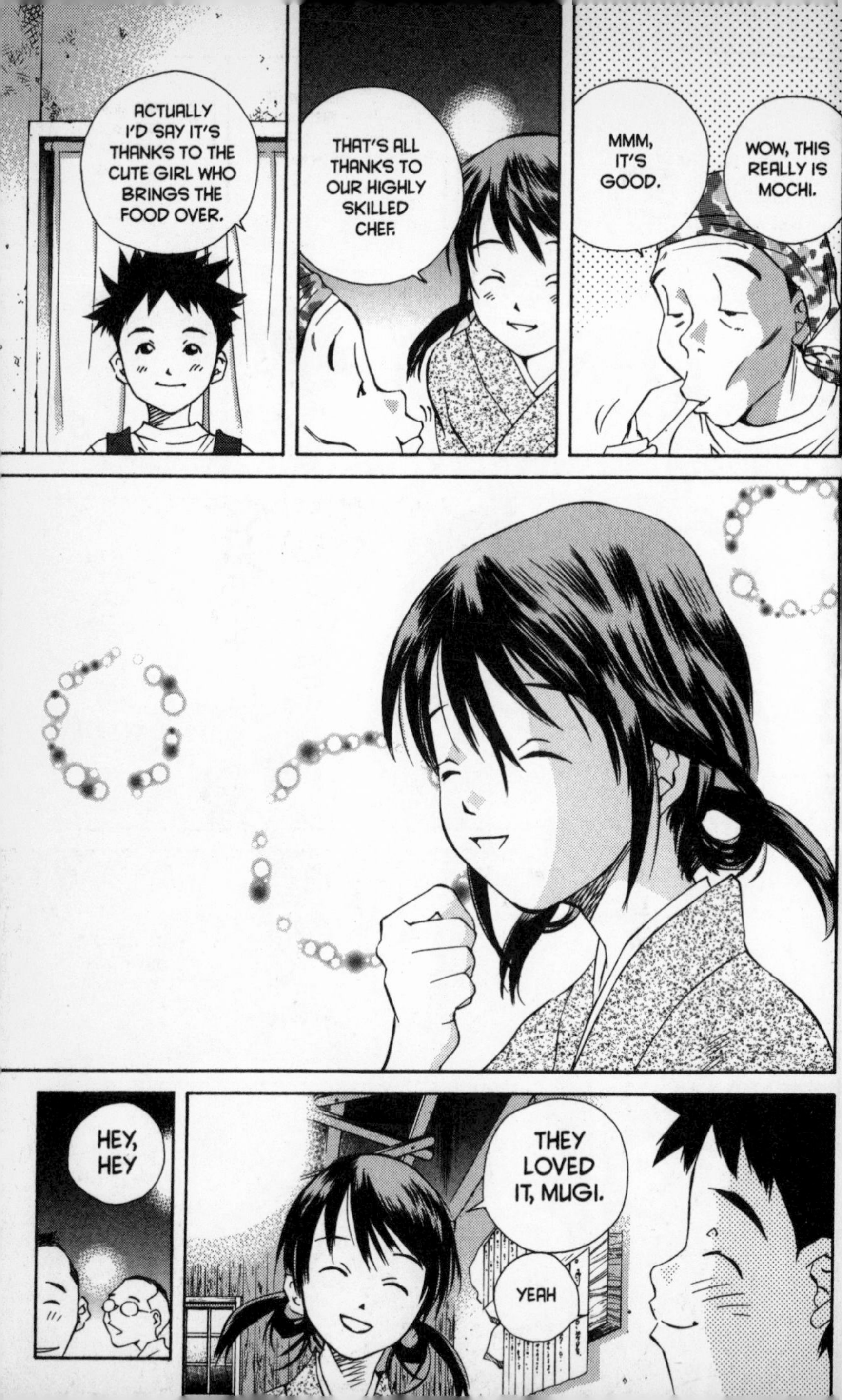
WOW, THIS REALLY IS MOCHI.
MMM, IT'S GOOD.
THAT'S ALL THANKS TO OUR HIGHLY SKILLED CHEF.
ACTUALLY I'D SAY IT'S THANKS TO THE CUTE GIRL WHO BRINGS THE FOOD OVER.
THEY LOVED IT, MUGI.
YEAH
HEY, HEY

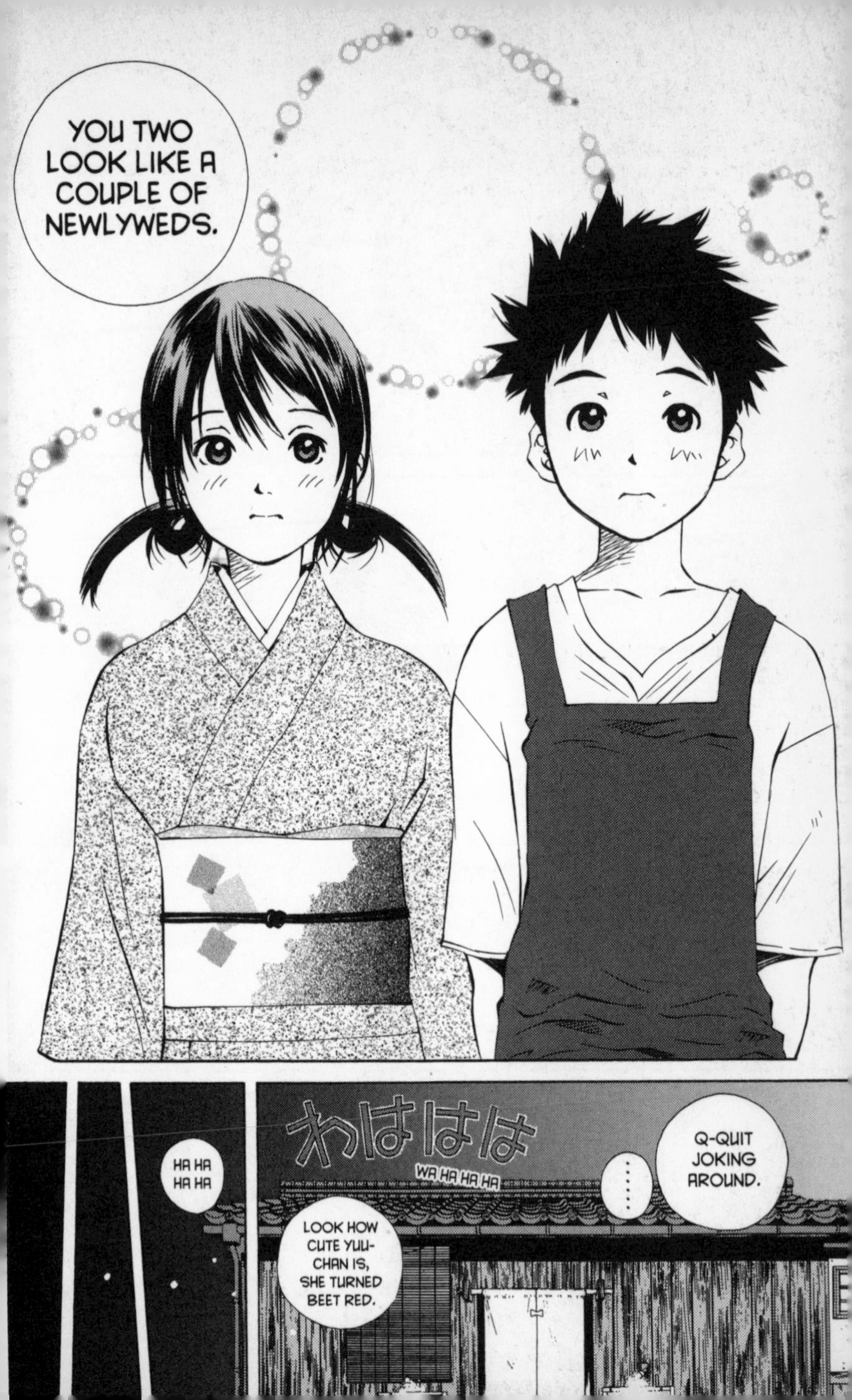
YOU TWO LOOK LIKE A COUPLE OF NEWLYWEDS.
Q-QUIT JOKING AROUND.
......
わははは
WA HA HA HA
LOOK HOW CUTE YUU-CHAN IS, SHE TURNED BEET RED.
HA HA HA HA

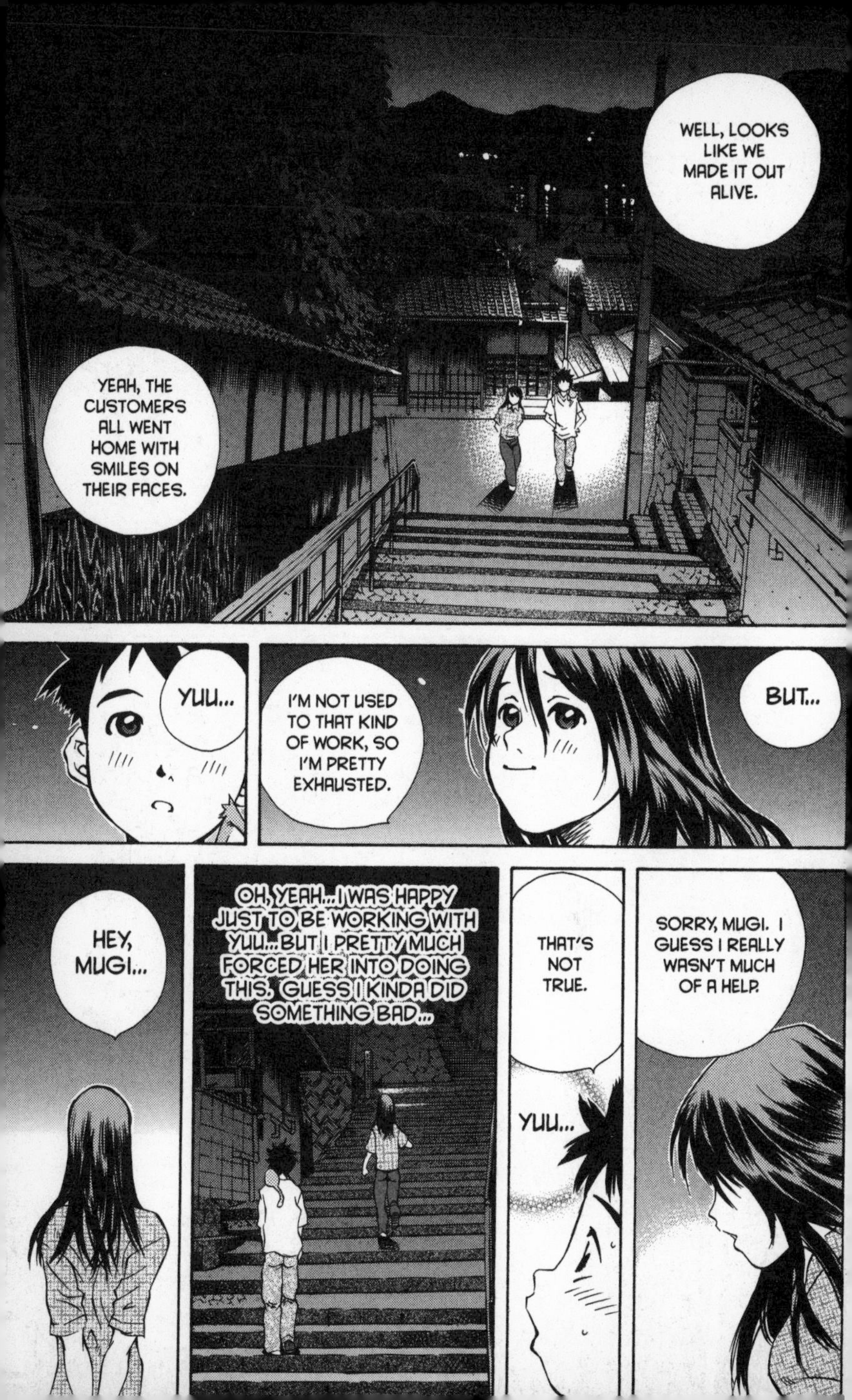
WELL, LOOKS LIKE WE MADE IT OUT ALIVE.
YEAH, THE CUSTOMERS ALL WENT HOME WITH SMILES ON THEIR FACES.
BUT...
I'M NOT USED TO THAT KIND OF WORK, SO I'M PRETTY EXHAUSTED.
YUU...
SORRY, MUGI. I GUESS I REALLY WASN'T MUCH OF A HELP.
THAT'S NOT TRUE.
YUU...
OH, YEAH...I WAS HAPPY JUST TO BE WORKING WITH YUU...BUT I PRETTY MUCH FORCED HER INTO DOING THIS. GUESS I KINDA DID SOMETHING BAD...
HEY, MUGI...

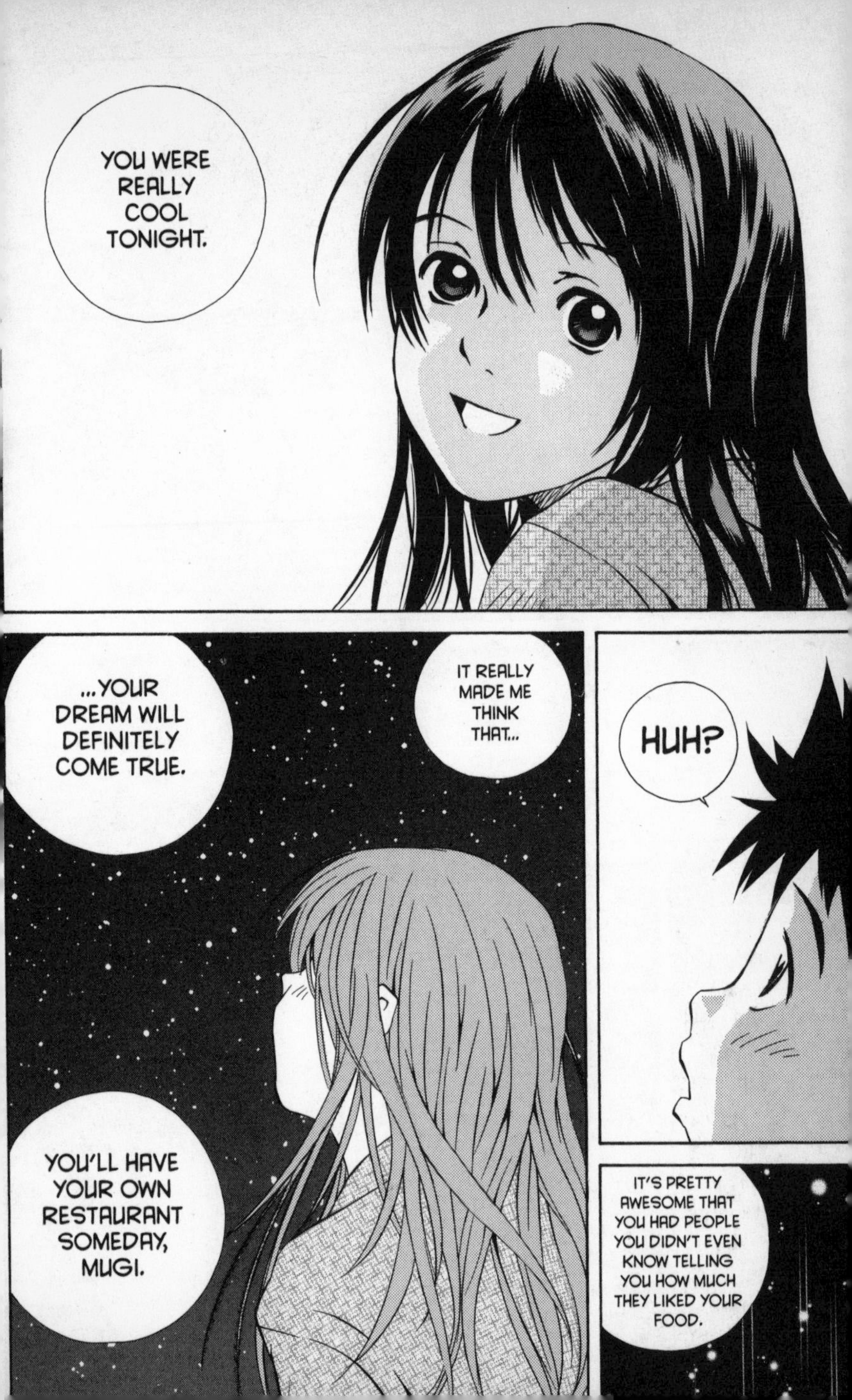
YOU WERE REALLY COOL TONIGHT.
HUH?
IT'S PRETTY AWESOME THAT YOU HAD PEOPLE YOU DIDN'T EVEN KNOW TELLING YOU HOW MUCH THEY LIKED YOUR FOOD.
IT REALLY MADE ME THINK THAT...
...YOUR DREAM WILL DEFINITELY COME TRUE.
YOU'LL HAVE YOUR OWN RESTAURANT SOMEDAY, MUGI.

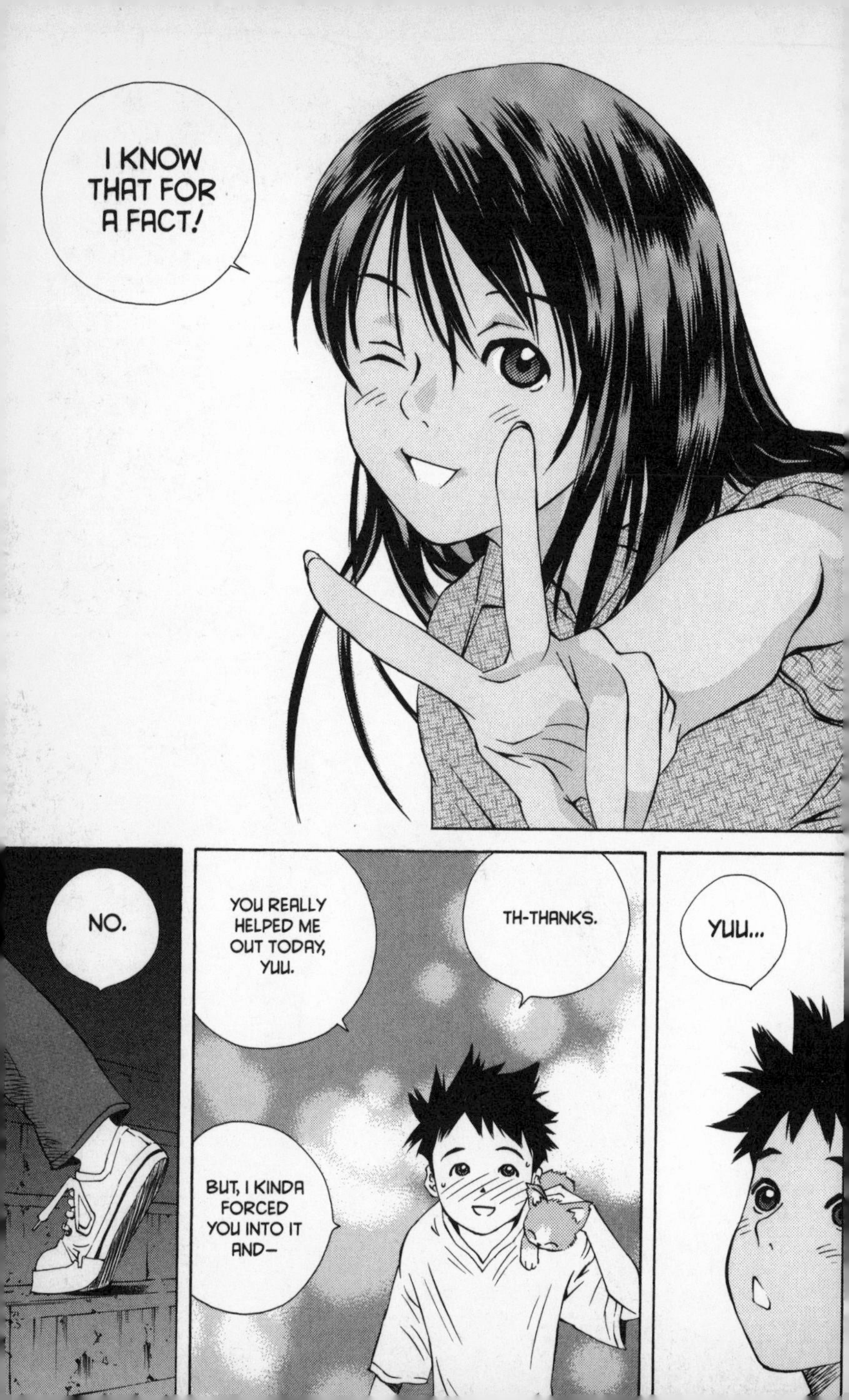
I KNOW THAT FOR A FACT!
YUU...
TH-THANKS.
YOU REALLY HELPED ME OUT TODAY, YUU.
BUT, I KINDA FORCED YOU INTO IT AND–
NO.

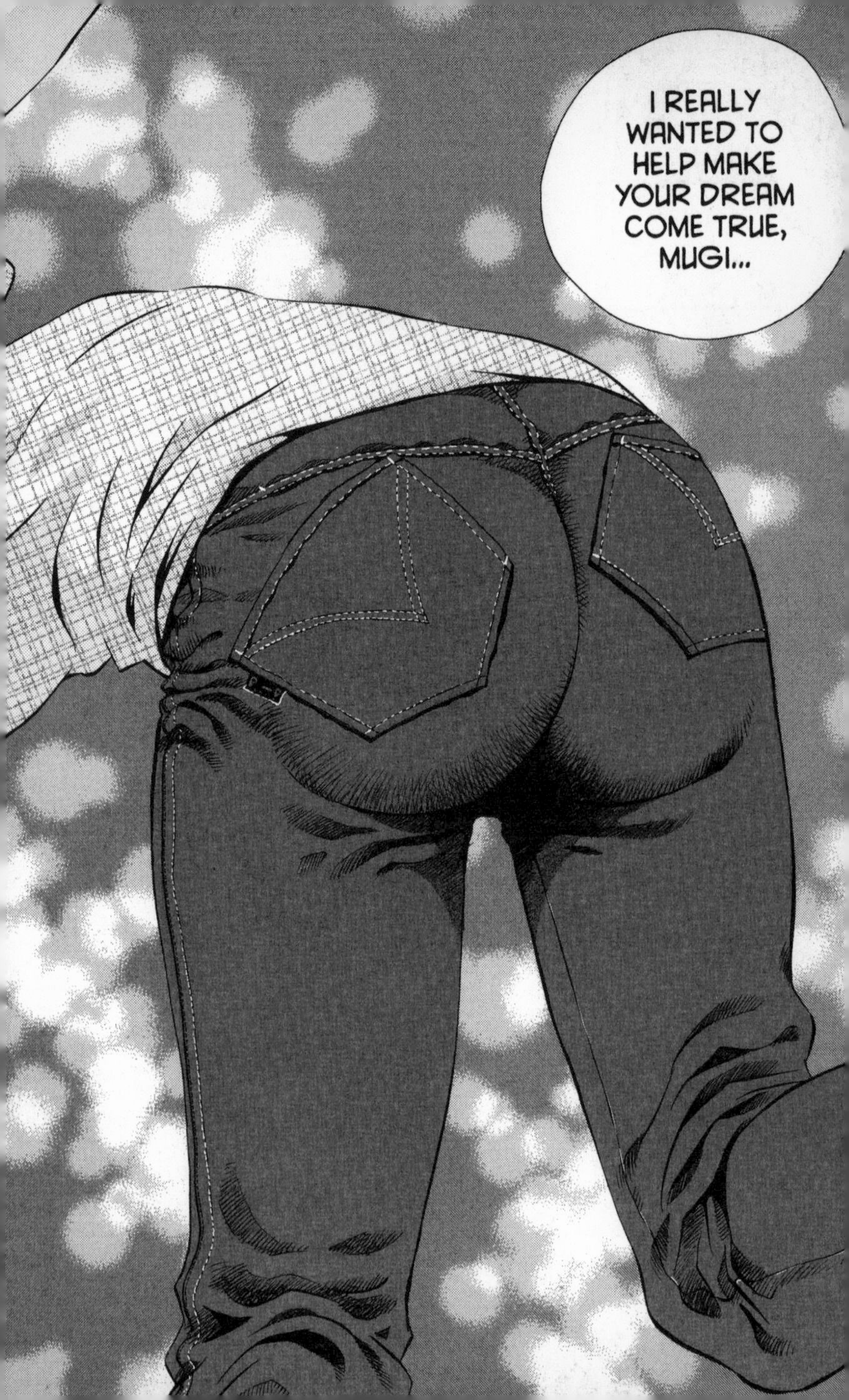
I REALLY WANTED TO HELP MAKE YOUR DREAM COME TRUE, MUGI...

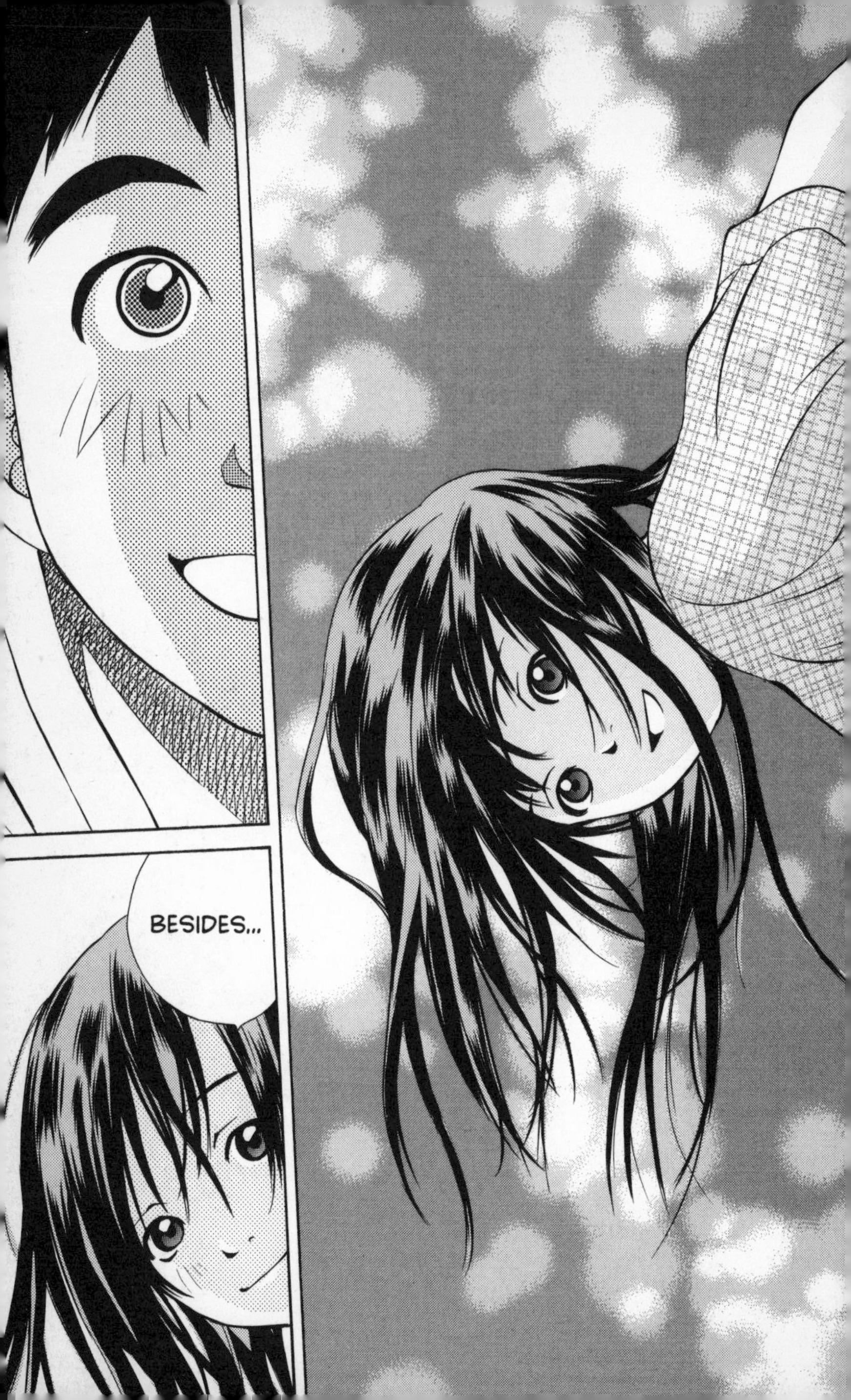
BESIDES...

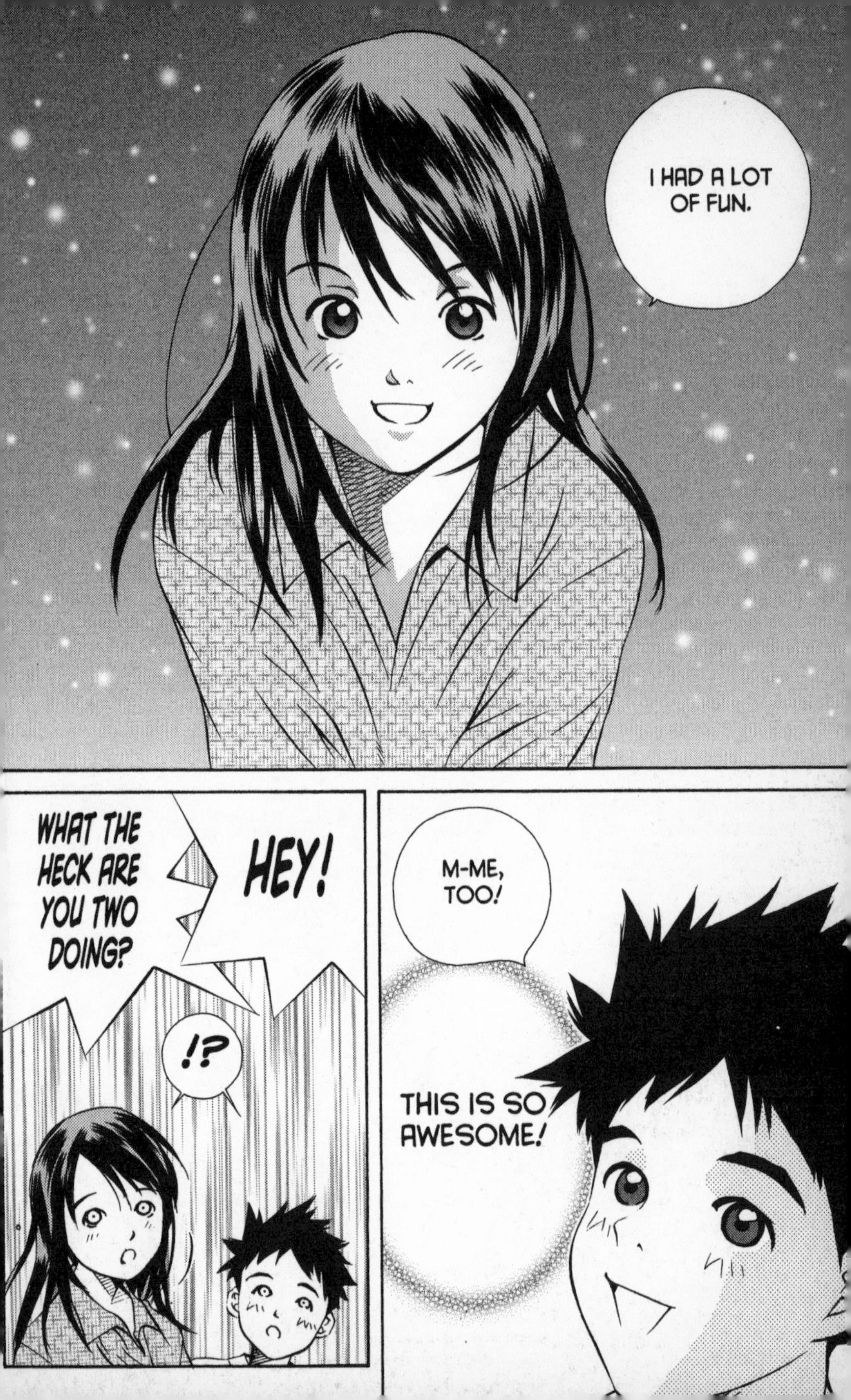
I HAD A LOT OF FUN.
M-ME, TOO!
THIS IS SO AWESOME!
HEY!
WHAT THE HECK ARE YOU TWO DOING?
!?

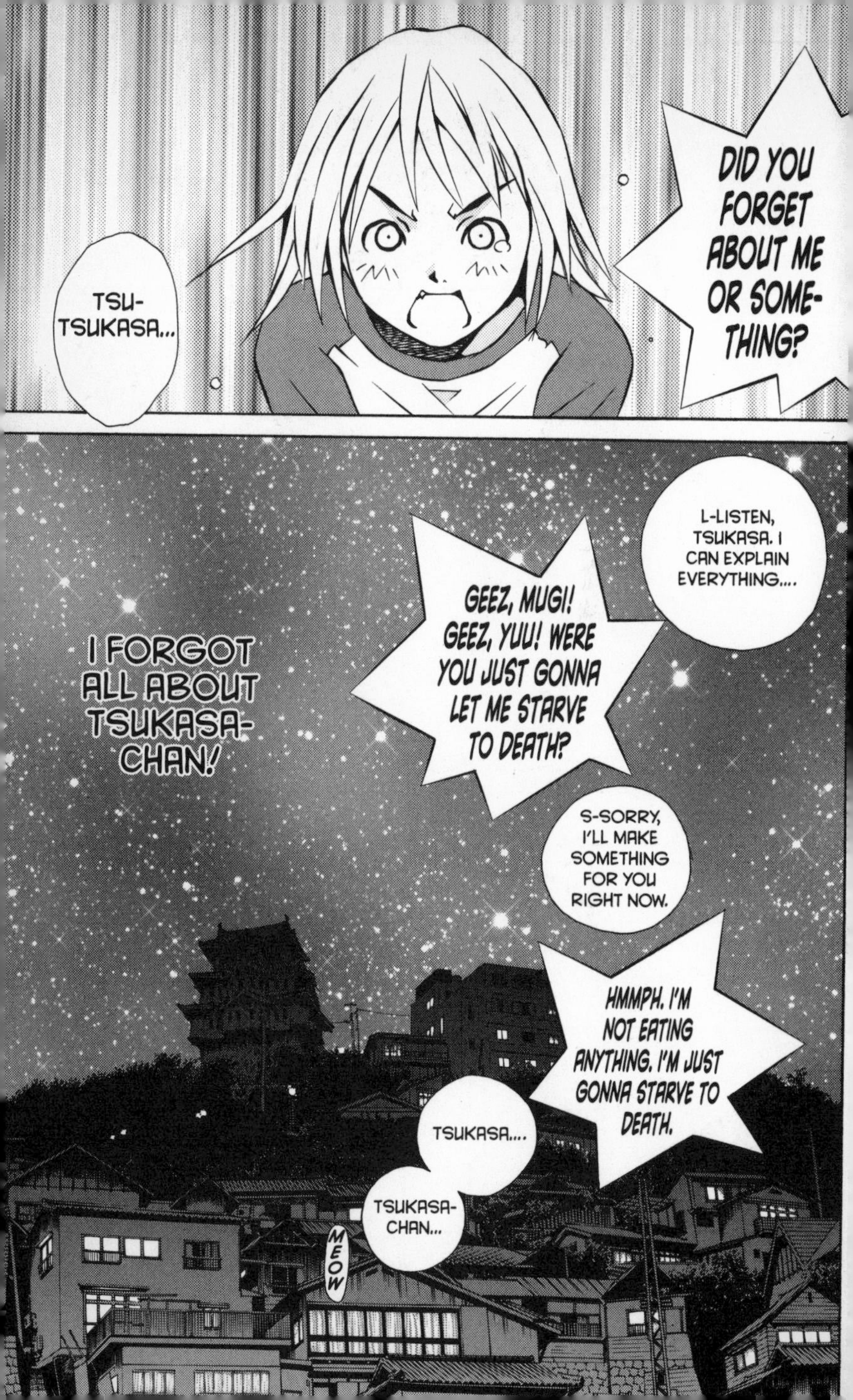
DID YOU FORGET ABOUT ME OR SOME-THING?
TSU-TSUKASA...
L-LISTEN, TSUKASA. I CAN EXPLAIN EVERYTHING....
GEEZ, MUGI! GEEZ, YUU! WERE YOU JUST GONNA LET ME STARVE TO DEATH?
I FORGOT ALL ABOUT TSUKASA-CHAN!
S-SORRY, I'LL MAKE SOMETHING FOR YOU RIGHT NOW.
HMMPH. I'M NOT EATING ANYTHING. I'M JUST GONNA STARVE TO DEATH.
TSUKASA....
TSUKASA-CHAN...
MEOW

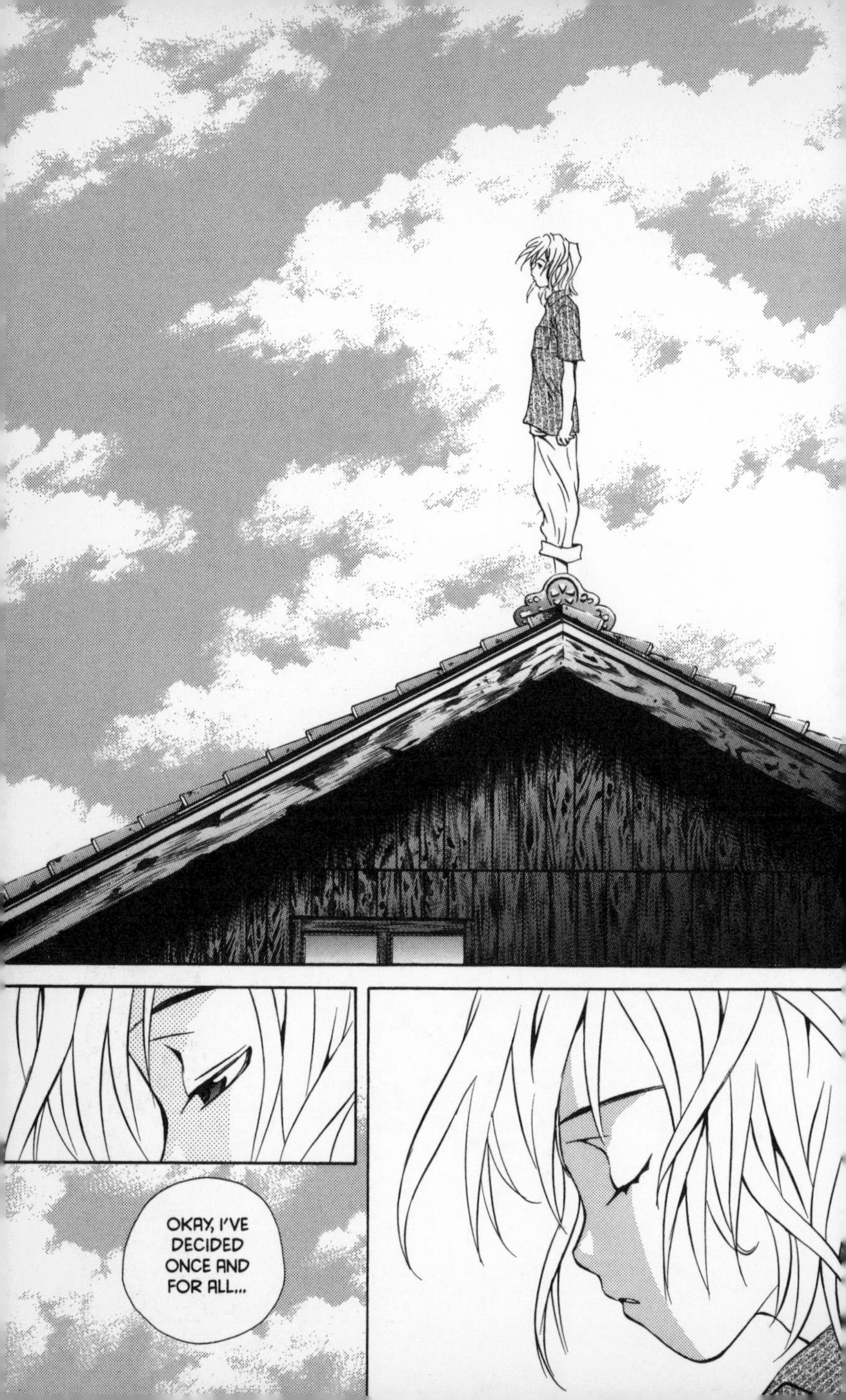
OKAY, I'VE DECIDED ONCE AND FOR ALL...

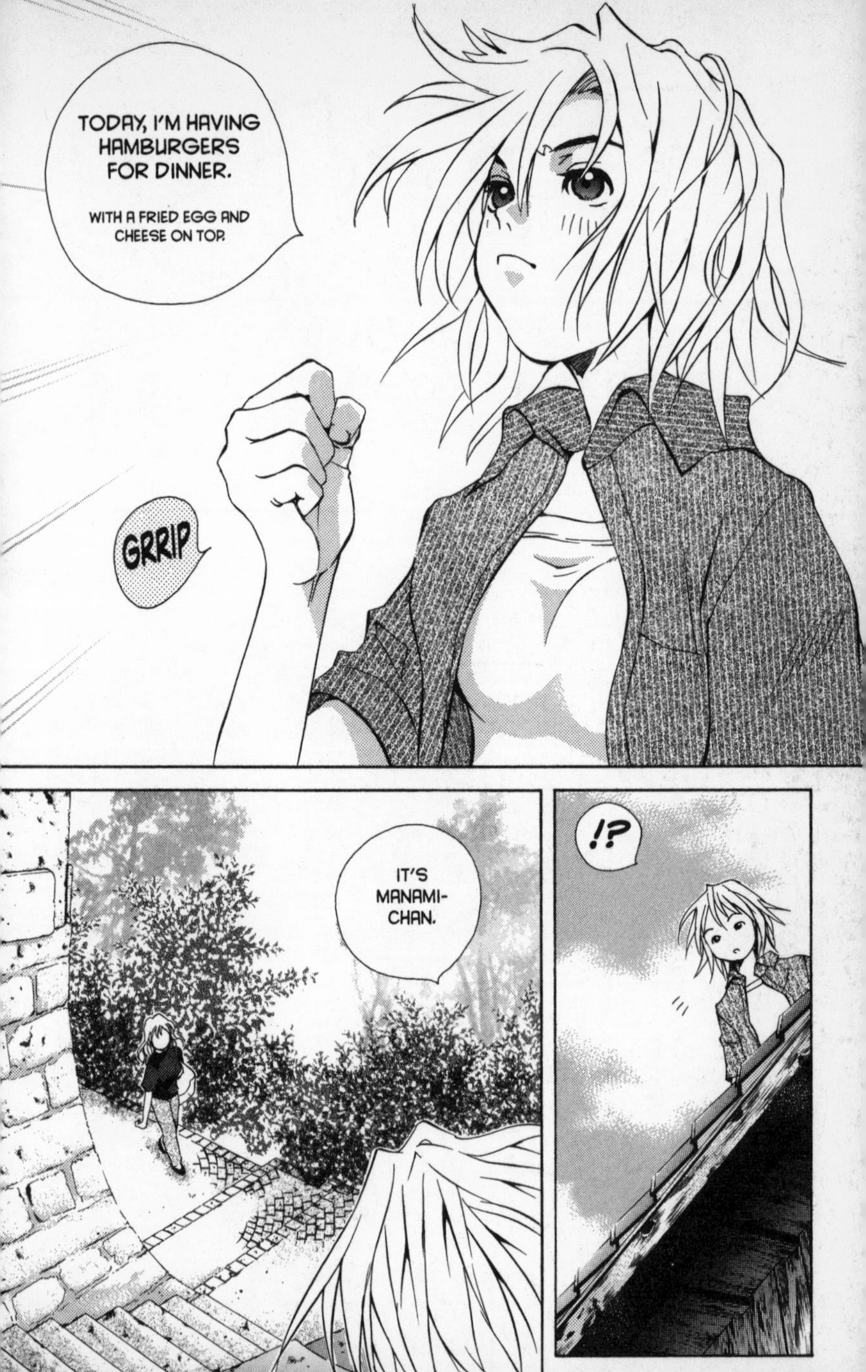
TODAY, I'M HAVING HAMBURGERS FOR DINNER.
WITH A FRIED EGG AND CHEESE ON TOP.
GRRIP
!?
IT'S MANAMI-CHAN.

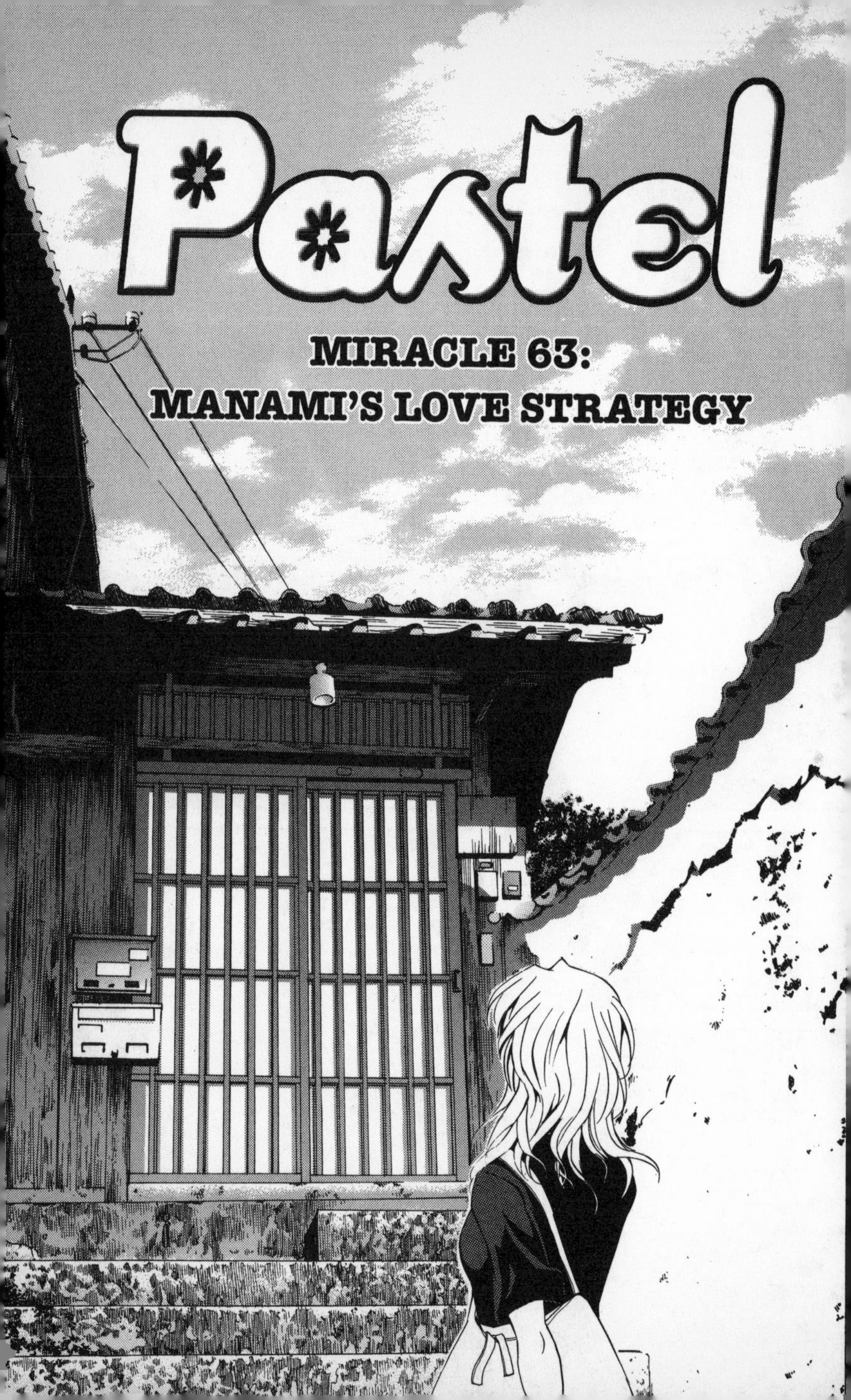
Pastel
MIRACLE 63:
MANAMI'S LOVE STRATEGY

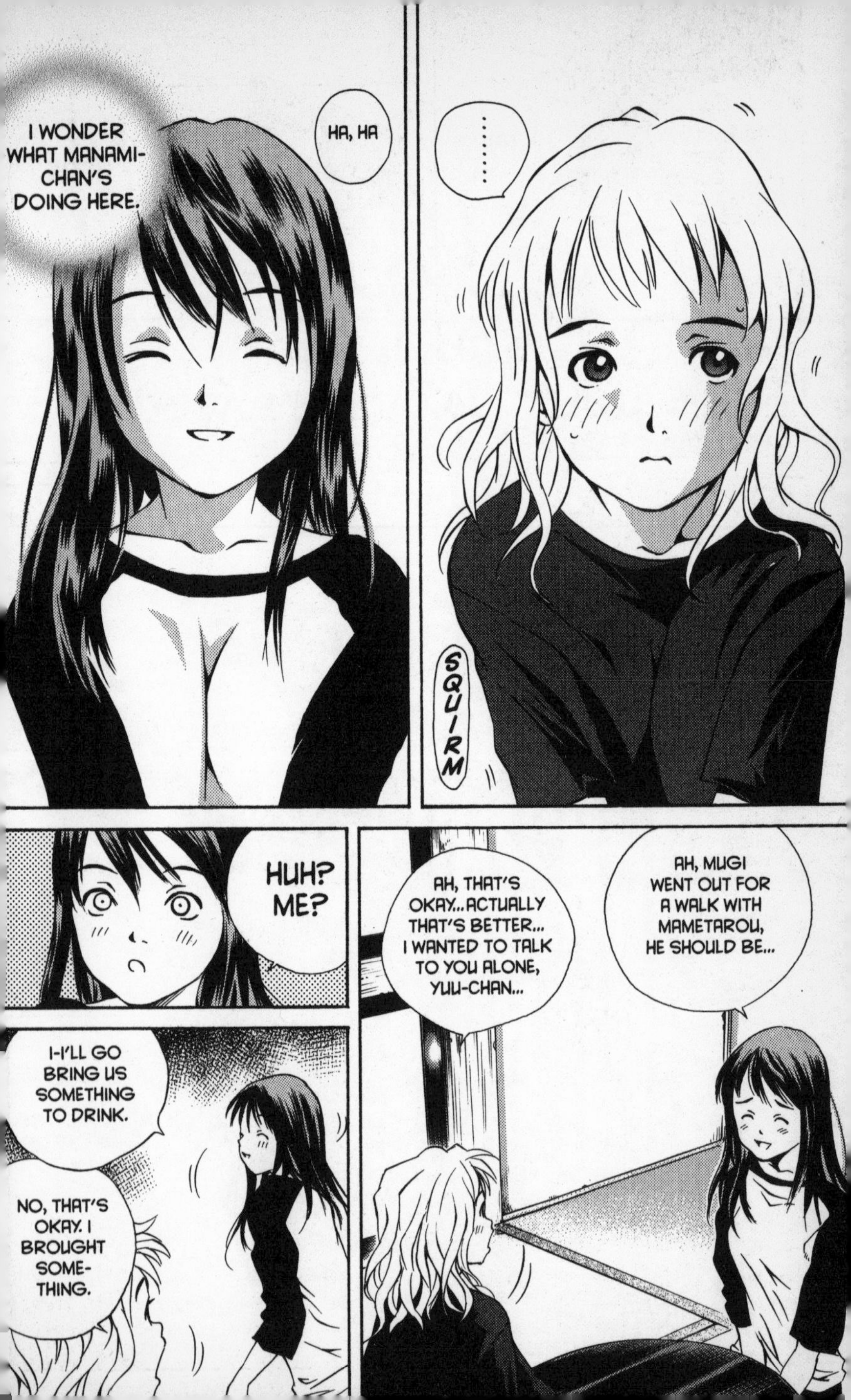
......
SQUIRM
HA, HA
I WONDER WHAT MANAMI-CHAN'S DOING HERE.
AH, MUGI WENT OUT FOR A WALK WITH MAMETAROU, HE SHOULD BE...
AH, THAT'S OKAY...ACTUALLY THAT'S BETTER... I WANTED TO TALK TO YOU ALONE, YUU-CHAN...
HUH? ME?
I-I'LL GO BRING US SOMETHING TO DRINK.
NO, THAT'S OKAY. I BROUGHT SOME-THING.

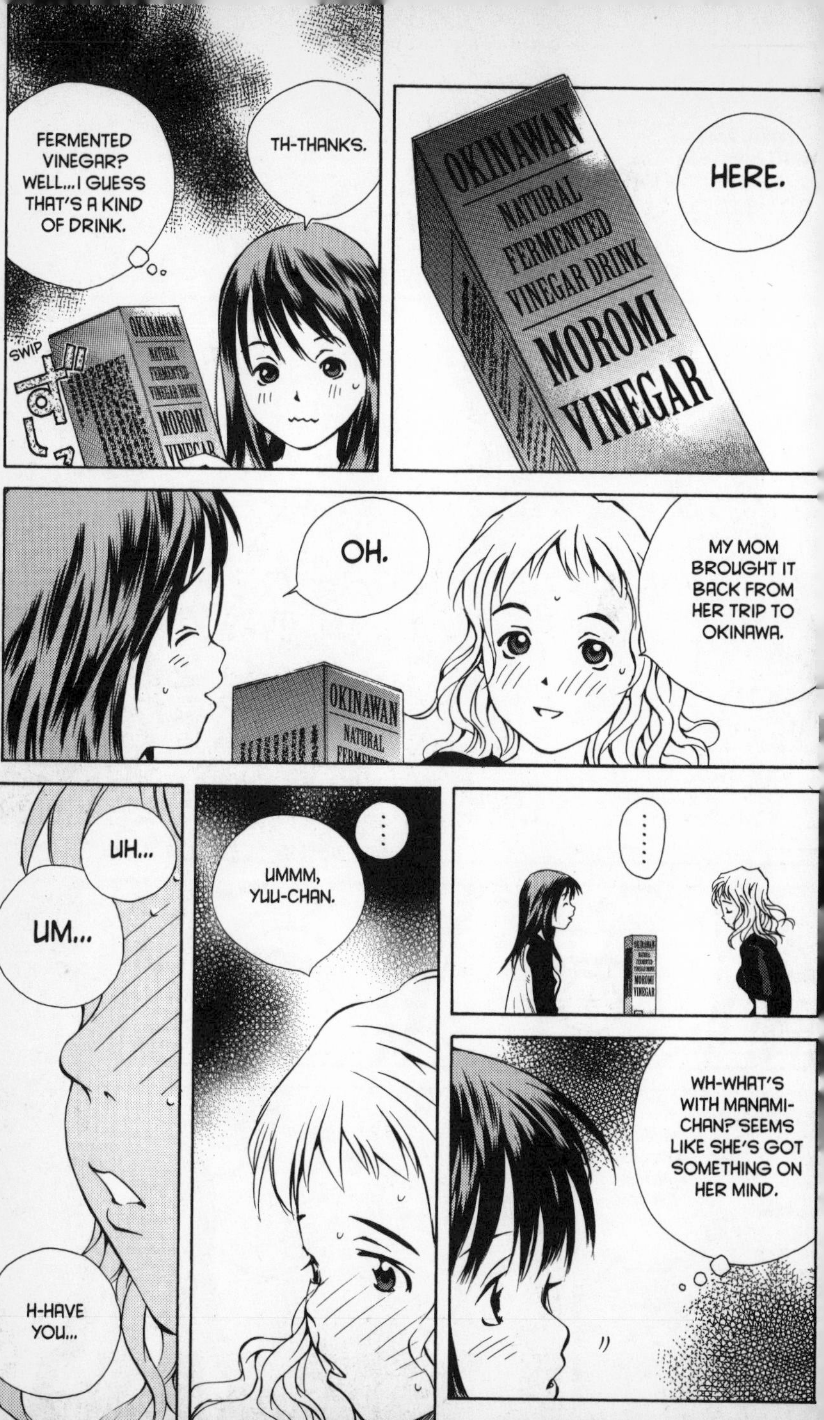
HERE.
OKINAWAN
NATURAL FERMENTED VINEGAR DRINK
MOROMI VINEGAR
TH-THANKS.
FERMENTED VINEGAR? WELL...I GUESS THAT'S A KIND OF DRINK.
SWIP
MY MOM BROUGHT IT BACK FROM HER TRIP TO OKINAWA.
OH.
......
WH-WHAT'S WITH MANAMI-CHAN? SEEMS LIKE SHE'S GOT SOMETHING ON HER MIND.
.....
UMMM, YUU-CHAN.
UH...
UM...
H-HAVE YOU...

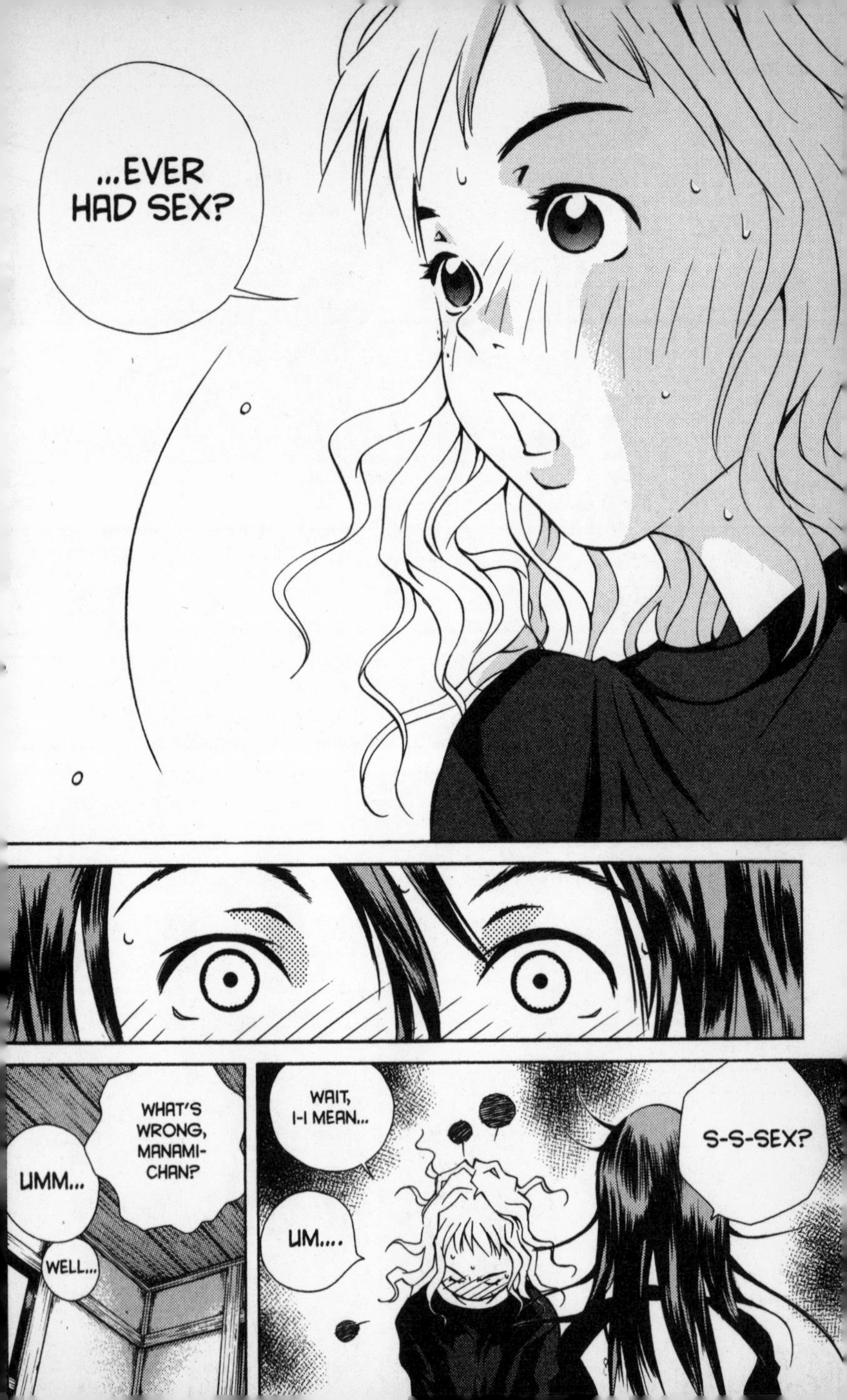
...EVER HAD SEX?
S-S-SEX?
WAIT, I-I MEAN...
UM....
WHAT'S WRONG, MANAMI-CHAN?
UMM...
WELL...

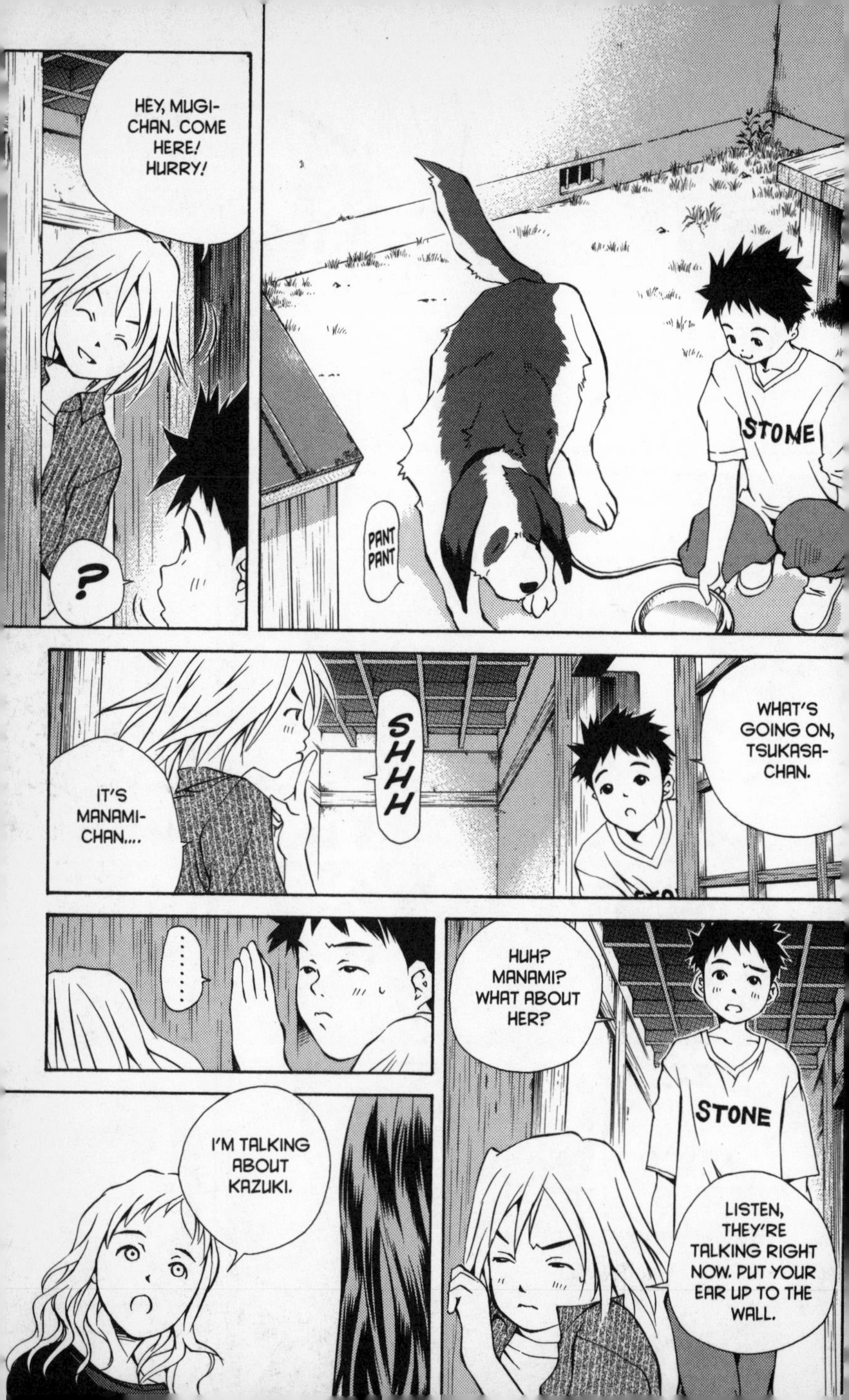
PANT PANT
HEY, MUGI-CHAN. COME HERE! HURRY!
?
WHAT'S GOING ON, TSUKASA-CHAN.
SHHH
IT'S MANAMI-CHAN....
HUH? MANAMI? WHAT ABOUT HER?
LISTEN, THEY'RE TALKING RIGHT NOW. PUT YOUR EAR UP TO THE WALL.
....
I'M TALKING ABOUT KAZUKI.

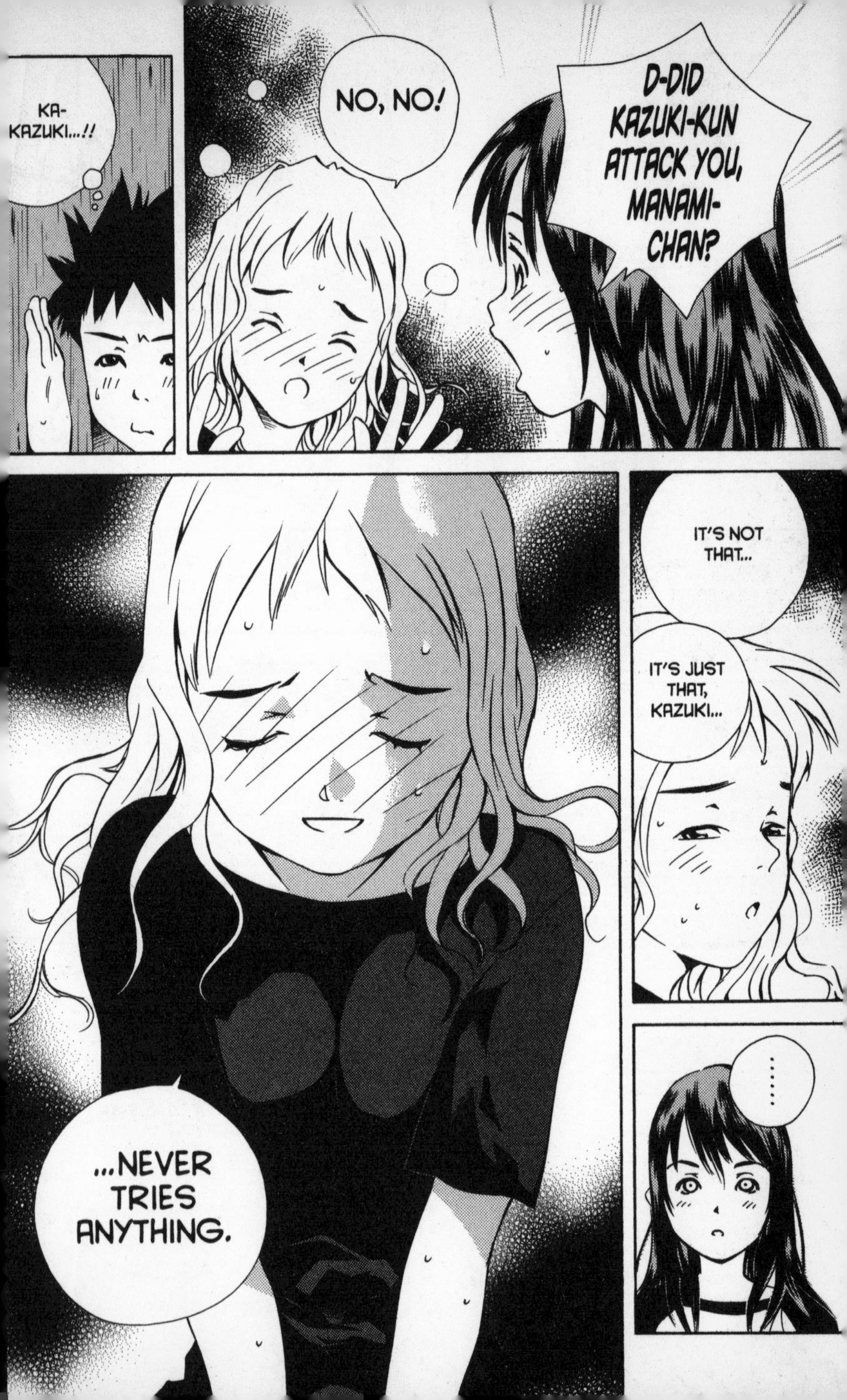
D-DID KAZUKI-KUN ATTACK YOU, MANAMI-CHAN?
NO, NO!
KA-KAZUKI...!!
IT'S NOT THAT...
IT'S JUST THAT, KAZUKI...
......
...NEVER TRIES ANYTHING.

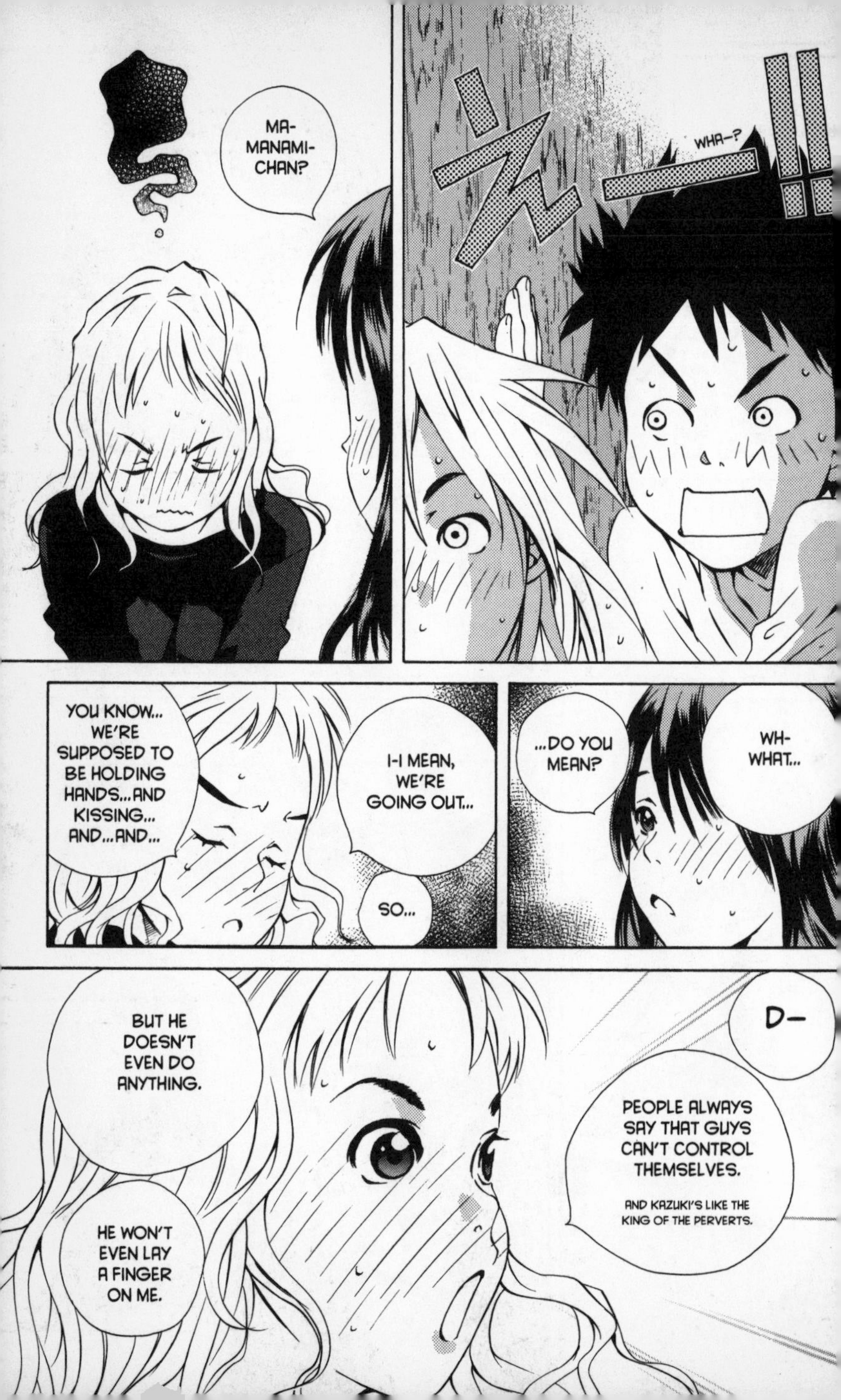
WHA–?
MA-MANAMI-CHAN?
WH-WHAT...
...DO YOU MEAN?
I-I MEAN, WE'RE GOING OUT...
SO...
YOU KNOW... WE'RE SUPPOSED TO BE HOLDING HANDS...AND KISSING... AND...AND...
D–
PEOPLE ALWAYS SAY THAT GUYS CAN'T CONTROL THEMSELVES.
AND KAZUKI'S LIKE THE KING OF THE PERVERTS.
BUT HE DOESN'T EVEN DO ANYTHING.
HE WON'T EVEN LAY A FINGER ON ME.

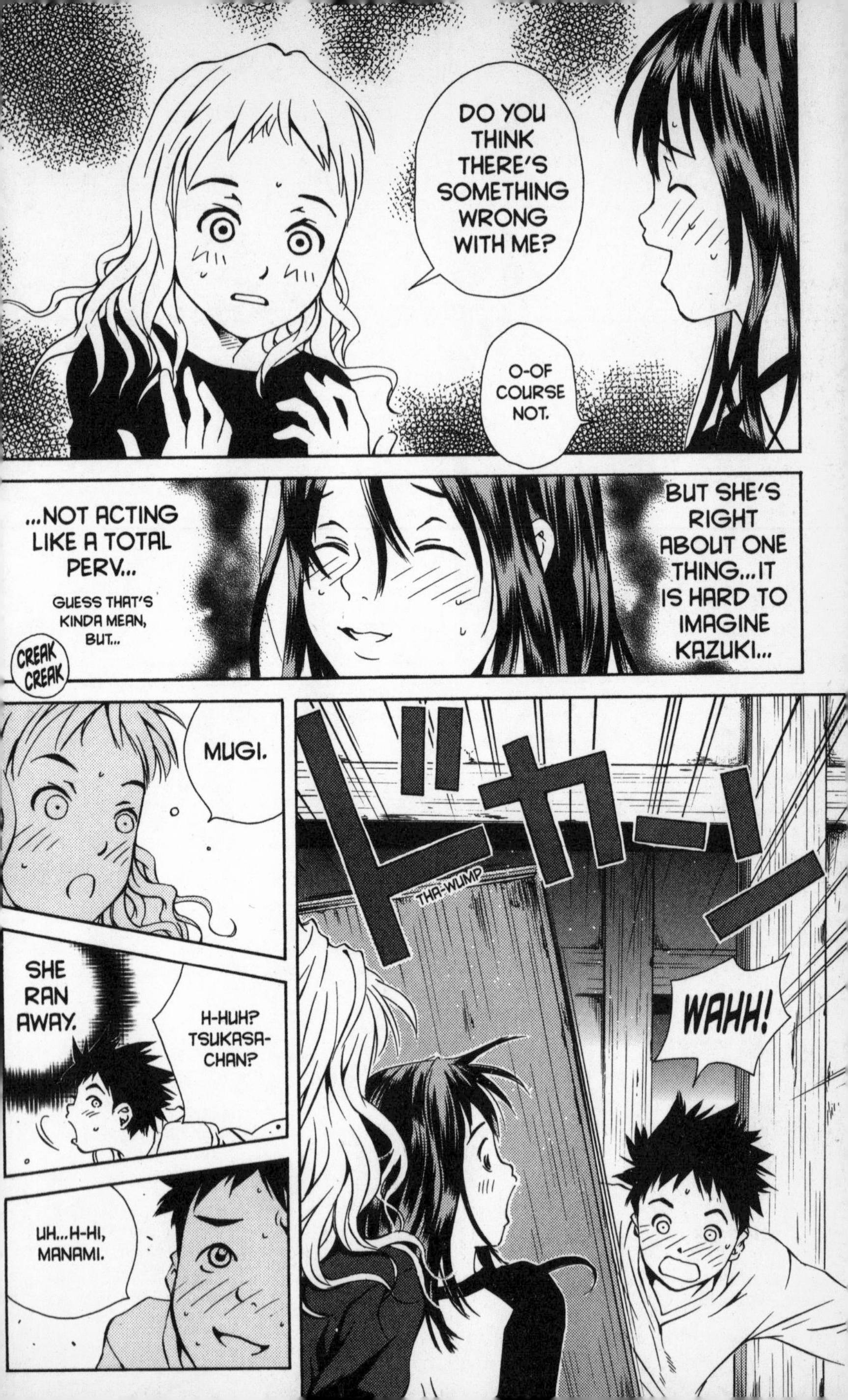
DO YOU THINK THERE'S SOMETHING WRONG WITH ME?
O-OF COURSE NOT.
BUT SHE'S RIGHT ABOUT ONE THING...IT IS HARD TO IMAGINE KAZUKI...
...NOT ACTING LIKE A TOTAL PERV...
GUESS THAT'S KINDA MEAN, BUT...
CREAK CREAK
ドカーン
THA-WUMP
WAHH!
MUGI.
H-HUH? TSUKASA-CHAN?
SHE RAN AWAY.
UH...H-HI, MANAMI.

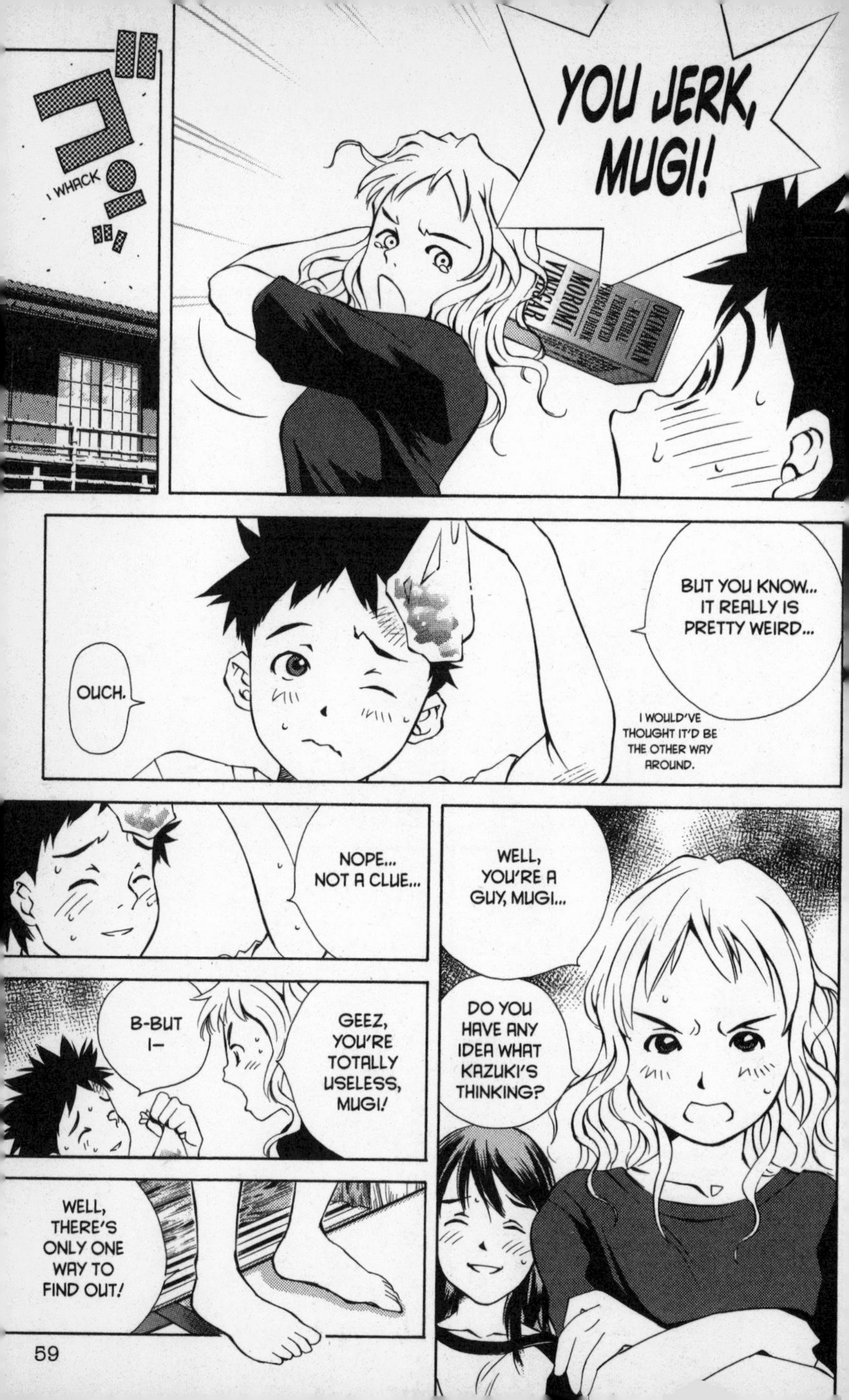
YOU JERK, MUGI!
OKINAWAN
MOROMI VINEGAR
WHACK
BUT YOU KNOW... IT REALLY IS PRETTY WEIRD...
I WOULD'VE THOUGHT IT'D BE THE OTHER WAY AROUND.
OUCH.
WELL, YOU'RE A GUY, MUGI...
DO YOU HAVE ANY IDEA WHAT KAZUKI'S THINKING?
NOPE... NOT A CLUE...
GEEZ, YOU'RE TOTALLY USELESS, MUGI!
B-BUT I—
WELL, THERE'S ONLY ONE WAY TO FIND OUT!

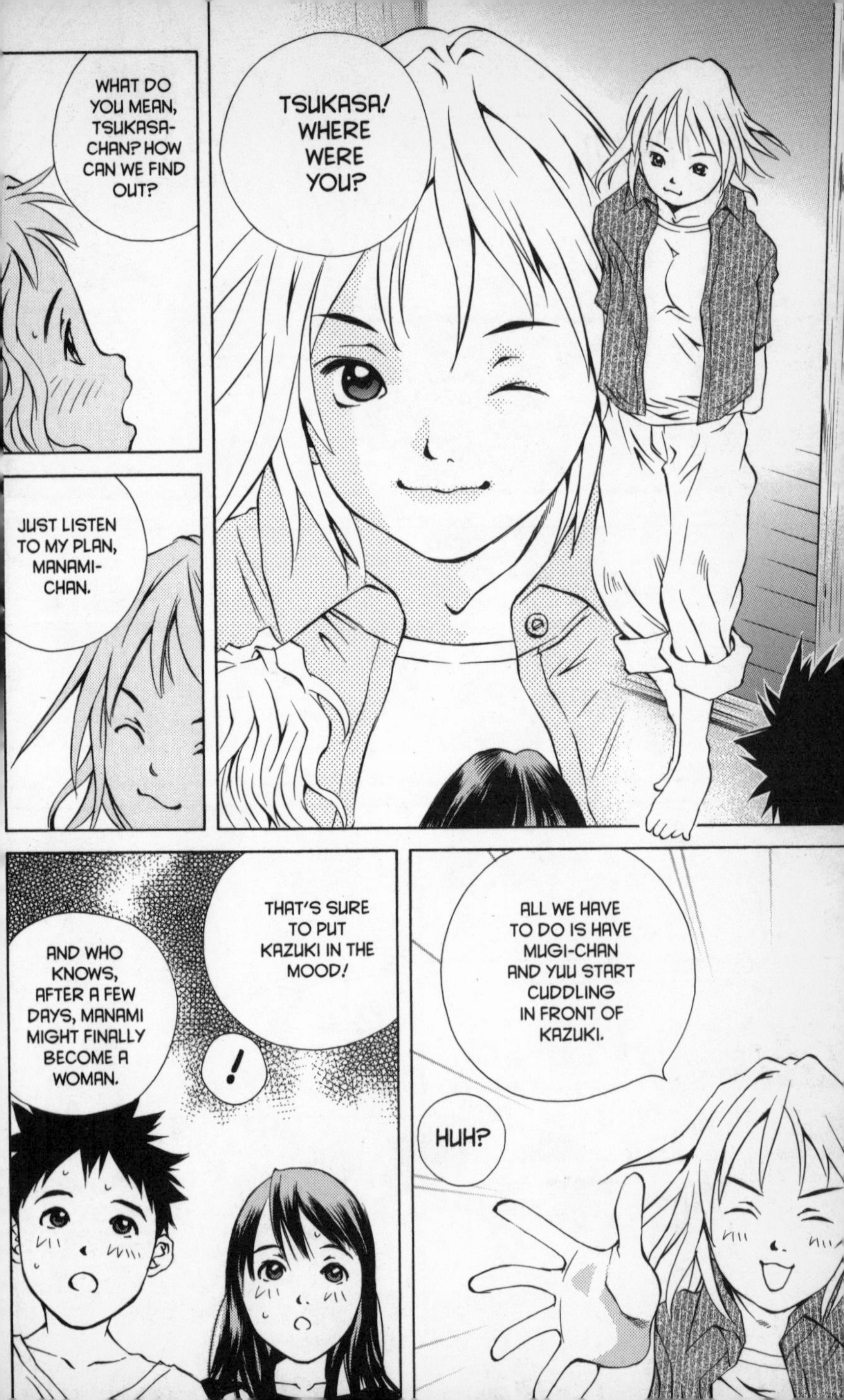
TSUKASA! WHERE WERE YOU?
WHAT DO YOU MEAN, TSUKASA-CHAN? HOW CAN WE FIND OUT?
JUST LISTEN TO MY PLAN, MANAMI-CHAN.
ALL WE HAVE TO DO IS HAVE MUGI-CHAN AND YUU START CUDDLING IN FRONT OF KAZUKI.
HUH?
THAT'S SURE TO PUT KAZUKI IN THE MOOD!
!
AND WHO KNOWS, AFTER A FEW DAYS, MANAMI MIGHT FINALLY BECOME A WOMAN.

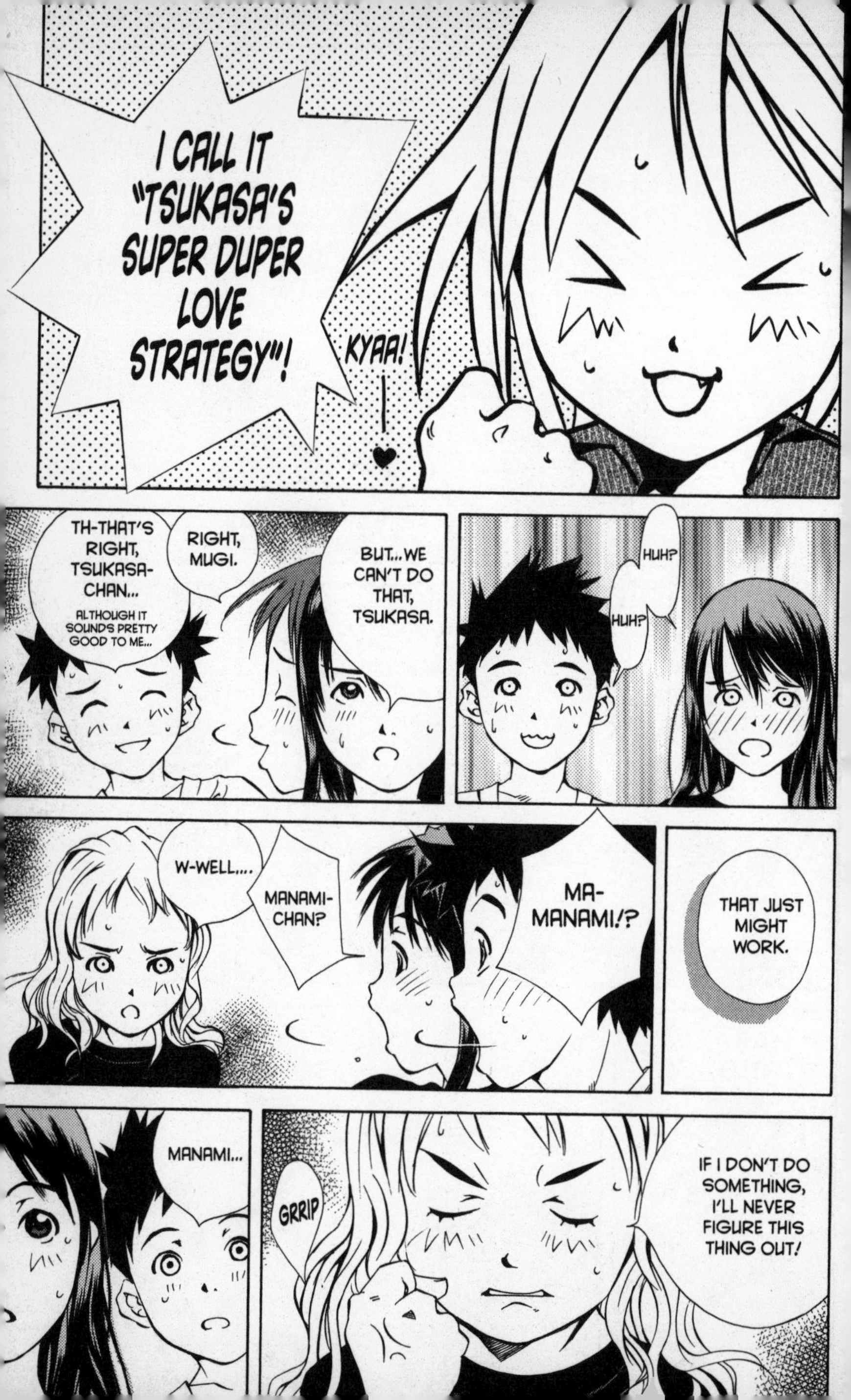
I CALL IT "TSUKASA'S SUPER DUPER LOVE STRATEGY"!
KYAA! ♥
HUH?
HUH?
BUT...WE CAN'T DO THAT, TSUKASA.
RIGHT, MUGI.
TH-THAT'S RIGHT, TSUKASA-CHAN...
ALTHOUGH IT SOUNDS PRETTY GOOD TO ME...
THAT JUST MIGHT WORK.
MA-MANAMI!?
MANAMI-CHAN?
W-WELL....
IF I DON'T DO SOMETHING, I'LL NEVER FIGURE THIS THING OUT!
GRRIP
MANAMI...

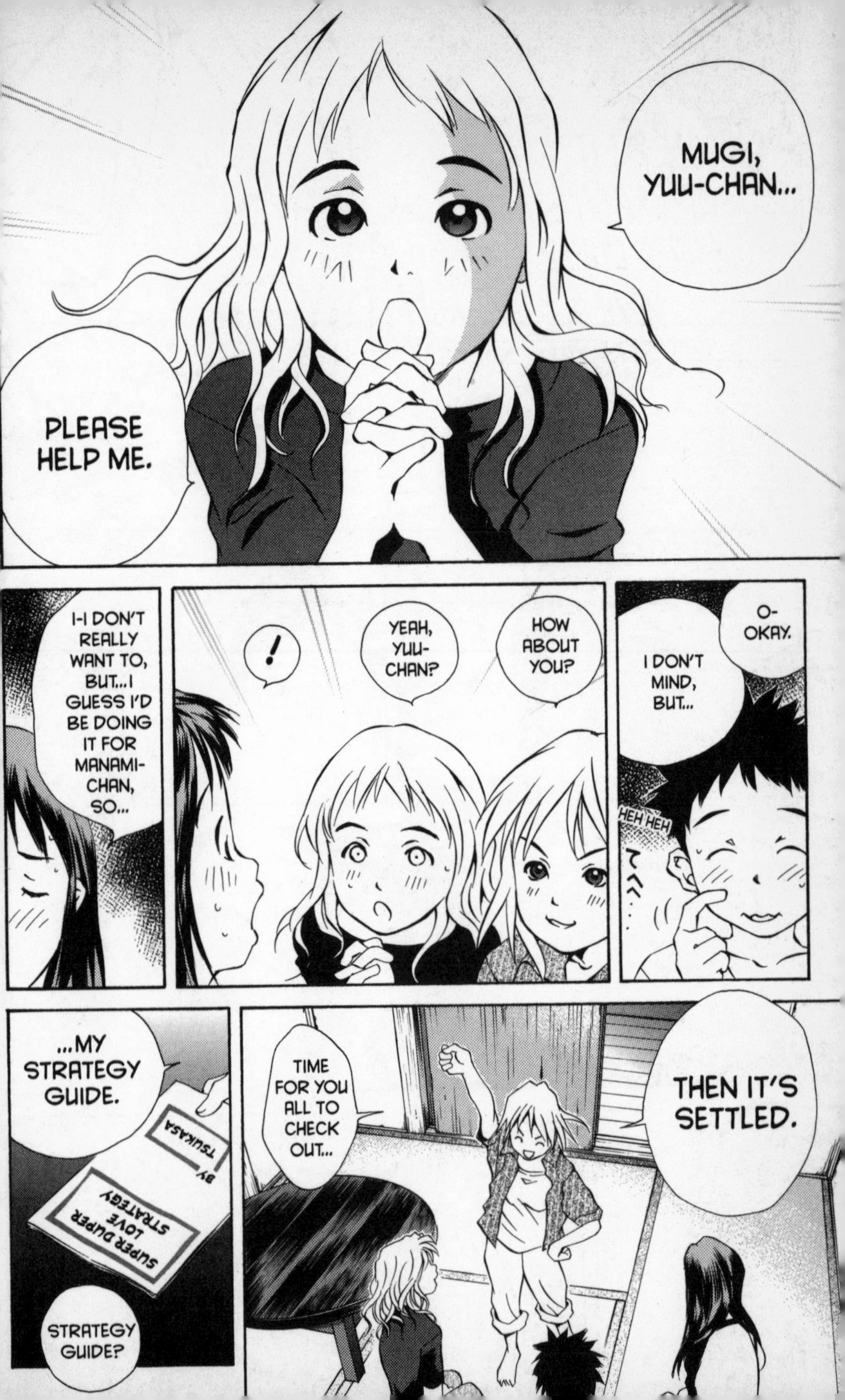
MUGI, YUU-CHAN...
PLEASE HELP ME.
O-OKAY.
I DON'T MIND, BUT...
HEH HEH
HOW ABOUT YOU?
YEAH, YUU-CHAN?
!
I-I DON'T REALLY WANT TO, BUT...I GUESS I'D BE DOING IT FOR MANAMI-CHAN, SO...
THEN IT'S SETTLED.
TIME FOR YOU ALL TO CHECK OUT...
...MY STRATEGY GUIDE.
SUPER DUPER LOVE STRATEGY
BY TSUKASA
STRATEGY GUIDE?

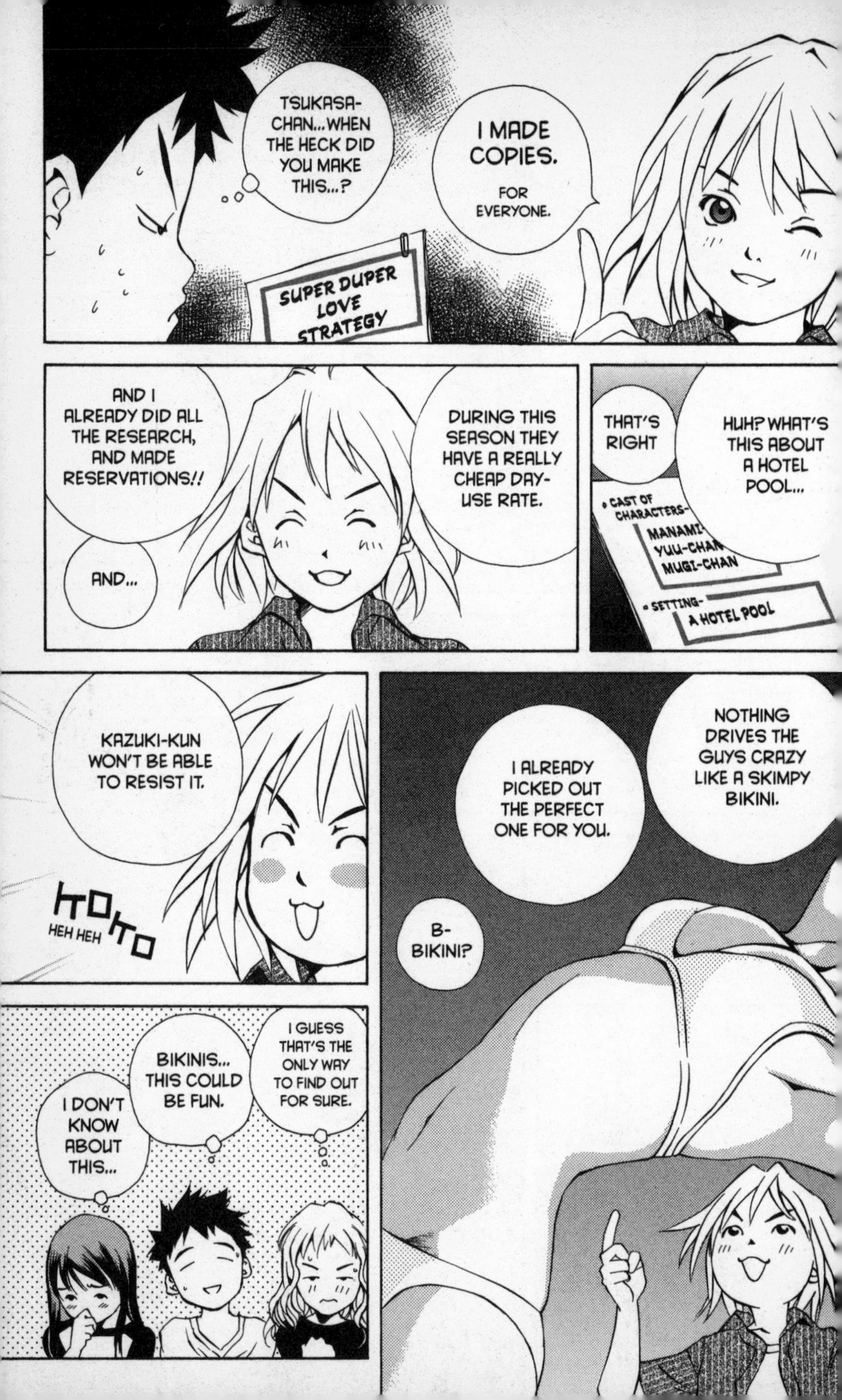
I MADE COPIES.
FOR EVERYONE.
TSUKASA-CHAN...WHEN THE HECK DID YOU MAKE THIS...?
SUPER DUPER LOVE STRATEGY
HUH? WHAT'S THIS ABOUT A HOTEL POOL...
THAT'S RIGHT
CAST OF CHARACTERS-
MANAMI-
YUU-CHAN
MUGI-CHAN
SETTING-
A HOTEL POOL
DURING THIS SEASON THEY HAVE A REALLY CHEAP DAY-USE RATE.
AND I ALREADY DID ALL THE RESEARCH, AND MADE RESERVATIONS!!
AND...
NOTHING DRIVES THE GUYS CRAZY LIKE A SKIMPY BIKINI.
I ALREADY PICKED OUT THE PERFECT ONE FOR YOU.
B-BIKINI?
KAZUKI-KUN WON'T BE ABLE TO RESIST IT.
HEH HEH
I GUESS THAT'S THE ONLY WAY TO FIND OUT FOR SURE.
BIKINIS... THIS COULD BE FUN.
I DON'T KNOW ABOUT THIS...

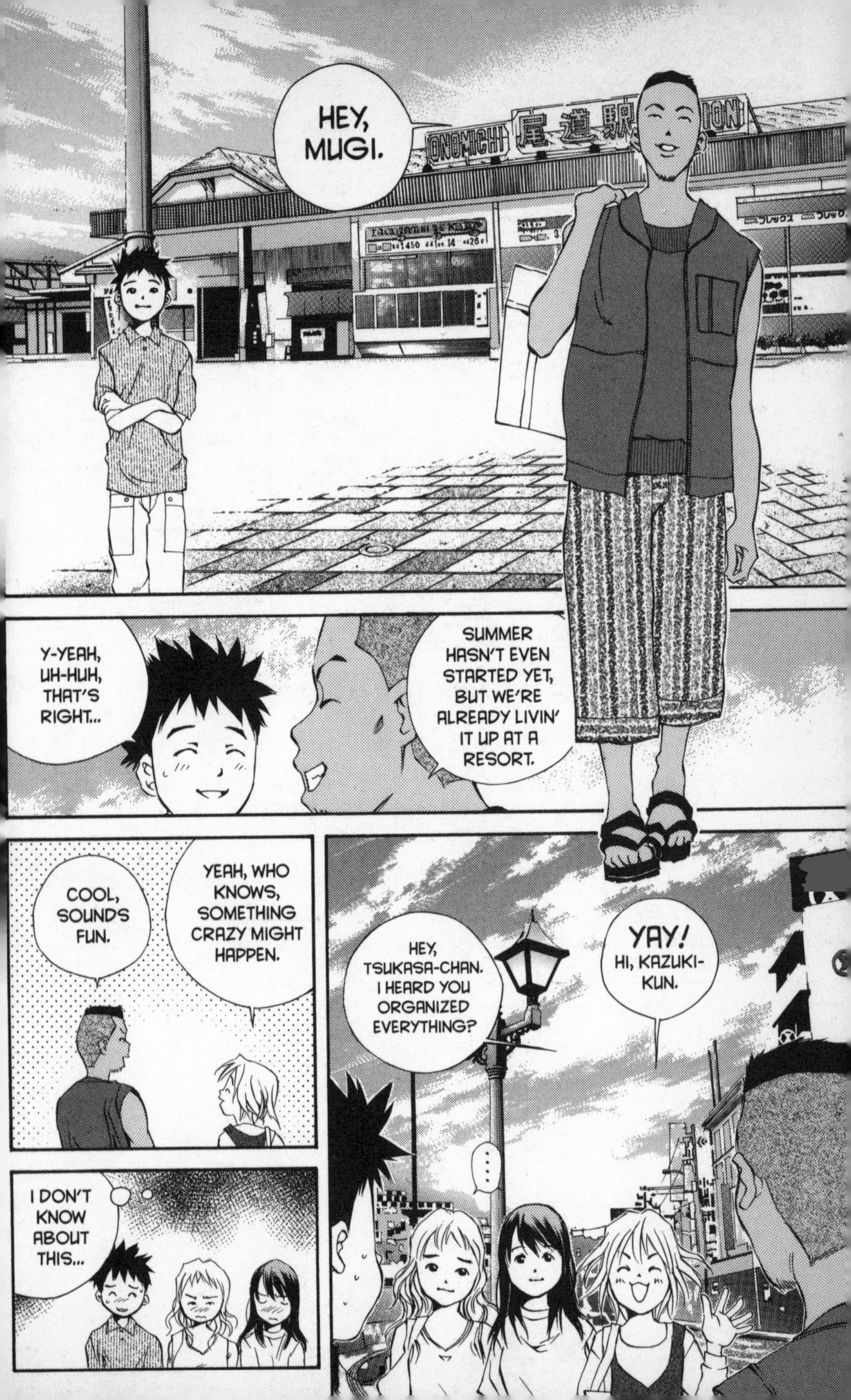
ONOMICHI 尾道駅
HEY, MUGI.
SUMMER HASN'T EVEN STARTED YET, BUT WE'RE ALREADY LIVIN' IT UP AT A RESORT.
Y-YEAH, UH-HUH, THAT'S RIGHT...
YAY! HI, KAZUKI-KUN.
HEY, TSUKASA-CHAN. I HEARD YOU ORGANIZED EVERYTHING?
....
YEAH, WHO KNOWS, SOMETHING CRAZY MIGHT HAPPEN.
COOL, SOUNDS FUN.
I DON'T KNOW ABOUT THIS...

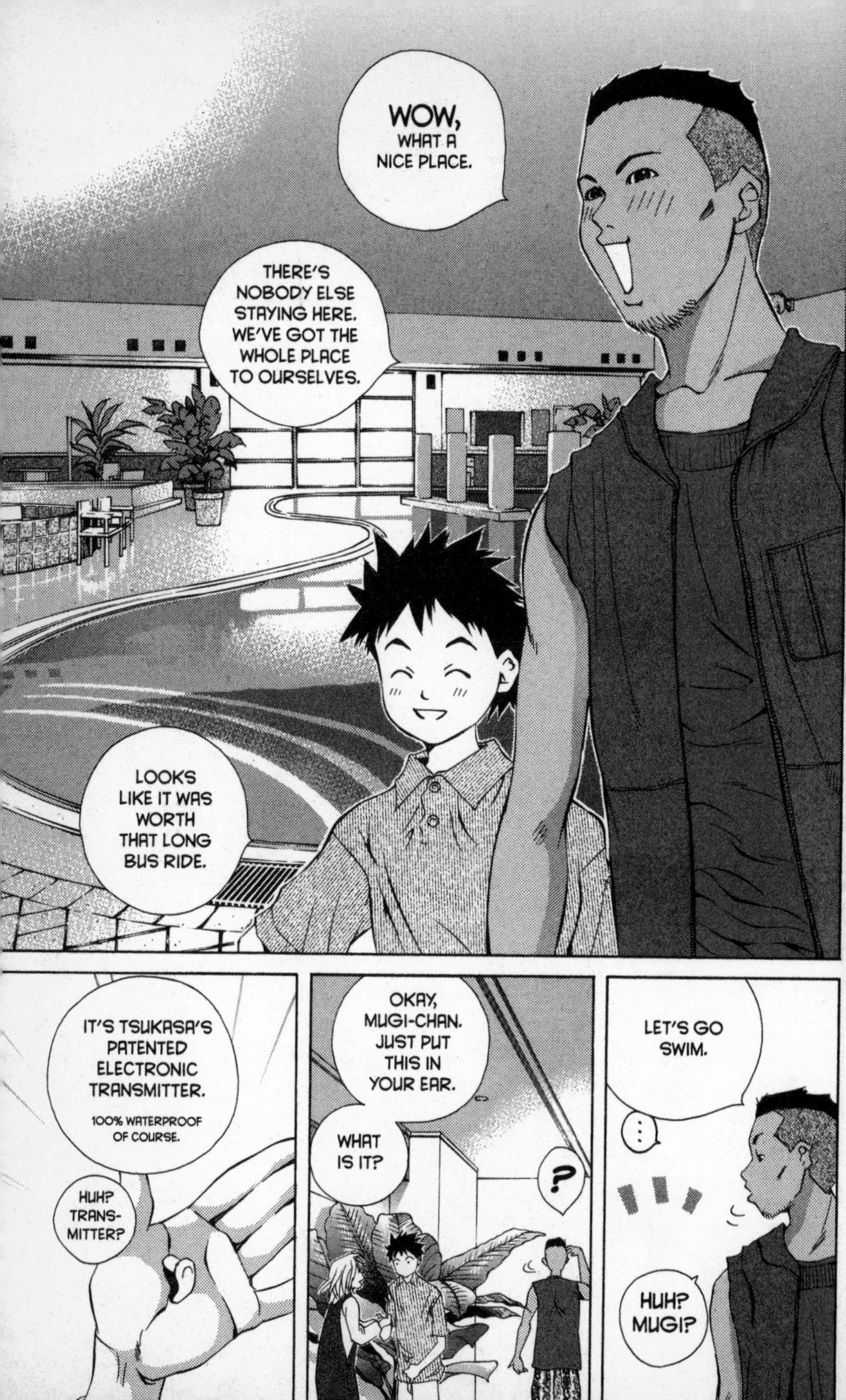
WOW, WHAT A NICE PLACE.
THERE'S NOBODY ELSE STAYING HERE. WE'VE GOT THE WHOLE PLACE TO OURSELVES.
LOOKS LIKE IT WAS WORTH THAT LONG BUS RIDE.
LET'S GO SWIM.
...
HUH? MUGI?
OKAY, MUGI-CHAN. JUST PUT THIS IN YOUR EAR.
WHAT IS IT?
?
IT'S TSUKASA'S PATENTED ELECTRONIC TRANSMITTER.
100% WATERPROOF OF COURSE.
HUH? TRANS-MITTER?

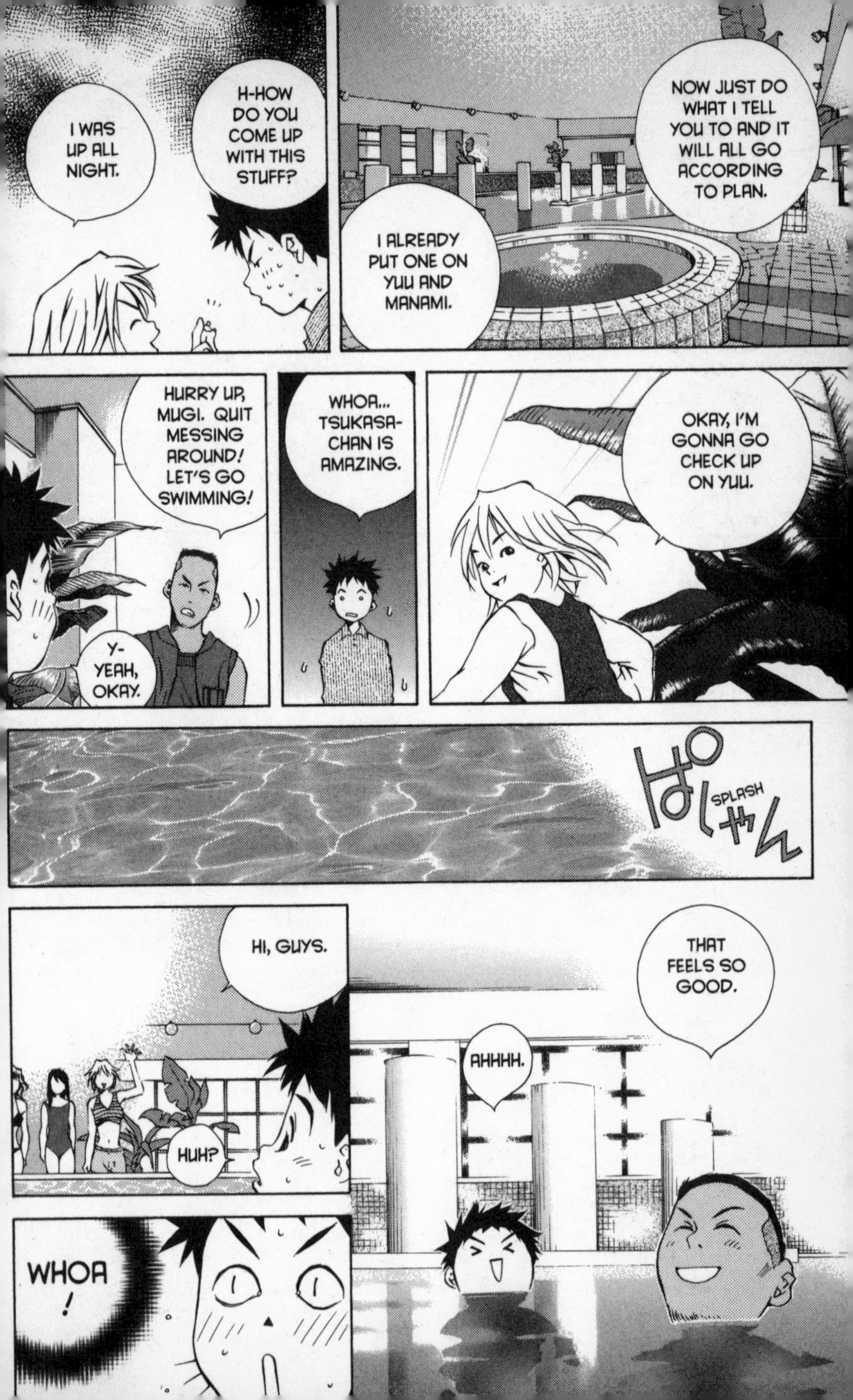
NOW JUST DO WHAT I TELL YOU TO AND IT WILL ALL GO ACCORDING TO PLAN.
I ALREADY PUT ONE ON YUU AND MANAMI.
H-HOW DO YOU COME UP WITH THIS STUFF?
I WAS UP ALL NIGHT.
OKAY, I'M GONNA GO CHECK UP ON YUU.
WHOA... TSUKASA-CHAN IS AMAZING.
HURRY UP, MUGI. QUIT MESSING AROUND! LET'S GO SWIMMING!
Y-YEAH, OKAY.
ぱしゃん
SPLASH
THAT FEELS SO GOOD.
AHHHH.
HI, GUYS.
HUH?
WHOA!

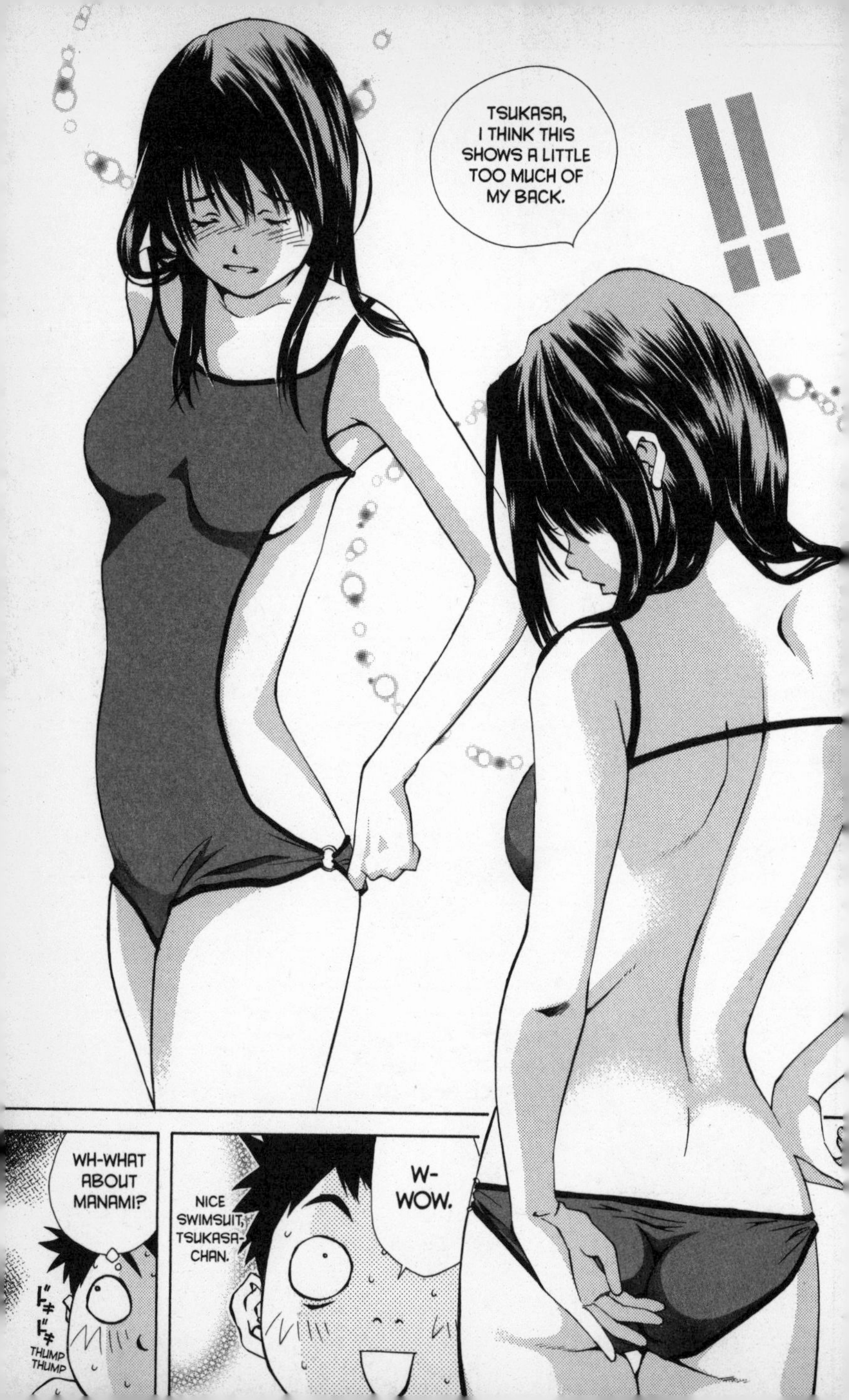

TSUKASA, I THINK THIS SHOWS A LITTLE TOO MUCH OF MY BACK.
!!
W-WOW.
NICE SWIMSUIT, TSUKASA-CHAN.
WH-WHAT ABOUT MANAMI?
ドキドキ
THUMP THUMP

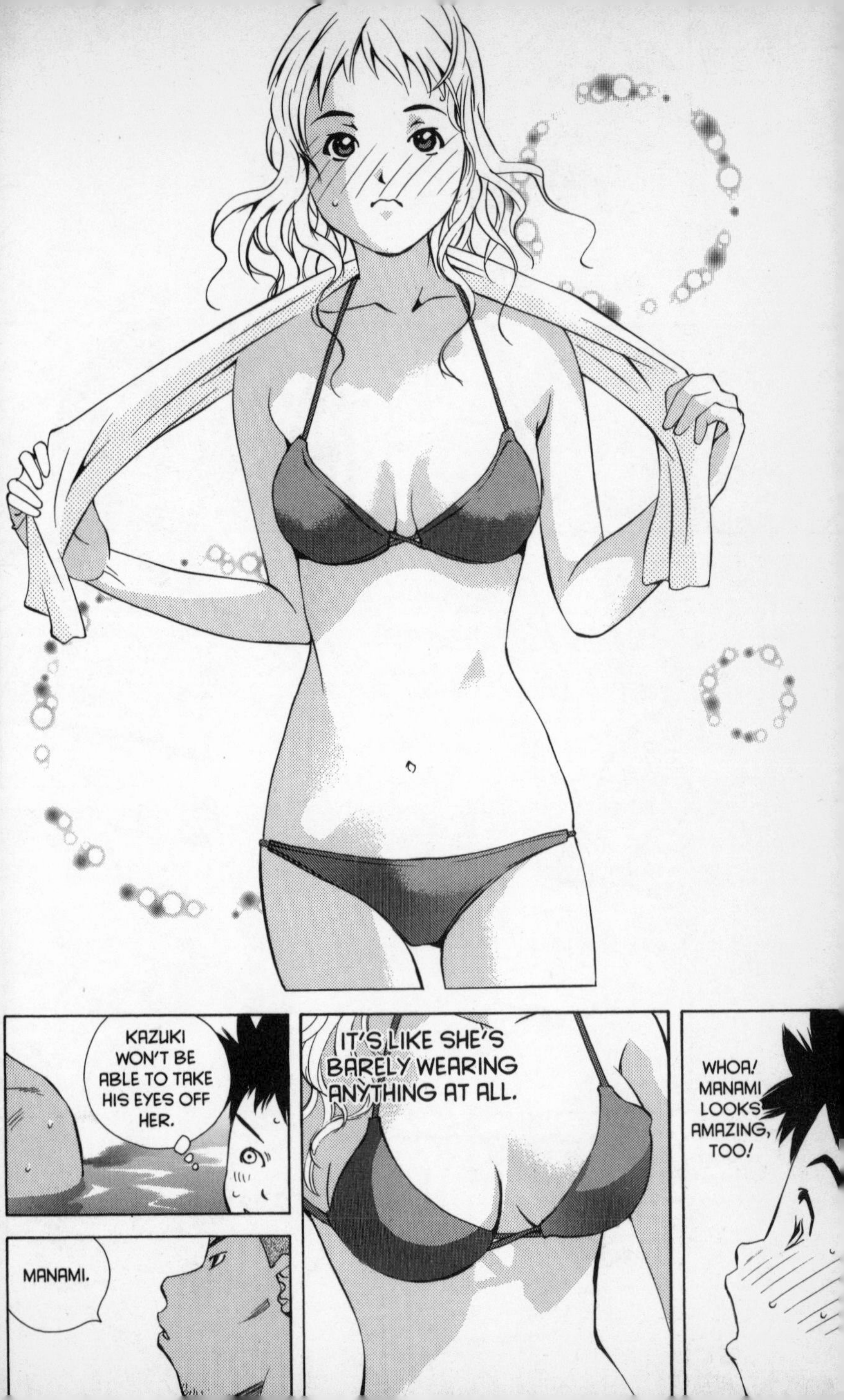
WHOA! MANAMI LOOKS AMAZING, TOO!
IT'S LIKE SHE'S BARELY WEARING ANYTHING AT ALL.
KAZUKI WON'T BE ABLE TO TAKE HIS EYES OFF HER.
MANAMI.

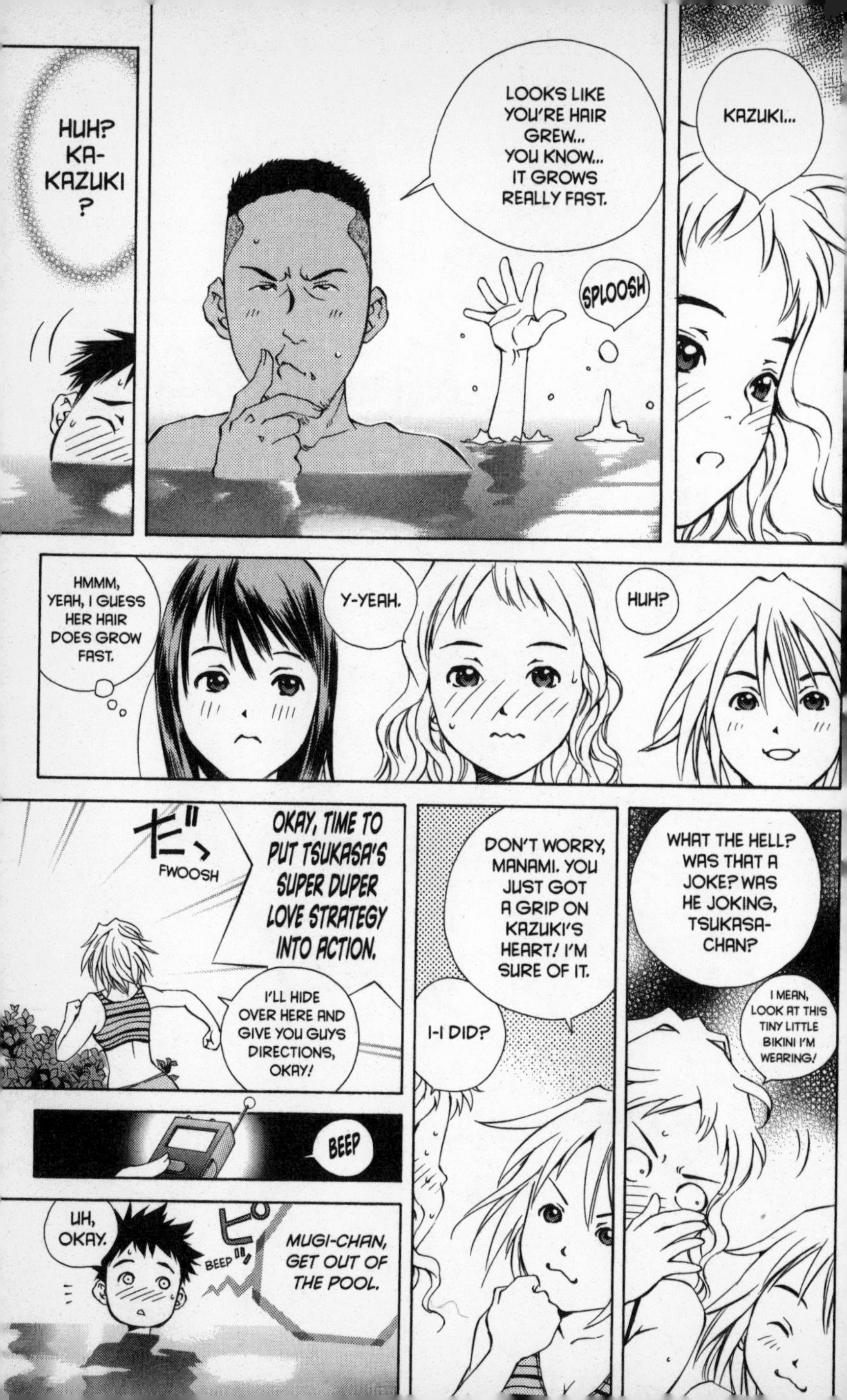
KAZUKI...
LOOKS LIKE YOU'RE HAIR GREW... YOU KNOW... IT GROWS REALLY FAST.
SPLOOSH
HUH? KA-KAZUKI?
HUH?
Y-YEAH.
HMMM, YEAH, I GUESS HER HAIR DOES GROW FAST.
WHAT THE HELL? WAS THAT A JOKE? WAS HE JOKING, TSUKASA-CHAN?
I MEAN, LOOK AT THIS TINY LITTLE BIKINI I'M WEARING!
DON'T WORRY, MANAMI. YOU JUST GOT A GRIP ON KAZUKI'S HEART! I'M SURE OF IT.
I-I DID?
OKAY, TIME TO PUT TSUKASA'S SUPER DUPER LOVE STRATEGY INTO ACTION.
FWOOSH
I'LL HIDE OVER HERE AND GIVE YOU GUYS DIRECTIONS, OKAY!
BEEP
MUGI-CHAN, GET OUT OF THE POOL.
BEEP
UH, OKAY.

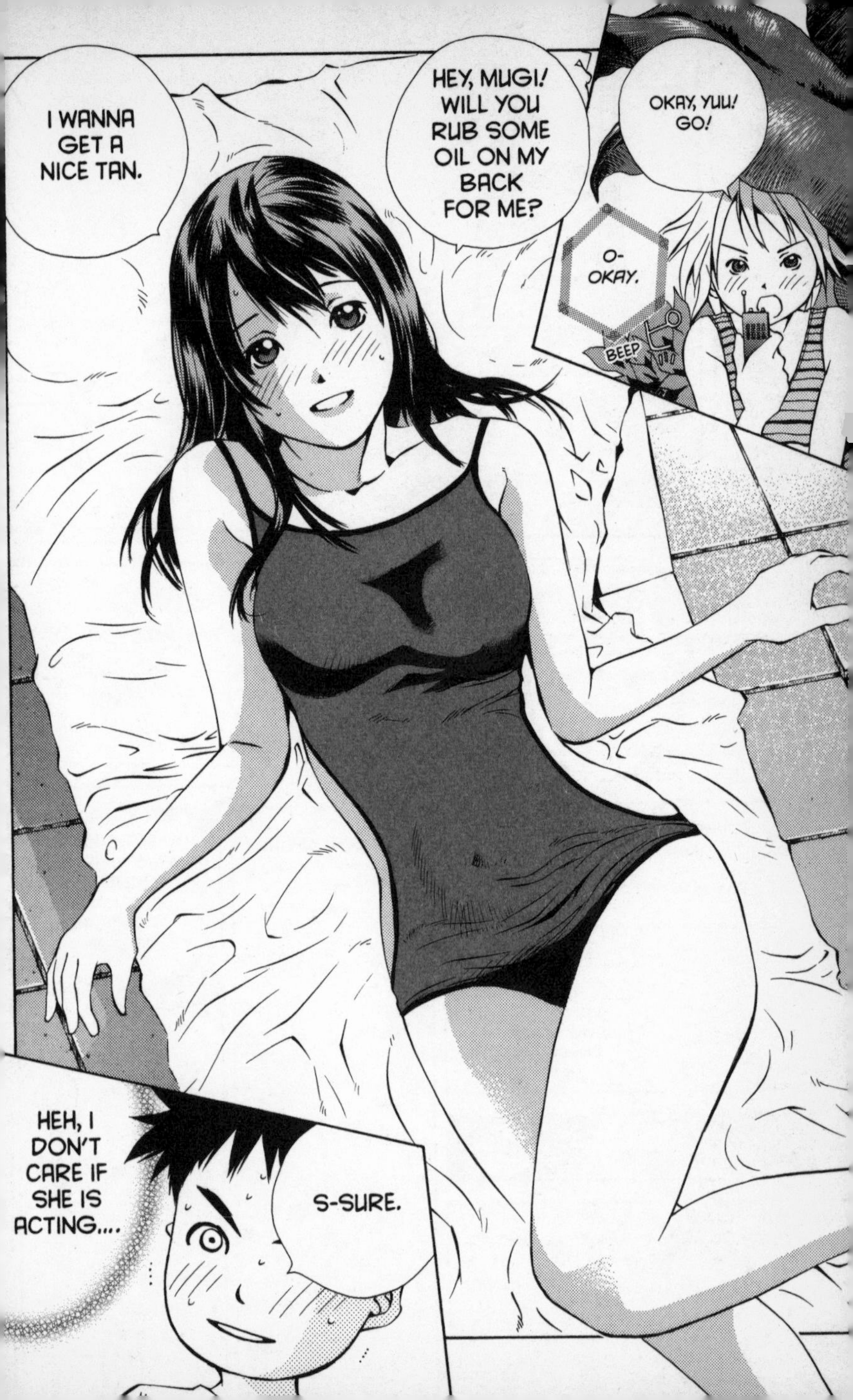
OKAY, YUU! GO!
O-OKAY.
BEEP
HEY, MUGI! WILL YOU RUB SOME OIL ON MY BACK FOR ME?
I WANNA GET A NICE TAN.
S-SURE.
HEH, I DON'T CARE IF SHE IS ACTING....

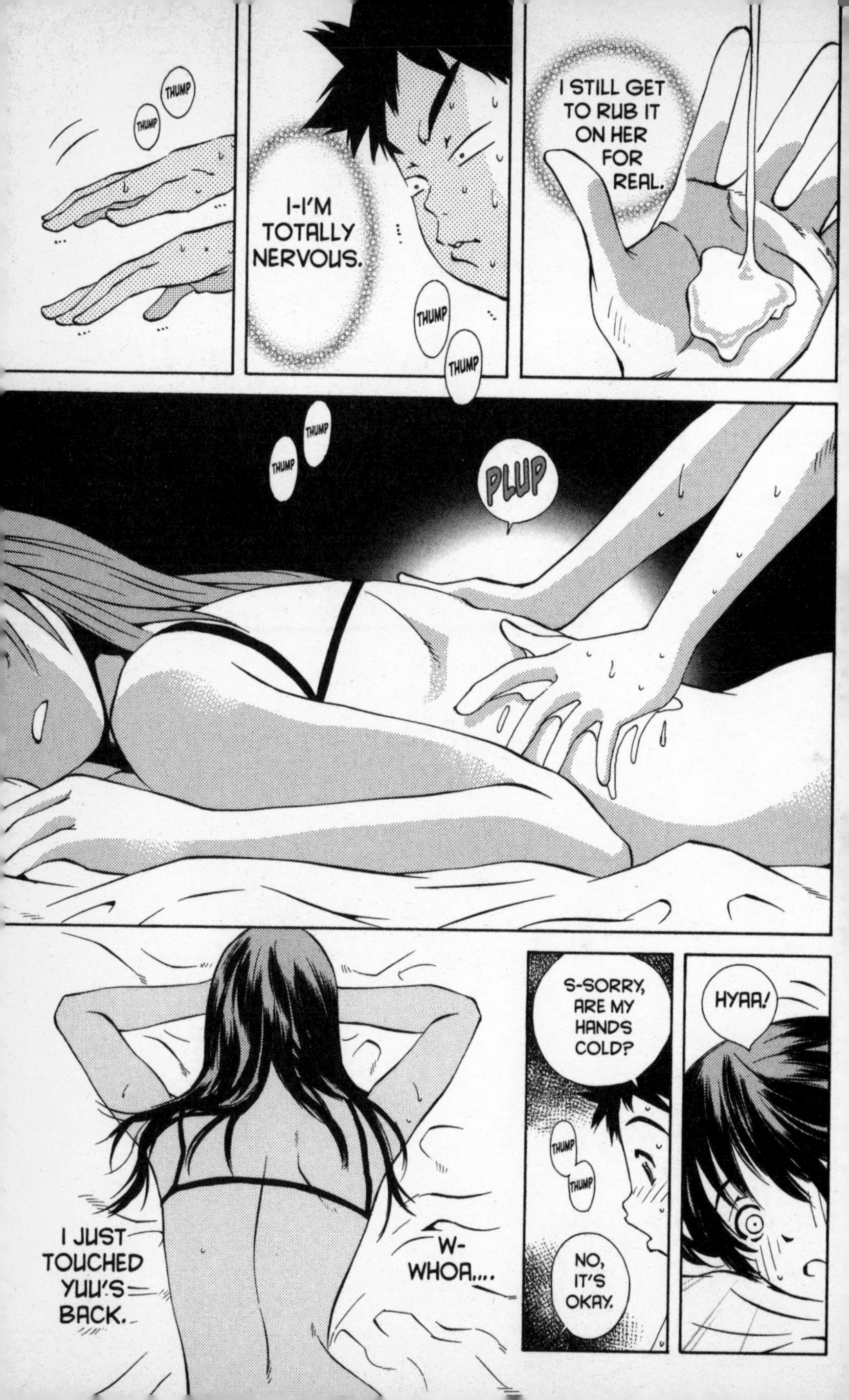
I STILL GET TO RUB IT ON HER FOR REAL.
I-I'M TOTALLY NERVOUS.
THUMP
THUMP
THUMP
THUMP
THUMP
THUMP
PLUP
HYAA!
S-SORRY, ARE MY HANDS COLD?
THUMP
THUMP
NO, IT'S OKAY.
W-WHOA....
I JUST TOUCHED YUU'S BACK.

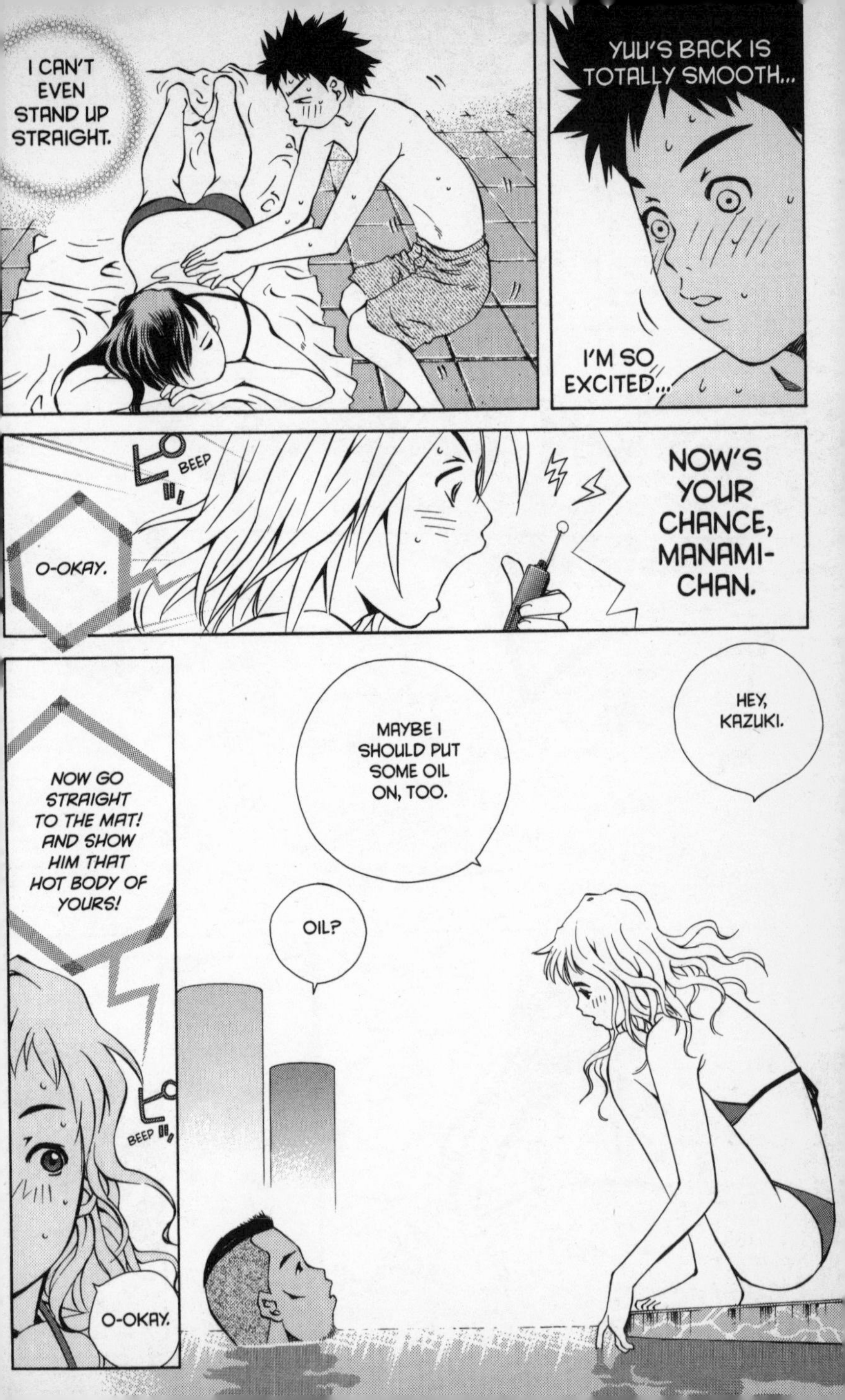
YUU'S BACK IS TOTALLY SMOOTH...
I'M SO EXCITED...
I CAN'T EVEN STAND UP STRAIGHT.
NOW'S YOUR CHANCE, MANAMI-CHAN.
BEEP
O-OKAY.
HEY, KAZUKI.
MAYBE I SHOULD PUT SOME OIL ON, TOO.
OIL?
NOW GO STRAIGHT TO THE MAT! AND SHOW HIM THAT HOT BODY OF YOURS!
BEEP
O-OKAY.

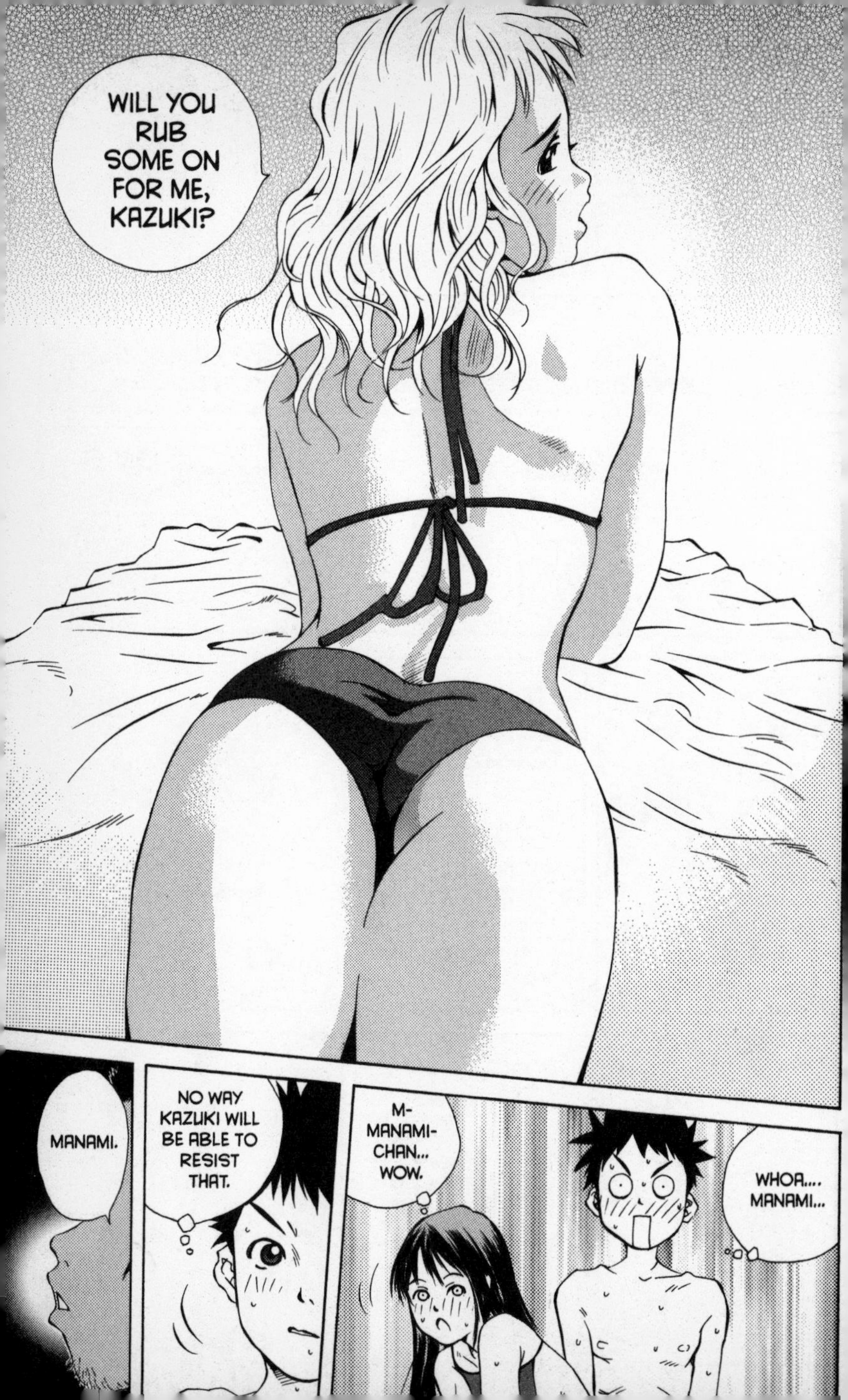
WILL YOU RUB SOME ON FOR ME, KAZUKI?
WHOA.... MANAMI...
M-MANAMI-CHAN... WOW.
NO WAY KAZUKI WILL BE ABLE TO RESIST THAT.
MANAMI.

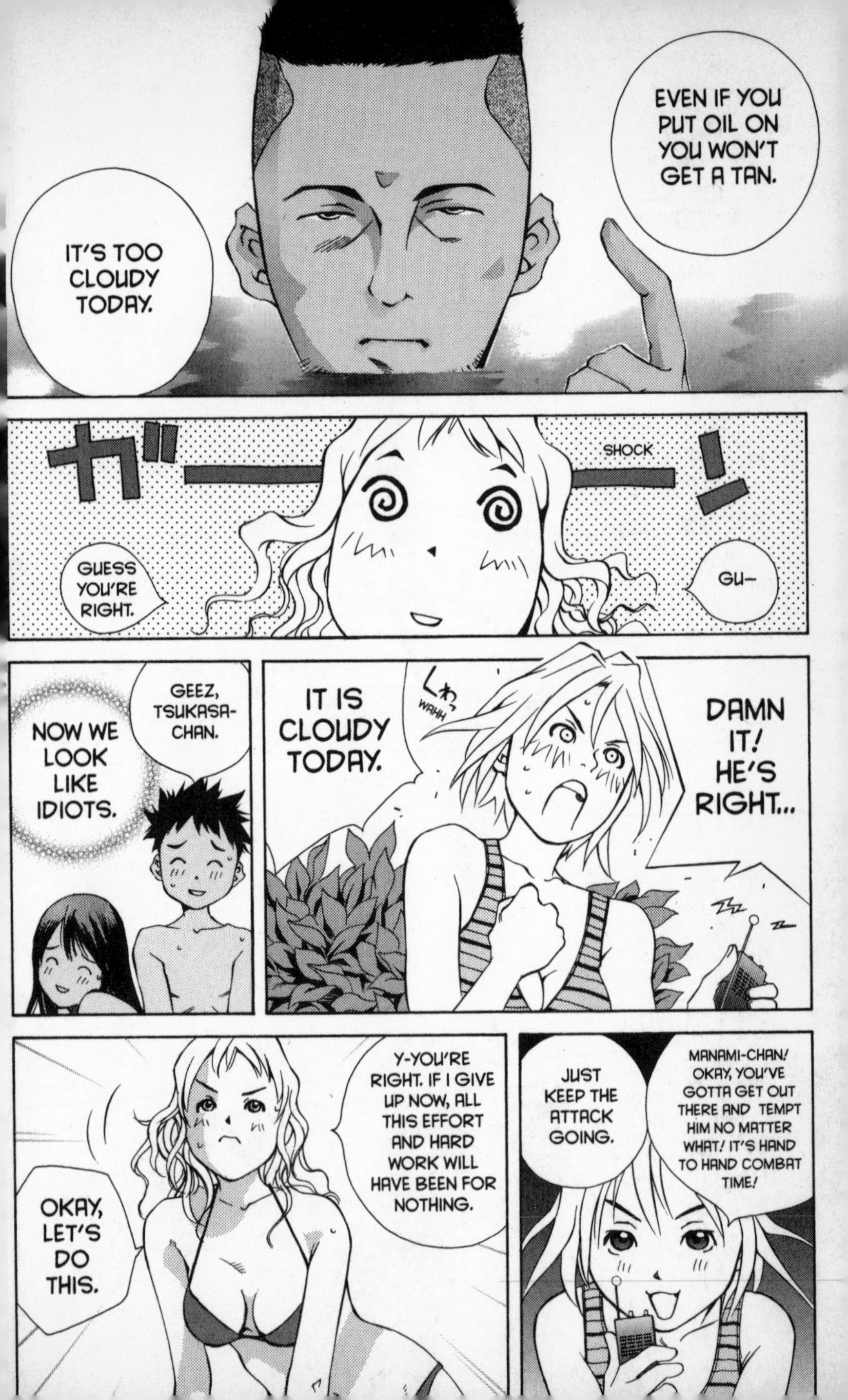

EVEN IF YOU PUT OIL ON YOU WON'T GET A TAN.
IT'S TOO CLOUDY TODAY.
ガーン
SHOCK
GU–
GUESS YOU'RE RIGHT.
DAMN IT! HE'S RIGHT...
WAHH
IT IS CLOUDY TODAY.
GEEZ, TSUKASA-CHAN.
NOW WE LOOK LIKE IDIOTS.
MANAMI-CHAN! OKAY, YOU'VE GOTTA GET OUT THERE AND TEMPT HIM NO MATTER WHAT! IT'S HAND TO HAND COMBAT TIME!
JUST KEEP THE ATTACK GOING.
Y-YOU'RE RIGHT. IF I GIVE UP NOW, ALL THIS EFFORT AND HARD WORK WILL HAVE BEEN FOR NOTHING.
OKAY, LET'S DO THIS.

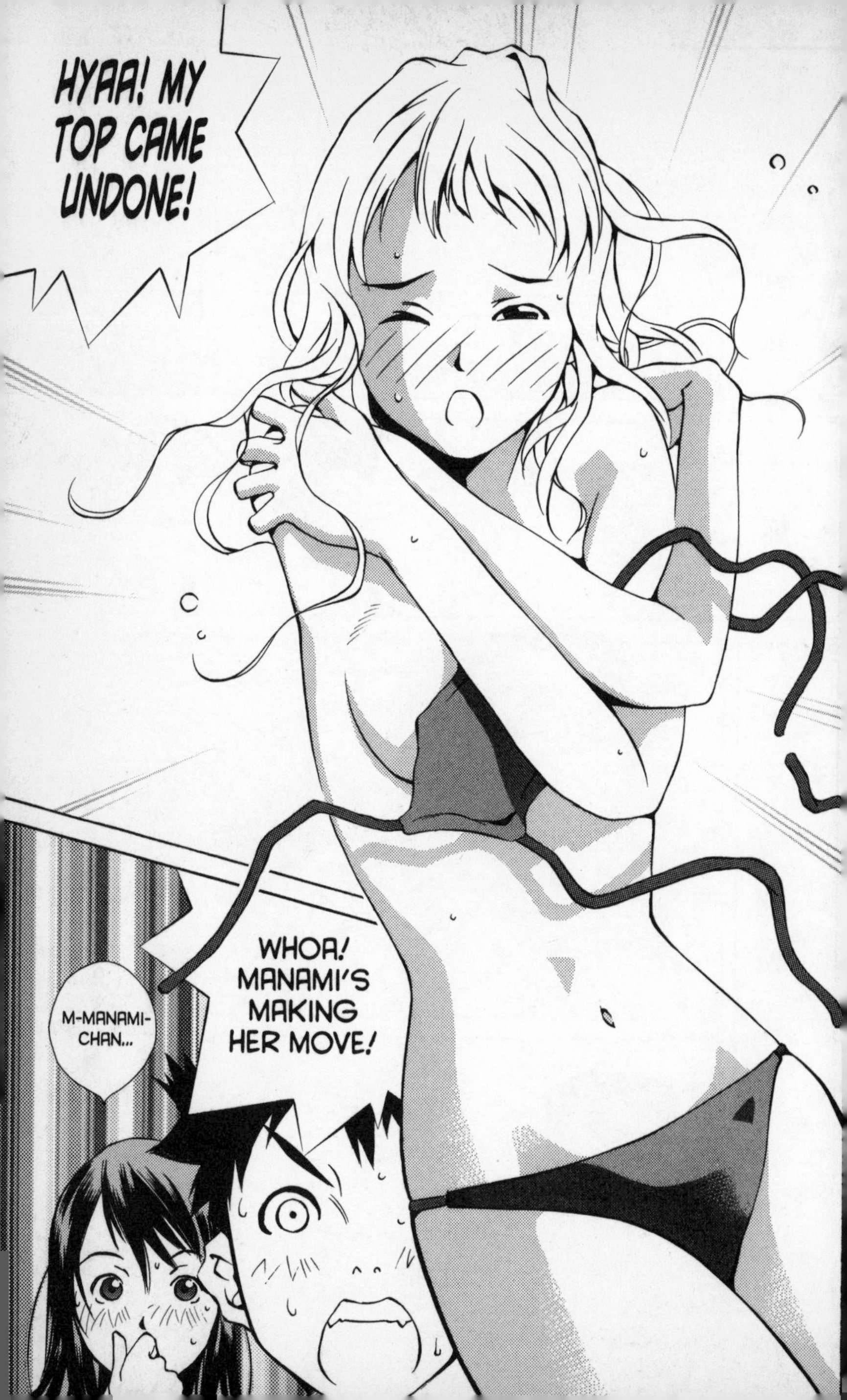
HYAA! MY TOP CAME UNDONE!
WHOA! MANAMI'S MAKING HER MOVE!
M-MANAMI-CHAN...

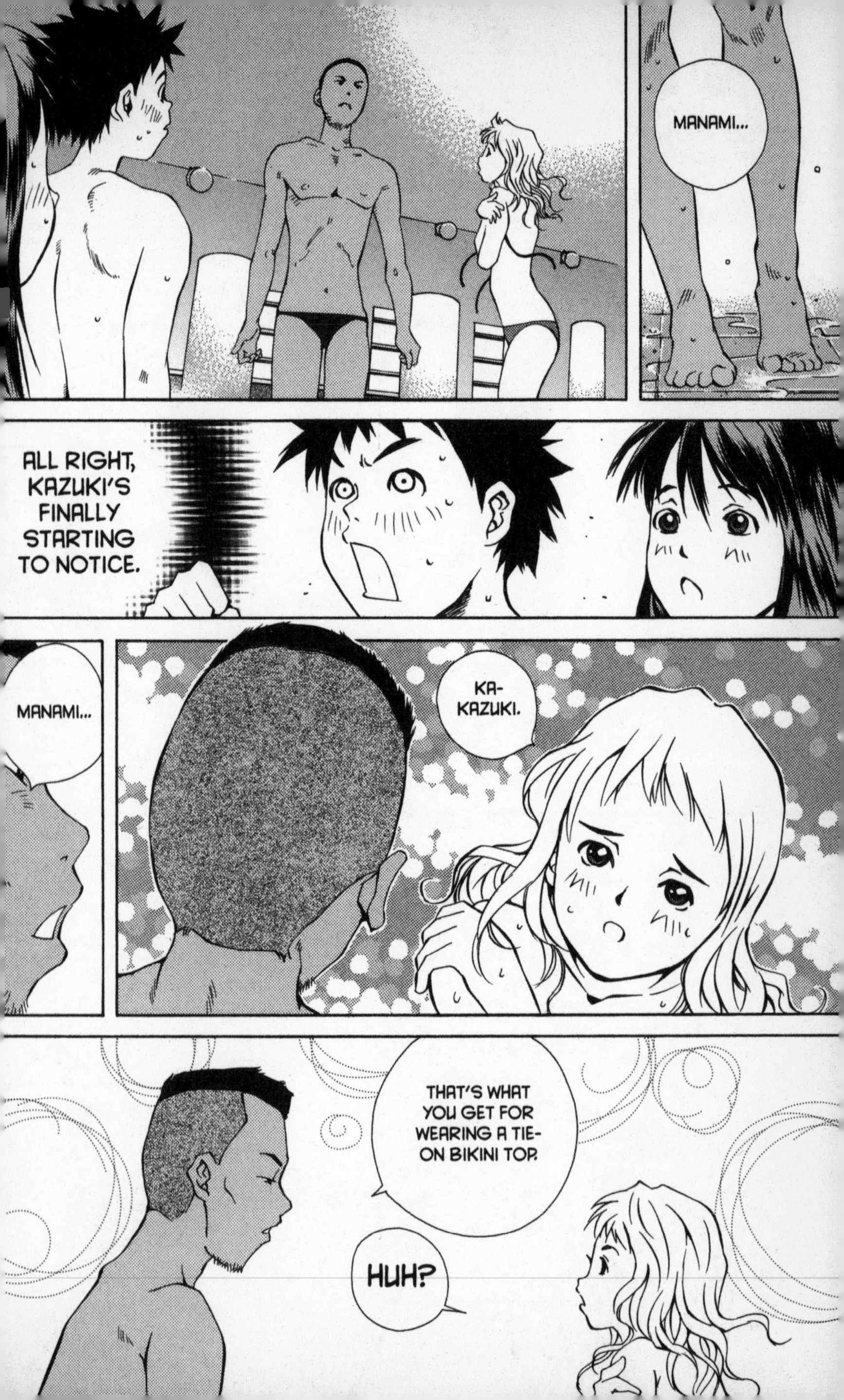
MANAMI...
ALL RIGHT, KAZUKI'S FINALLY STARTING TO NOTICE.
KA-KAZUKI.
MANAMI...
THAT'S WHAT YOU GET FOR WEARING A TIE-ON BIKINI TOP.
HUH?

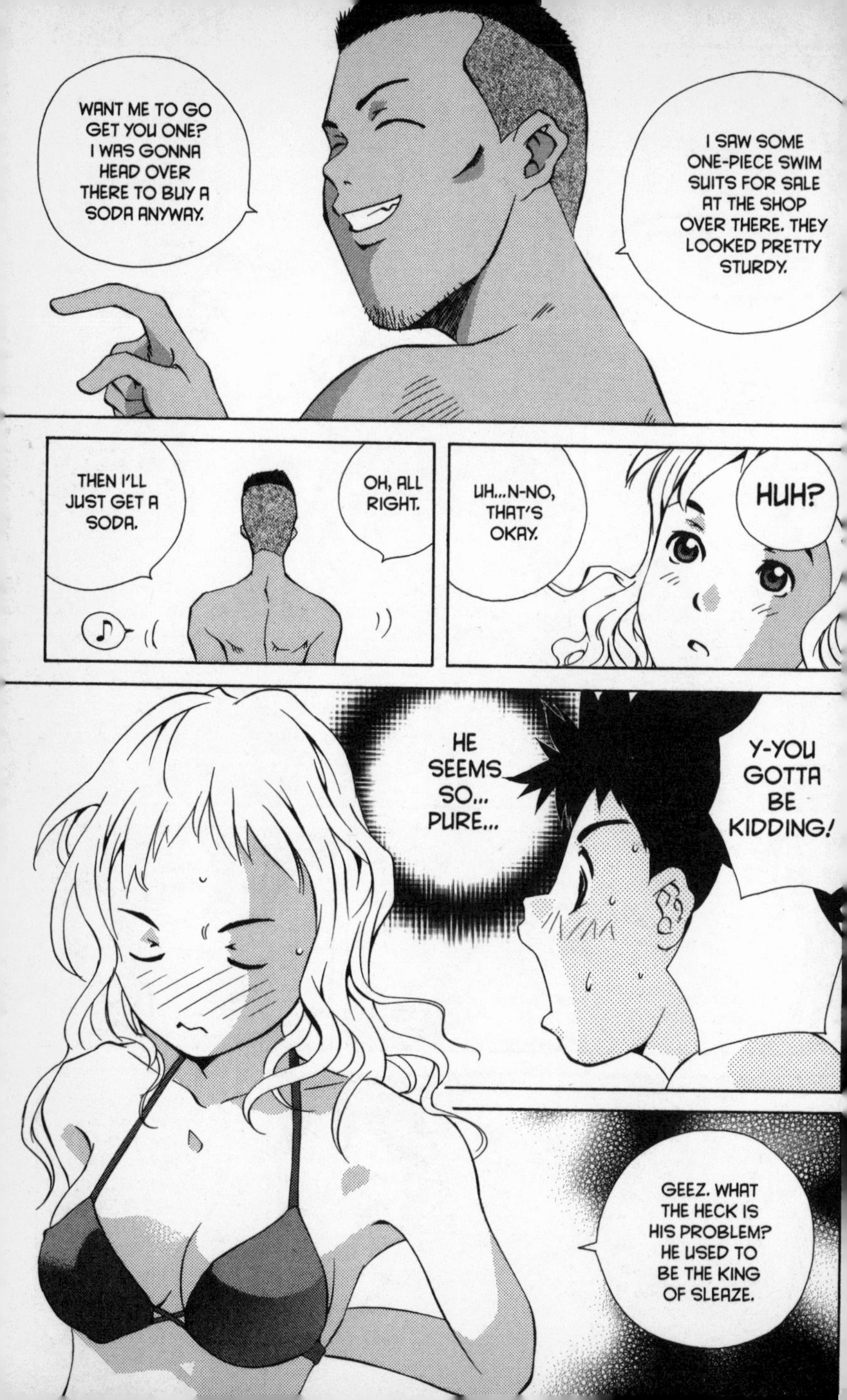
I SAW SOME ONE-PIECE SWIM SUITS FOR SALE AT THE SHOP OVER THERE. THEY LOOKED PRETTY STURDY.
WANT ME TO GO GET YOU ONE? I WAS GONNA HEAD OVER THERE TO BUY A SODA ANYWAY.
HUH?
UH...N-NO, THAT'S OKAY.
OH, ALL RIGHT.
THEN I'LL JUST GET A SODA.
Y-YOU GOTTA BE KIDDING!
HE SEEMS SO... PURE...
GEEZ. WHAT THE HECK IS HIS PROBLEM? HE USED TO BE THE KING OF SLEAZE.

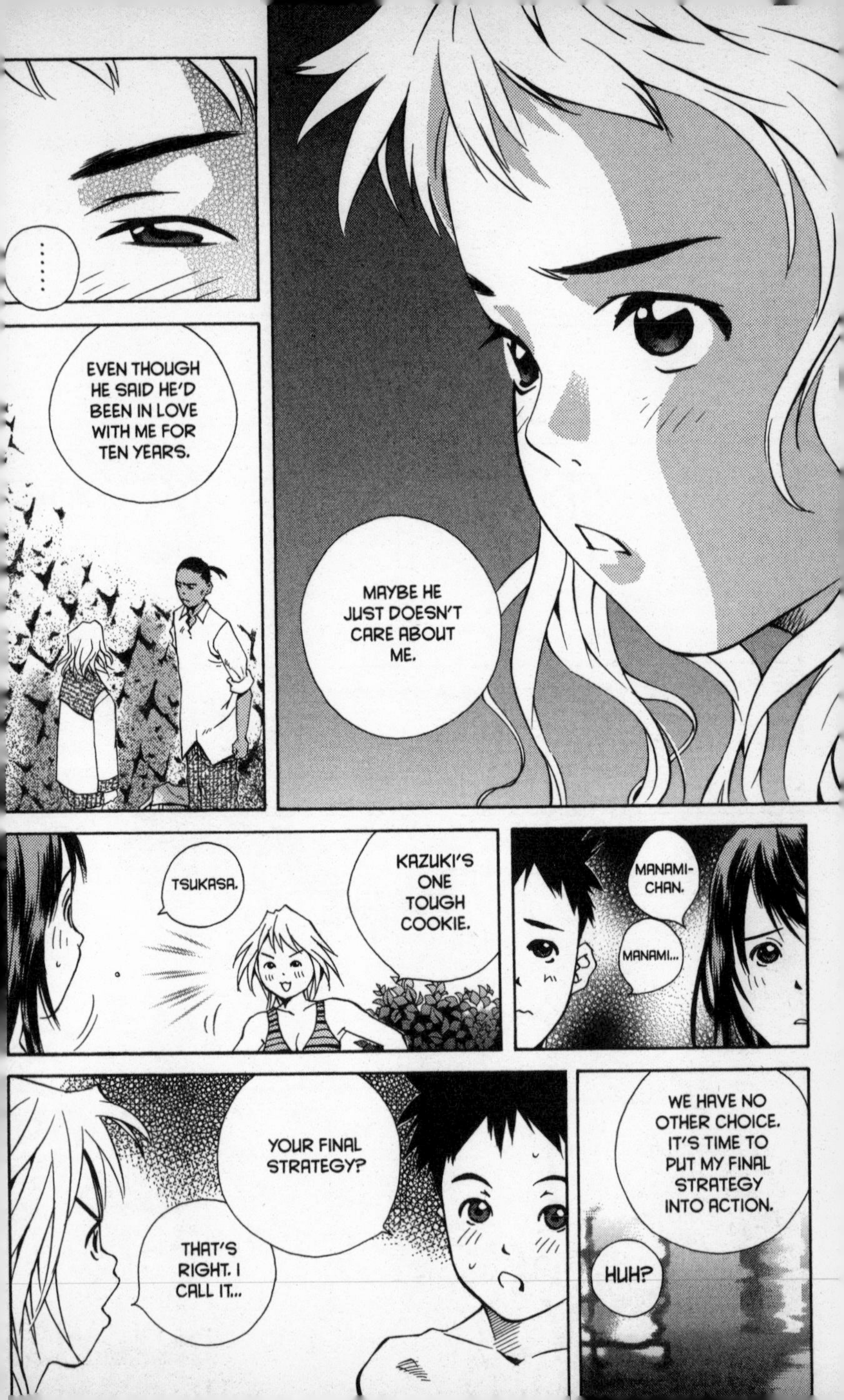
MAYBE HE JUST DOESN'T CARE ABOUT ME.
……
EVEN THOUGH HE SAID HE'D BEEN IN LOVE WITH ME FOR TEN YEARS.
MANAMI-CHAN.
MANAMI...
KAZUKI'S ONE TOUGH COOKIE.
TSUKASA.
WE HAVE NO OTHER CHOICE. IT'S TIME TO PUT MY FINAL STRATEGY INTO ACTION.
HUH?
YOUR FINAL STRATEGY?
THAT'S RIGHT. I CALL IT...

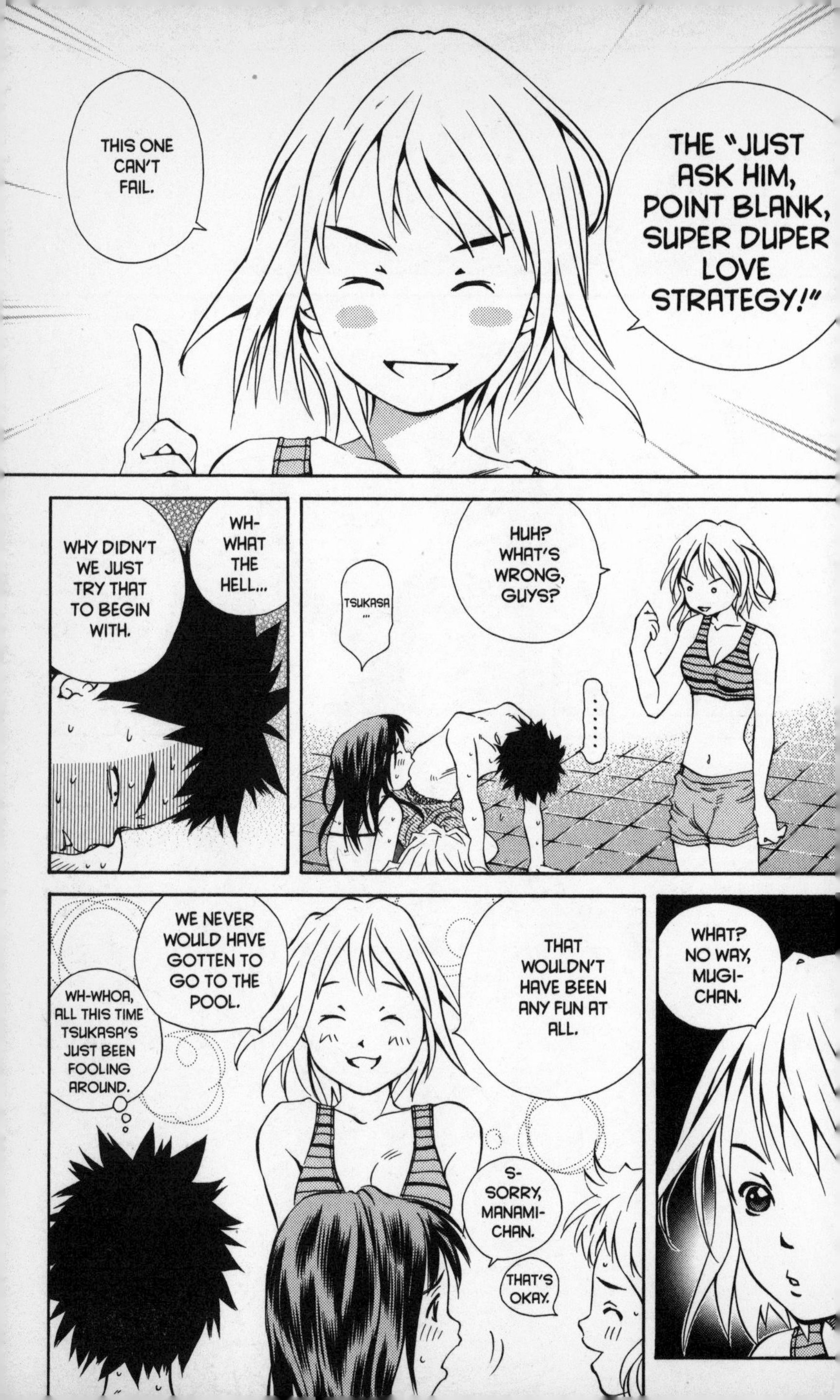
THE "JUST ASK HIM, POINT BLANK, SUPER DUPER LOVE STRATEGY!"
THIS ONE CAN'T FAIL.
HUH? WHAT'S WRONG, GUYS?
TSUKASA...
......
WH- WHAT THE HELL...
WHY DIDN'T WE JUST TRY THAT TO BEGIN WITH.
WHAT? NO WAY, MUGI-CHAN.
THAT WOULDN'T HAVE BEEN ANY FUN AT ALL.
WE NEVER WOULD HAVE GOTTEN TO GO TO THE POOL.
WH-WHOA, ALL THIS TIME TSUKASA'S JUST BEEN FOOLING AROUND.
S-SORRY, MANAMI-CHAN.
THAT'S OKAY.

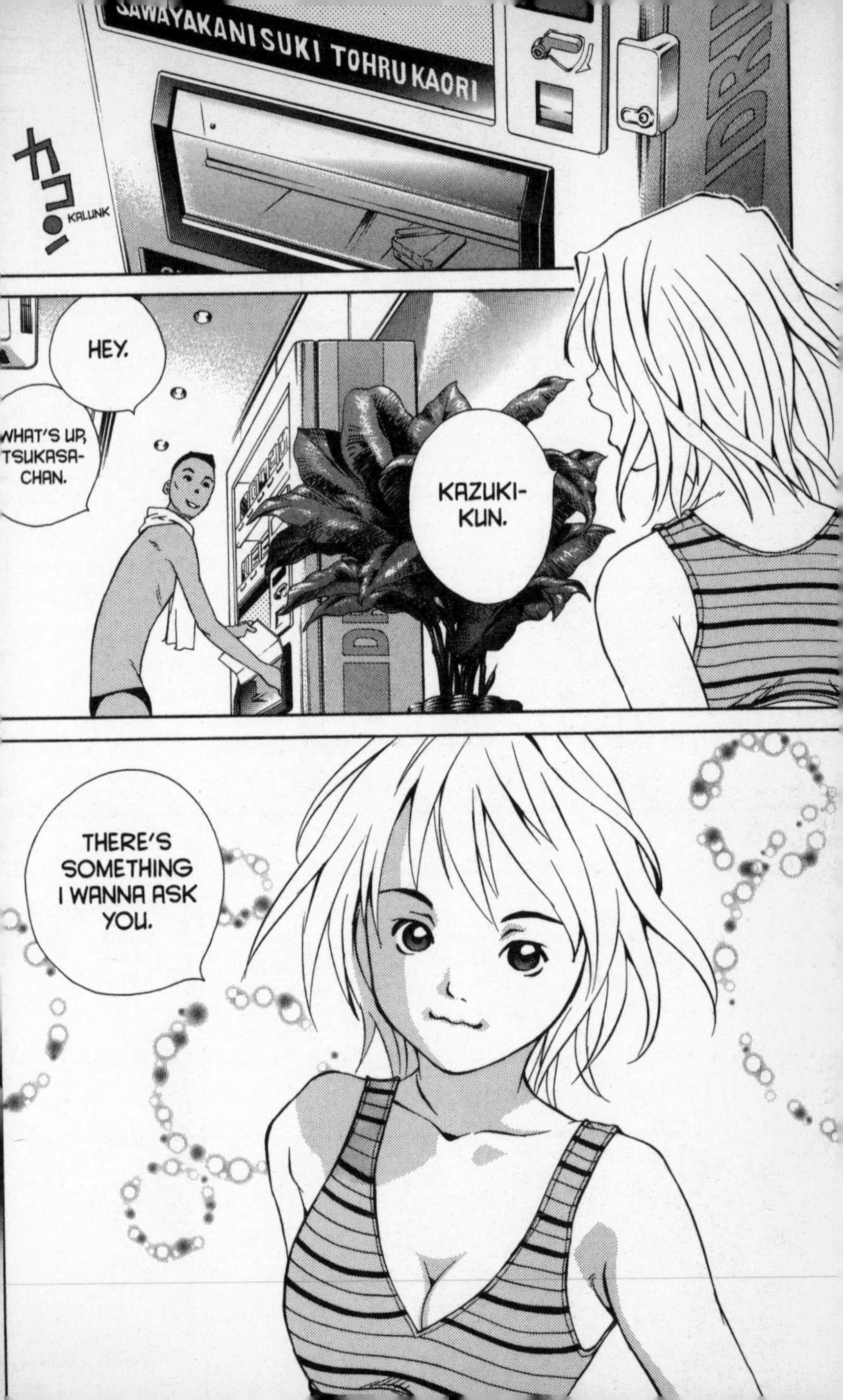
SAWAYAKANI SUKI TOHRU KAORI
KALUNK
KAZUKI-KUN.
HEY.
WHAT'S UP, TSUKASA-CHAN.
THERE'S SOMETHING I WANNA ASK YOU.

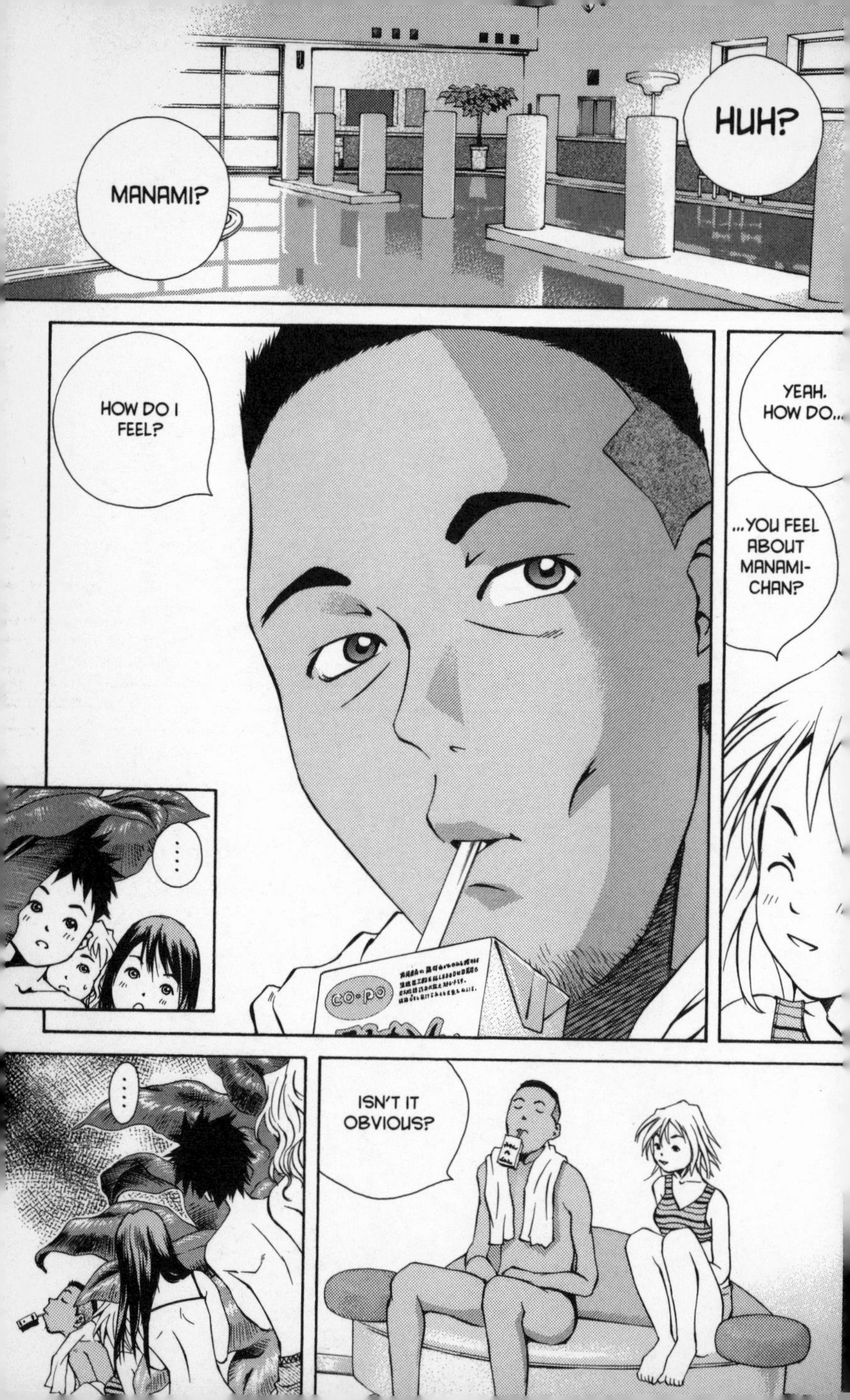

HUH?
MANAMI?
YEAH. HOW DO...
...YOU FEEL ABOUT MANAMI-CHAN?
HOW DO I FEEL?
....
ISN'T IT OBVIOUS?
....

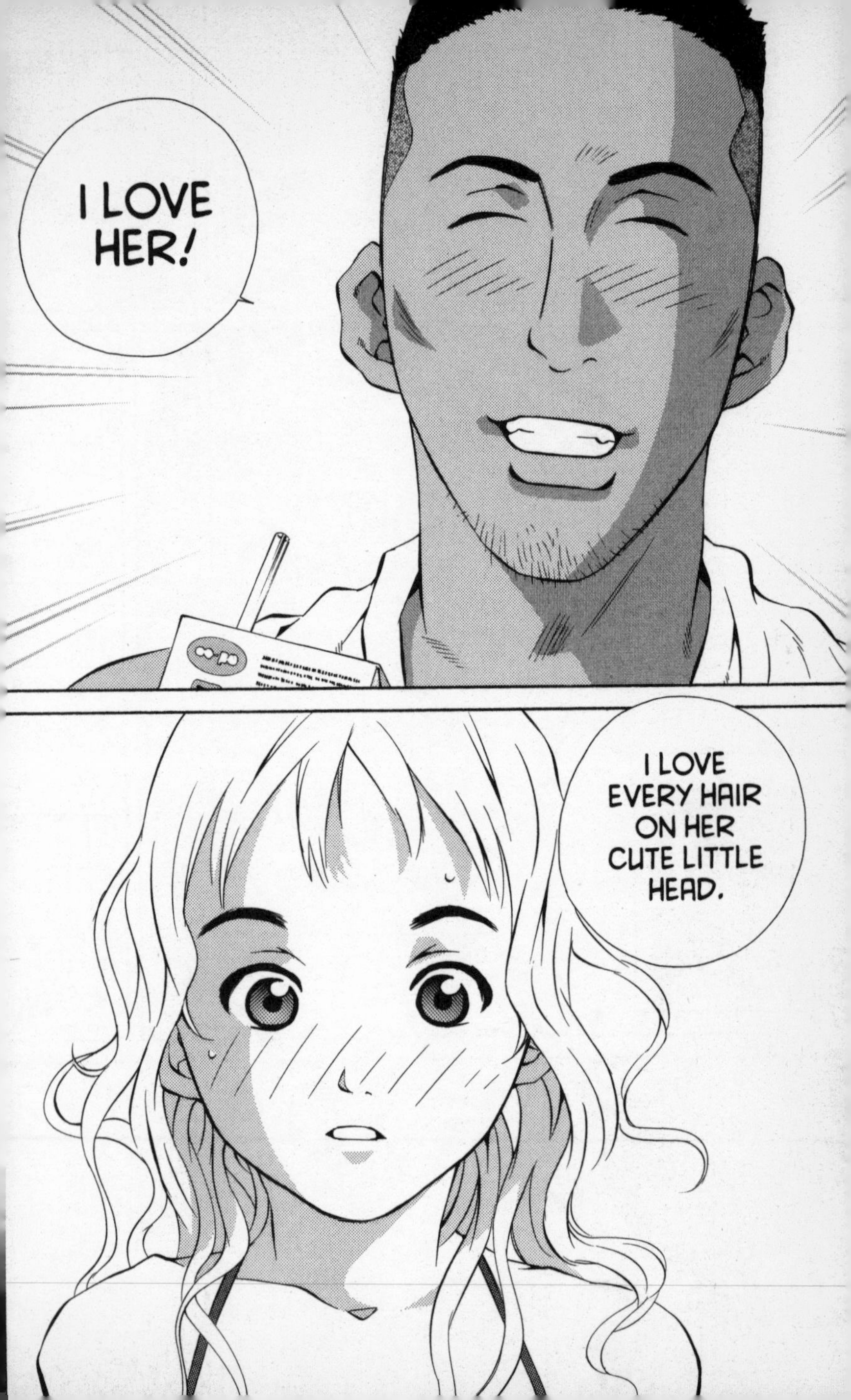
I LOVE HER!
I LOVE EVERY HAIR ON HER CUTE LITTLE HEAD.

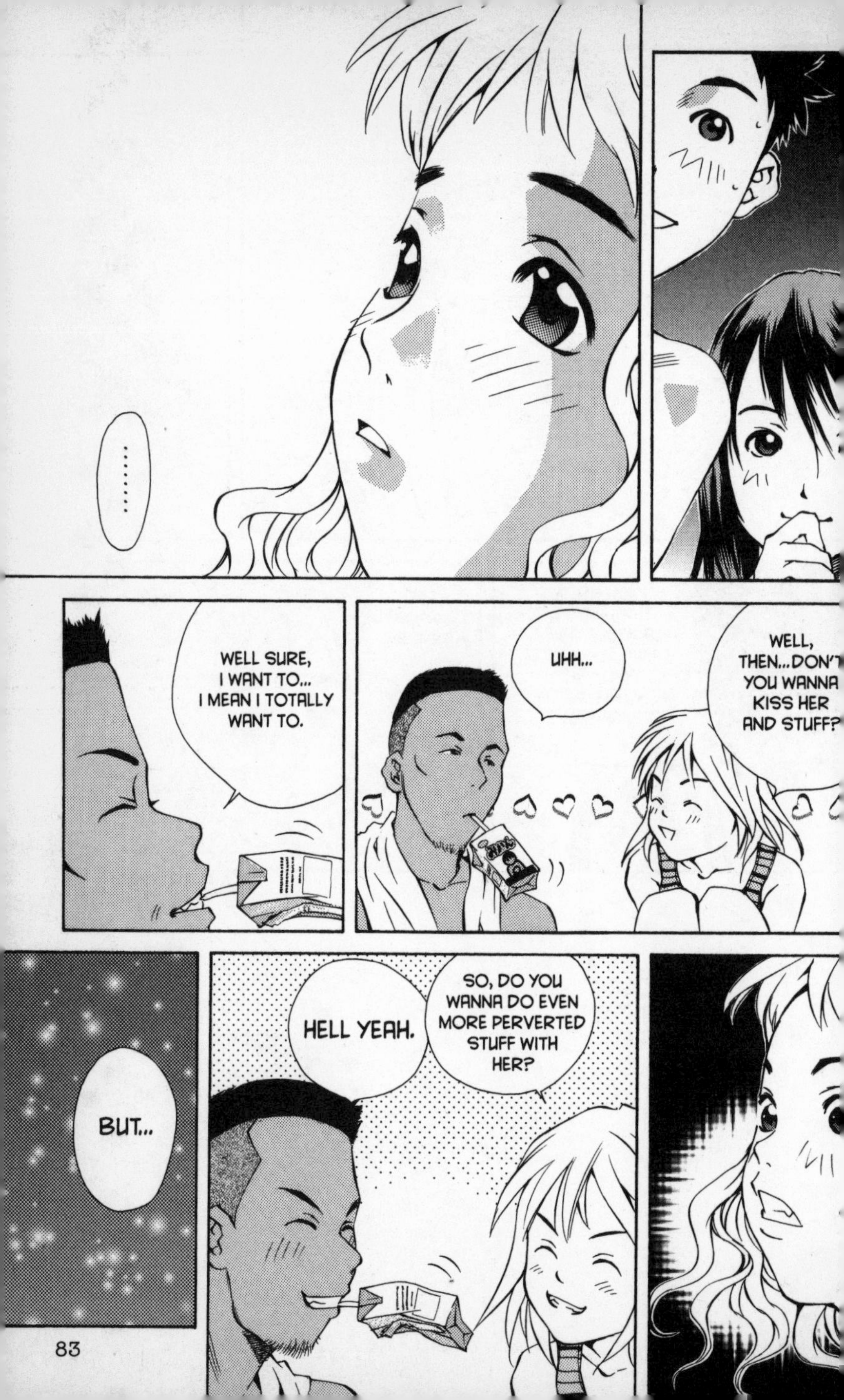
......
WELL, THEN...DON'T YOU WANNA KISS HER AND STUFF?
UHH...
WELL SURE, I WANT TO... I MEAN I TOTALLY WANT TO.
SO, DO YOU WANNA DO EVEN MORE PERVERTED STUFF WITH HER?
HELL YEAH.
BUT...

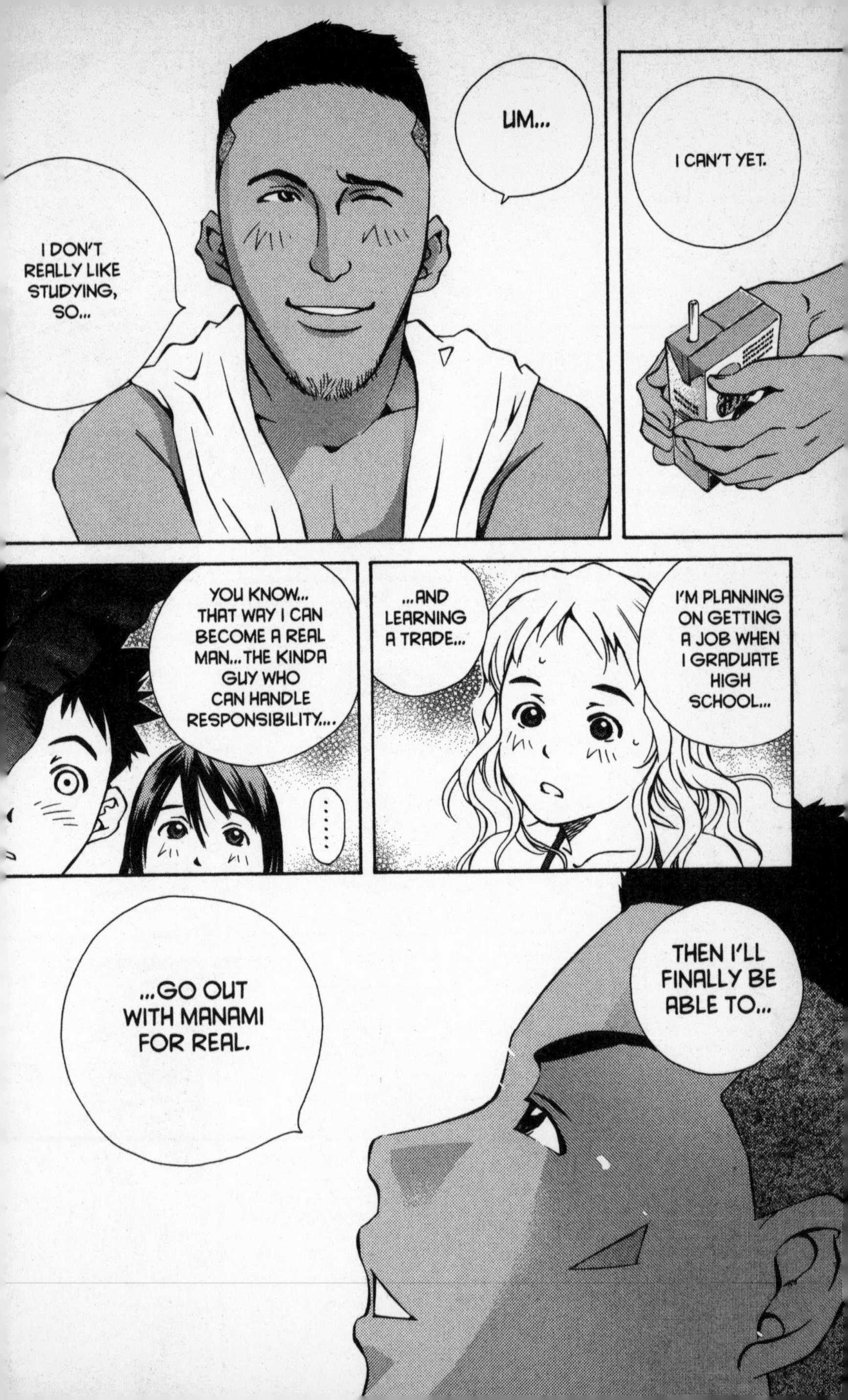
I CAN'T YET.
UM...
I DON'T REALLY LIKE STUDYING, SO...
I'M PLANNING ON GETTING A JOB WHEN I GRADUATE HIGH SCHOOL...
...AND LEARNING A TRADE...
YOU KNOW... THAT WAY I CAN BECOME A REAL MAN...THE KINDA GUY WHO CAN HANDLE RESPONSIBILITY....
......
THEN I'LL FINALLY BE ABLE TO...
...GO OUT WITH MANAMI FOR REAL.

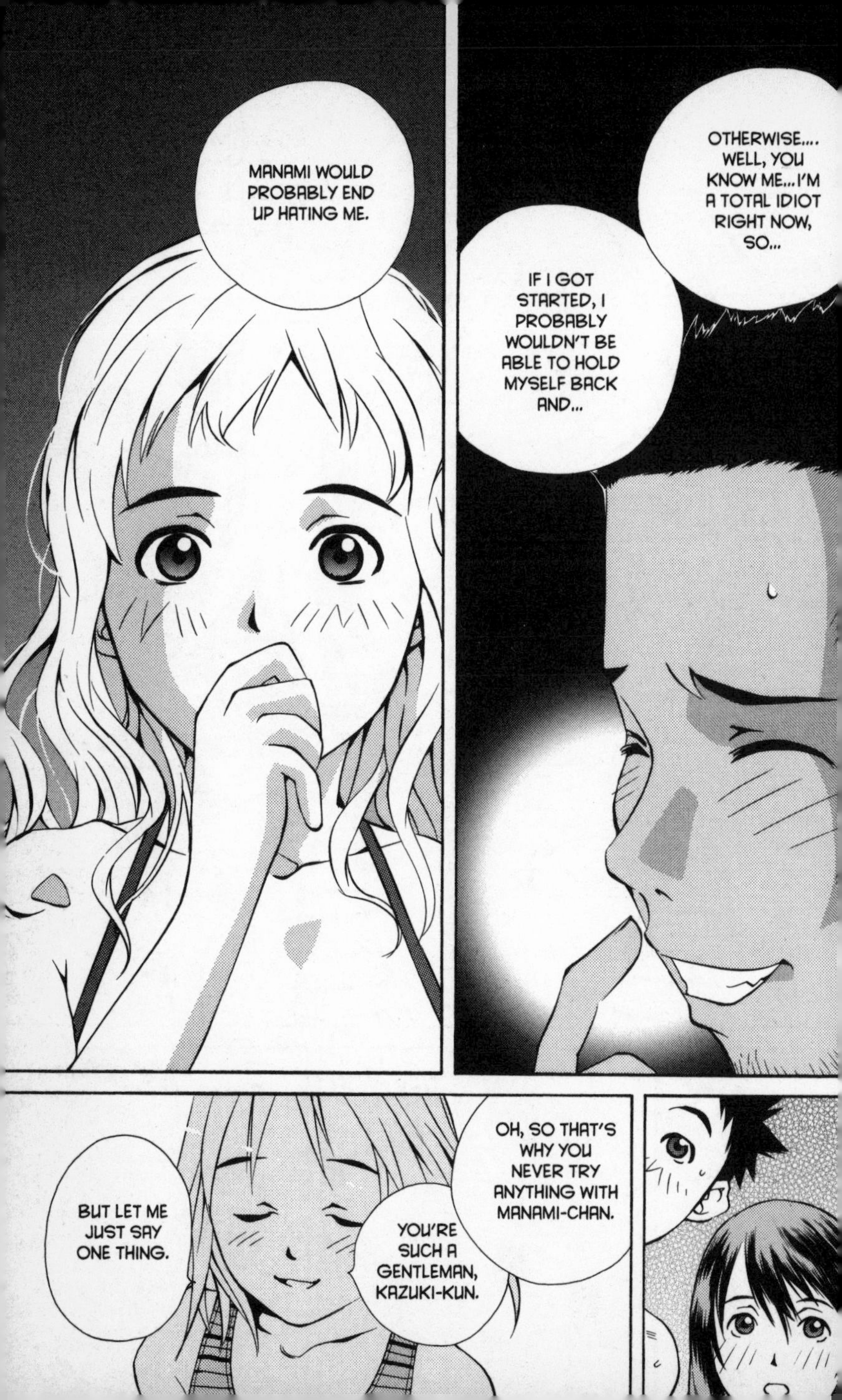

OTHERWISE.... WELL, YOU KNOW ME...I'M A TOTAL IDIOT RIGHT NOW, SO...
IF I GOT STARTED, I PROBABLY WOULDN'T BE ABLE TO HOLD MYSELF BACK AND...
MANAMI WOULD PROBABLY END UP HATING ME.
OH, SO THAT'S WHY YOU NEVER TRY ANYTHING WITH MANAMI-CHAN.
YOU'RE SUCH A GENTLEMAN, KAZUKI-KUN.
BUT LET ME JUST SAY ONE THING.

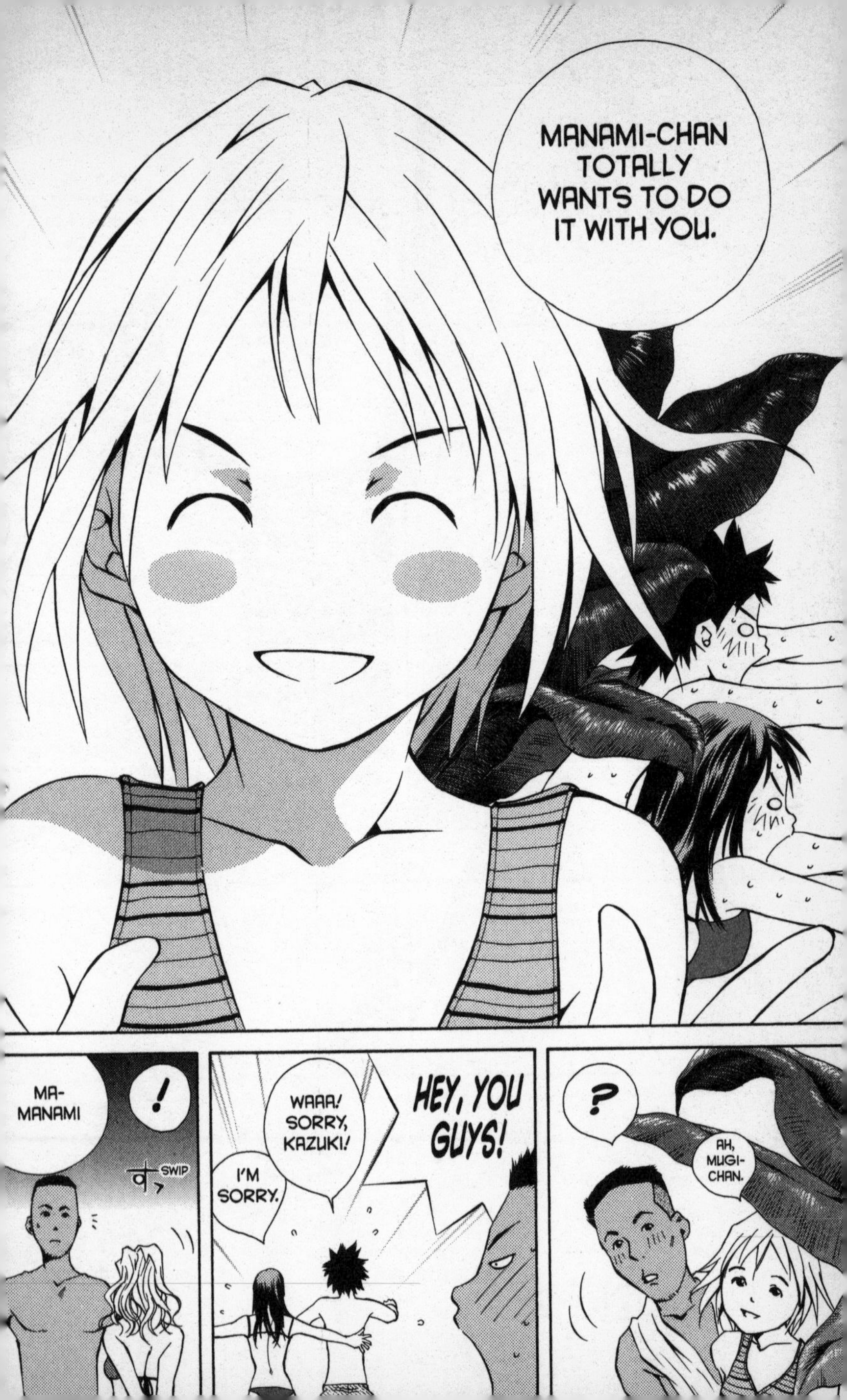
MANAMI-CHAN TOTALLY WANTS TO DO IT WITH YOU.
?
AH, MUGI-CHAN.
HEY, YOU GUYS!
WAAA! SORRY, KAZUKI!
I'M SORRY.
!
MA-MANAMI
す SWIP

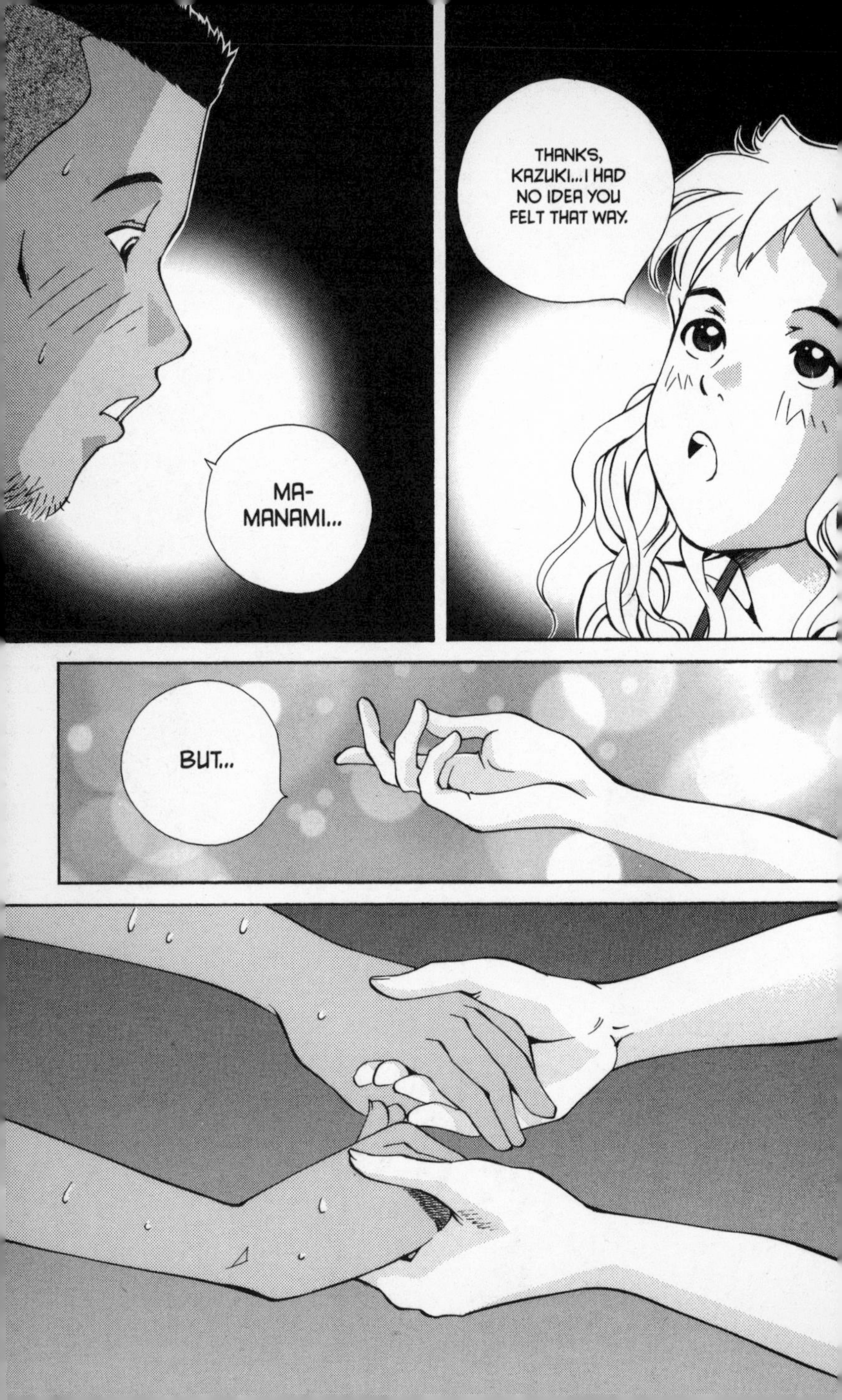
THANKS, KAZUKI...I HAD NO IDEA YOU FELT THAT WAY.
MA- MANAMI...
BUT...

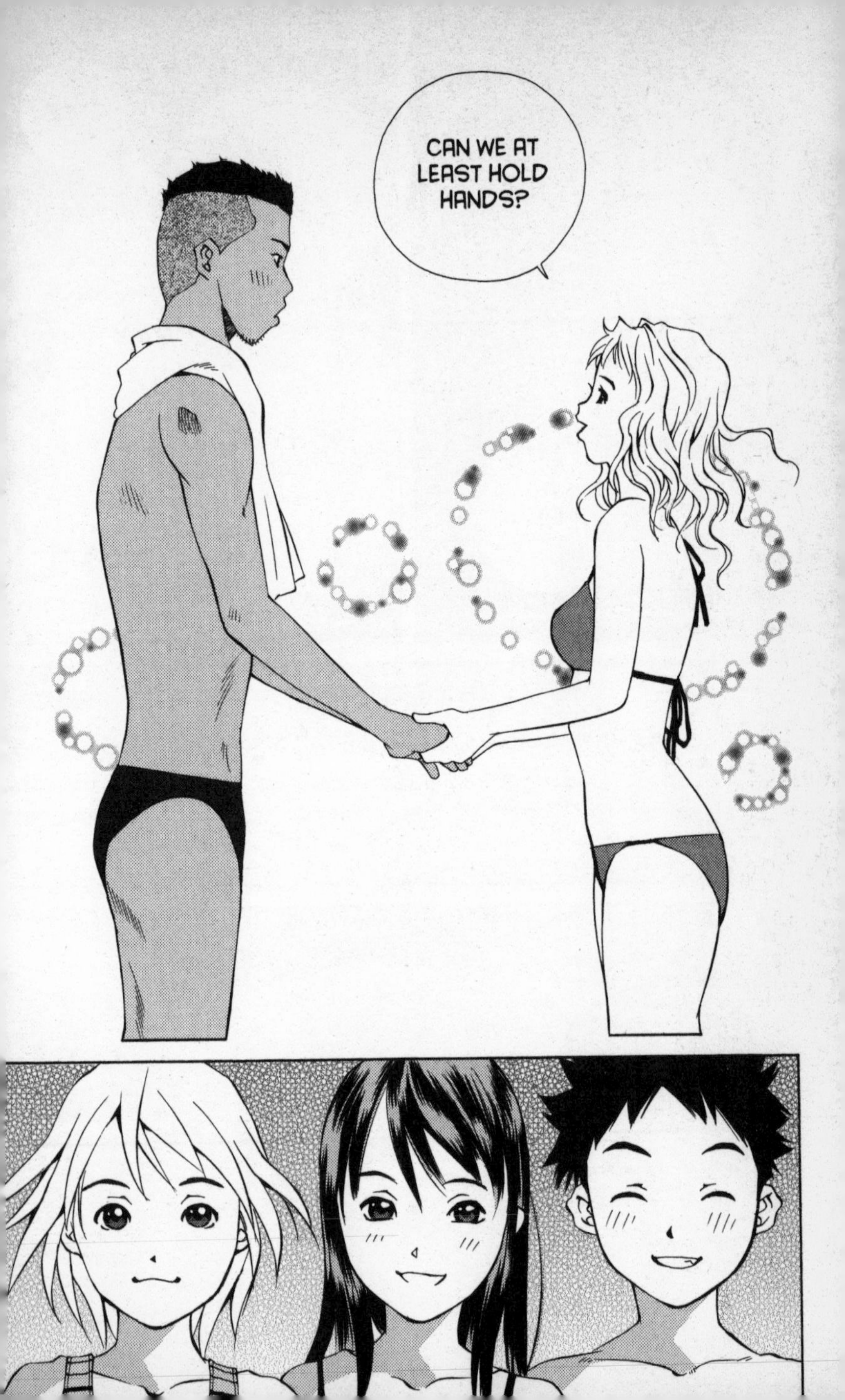
CAN WE AT LEAST HOLD HANDS?

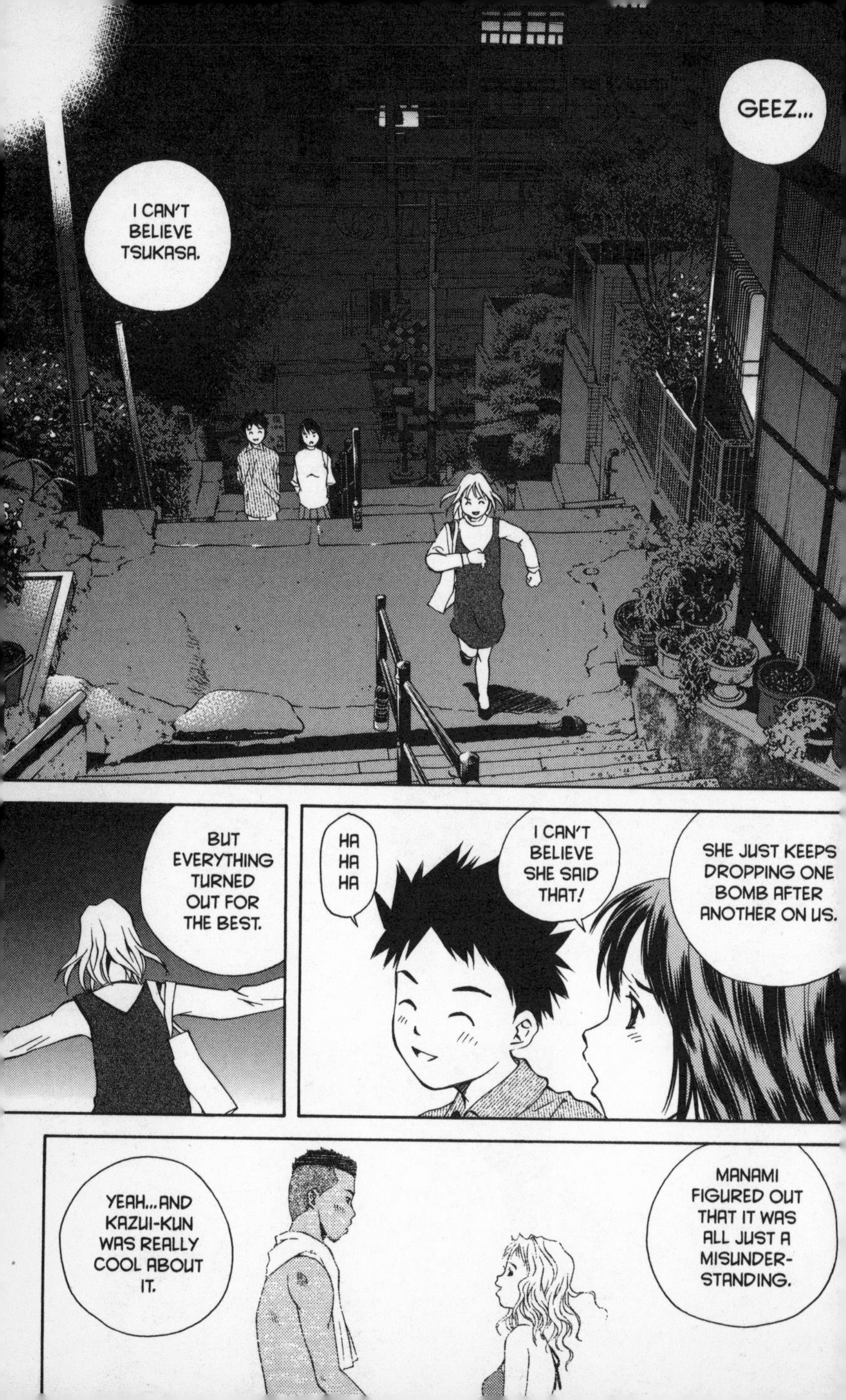
GEEZ...
I CAN'T BELIEVE TSUKASA.
SHE JUST KEEPS DROPPING ONE BOMB AFTER ANOTHER ON US.
I CAN'T BELIEVE SHE SAID THAT!
HA HA HA
BUT EVERYTHING TURNED OUT FOR THE BEST.
MANAMI FIGURED OUT THAT IT WAS ALL JUST A MISUNDER-STANDING.
YEAH...AND KAZUI-KUN WAS REALLY COOL ABOUT IT.

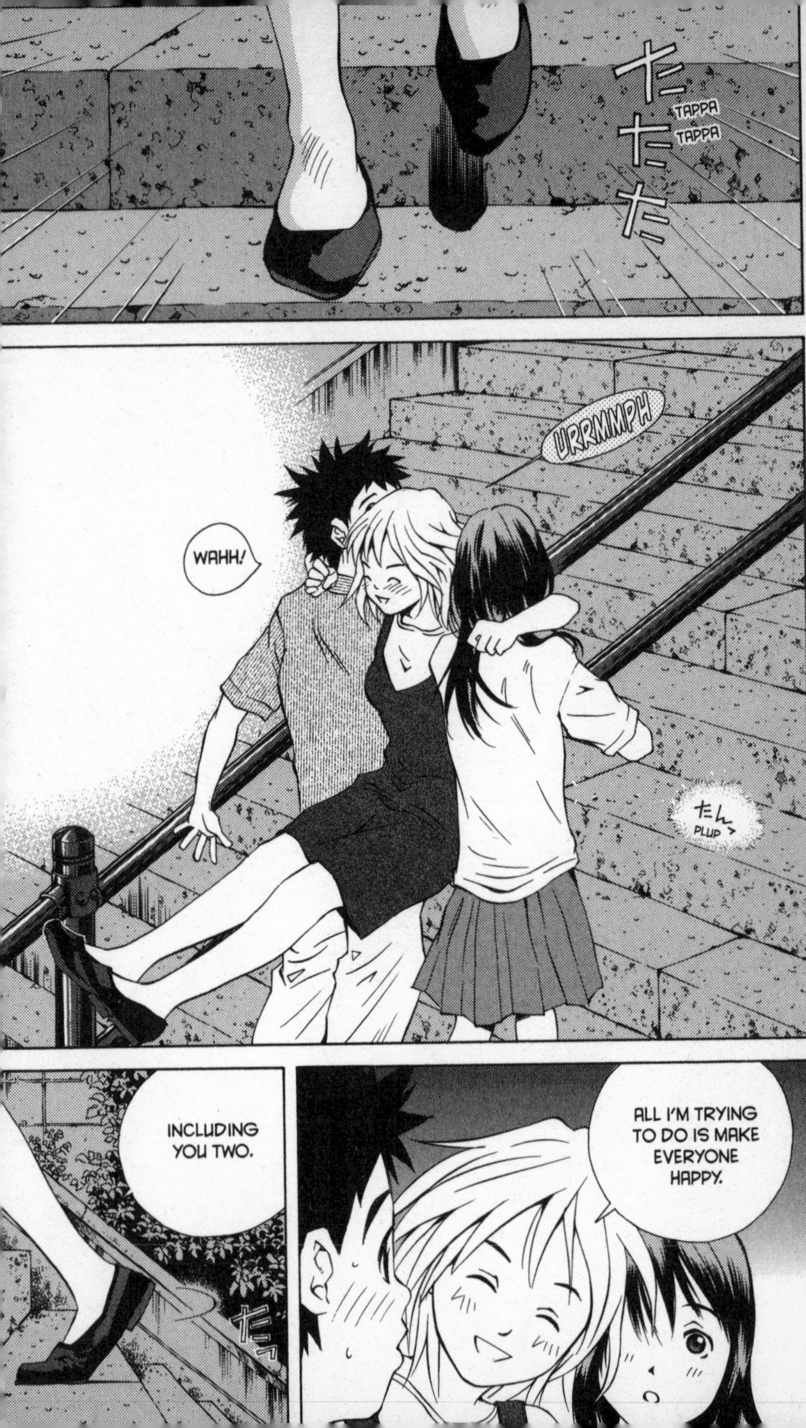
たたたた
TAPPA TAPPA
URRMMPH
WAHH!
たん
PLUP
ALL I'M TRYING TO DO IS MAKE EVERYONE HAPPY.
INCLUDING YOU TWO.
たっ

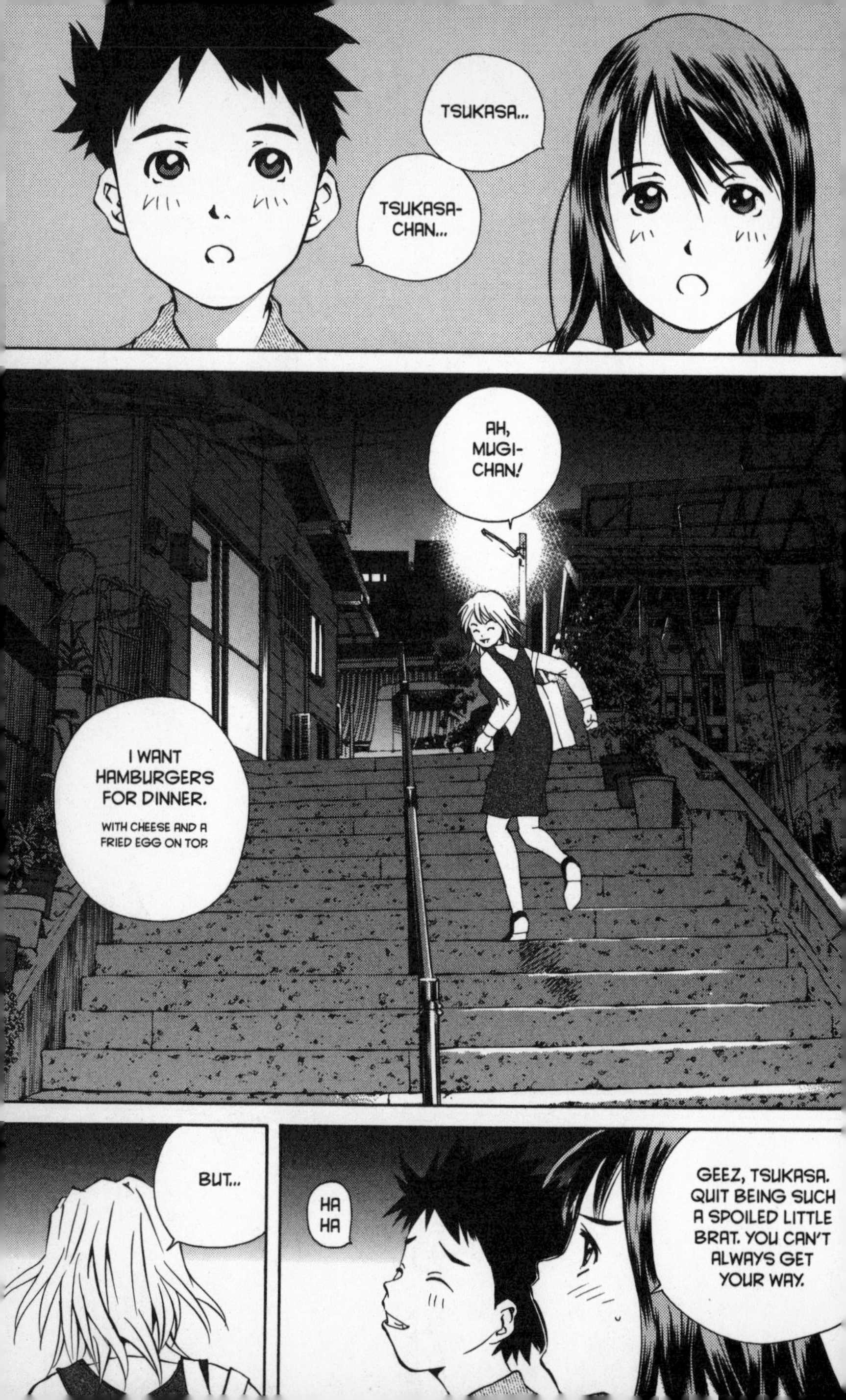
TSUKASA...
TSUKASA-CHAN...
AH, MUGI-CHAN!
I WANT HAMBURGERS FOR DINNER.
WITH CHEESE AND A FRIED EGG ON TOP.
GEEZ, TSUKASA. QUIT BEING SUCH A SPOILED LITTLE BRAT. YOU CAN'T ALWAYS GET YOUR WAY.
HA HA
BUT...

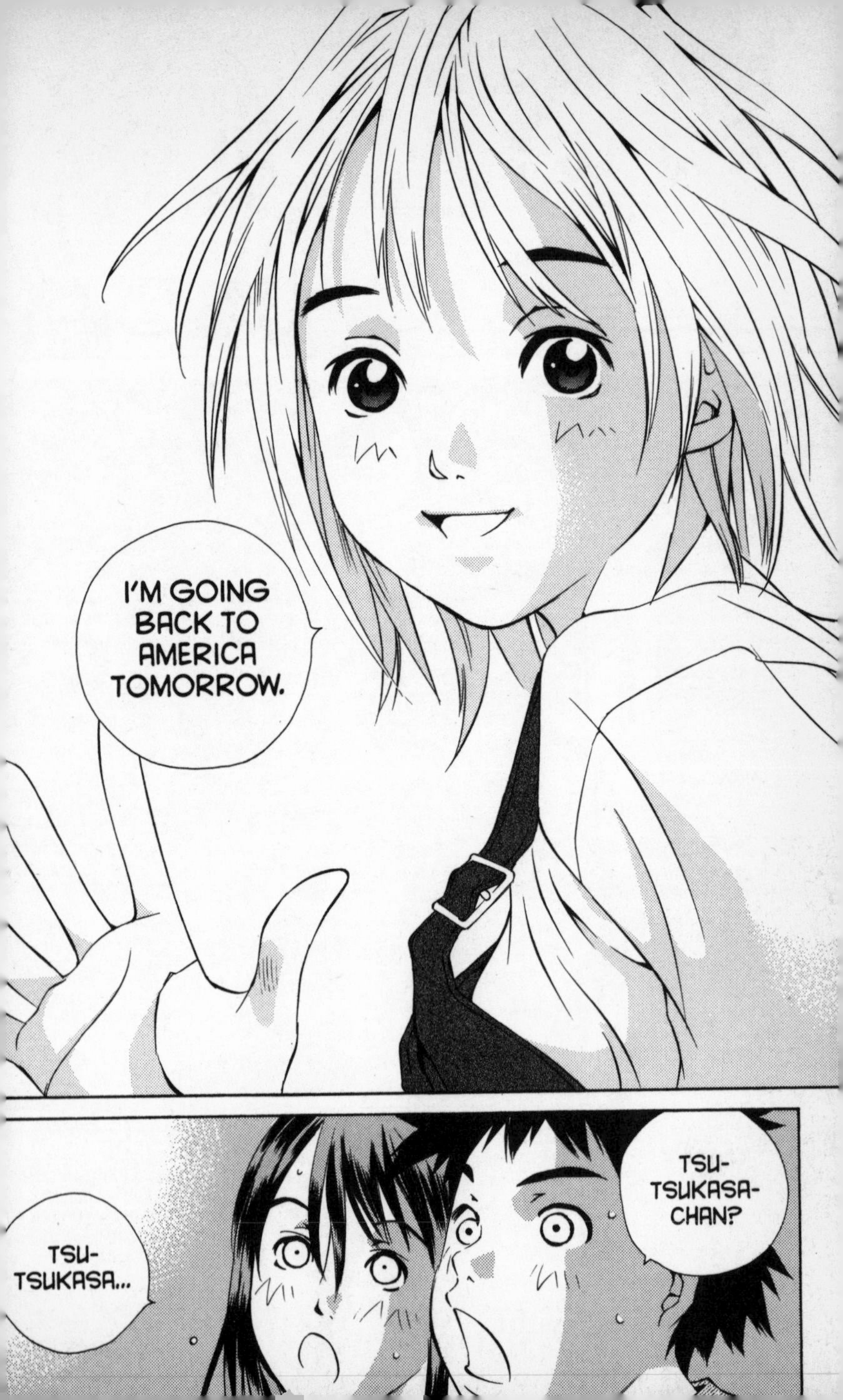
I'M GOING BACK TO AMERICA TOMORROW.
TSU- TSUKASA-CHAN?
TSU- TSUKASA...

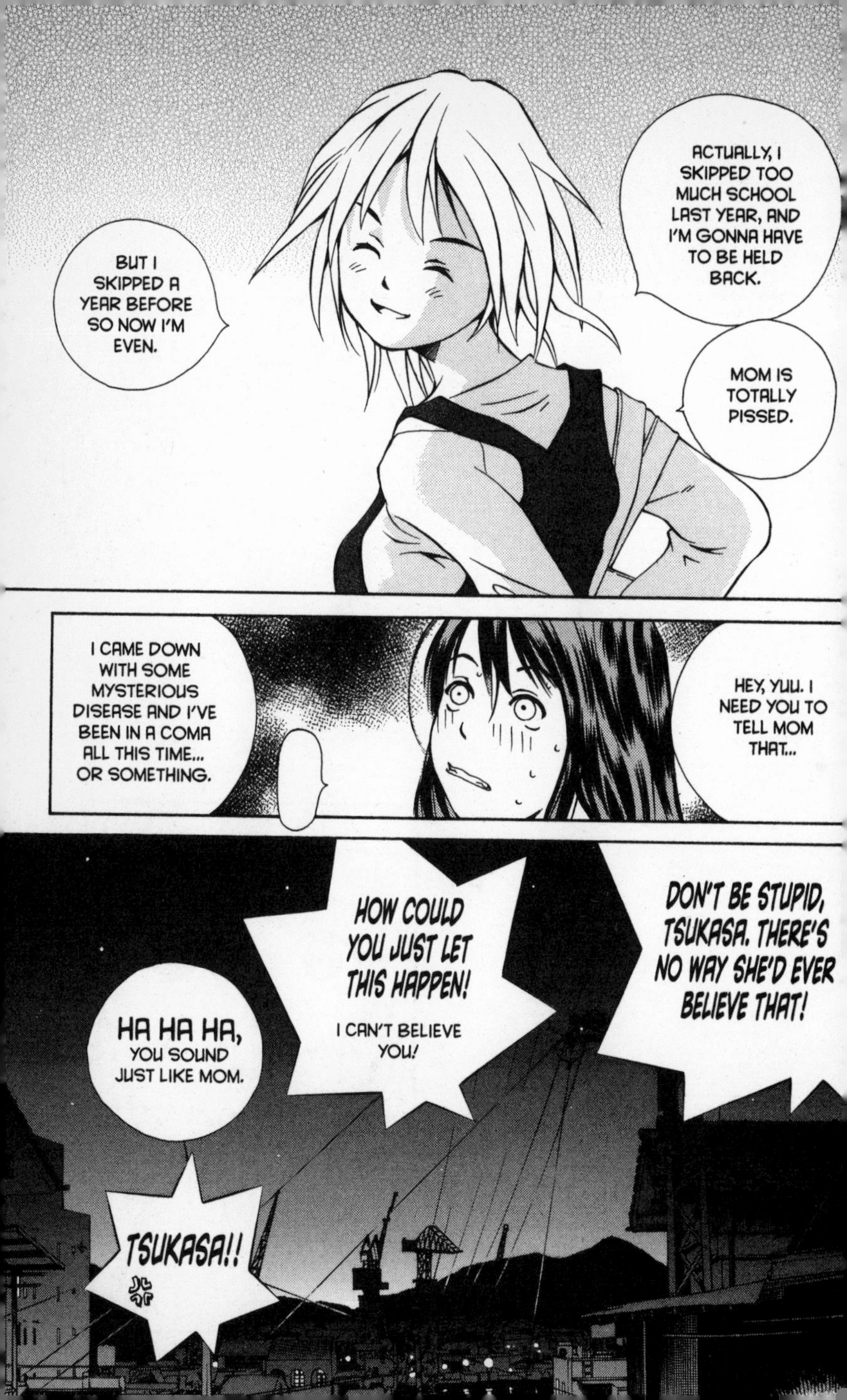
ACTUALLY, I SKIPPED TOO MUCH SCHOOL LAST YEAR, AND I'M GONNA HAVE TO BE HELD BACK.
BUT I SKIPPED A YEAR BEFORE SO NOW I'M EVEN.
MOM IS TOTALLY PISSED.
HEY, YUU. I NEED YOU TO TELL MOM THAT...
I CAME DOWN WITH SOME MYSTERIOUS DISEASE AND I'VE BEEN IN A COMA ALL THIS TIME... OR SOMETHING.
DON'T BE STUPID, TSUKASA. THERE'S NO WAY SHE'D EVER BELIEVE THAT!
HOW COULD YOU JUST LET THIS HAPPEN!
I CAN'T BELIEVE YOU!
HA HA HA, YOU SOUND JUST LIKE MOM.
TSUKASA!!

MIRACLE 64: OSAKA LOVE QUARREL

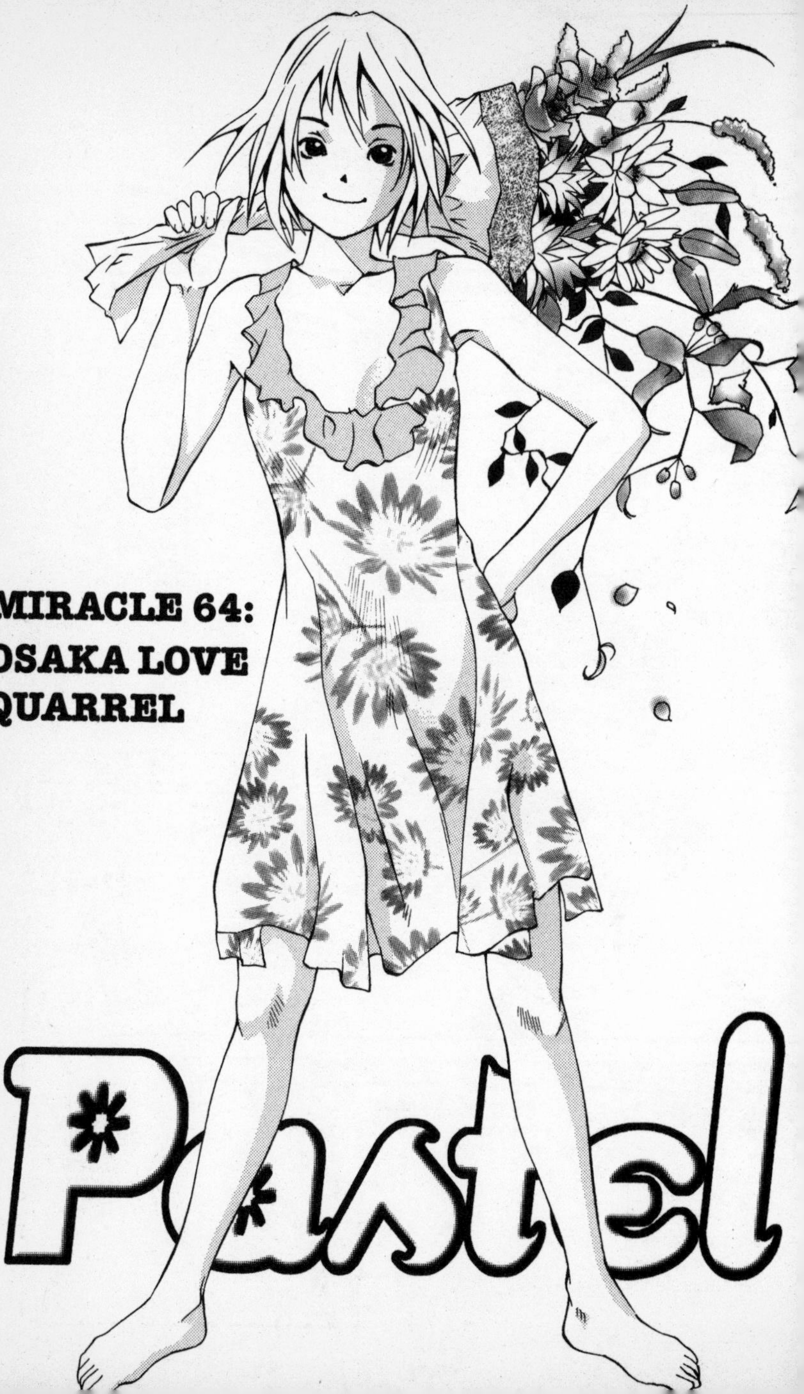
Pastel

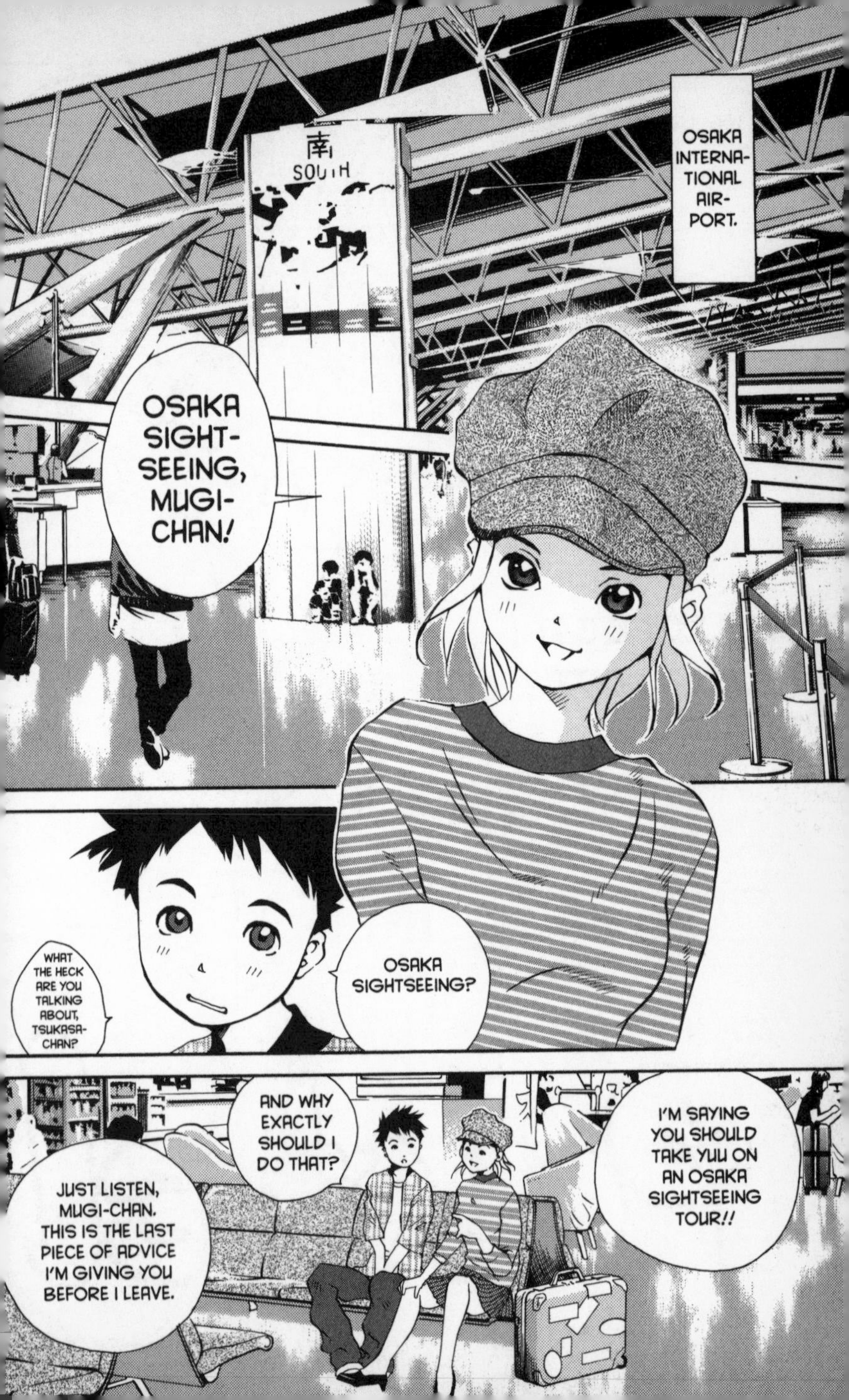
OSAKA INTERNATIONAL AIRPORT.
南
SOUTH
OSAKA SIGHTSEEING, MUGI-CHAN!
OSAKA SIGHTSEEING?
WHAT THE HECK ARE YOU TALKING ABOUT, TSUKASA-CHAN?
I'M SAYING YOU SHOULD TAKE YUU ON AN OSAKA SIGHTSEEING TOUR!!
AND WHY EXACTLY SHOULD I DO THAT?
JUST LISTEN, MUGI-CHAN. THIS IS THE LAST PIECE OF ADVICE I'M GIVING YOU BEFORE I LEAVE.

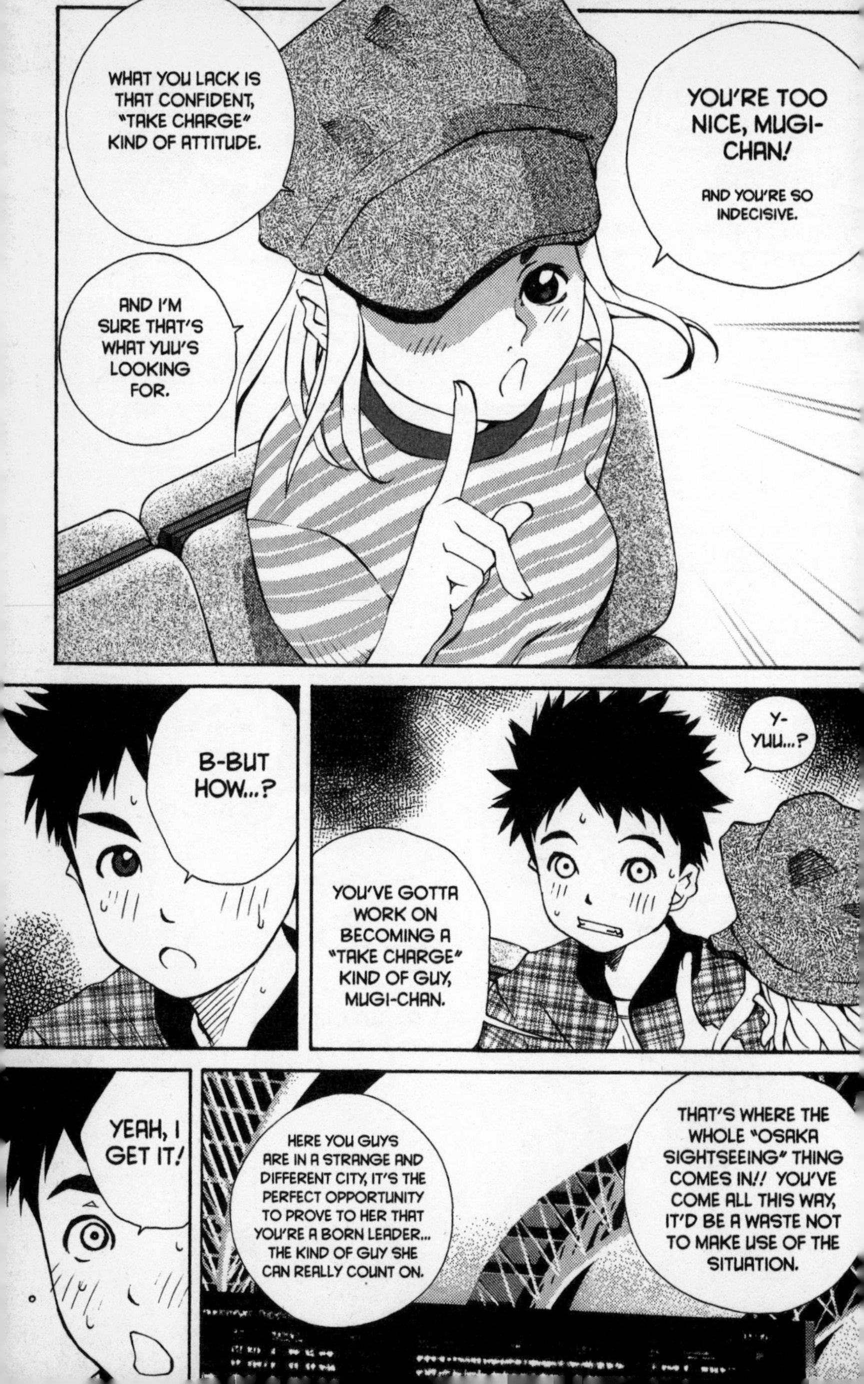
YOU'RE TOO NICE, MUGI-CHAN!
AND YOU'RE SO INDECISIVE.
WHAT YOU LACK IS THAT CONFIDENT, "TAKE CHARGE" KIND OF ATTITUDE.
AND I'M SURE THAT'S WHAT YUU'S LOOKING FOR.
Y-YUU...?
YOU'VE GOTTA WORK ON BECOMING A "TAKE CHARGE" KIND OF GUY, MUGI-CHAN.
B-BUT HOW...?
THAT'S WHERE THE WHOLE "OSAKA SIGHTSEEING" THING COMES IN!! YOU'VE COME ALL THIS WAY, IT'D BE A WASTE NOT TO MAKE USE OF THE SITUATION.
HERE YOU GUYS ARE IN A STRANGE AND DIFFERENT CITY, IT'S THE PERFECT OPPORTUNITY TO PROVE TO HER THAT YOU'RE A BORN LEADER... THE KIND OF GUY SHE CAN REALLY COUNT ON.
YEAH, I GET IT!

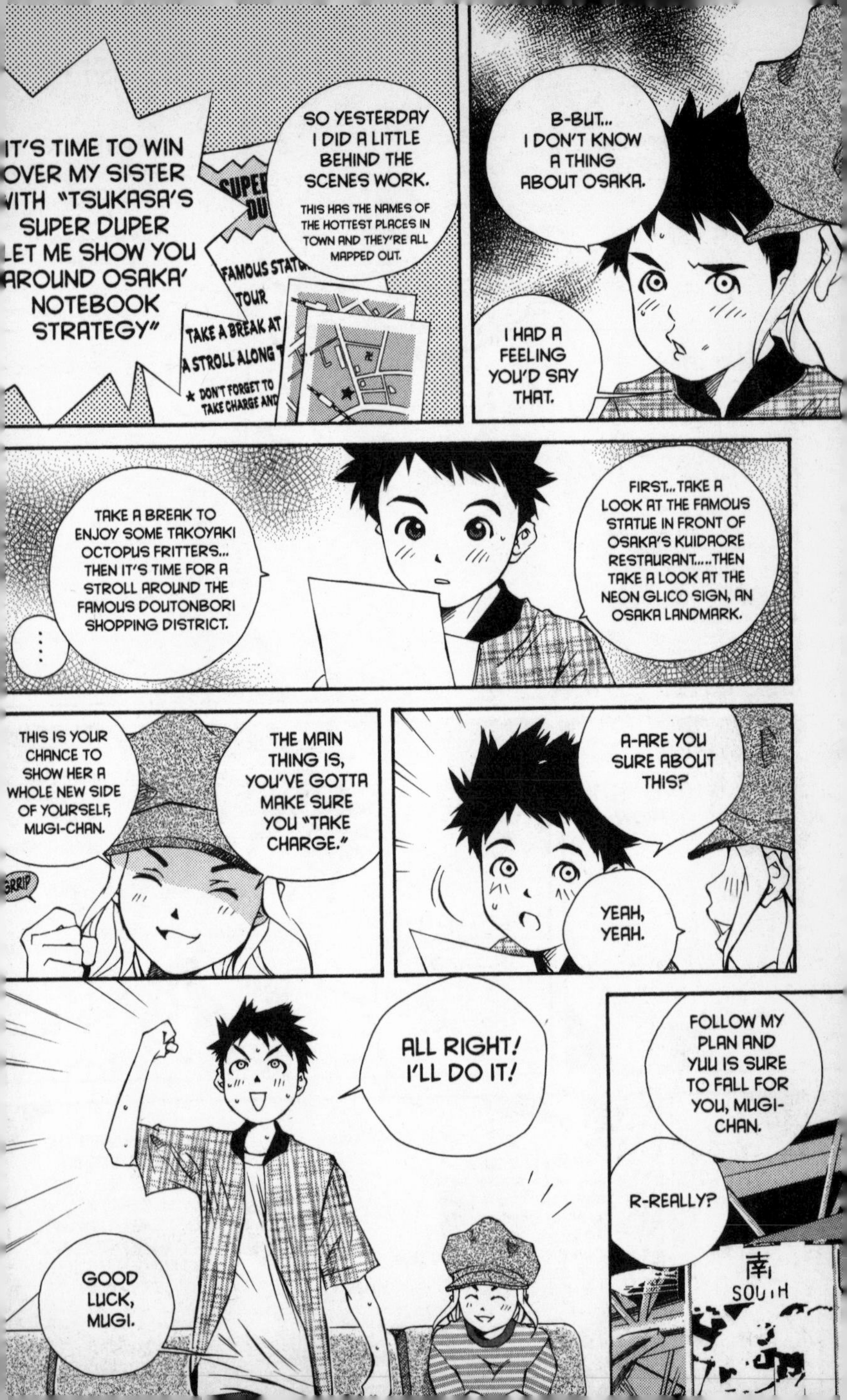
B-BUT... I DON'T KNOW A THING ABOUT OSAKA.
I HAD A FEELING YOU'D SAY THAT.
SO YESTERDAY I DID A LITTLE BEHIND THE SCENES WORK.
THIS HAS THE NAMES OF THE HOTTEST PLACES IN TOWN AND THEY'RE ALL MAPPED OUT.
IT'S TIME TO WIN OVER MY SISTER WITH "TSUKASA'S SUPER DUPER LET ME SHOW YOU AROUND OSAKA' NOTEBOOK STRATEGY"
TOUR
TAKE A BREAK AT
FIRST...TAKE A LOOK AT THE FAMOUS STATUE IN FRONT OF OSAKA'S KUIDAORE RESTAURANT.....THEN TAKE A LOOK AT THE NEON GLICO SIGN, AN OSAKA LANDMARK.
TAKE A BREAK TO ENJOY SOME TAKOYAKI OCTOPUS FRITTERS... THEN IT'S TIME FOR A STROLL AROUND THE FAMOUS DOUTONBORI SHOPPING DISTRICT.
.....
A-ARE YOU SURE ABOUT THIS?
YEAH, YEAH.
THE MAIN THING IS, YOU'VE GOTTA MAKE SURE YOU "TAKE CHARGE."
THIS IS YOUR CHANCE TO SHOW HER A WHOLE NEW SIDE OF YOURSELF, MUGI-CHAN.
GRRIP
FOLLOW MY PLAN AND YUU IS SURE TO FALL FOR YOU, MUGI-CHAN.
R-REALLY?
南
SOUTH
ALL RIGHT! I'LL DO IT!
GOOD LUCK, MUGI.

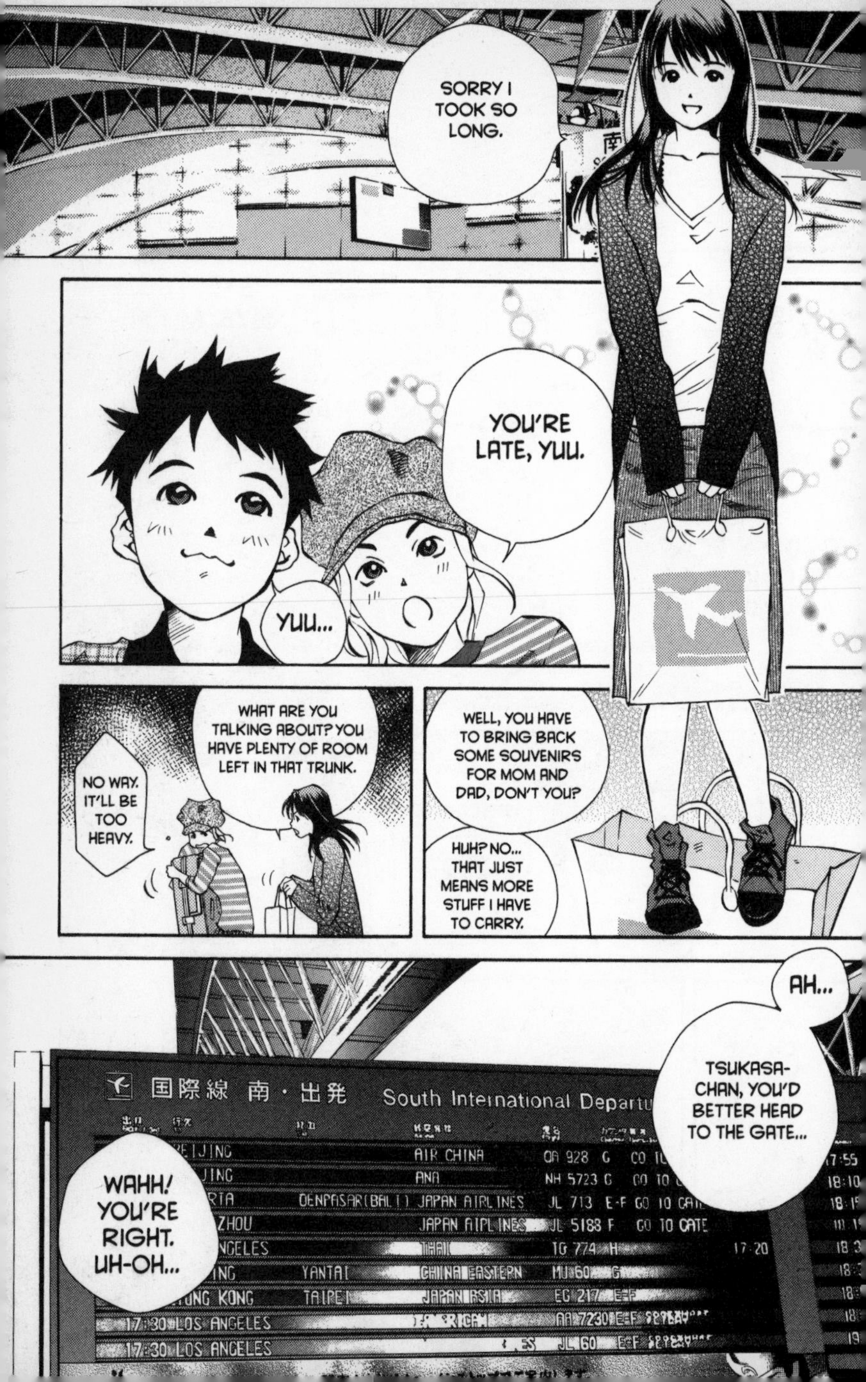
SORRY I TOOK SO LONG.
YOU'RE LATE, YUU.
YUU...
WELL, YOU HAVE TO BRING BACK SOME SOUVENIRS FOR MOM AND DAD, DON'T YOU?
HUH? NO... THAT JUST MEANS MORE STUFF I HAVE TO CARRY.
WHAT ARE YOU TALKING ABOUT? YOU HAVE PLENTY OF ROOM LEFT IN THAT TRUNK.
NO WAY. IT'LL BE TOO HEAVY.
AH...
TSUKASA-CHAN, YOU'D BETTER HEAD TO THE GATE...
国際線 南・出発
WAHH! YOU'RE RIGHT. UH-OH...

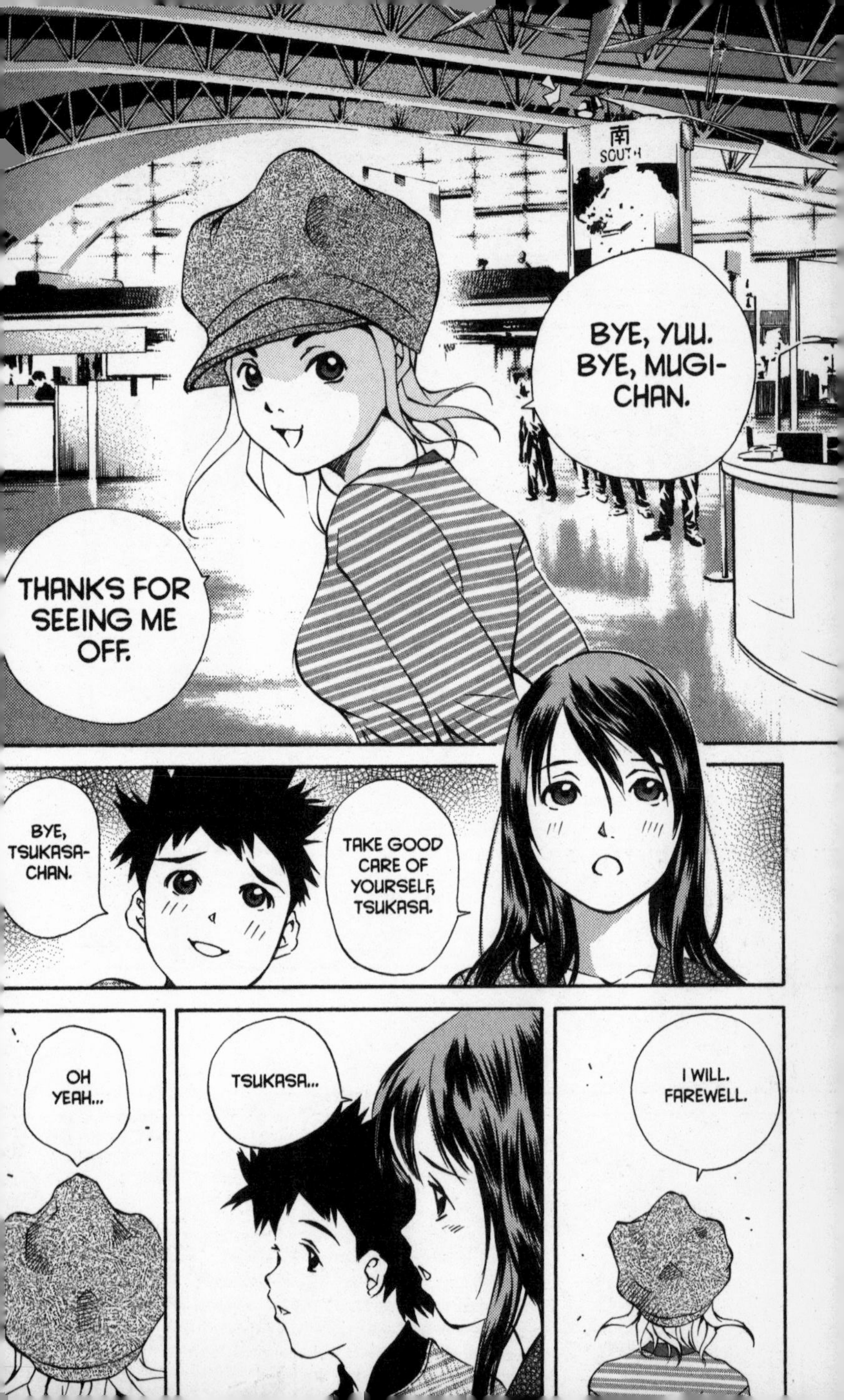
南
BYE, YUU. BYE, MUGI-CHAN.
THANKS FOR SEEING ME OFF.
TAKE GOOD CARE OF YOURSELF, TSUKASA.
BYE, TSUKASA-CHAN.
I WILL. FAREWELL.
TSUKASA...
OH YEAH...

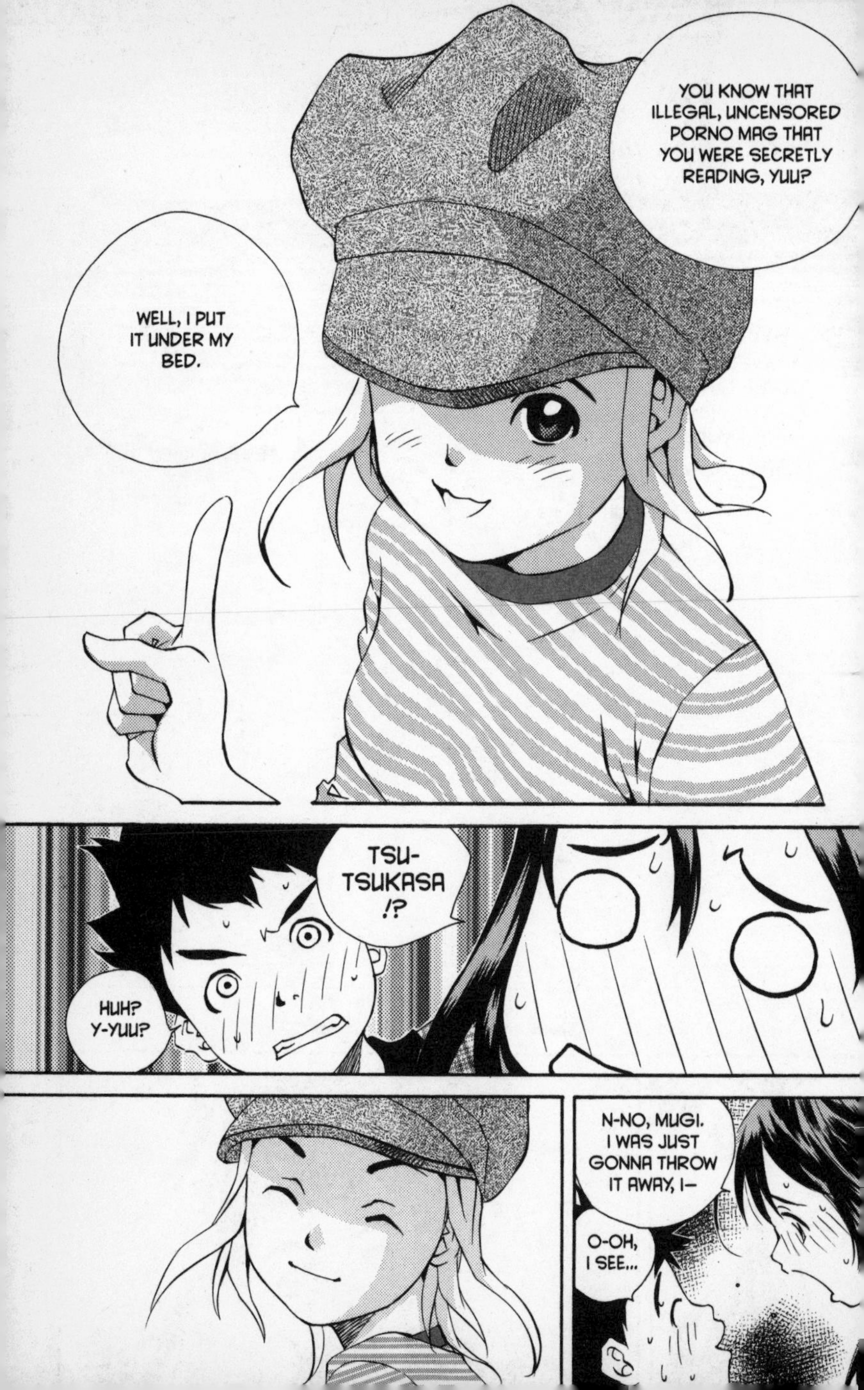
YOU KNOW THAT ILLEGAL, UNCENSORED PORNO MAG THAT YOU WERE SECRETLY READING, YUU?
WELL, I PUT IT UNDER MY BED.
TSU-TSUKASA!?
HUH? Y-YUU?
N-NO, MUGI. I WAS JUST GONNA THROW IT AWAY, I—
O-OH, I SEE...

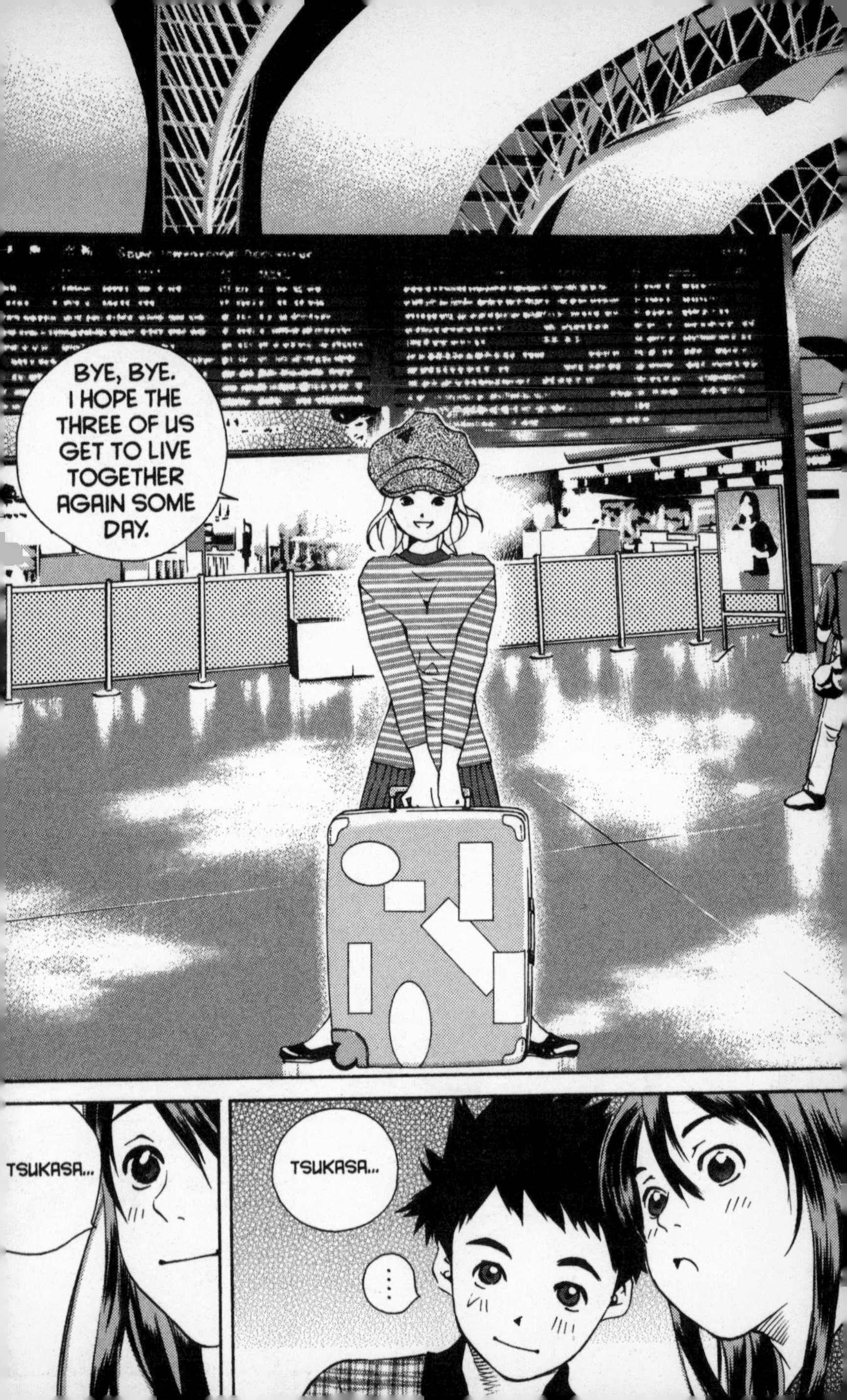
BYE, BYE. I HOPE THE THREE OF US GET TO LIVE TOGETHER AGAIN SOME DAY.
TSUKASA...
....
TSUKASA...

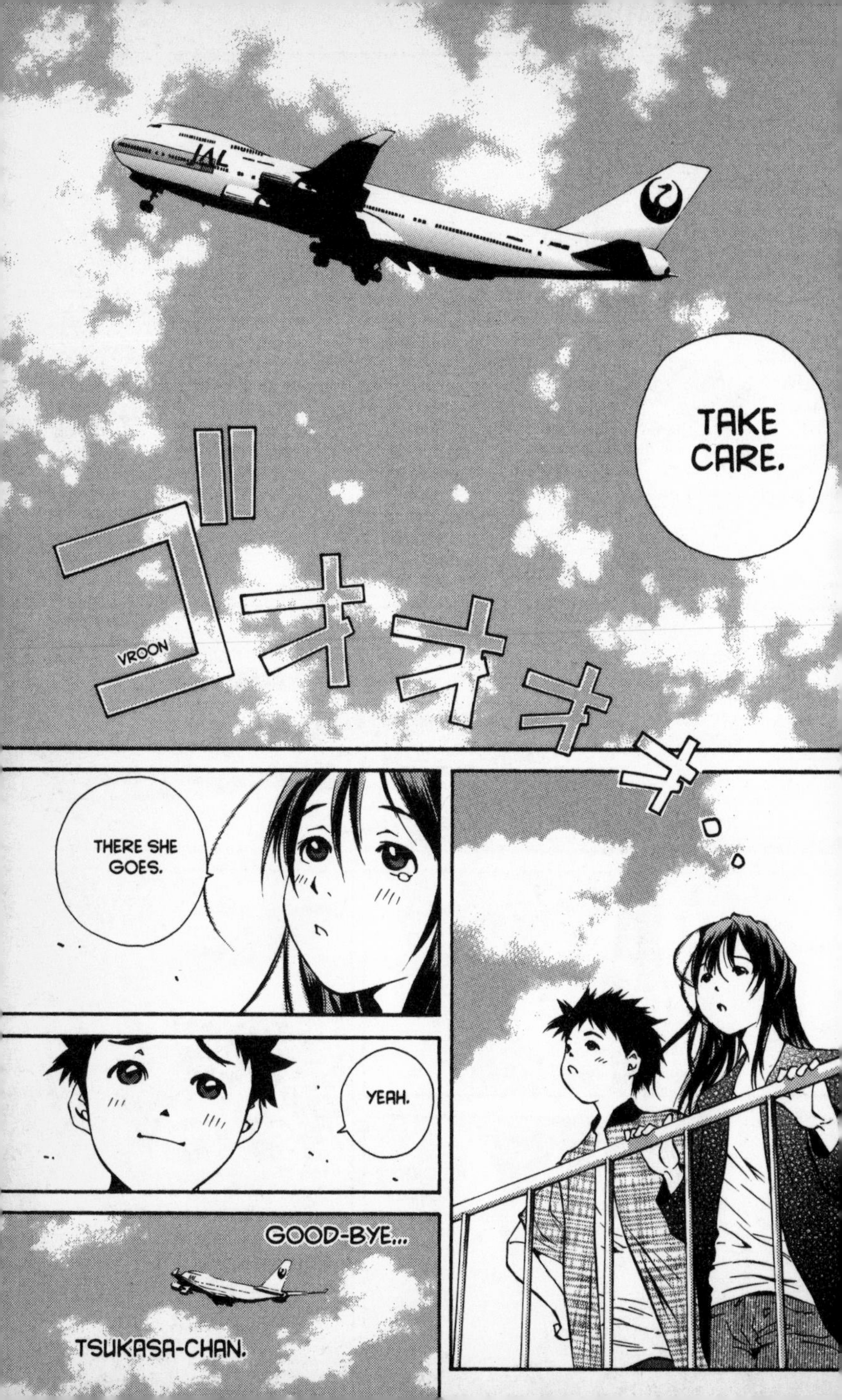
TAKE CARE.
ゴオオオオ
VROON
THERE SHE GOES.
YEAH.
GOOD-BYE...
TSUKASA-CHAN.

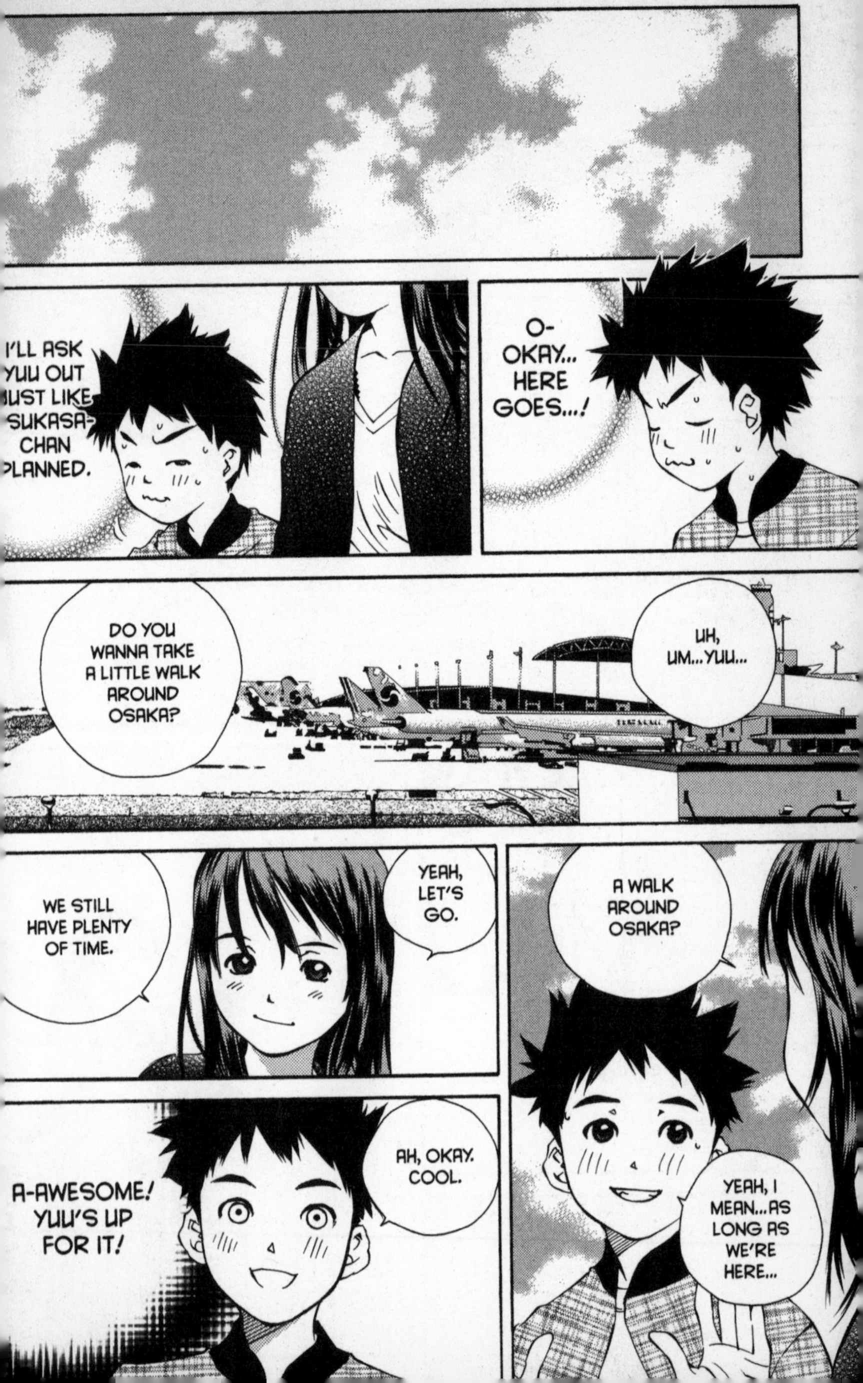
O-OKAY... HERE GOES...!
I'LL ASK YUU OUT JUST LIKE SUKASA-CHAN PLANNED.
UH, UM...YUU...
DO YOU WANNA TAKE A LITTLE WALK AROUND OSAKA?
A WALK AROUND OSAKA?
YEAH, I MEAN...AS LONG AS WE'RE HERE...
YEAH, LET'S GO.
WE STILL HAVE PLENTY OF TIME.
AH, OKAY. COOL.
A-AWESOME! YUU'S UP FOR IT!

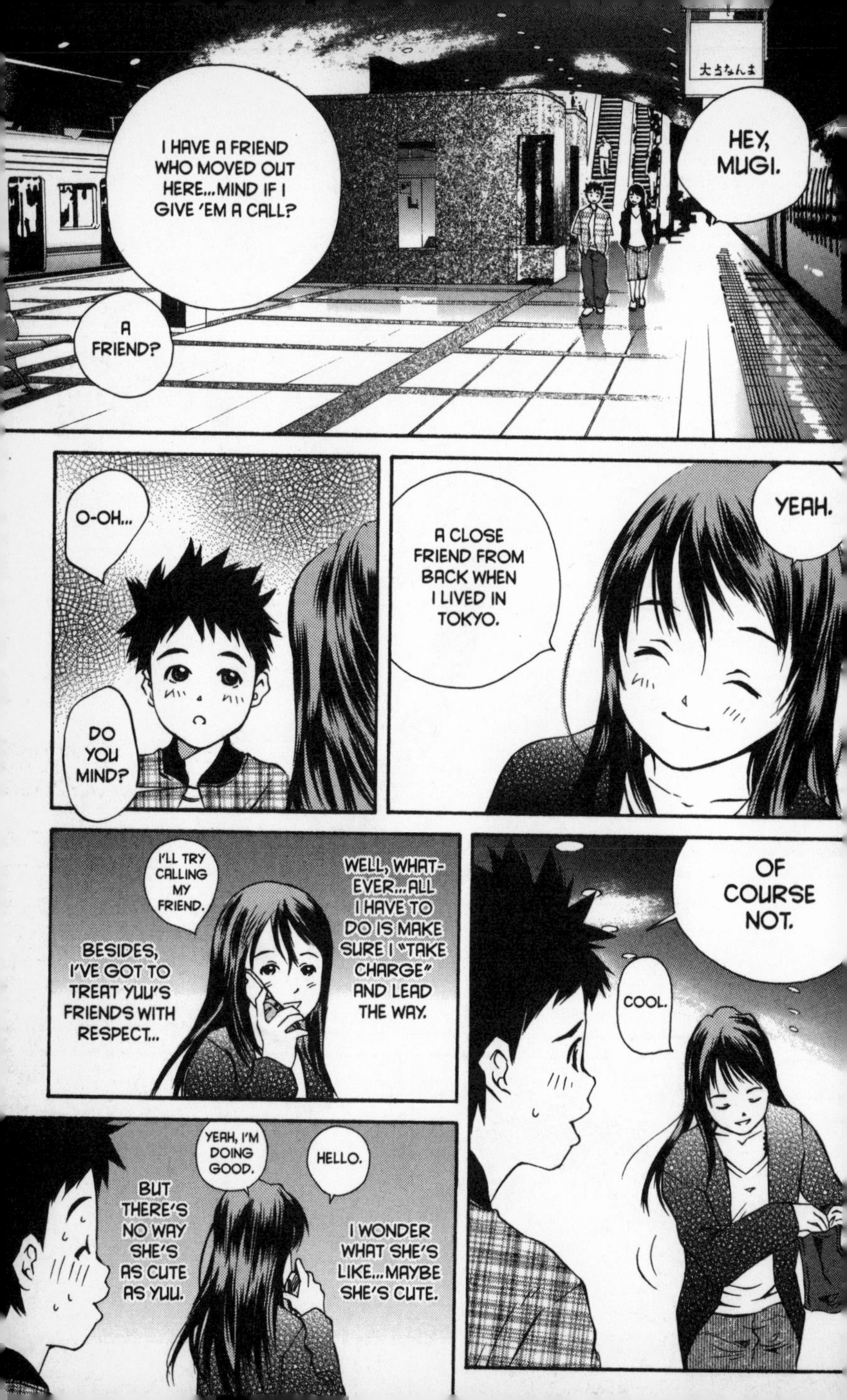
HEY, MUGI.
I HAVE A FRIEND WHO MOVED OUT HERE...MIND IF I GIVE 'EM A CALL?
A FRIEND?
YEAH.
A CLOSE FRIEND FROM BACK WHEN I LIVED IN TOKYO.
O-OH...
DO YOU MIND?
OF COURSE NOT.
COOL.
WELL, WHAT-EVER...ALL I HAVE TO DO IS MAKE SURE I "TAKE CHARGE" AND LEAD THE WAY.
I'LL TRY CALLING MY FRIEND.
BESIDES, I'VE GOT TO TREAT YUU'S FRIENDS WITH RESPECT...
HELLO.
YEAH, I'M DOING GOOD.
I WONDER WHAT SHE'S LIKE...MAYBE SHE'S CUTE.
BUT THERE'S NO WAY SHE'S AS CUTE AS YUU.

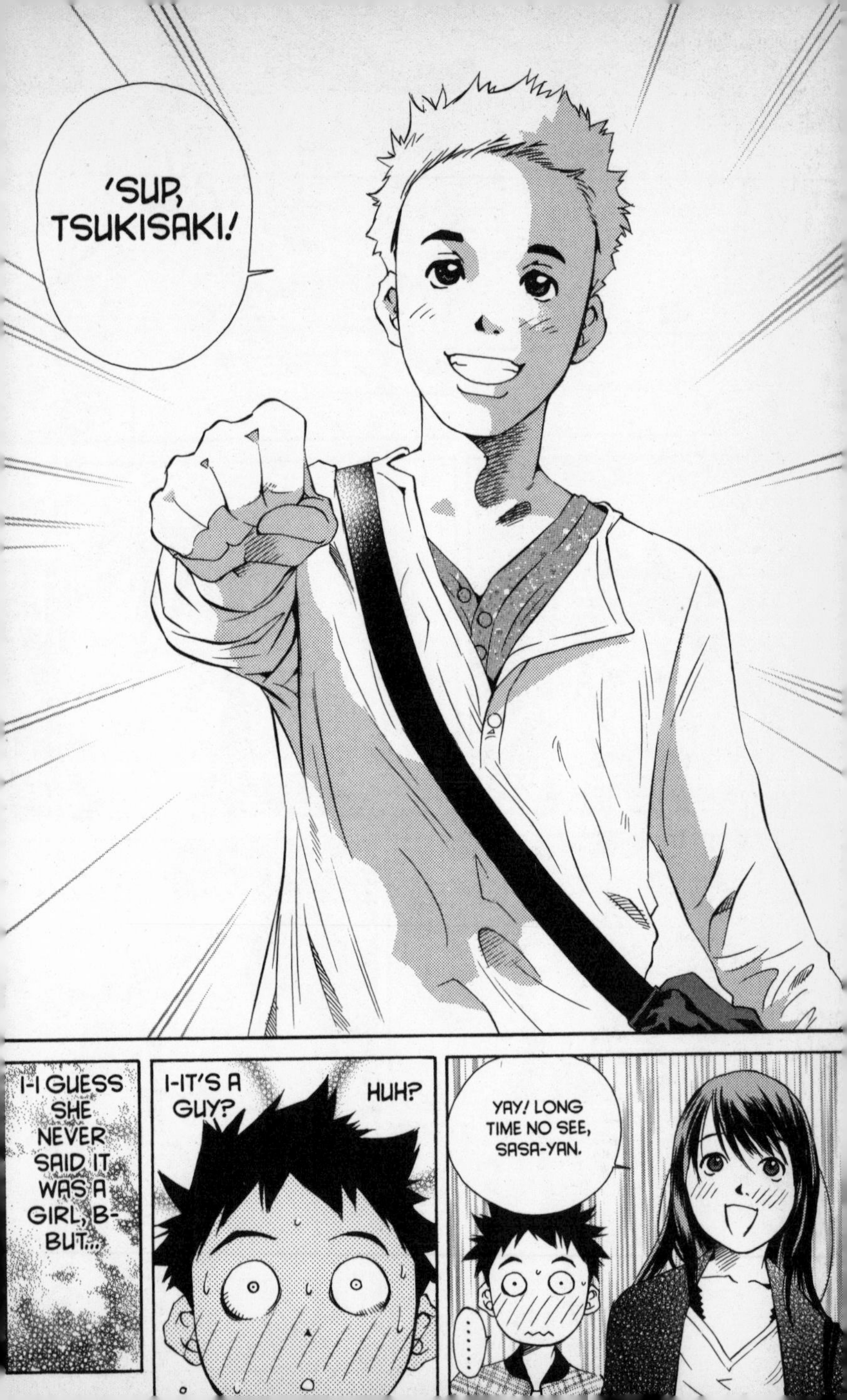
'SUP, TSUKISAKI!
YAY! LONG TIME NO SEE, SASA-YAN.
......
HUH?
I-IT'S A GUY?
I-I GUESS SHE NEVER SAID IT WAS A GIRL, B-BUT...

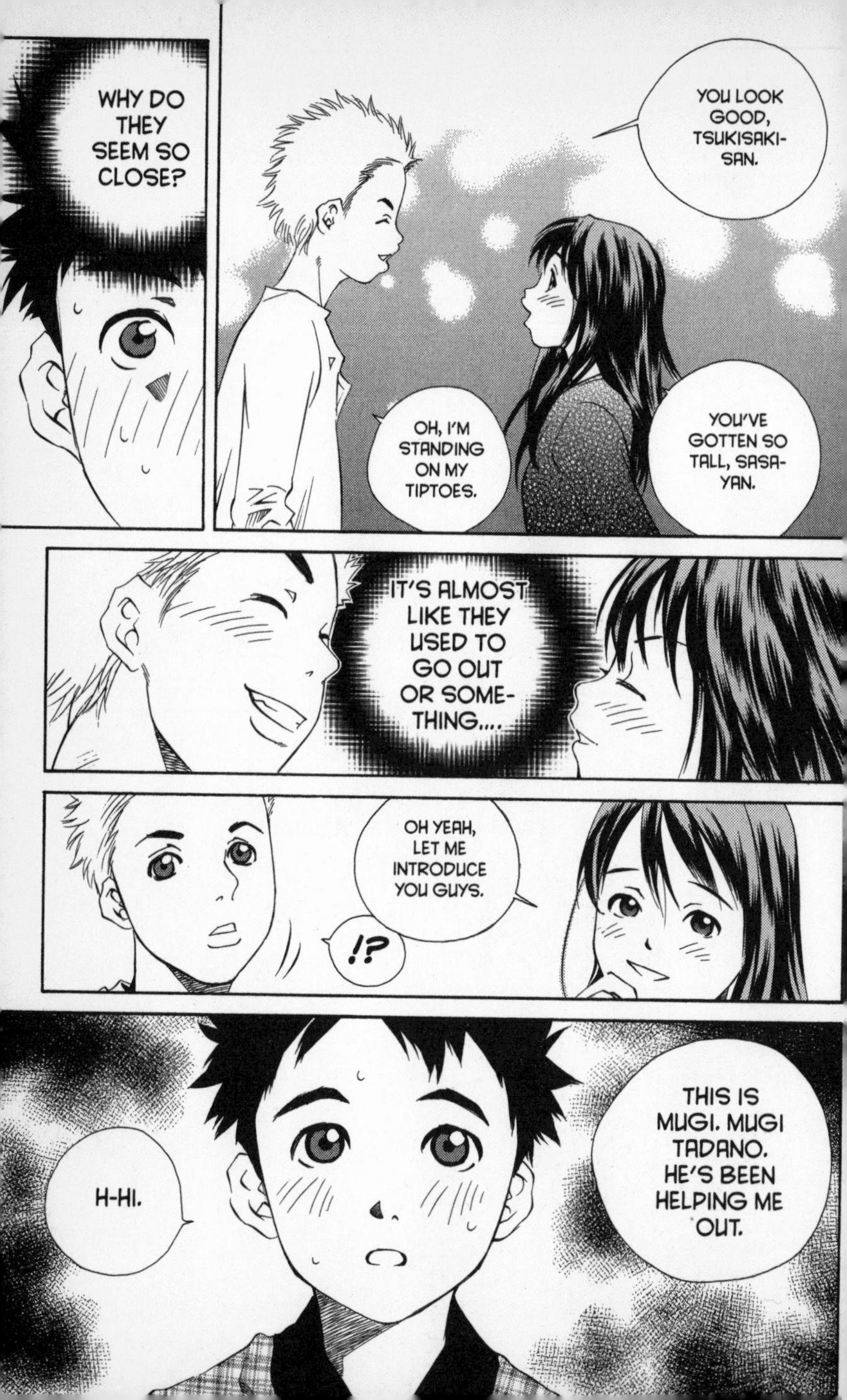
YOU LOOK GOOD, TSUKISAKI-SAN.
YOU'VE GOTTEN SO TALL, SASA-YAN.
OH, I'M STANDING ON MY TIPTOES.
WHY DO THEY SEEM SO CLOSE?
IT'S ALMOST LIKE THEY USED TO GO OUT OR SOME-THING....
OH YEAH, LET ME INTRODUCE YOU GUYS.
!?
THIS IS MUGI. MUGI TADANO. HE'S BEEN HELPING ME OUT.
H-HI.

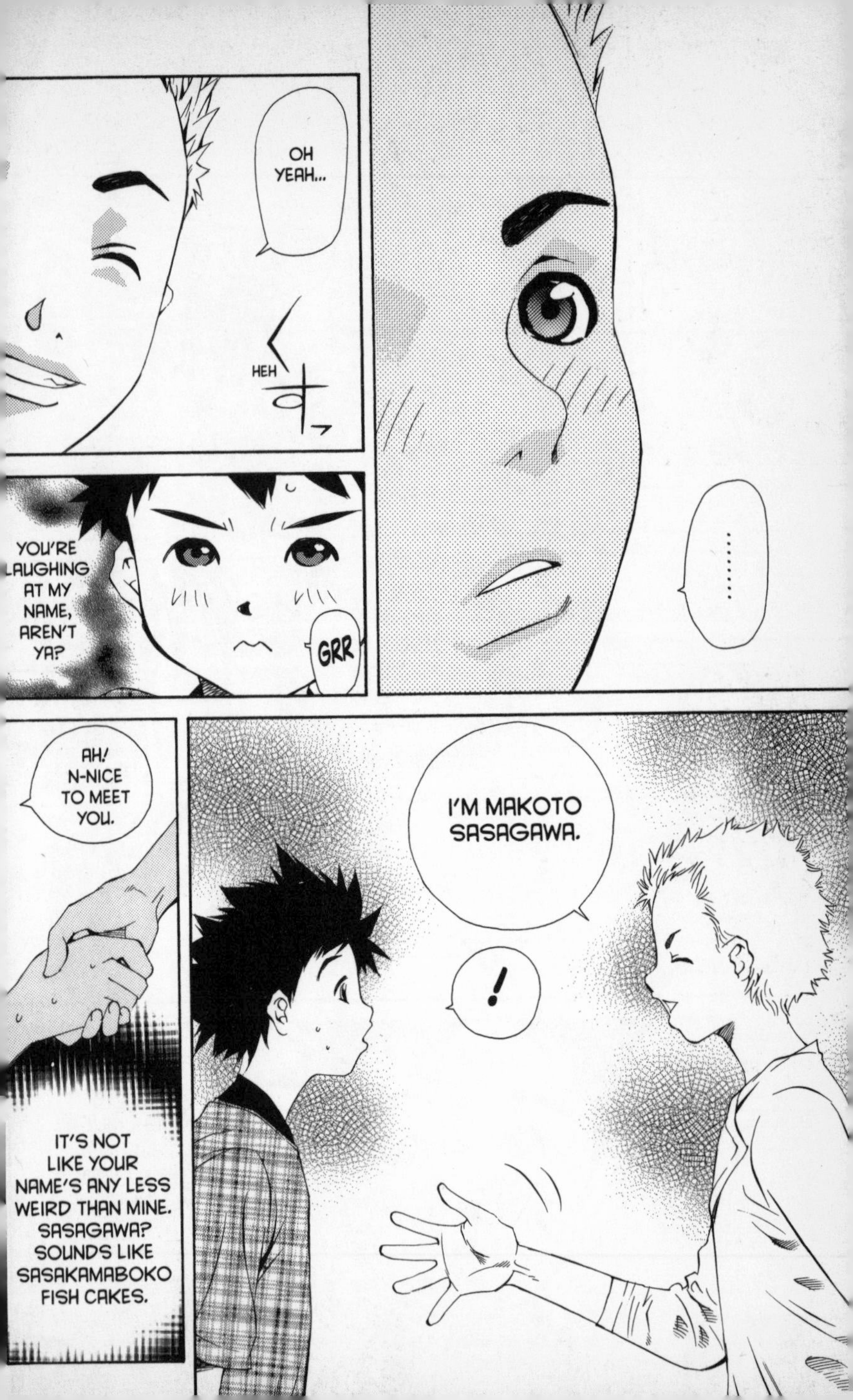
......
OH YEAH...
HEH
YOU'RE LAUGHING AT MY NAME, AREN'T YA?
GRR
I'M MAKOTO SASAGAWA.
!
AH! N-NICE TO MEET YOU.
IT'S NOT LIKE YOUR NAME'S ANY LESS WEIRD THAN MINE. SASAGAWA? SOUNDS LIKE SASAKAMABOKO FISH CAKES.

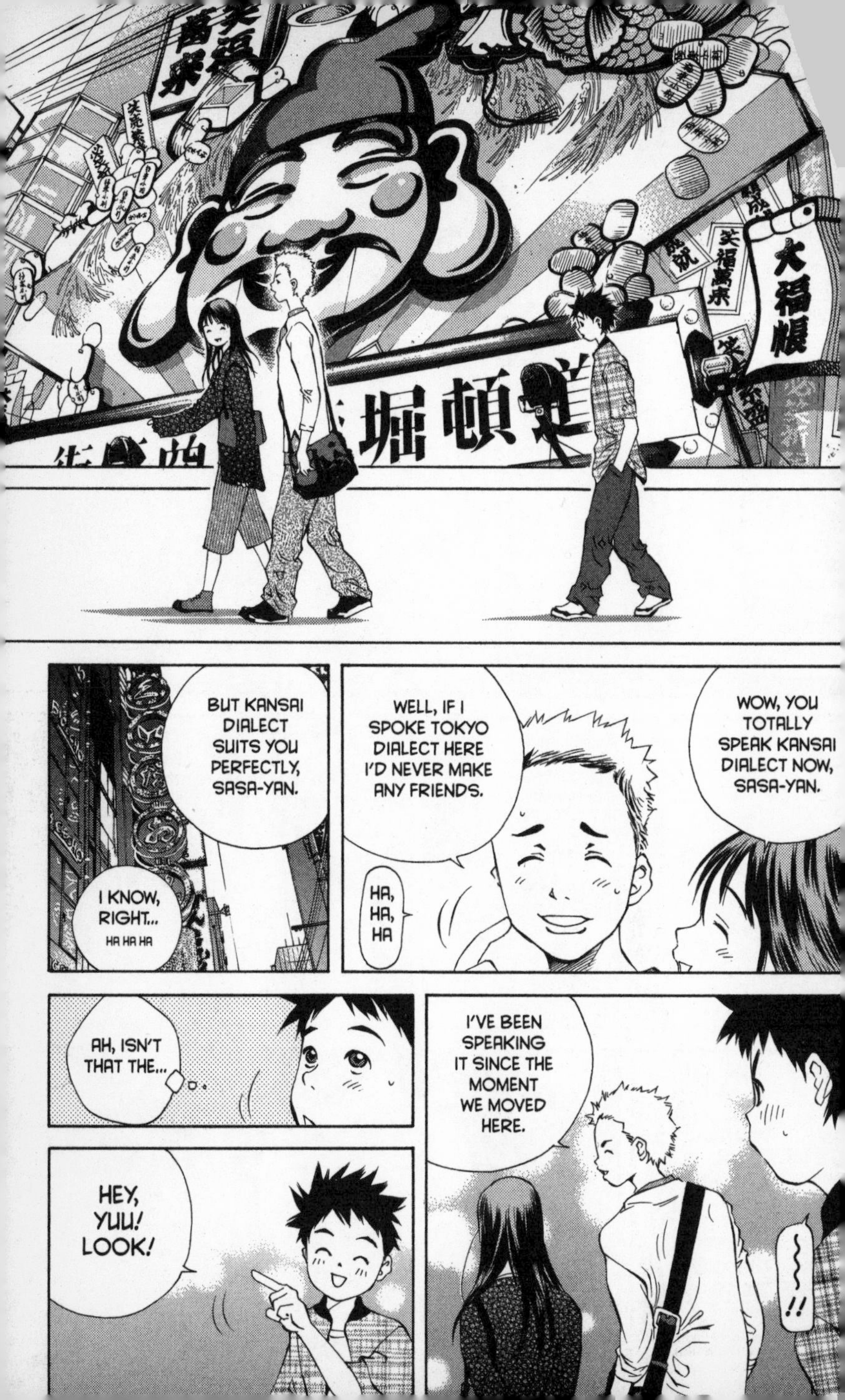

大福帳
WOW, YOU TOTALLY SPEAK KANSAI DIALECT NOW, SASA-YAN.
WELL, IF I SPOKE TOKYO DIALECT HERE I'D NEVER MAKE ANY FRIENDS.
HA, HA, HA
BUT KANSAI DIALECT SUITS YOU PERFECTLY, SASA-YAN.
I KNOW, RIGHT... HA HA HA
I'VE BEEN SPEAKING IT SINCE THE MOMENT WE MOVED HERE.
~~~!!
AH, ISN'T THAT THE...
HEY, YUU! LOOK!
~~~

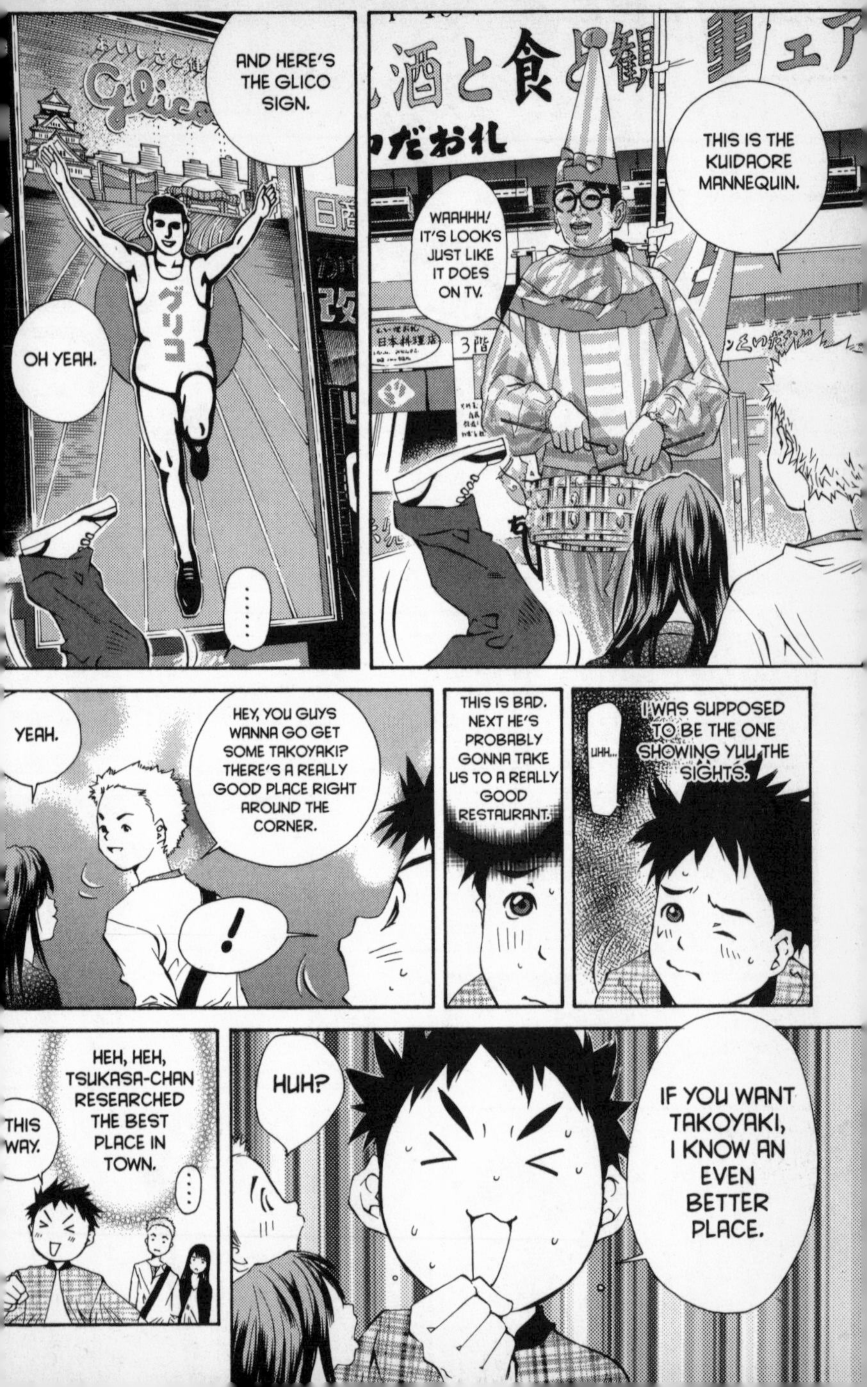
THIS IS THE KUIDAORE MANNEQUIN.
WAAHHH! IT'S LOOKS JUST LIKE IT DOES ON TV.
AND HERE'S THE GLICO SIGN.
OH YEAH.
......
I WAS SUPPOSED TO BE THE ONE SHOWING YUU THE SIGHTS.
UHH...
THIS IS BAD. NEXT HE'S PROBABLY GONNA TAKE US TO A REALLY GOOD RESTAURANT.
HEY, YOU GUYS WANNA GO GET SOME TAKOYAKI? THERE'S A REALLY GOOD PLACE RIGHT AROUND THE CORNER.
YEAH.
!
IF YOU WANT TAKOYAKI, I KNOW AN EVEN BETTER PLACE.
HUH?
HEH, HEH, TSUKASA-CHAN RESEARCHED THE BEST PLACE IN TOWN.
THIS WAY.
....

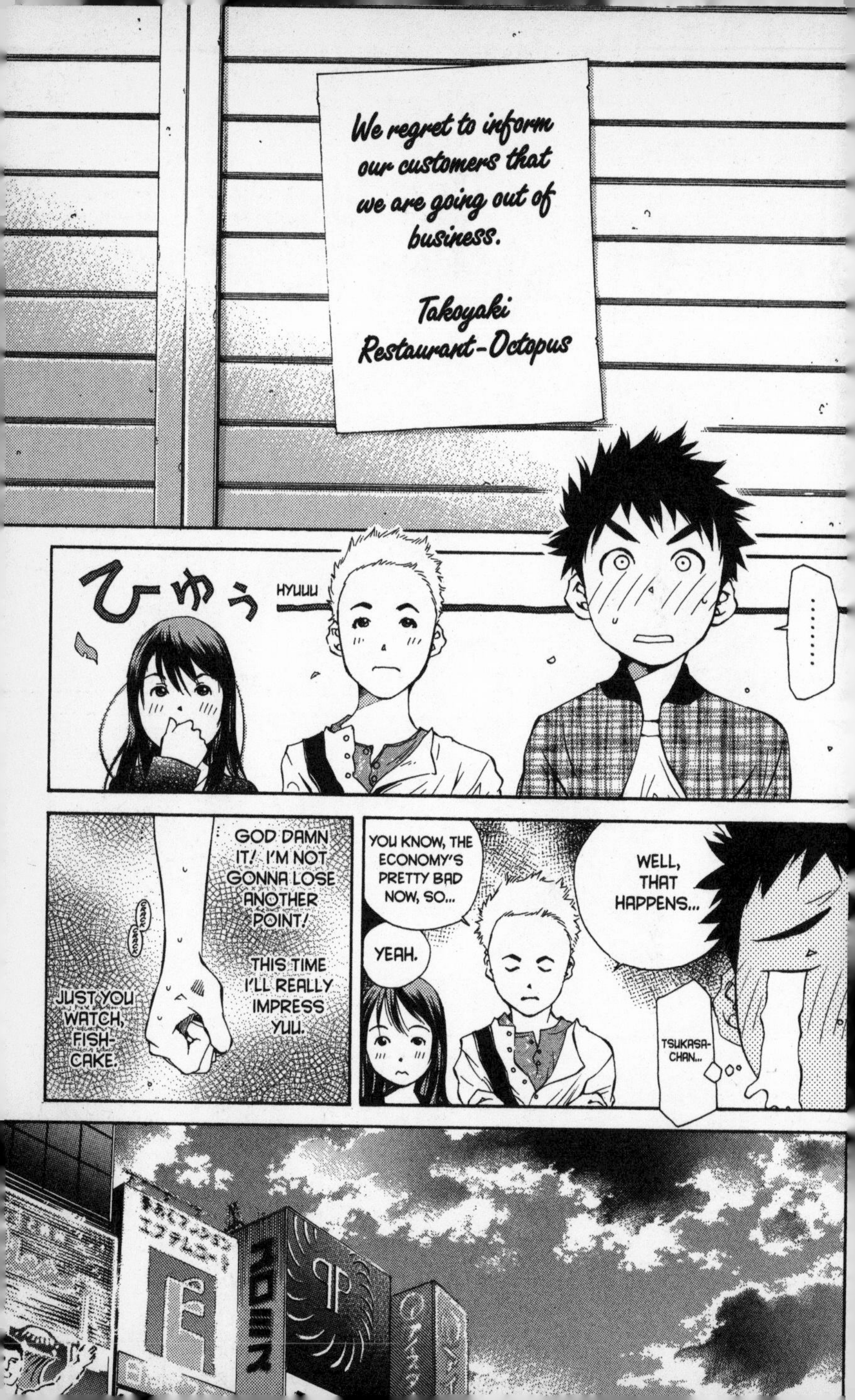
We regret to inform our customers that we are going out of business.
Takoyaki Restaurant-Octopus
....
ひゅう―
HYUUU
WELL, THAT HAPPENS...
TSUKASA-CHAN...
YOU KNOW, THE ECONOMY'S PRETTY BAD NOW, SO...
YEAH.
GOD DAMN IT! I'M NOT GONNA LOSE ANOTHER POINT!
THIS TIME I'LL REALLY IMPRESS YUU.
JUST YOU WATCH, FISH-CAKE.

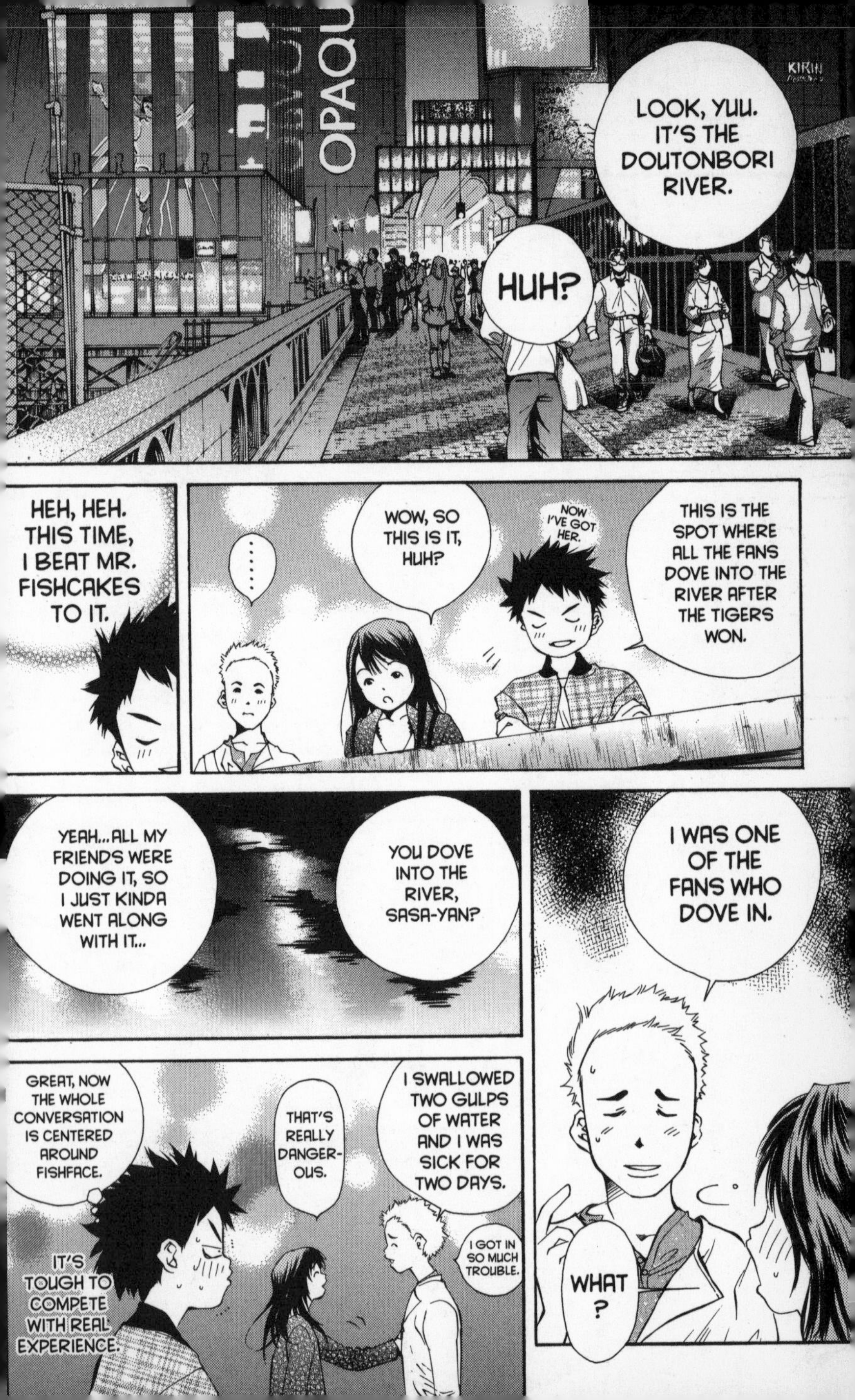
KIRIN
OPAQU
LOOK, YUU. IT'S THE DOUTONBORI RIVER.
HUH?
THIS IS THE SPOT WHERE ALL THE FANS DOVE INTO THE RIVER AFTER THE TIGERS WON.
NOW I'VE GOT HER.
WOW, SO THIS IS IT, HUH?
......
HEH, HEH. THIS TIME, I BEAT MR. FISHCAKES TO IT.
I WAS ONE OF THE FANS WHO DOVE IN.
WHAT?
YOU DOVE INTO THE RIVER, SASA-YAN?
YEAH...ALL MY FRIENDS WERE DOING IT, SO I JUST KINDA WENT ALONG WITH IT...
I SWALLOWED TWO GULPS OF WATER AND I WAS SICK FOR TWO DAYS.
I GOT IN SO MUCH TROUBLE.
THAT'S REALLY DANGER-OUS.
GREAT, NOW THE WHOLE CONVERSATION IS CENTERED AROUND FISHFACE.
IT'S TOUGH TO COMPETE WITH REAL EXPERIENCE.

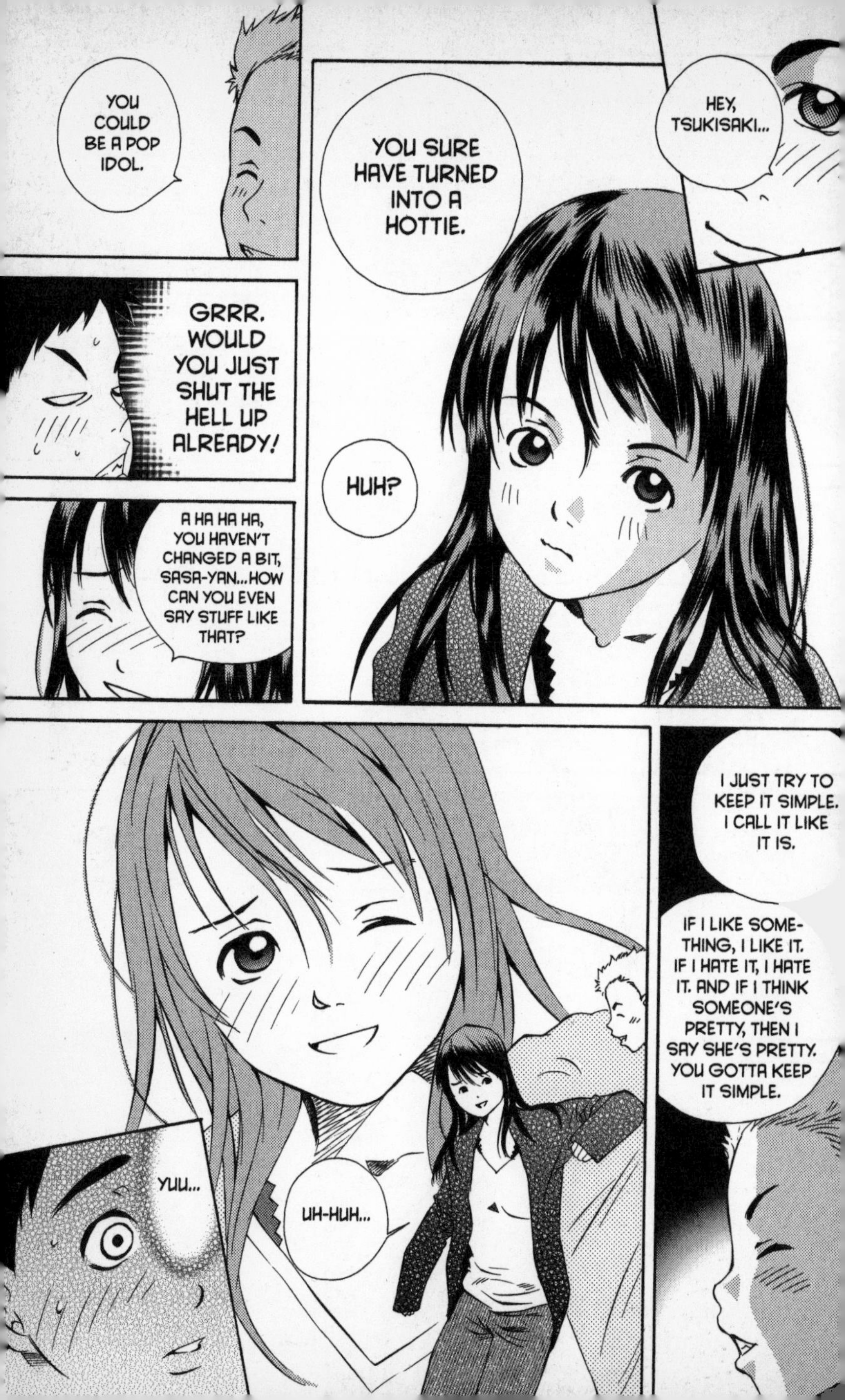
HEY, TSUKISAKI...
YOU SURE HAVE TURNED INTO A HOTTIE.
HUH?
YOU COULD BE A POP IDOL.
GRRR. WOULD YOU JUST SHUT THE HELL UP ALREADY!
A HA HA HA, YOU HAVEN'T CHANGED A BIT, SASA-YAN...HOW CAN YOU EVEN SAY STUFF LIKE THAT?
I JUST TRY TO KEEP IT SIMPLE. I CALL IT LIKE IT IS.
IF I LIKE SOME-THING, I LIKE IT. IF I HATE IT, I HATE IT. AND IF I THINK SOMEONE'S PRETTY, THEN I SAY SHE'S PRETTY. YOU GOTTA KEEP IT SIMPLE.
UH-HUH...
YUU...

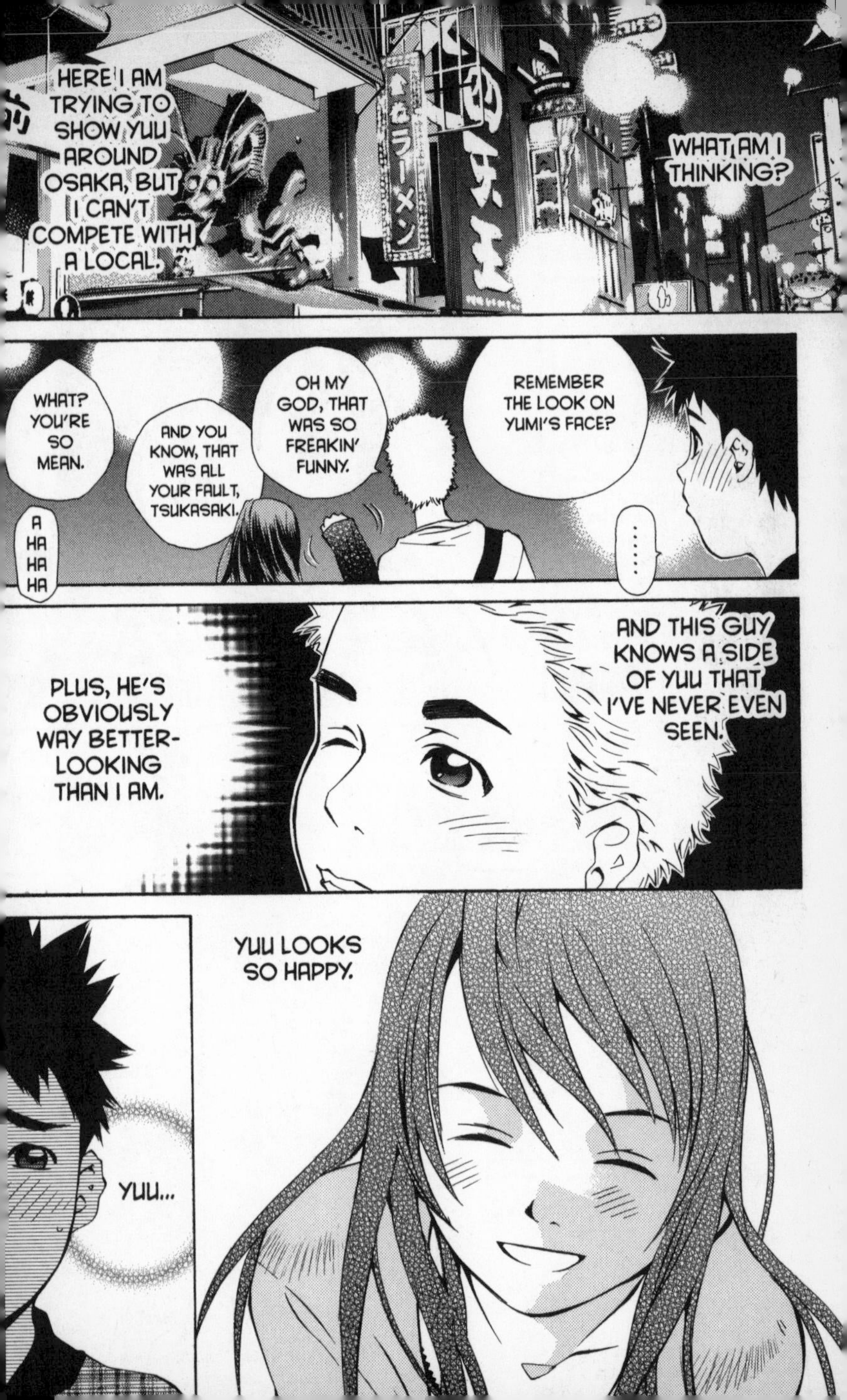
HERE I AM TRYING TO SHOW YUU AROUND OSAKA, BUT I CAN'T COMPETE WITH A LOCAL.
WHAT AM I THINKING?
REMEMBER THE LOOK ON YUMI'S FACE?
......
OH MY GOD, THAT WAS SO FREAKIN' FUNNY.
AND YOU KNOW, THAT WAS ALL YOUR FAULT, TSUKASAKI.
WHAT? YOU'RE SO MEAN.
A HA HA HA
AND THIS GUY KNOWS A SIDE OF YUU THAT I'VE NEVER EVEN SEEN.
PLUS, HE'S OBVIOUSLY WAY BETTER-LOOKING THAN I AM.
YUU LOOKS SO HAPPY.
YUU...

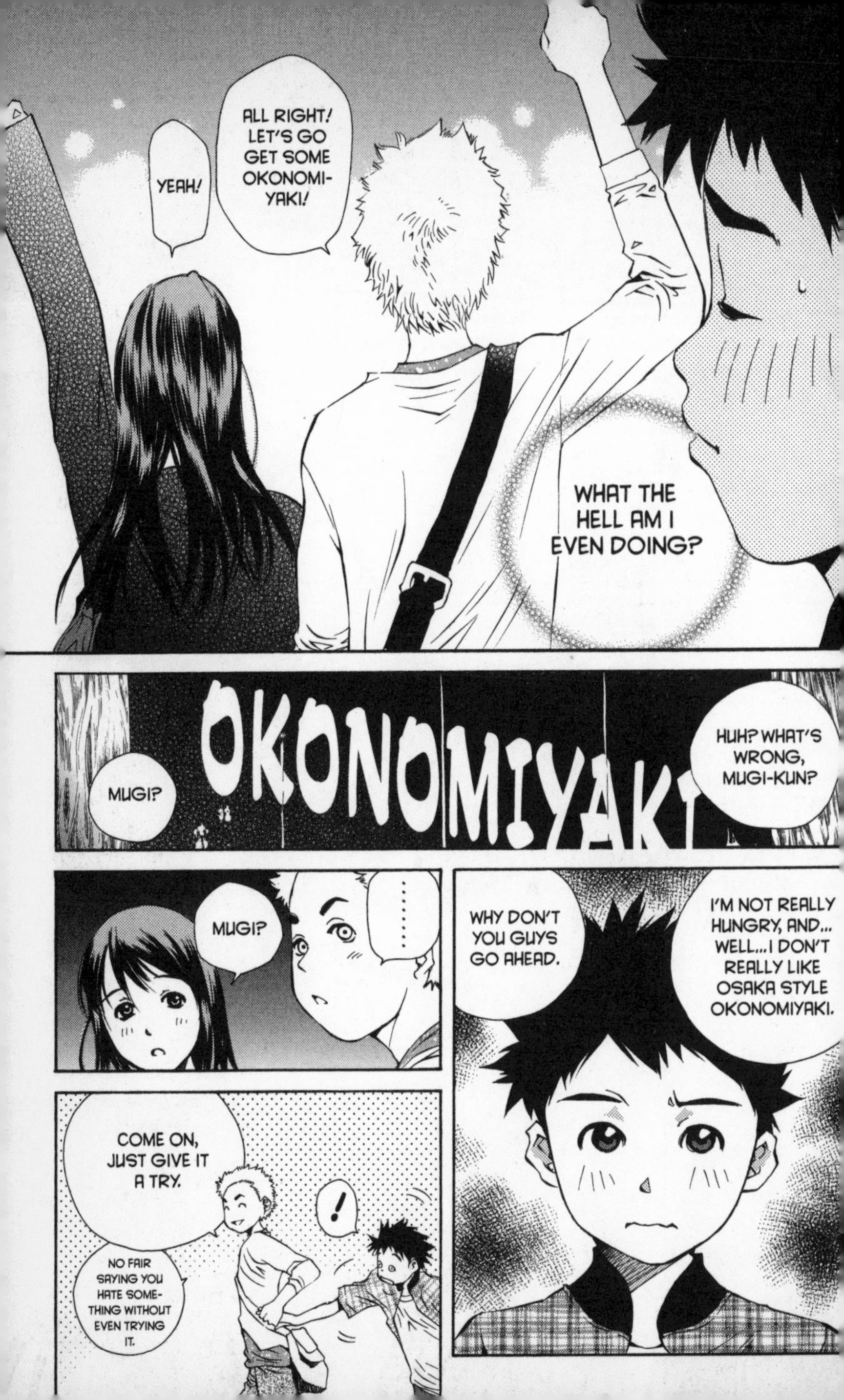
ALL RIGHT! LET'S GO GET SOME OKONOMI-YAKI!
YEAH!
WHAT THE HELL AM I EVEN DOING?
HUH? WHAT'S WRONG, MUGI-KUN?
OKONOMIYAKI
MUGI?
I'M NOT REALLY HUNGRY, AND... WELL...I DON'T REALLY LIKE OSAKA STYLE OKONOMIYAKI.
WHY DON'T YOU GUYS GO AHEAD.
......
MUGI?
!
COME ON, JUST GIVE IT A TRY.
NO FAIR SAYING YOU HATE SOME-THING WITHOUT EVEN TRYING IT.

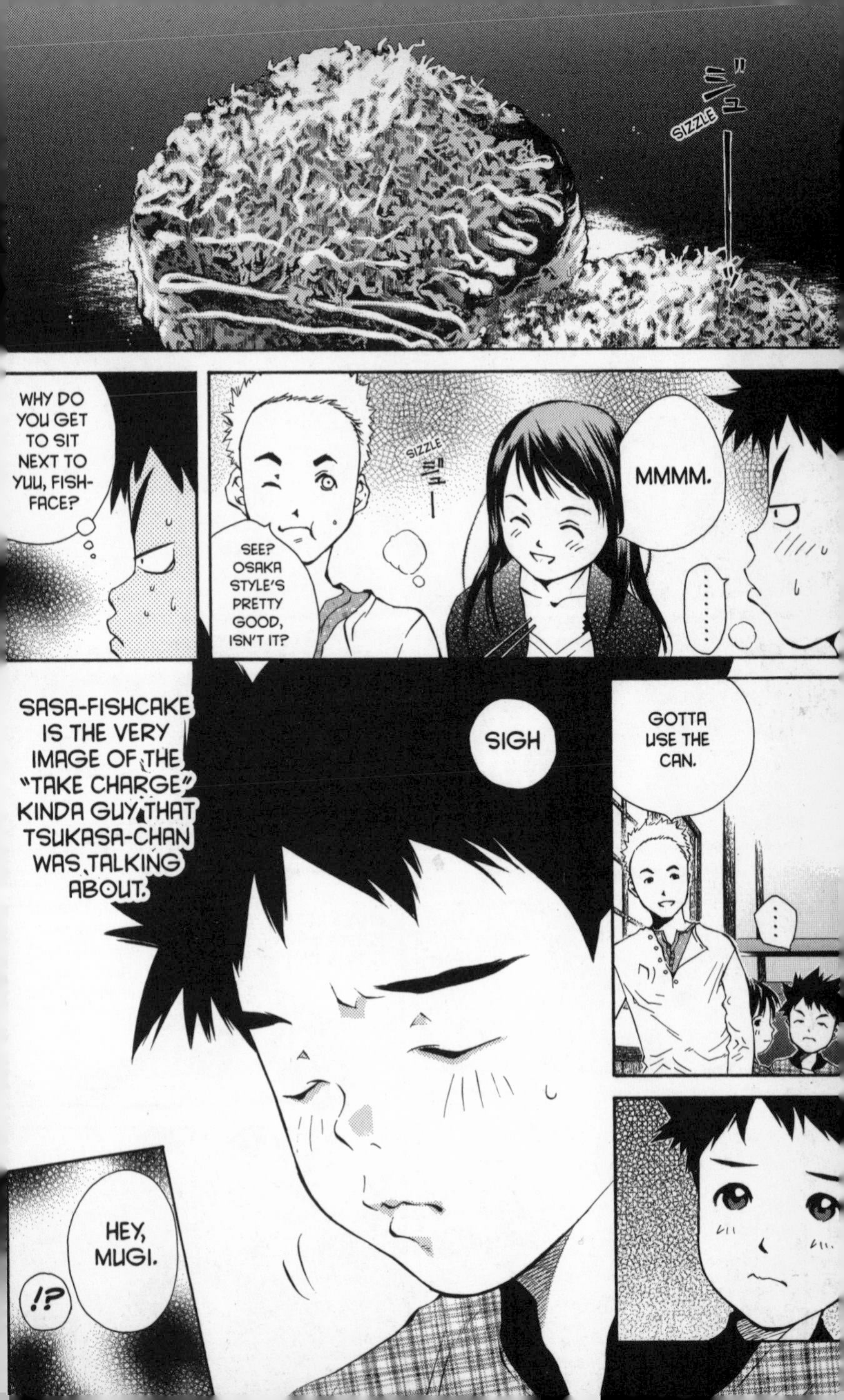
SIZZLE
MMMM.
......
SIZZLE
SEE? OSAKA STYLE'S PRETTY GOOD, ISN'T IT?
WHY DO YOU GET TO SIT NEXT TO YUU, FISH-FACE?
GOTTA USE THE CAN.
.....
SIGH
SASA-FISHCAKE IS THE VERY IMAGE OF THE "TAKE CHARGE" KINDA GUY THAT TSUKASA-CHAN WAS TALKING ABOUT.
HEY, MUGI.
!?

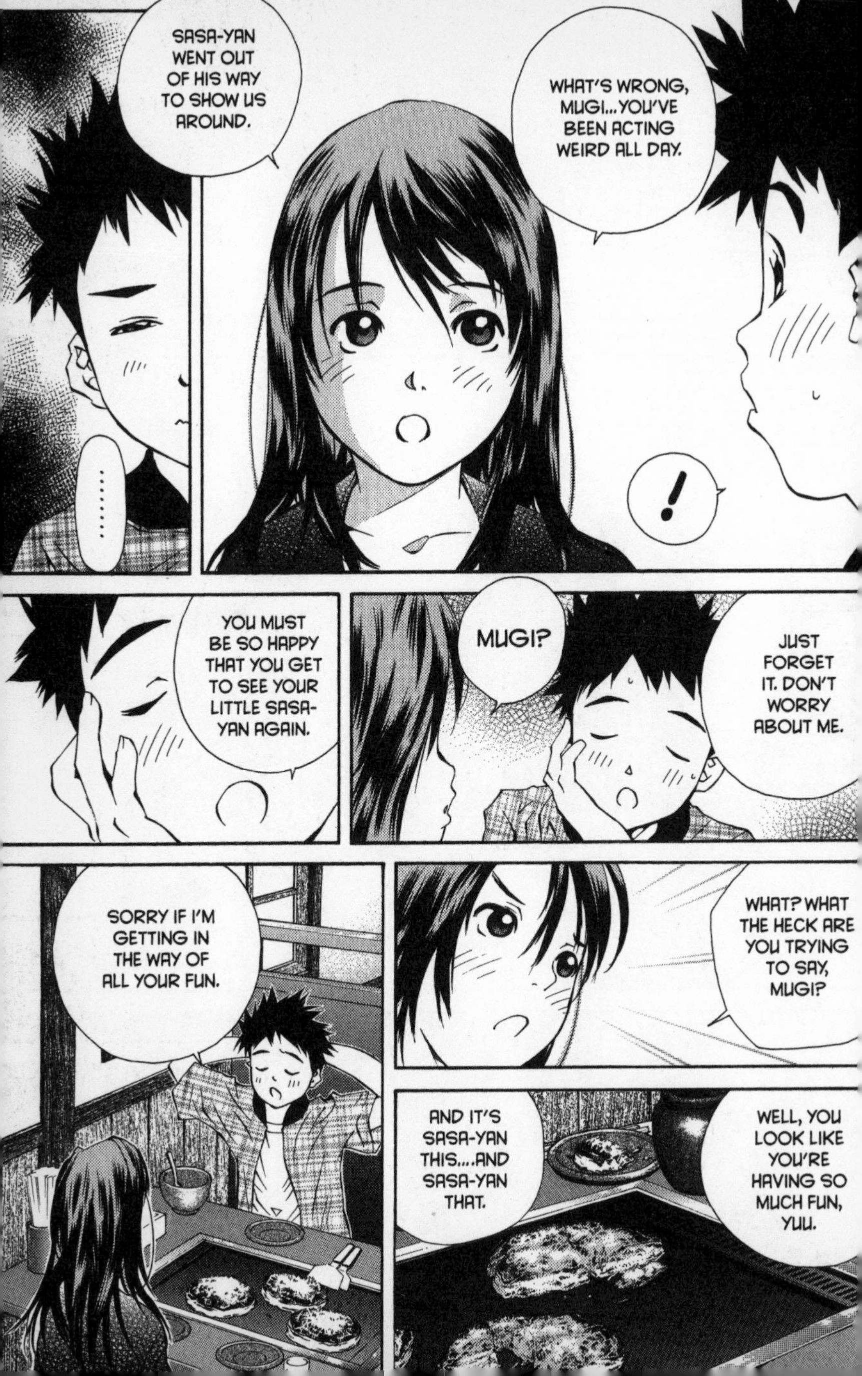
WHAT'S WRONG, MUGI...YOU'VE BEEN ACTING WEIRD ALL DAY.
!
SASA-YAN WENT OUT OF HIS WAY TO SHOW US AROUND.
......
MUGI?
JUST FORGET IT. DON'T WORRY ABOUT ME.
YOU MUST BE SO HAPPY THAT YOU GET TO SEE YOUR LITTLE SASA-YAN AGAIN.
WHAT? WHAT THE HECK ARE YOU TRYING TO SAY, MUGI?
WELL, YOU LOOK LIKE YOU'RE HAVING SO MUCH FUN, YUU.
AND IT'S SASA-YAN THIS....AND SASA-YAN THAT.
SORRY IF I'M GETTING IN THE WAY OF ALL YOUR FUN.

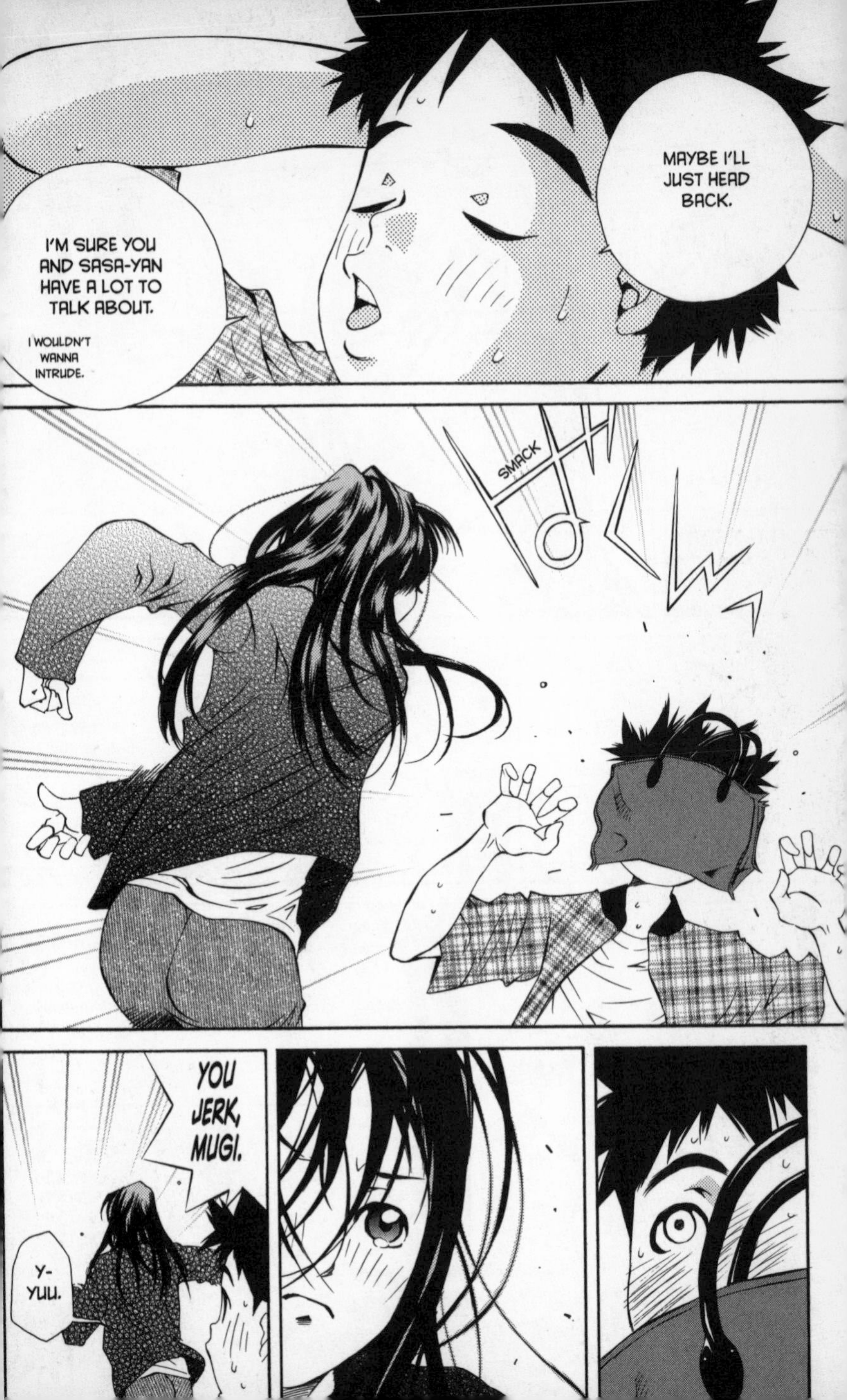
MAYBE I'LL JUST HEAD BACK.
I'M SURE YOU AND SASA-YAN HAVE A LOT TO TALK ABOUT.
I WOULDN'T WANNA INTRUDE.
SMACK
YOU JERK, MUGI.
Y-YUU.

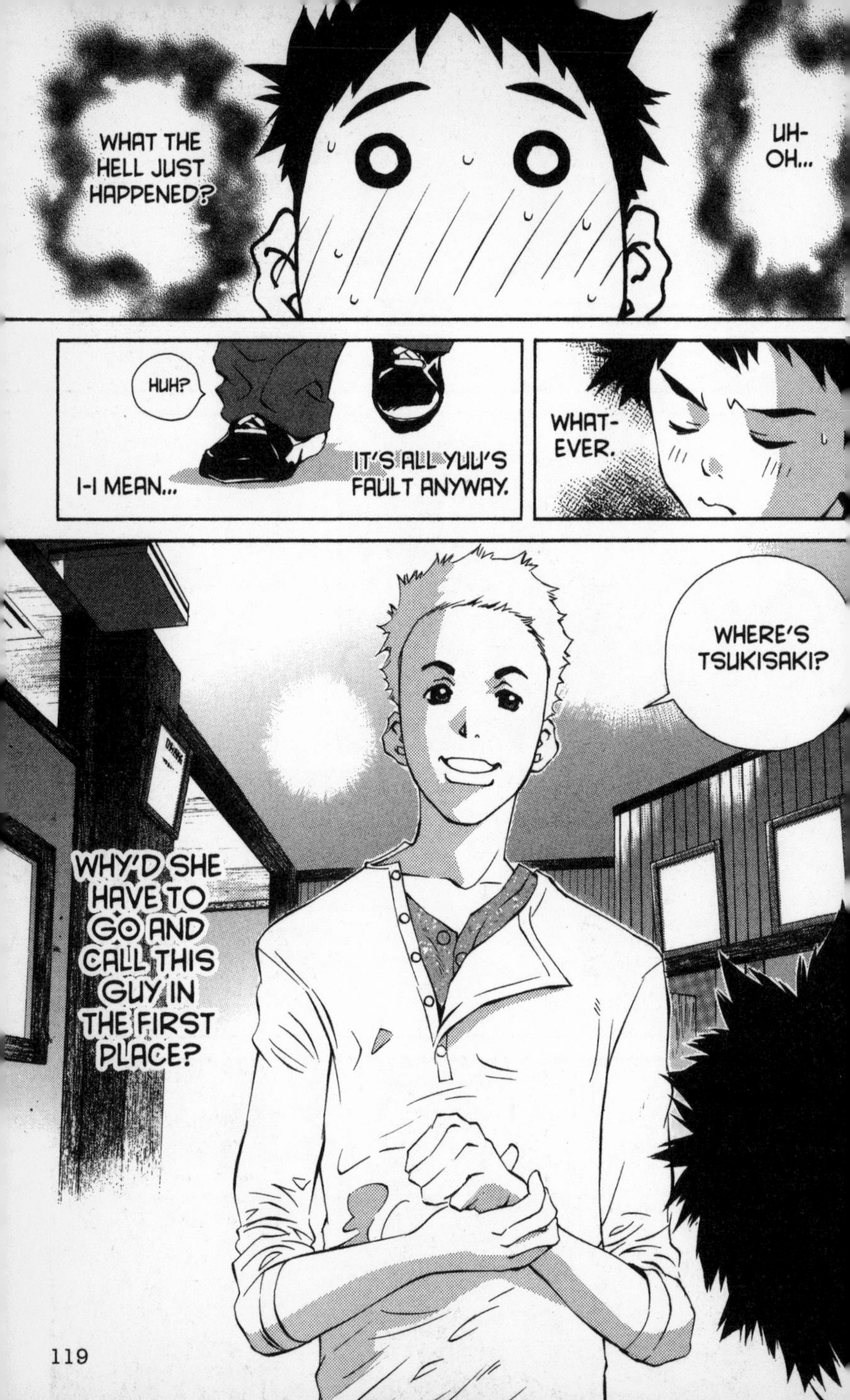
UH-OH...
WHAT THE HELL JUST HAPPENED?
WHAT-EVER.
HUH?
I-I MEAN...
IT'S ALL YUU'S FAULT ANYWAY.
WHERE'S TSUKISAKI?
WHY'D SHE HAVE TO GO AND CALL THIS GUY IN THE FIRST PLACE?

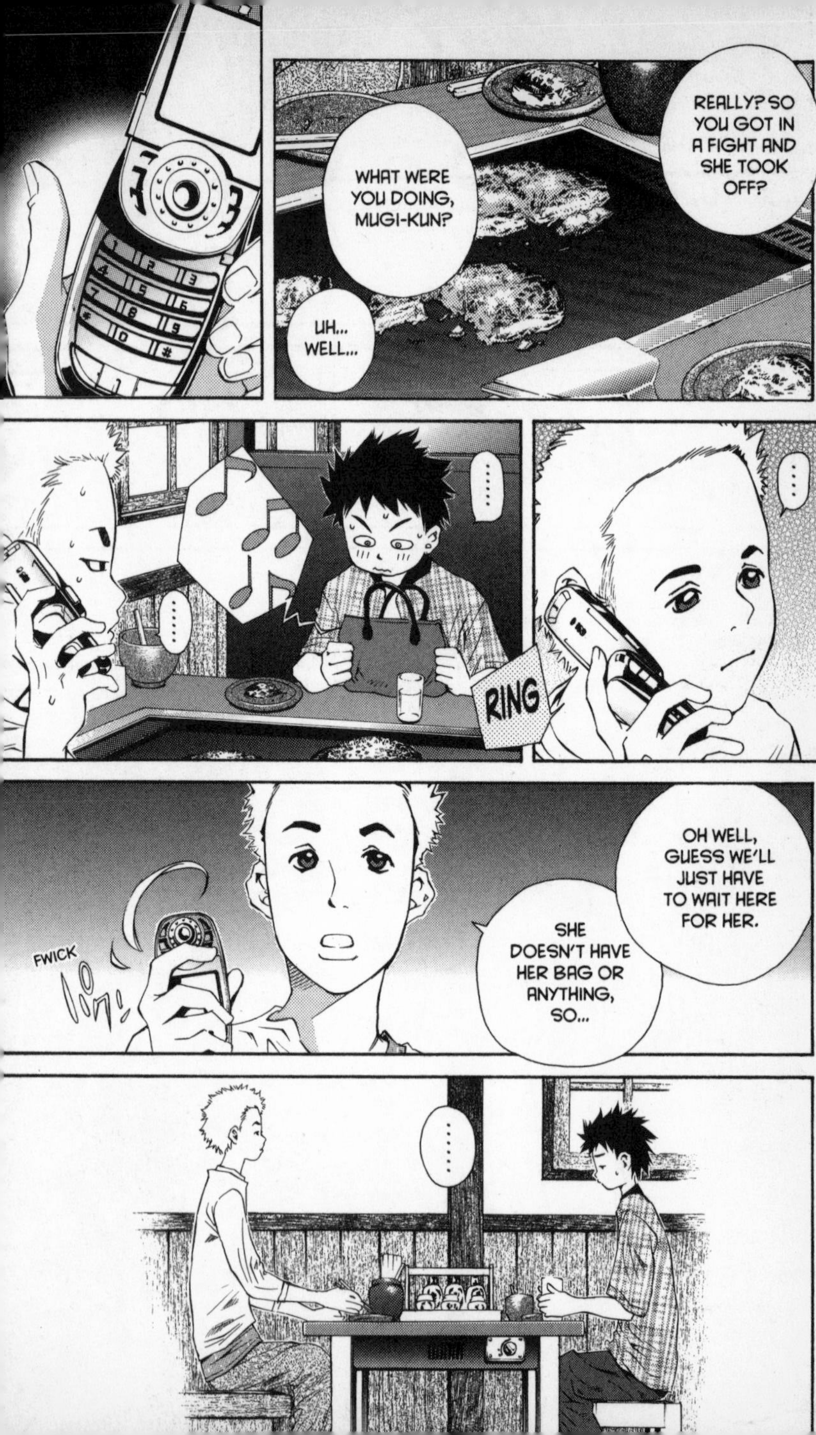
REALLY? SO YOU GOT IN A FIGHT AND SHE TOOK OFF?
WHAT WERE YOU DOING, MUGI-KUN?
UH... WELL...
......
RING
......
......
OH WELL, GUESS WE'LL JUST HAVE TO WAIT HERE FOR HER.
SHE DOESN'T HAVE HER BAG OR ANYTHING, SO...
FWICK
......

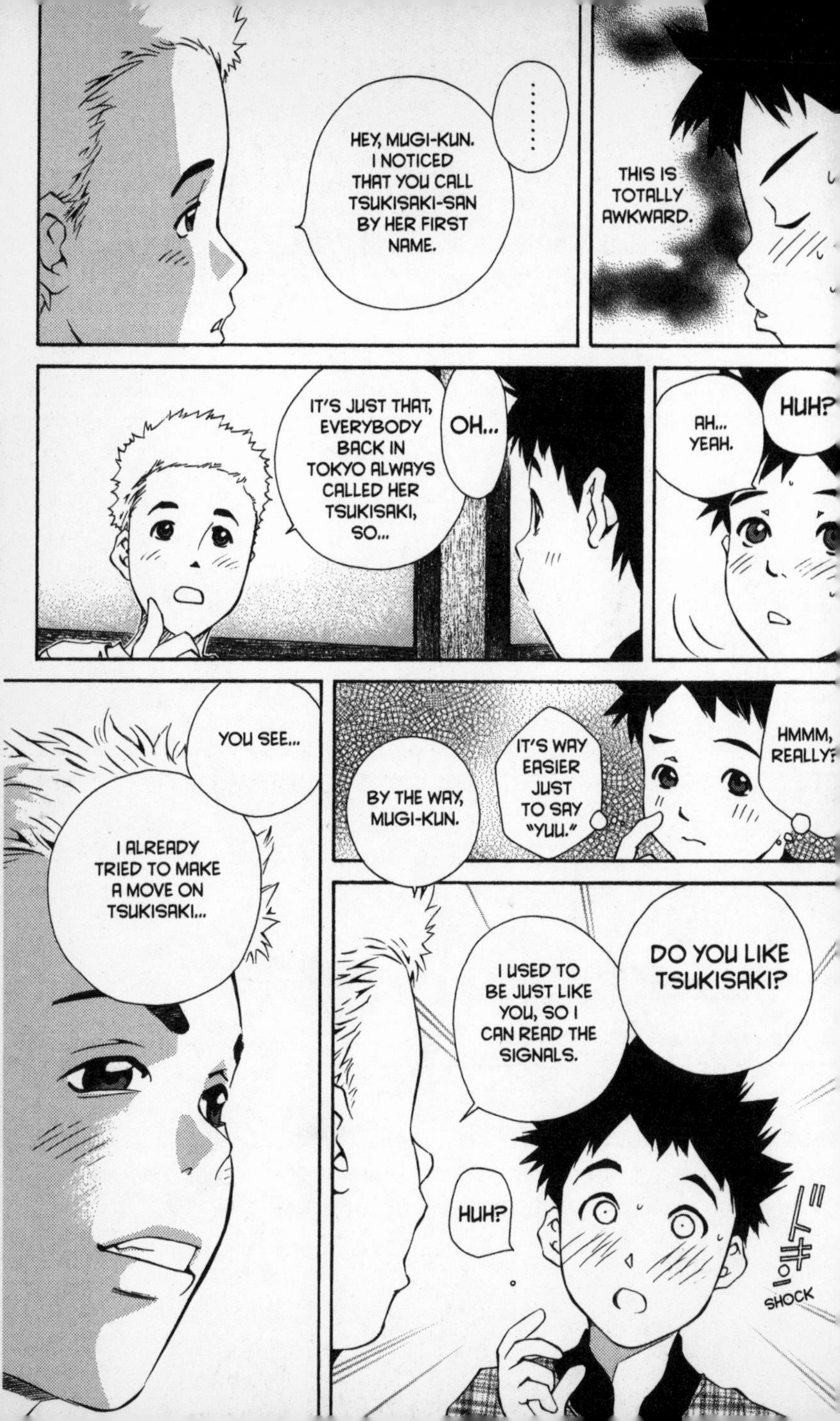
THIS IS TOTALLY AWKWARD.
....
HEY, MUGI-KUN. I NOTICED THAT YOU CALL TSUKISAKI-SAN BY HER FIRST NAME.
HUH?
AH... YEAH.
OH...
IT'S JUST THAT, EVERYBODY BACK IN TOKYO ALWAYS CALLED HER TSUKISAKI, SO...
HMMM, REALLY?
IT'S WAY EASIER JUST TO SAY "YUU."
BY THE WAY, MUGI-KUN.
DO YOU LIKE TSUKISAKI?
I USED TO BE JUST LIKE YOU, SO I CAN READ THE SIGNALS.
HUH?
SHOCK
YOU SEE...
I ALREADY TRIED TO MAKE A MOVE ON TSUKISAKI...

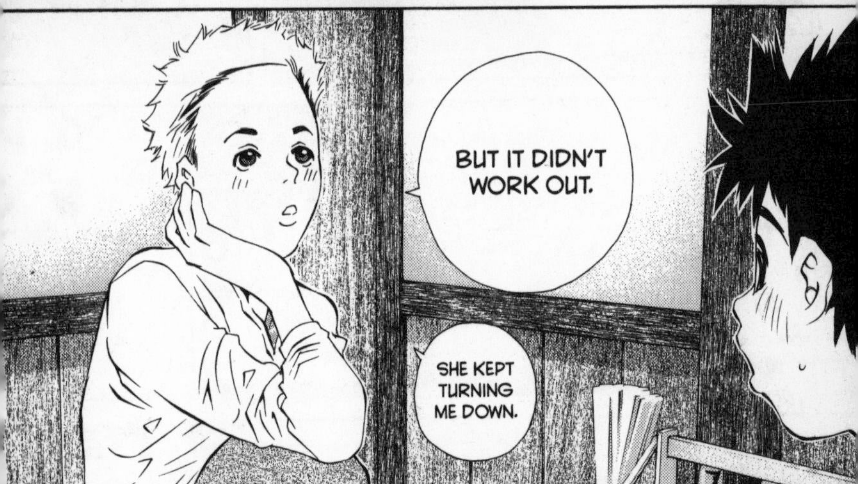
BUT IT DIDN'T WORK OUT.
SHE KEPT TURNING ME DOWN.
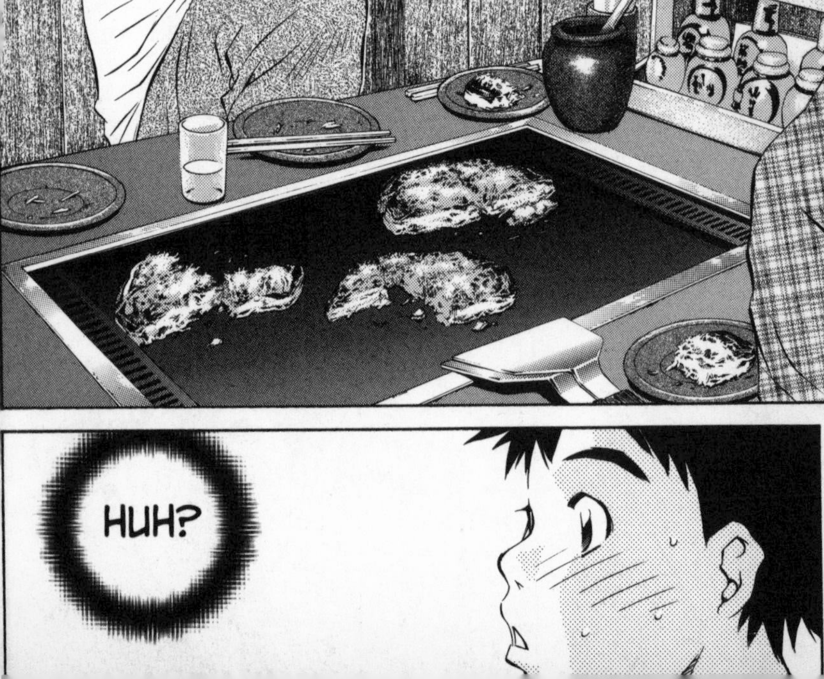
HUH?

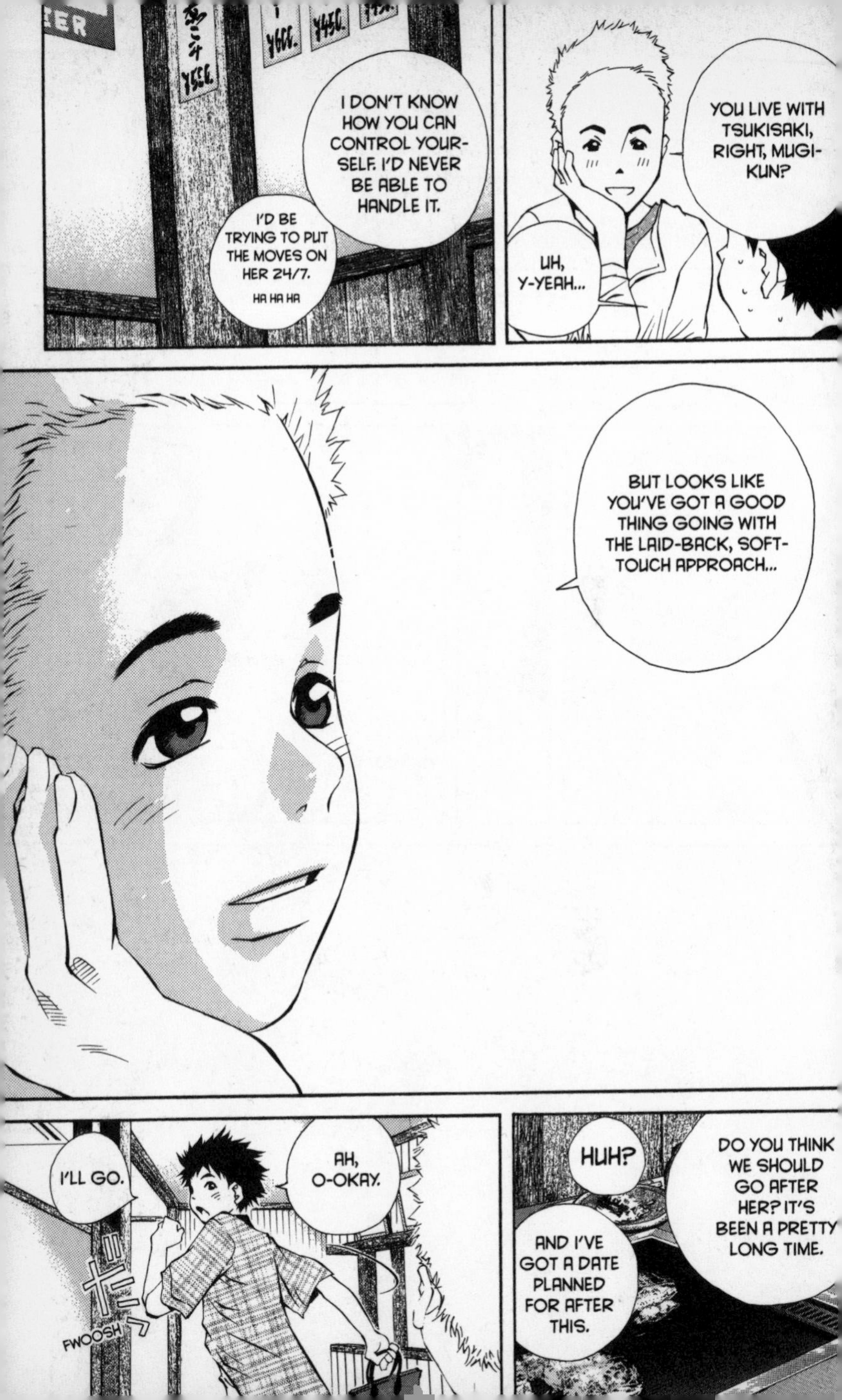
YOU LIVE WITH TSUKISAKI, RIGHT, MUGI-KUN?
UH, Y-YEAH...
I DON'T KNOW HOW YOU CAN CONTROL YOUR-SELF. I'D NEVER BE ABLE TO HANDLE IT.
I'D BE TRYING TO PUT THE MOVES ON HER 24/7.
HA HA HA
BUT LOOKS LIKE YOU'VE GOT A GOOD THING GOING WITH THE LAID-BACK, SOFT-TOUCH APPROACH...
DO YOU THINK WE SHOULD GO AFTER HER? IT'S BEEN A PRETTY LONG TIME.
HUH?
AND I'VE GOT A DATE PLANNED FOR AFTER THIS.
AH, O-OKAY.
I'LL GO.
FWOOSH

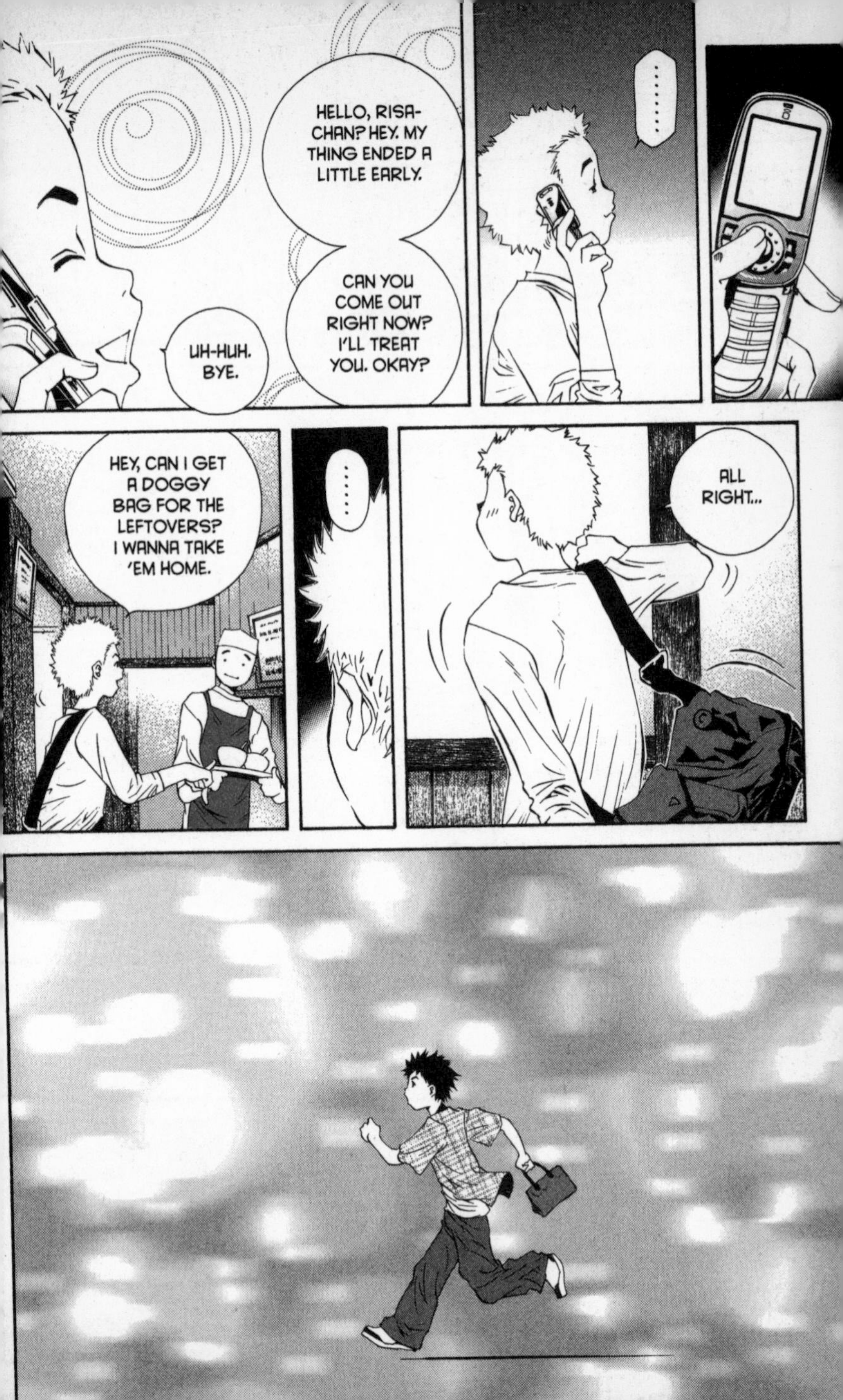

. . . .
HELLO, RISA-CHAN? HEY. MY THING ENDED A LITTLE EARLY.
CAN YOU COME OUT RIGHT NOW? I'LL TREAT YOU. OKAY?
UH-HUH. BYE.
ALL RIGHT...
. . . . . .
HEY, CAN I GET A DOGGY BAG FOR THE LEFTOVERS? I WANNA TAKE 'EM HOME.

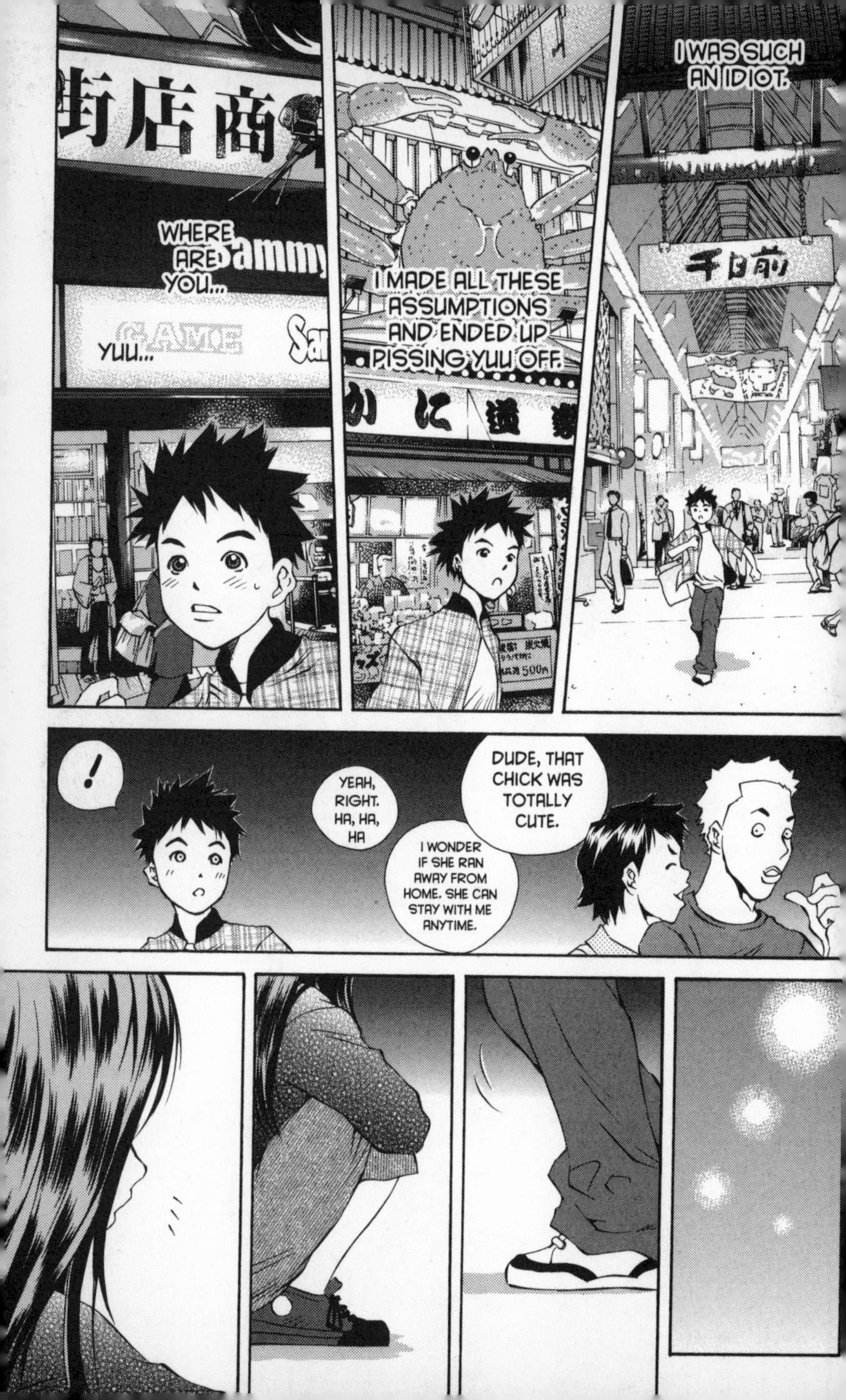
I WAS SUCH AN IDIOT.
I MADE ALL THESE ASSUMPTIONS AND ENDED UP PISSING YUU OFF.
WHERE ARE YOU...
YUU...
DUDE, THAT CHICK WAS TOTALLY CUTE.
YEAH, RIGHT. HA, HA, HA
I WONDER IF SHE RAN AWAY FROM HOME. SHE CAN STAY WITH ME ANYTIME.
!

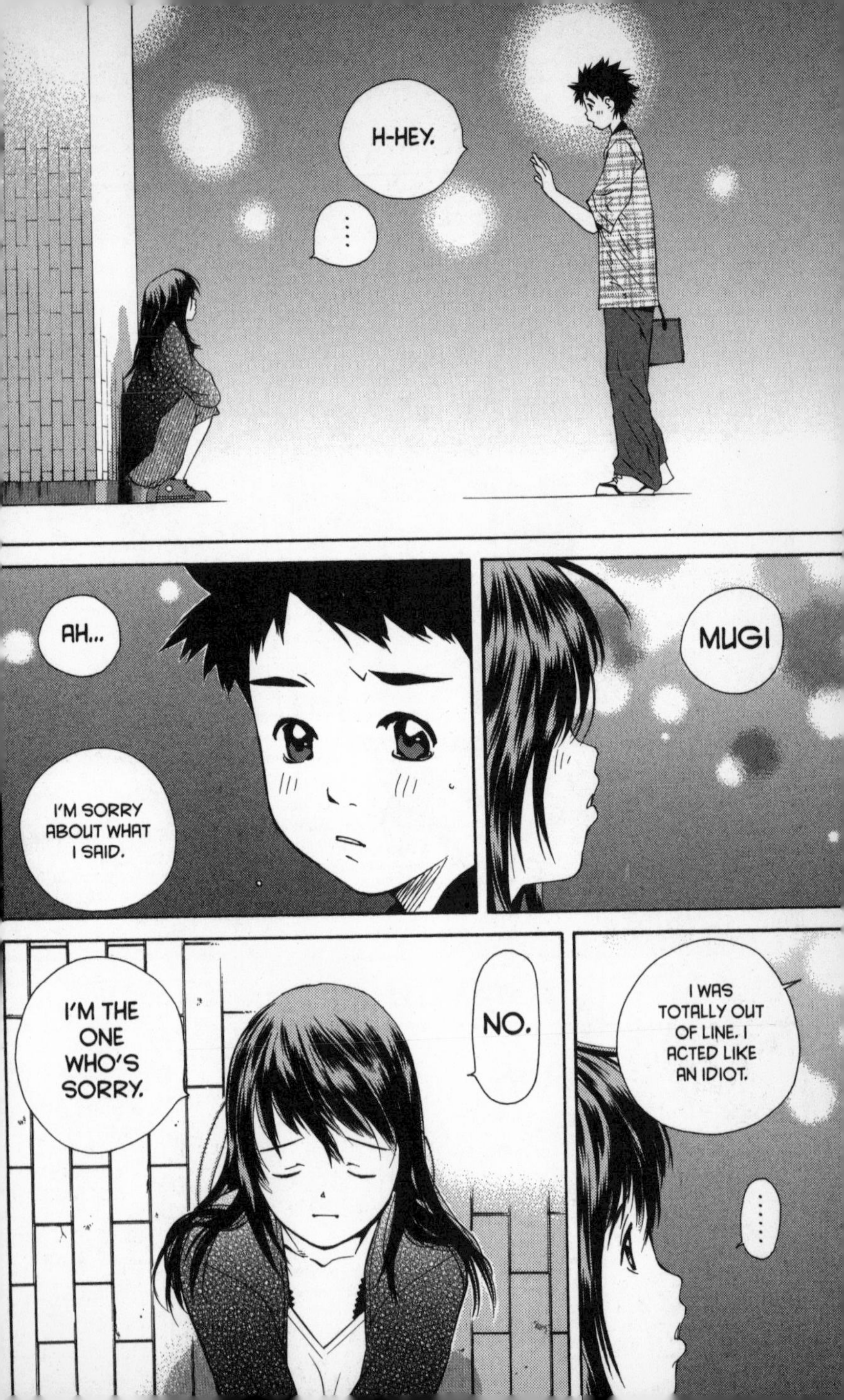
H-HEY.
....
MUGI
AH...
I'M SORRY ABOUT WHAT I SAID.
I WAS TOTALLY OUT OF LINE. I ACTED LIKE AN IDIOT.
......
NO.
I'M THE ONE WHO'S SORRY.

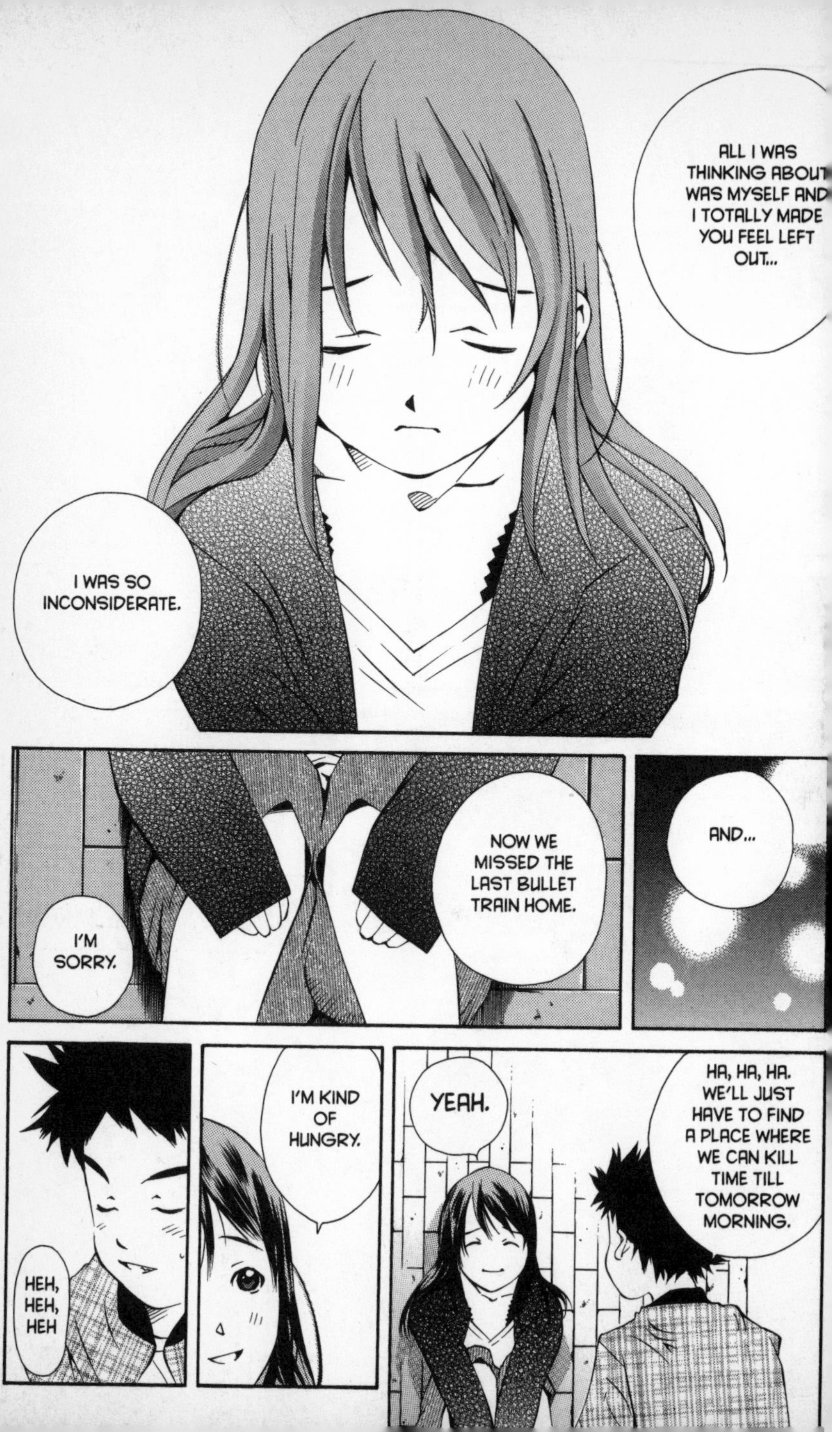
ALL I WAS THINKING ABOUT WAS MYSELF AND I TOTALLY MADE YOU FEEL LEFT OUT...
I WAS SO INCONSIDERATE.
AND...
NOW WE MISSED THE LAST BULLET TRAIN HOME.
I'M SORRY.
HA, HA, HA. WE'LL JUST HAVE TO FIND A PLACE WHERE WE CAN KILL TIME TILL TOMORROW MORNING.
YEAH.
I'M KIND OF HUNGRY.
HEH, HEH, HEH

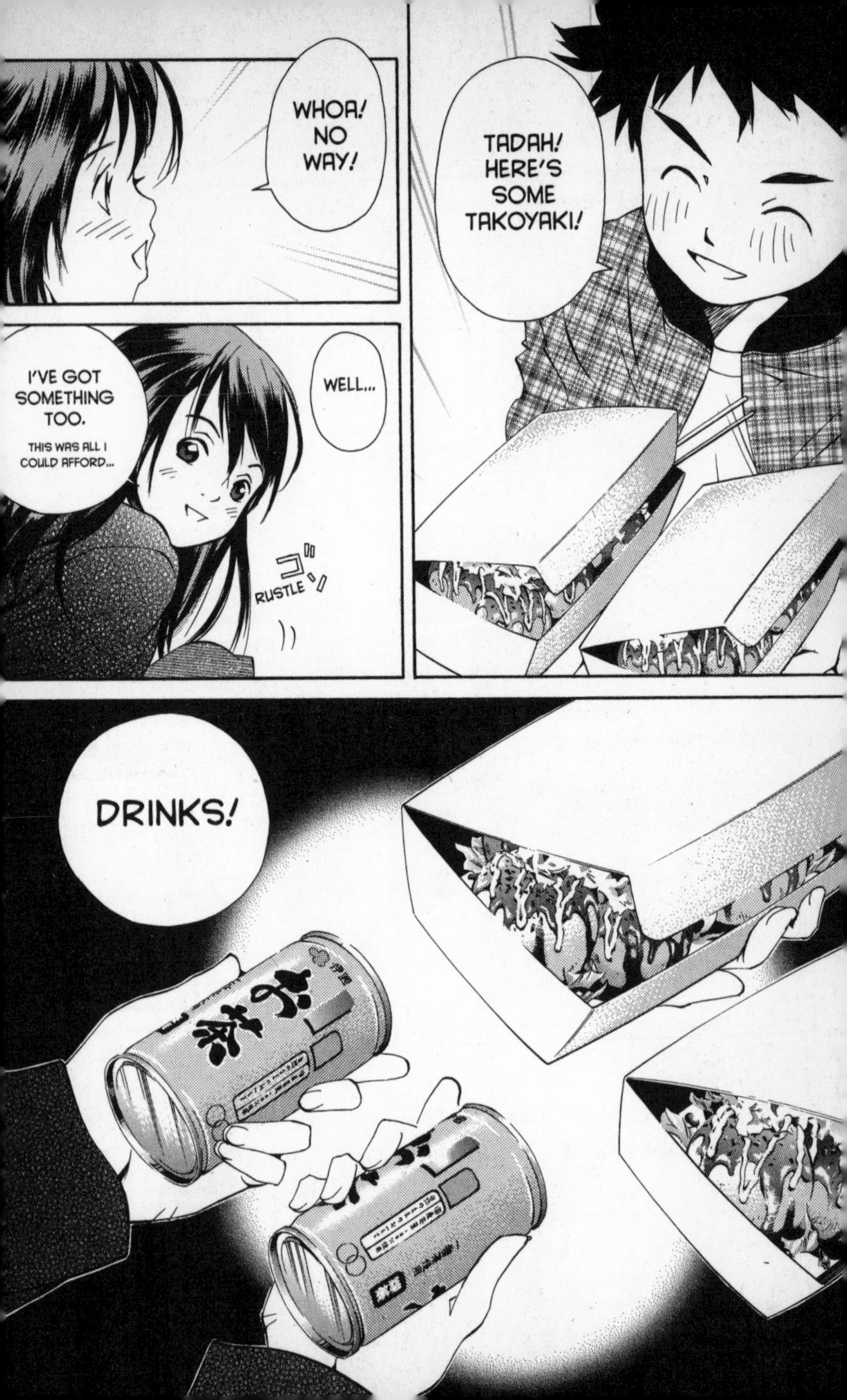
TADAH! HERE'S SOME TAKOYAKI!
WHOA! NO WAY!
WELL...
I'VE GOT SOMETHING TOO.
THIS WAS ALL I COULD AFFORD...
RUSTLE
DRINKS!

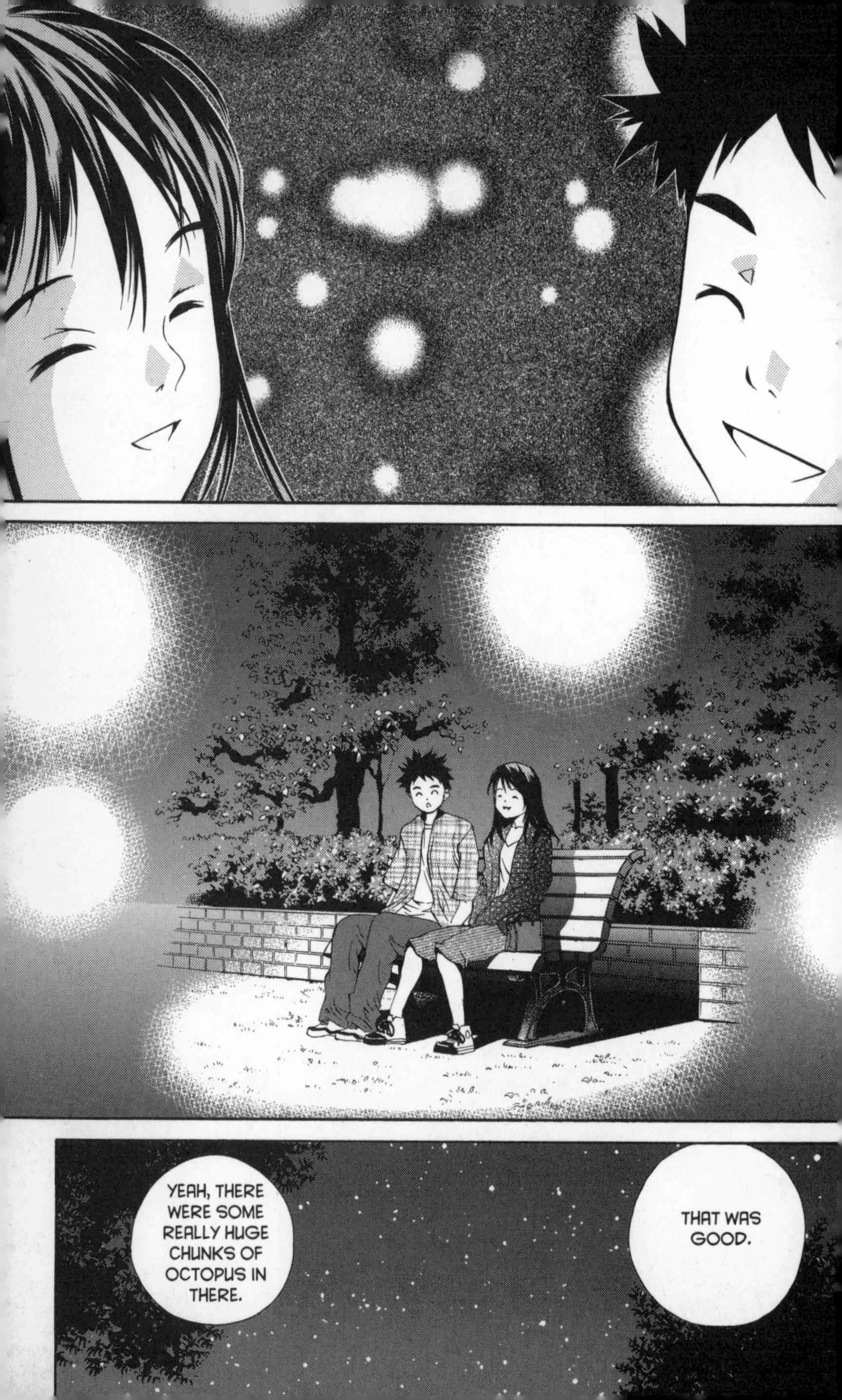
THAT WAS GOOD.
YEAH, THERE WERE SOME REALLY HUGE CHUNKS OF OCTOPUS IN THERE.

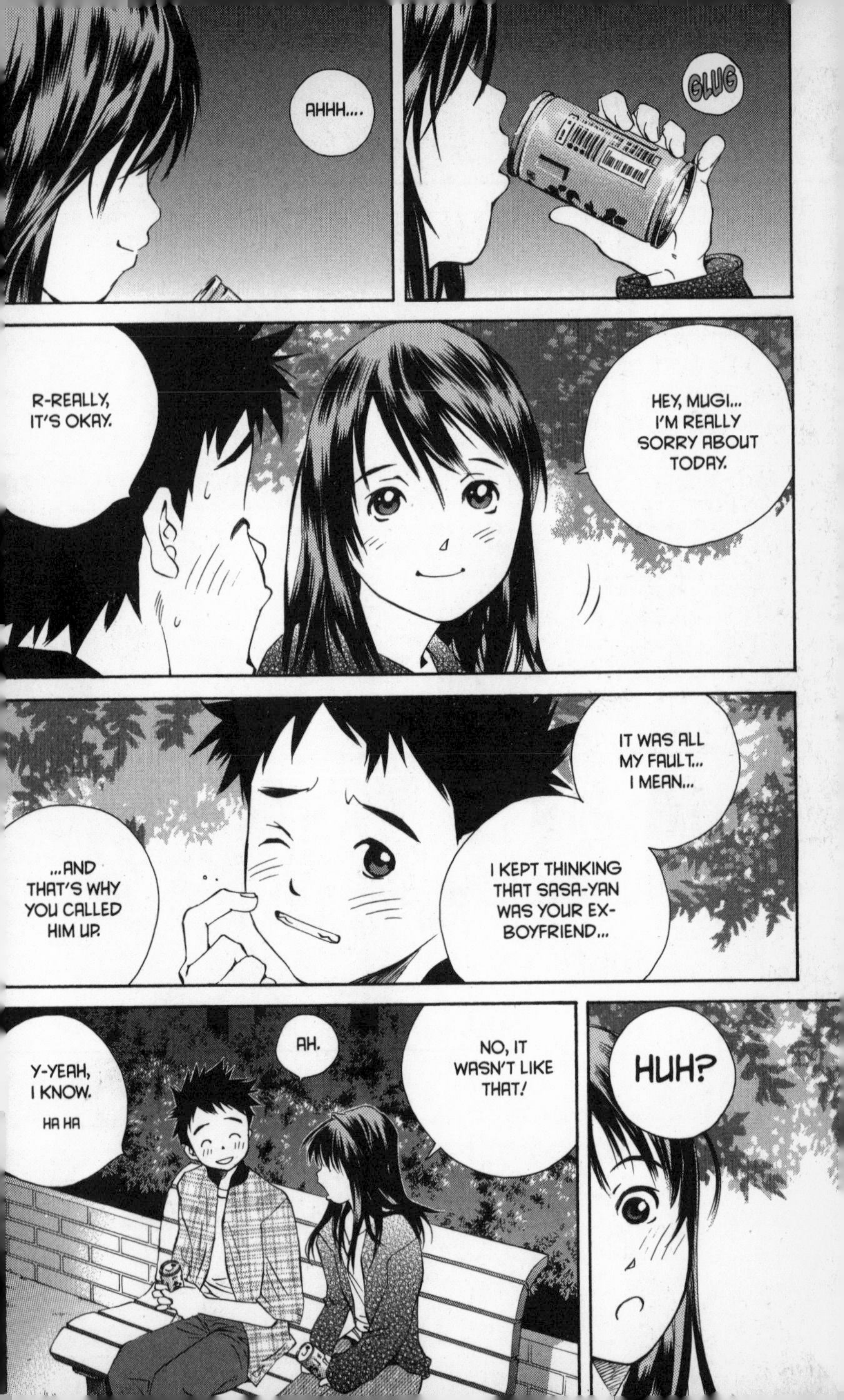
GLUG
AHHH....
HEY, MUGI... I'M REALLY SORRY ABOUT TODAY.
R-REALLY, IT'S OKAY.
IT WAS ALL MY FAULT... I MEAN...
I KEPT THINKING THAT SASA-YAN WAS YOUR EX-BOYFRIEND...
...AND THAT'S WHY YOU CALLED HIM UP.
HUH?
NO, IT WASN'T LIKE THAT!
AH.
Y-YEAH, I KNOW.
HA HA

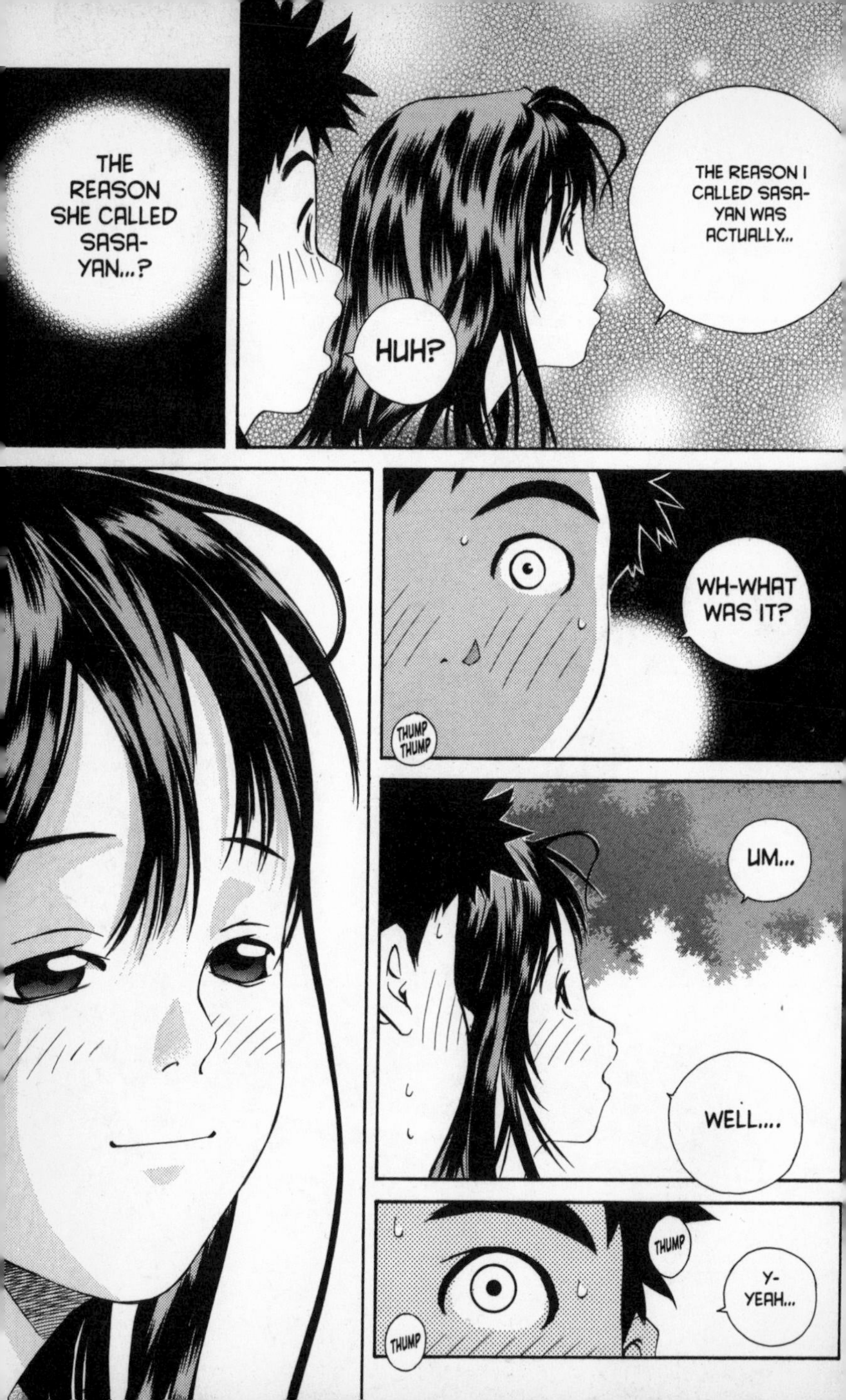
THE REASON I CALLED SASA-YAN WAS ACTUALLY...
HUH?
THE REASON SHE CALLED SASA-YAN...?
WH-WHAT WAS IT?
THUMP THUMP
UM...
WELL....
THUMP
Y-YEAH...
THUMP

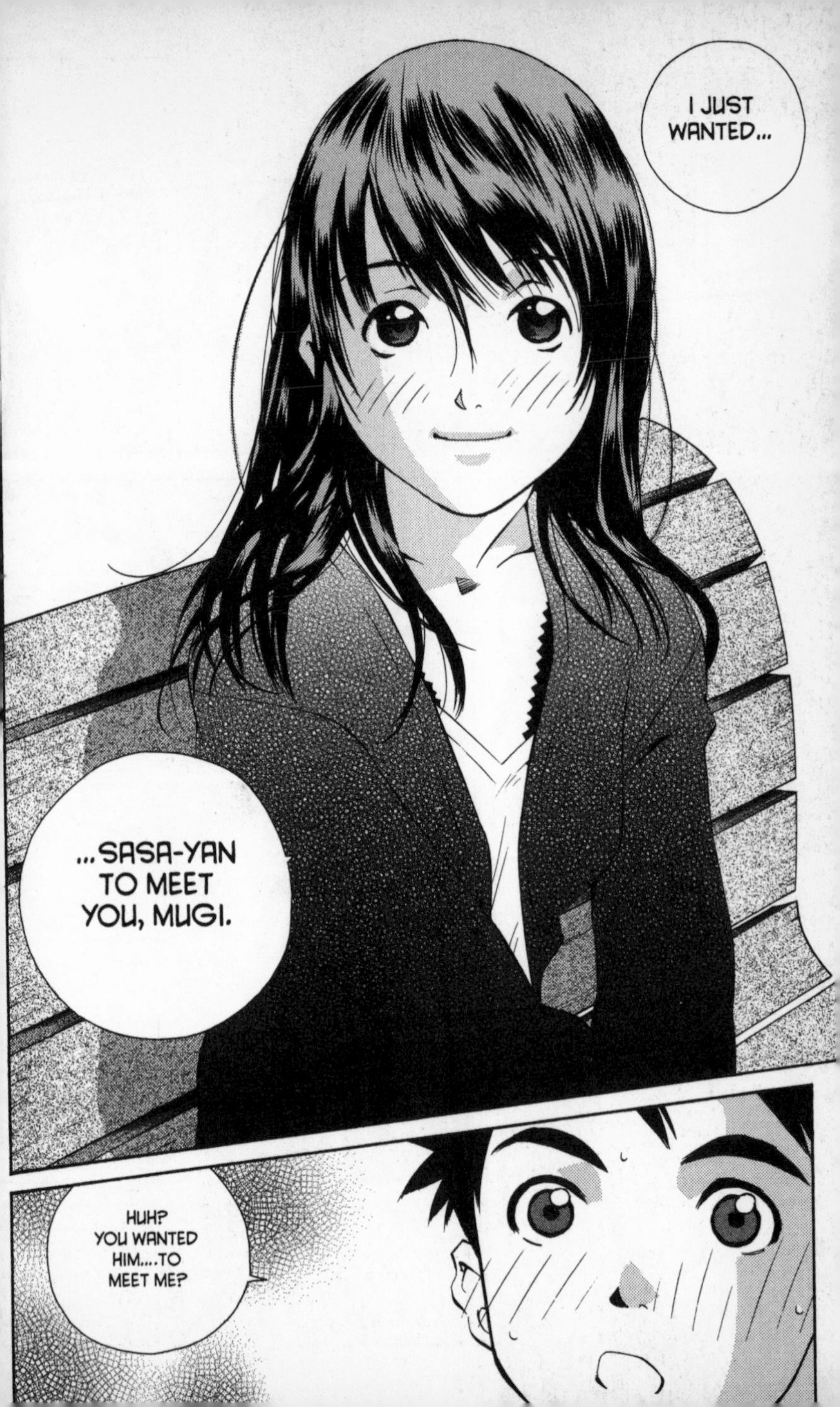
I JUST WANTED...
...SASA-YAN TO MEET YOU, MUGI.
HUH? YOU WANTED HIM....TO MEET ME?

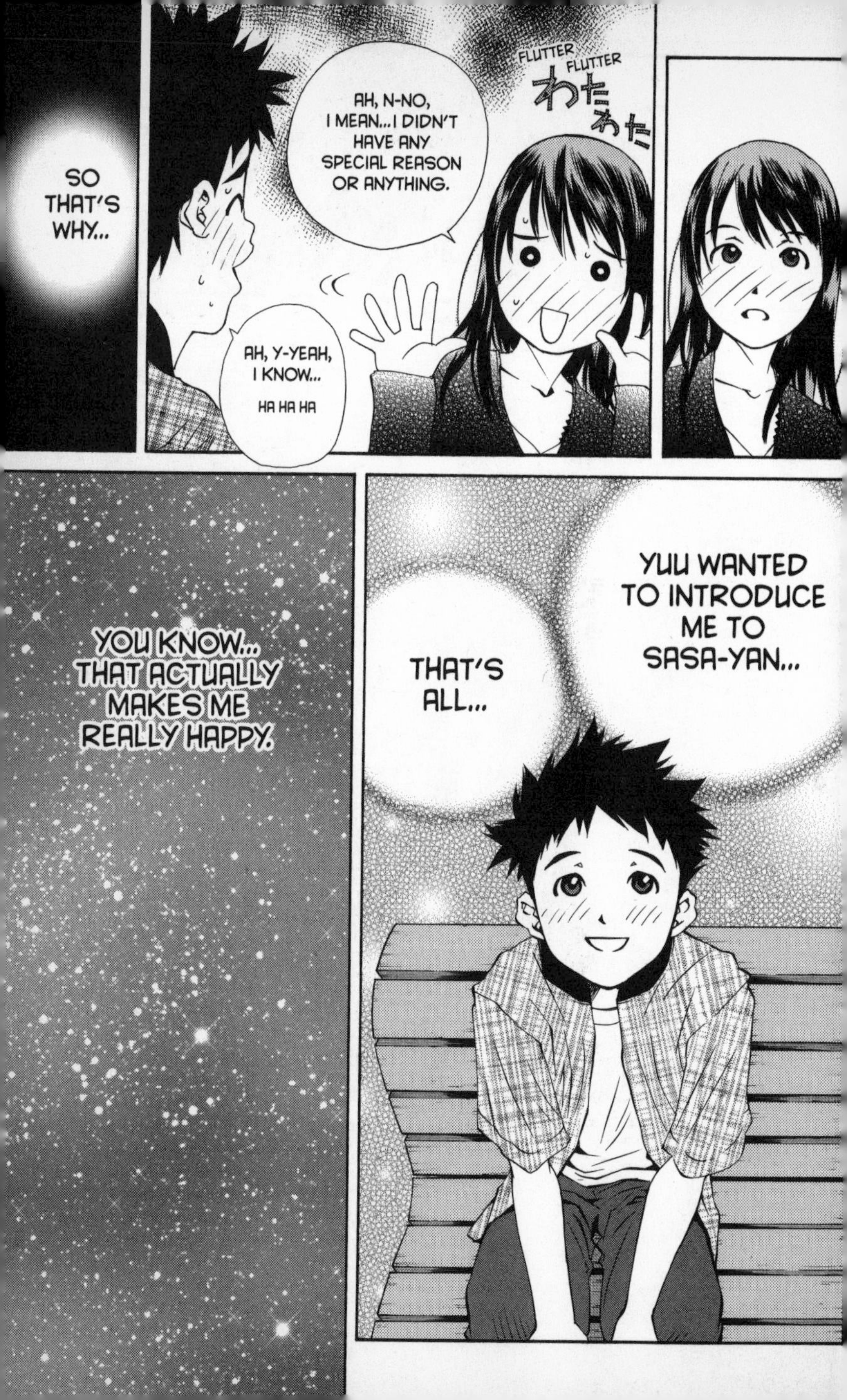
FLUTTER FLUTTER
わたわた
AH, N-NO, I MEAN...I DIDN'T HAVE ANY SPECIAL REASON OR ANYTHING.
AH, Y-YEAH, I KNOW... HA HA HA
SO THAT'S WHY...
YUU WANTED TO INTRODUCE ME TO SASA-YAN...
THAT'S ALL...
YOU KNOW... THAT ACTUALLY MAKES ME REALLY HAPPY.

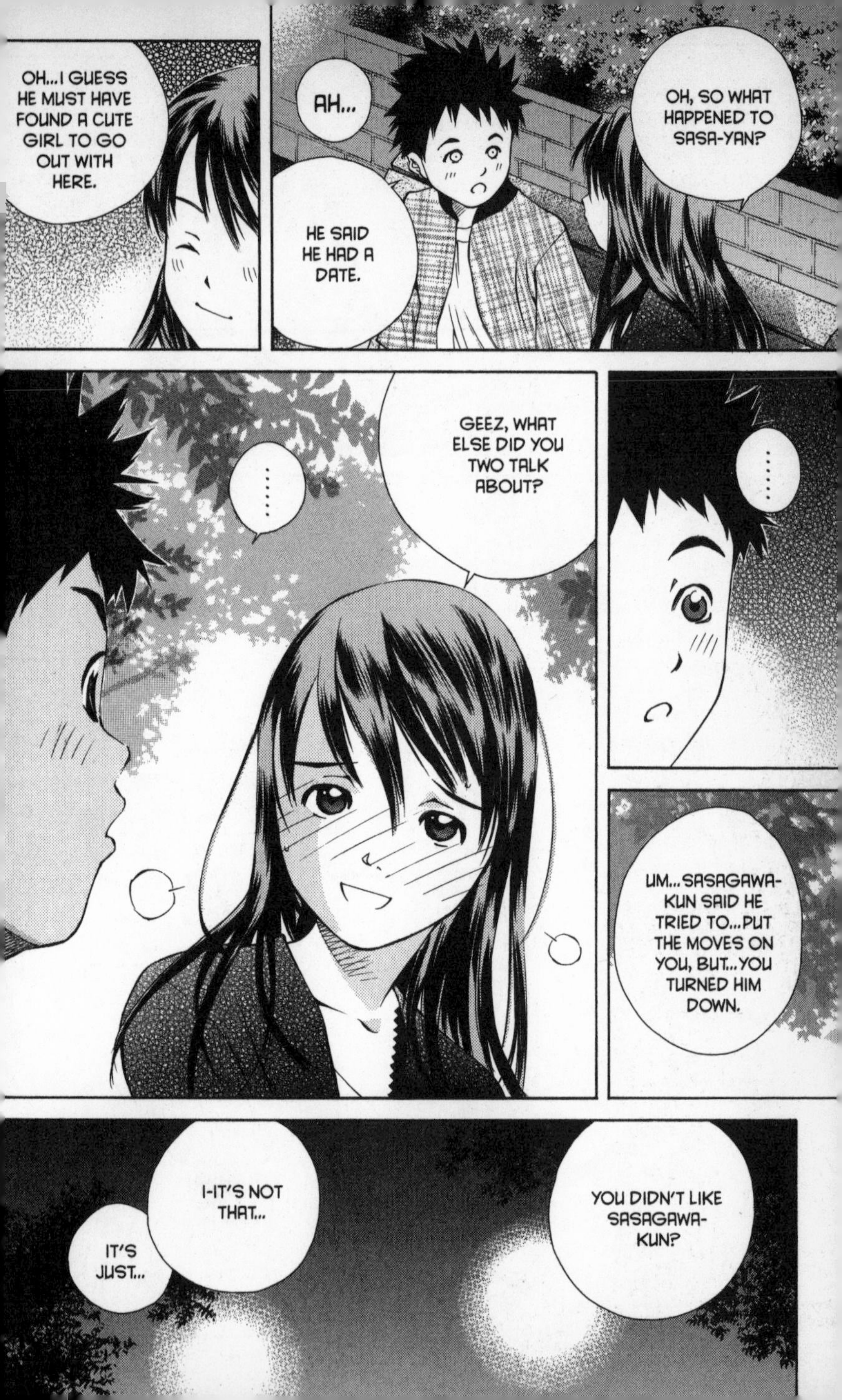
OH, SO WHAT HAPPENED TO SASA-YAN?
AH...
HE SAID HE HAD A DATE.
OH...I GUESS HE MUST HAVE FOUND A CUTE GIRL TO GO OUT WITH HERE.
......
UM...SASAGAWA-KUN SAID HE TRIED TO...PUT THE MOVES ON YOU, BUT...YOU TURNED HIM DOWN.
GEEZ, WHAT ELSE DID YOU TWO TALK ABOUT?
......
YOU DIDN'T LIKE SASAGAWA-KUN?
I-IT'S NOT THAT...
IT'S JUST...

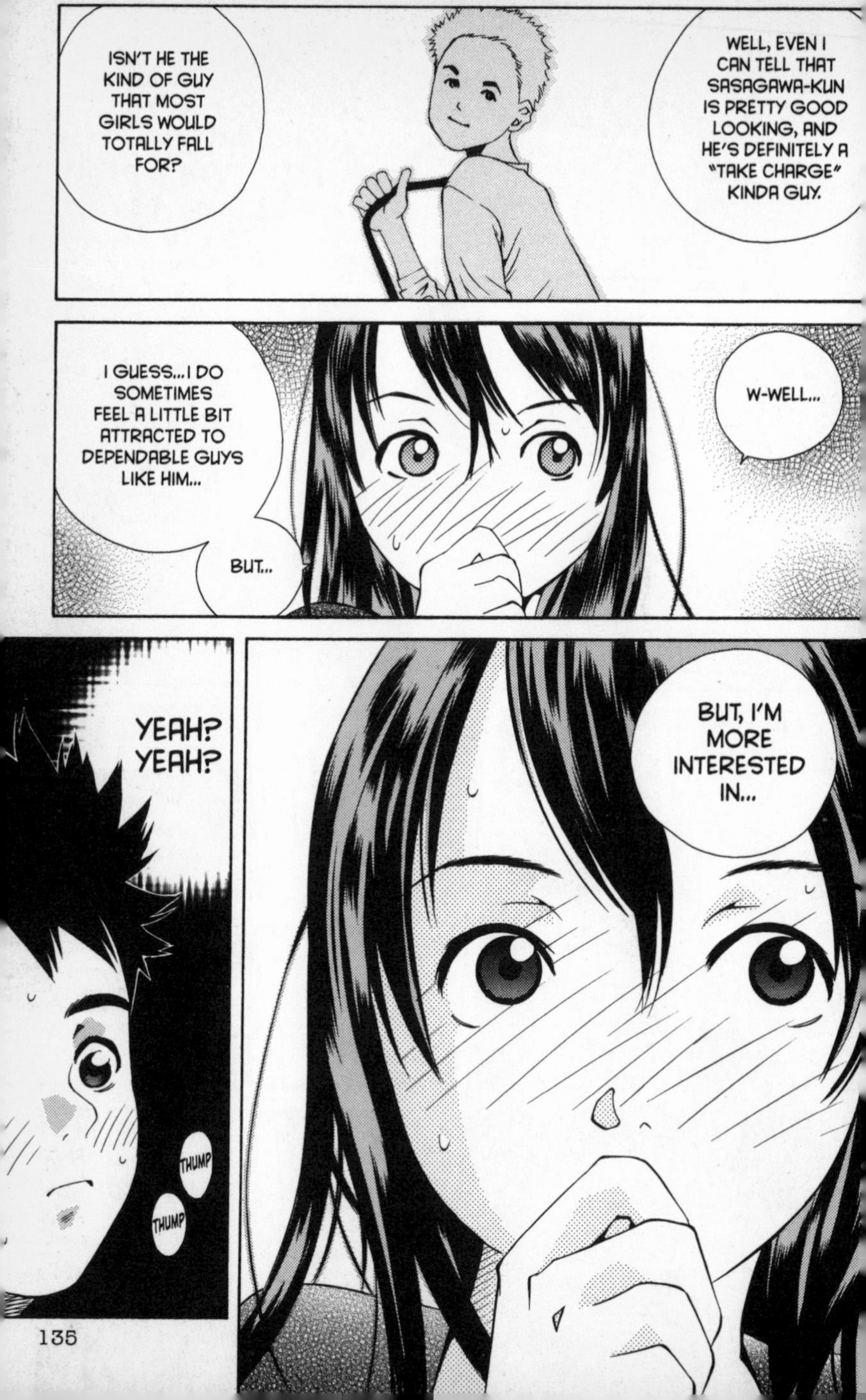
WELL, EVEN I CAN TELL THAT SASAGAWA-KUN IS PRETTY GOOD LOOKING, AND HE'S DEFINITELY A "TAKE CHARGE" KINDA GUY.
ISN'T HE THE KIND OF GUY THAT MOST GIRLS WOULD TOTALLY FALL FOR?
W-WELL...
I GUESS...I DO SOMETIMES FEEL A LITTLE BIT ATTRACTED TO DEPENDABLE GUYS LIKE HIM...
BUT...
BUT, I'M MORE INTERESTED IN...
YEAH? YEAH?
THUMP
THUMP

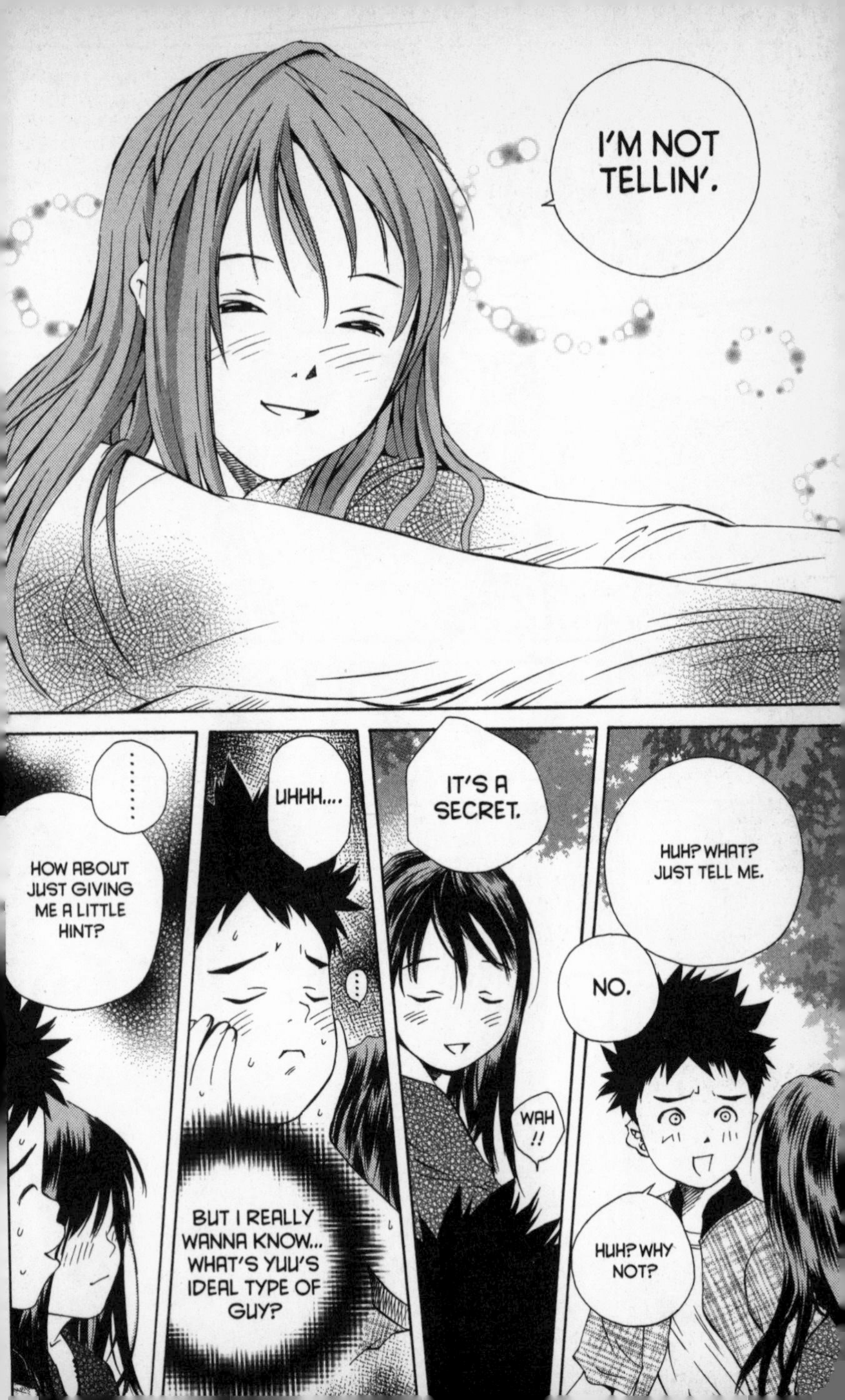
I'M NOT TELLIN'.
HUH? WHAT? JUST TELL ME.
NO.
HUH? WHY NOT?
IT'S A SECRET.
WAH !!
UHHH....
...
BUT I REALLY WANNA KNOW... WHAT'S YUU'S IDEAL TYPE OF GUY?
......
HOW ABOUT JUST GIVING ME A LITTLE HINT?

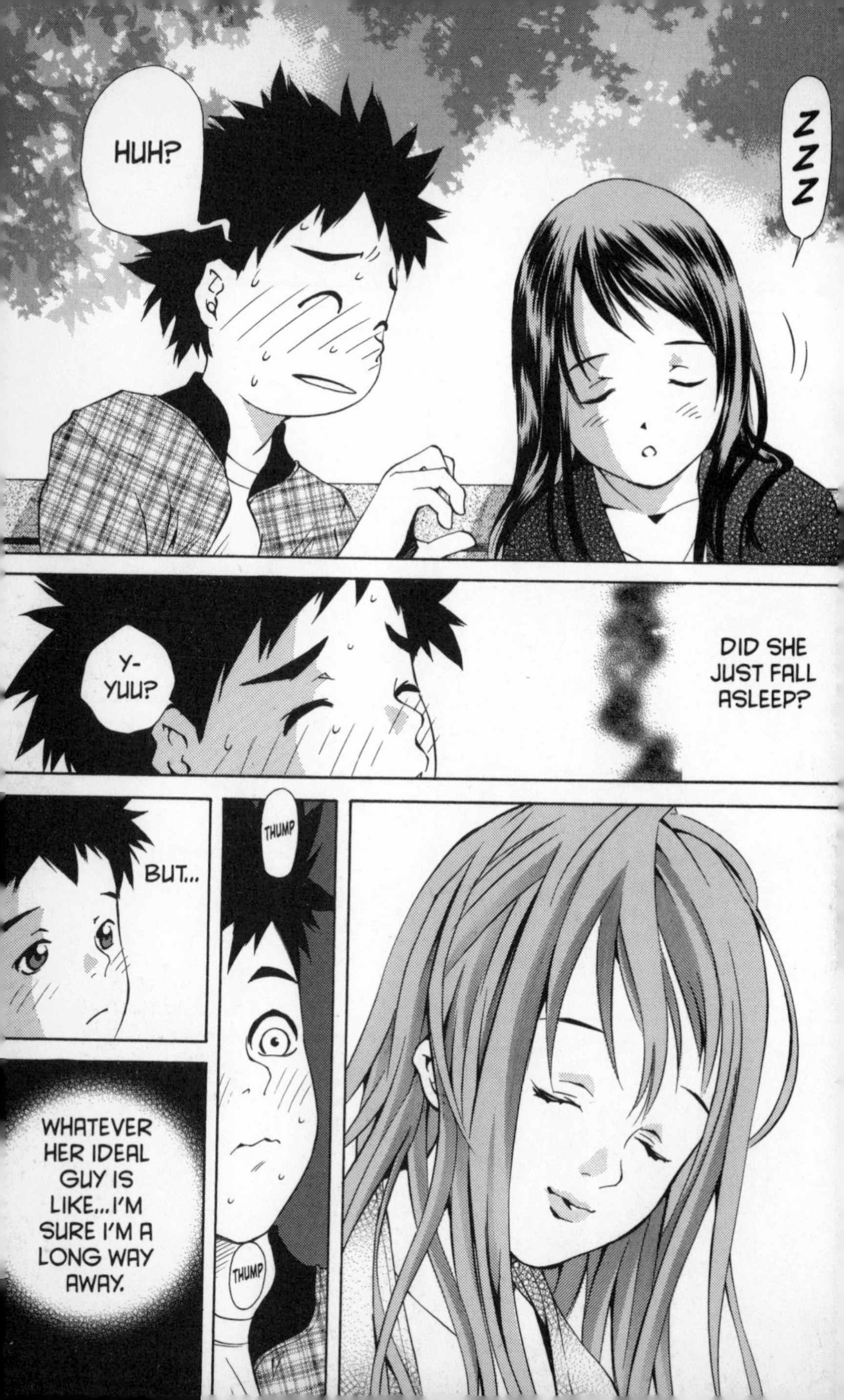
ZZZ
HUH?
DID SHE JUST FALL ASLEEP?
Y-YUU?
THUMP
THUMP
BUT...
WHATEVER HER IDEAL GUY IS LIKE...I'M SURE I'M A LONG WAY AWAY.

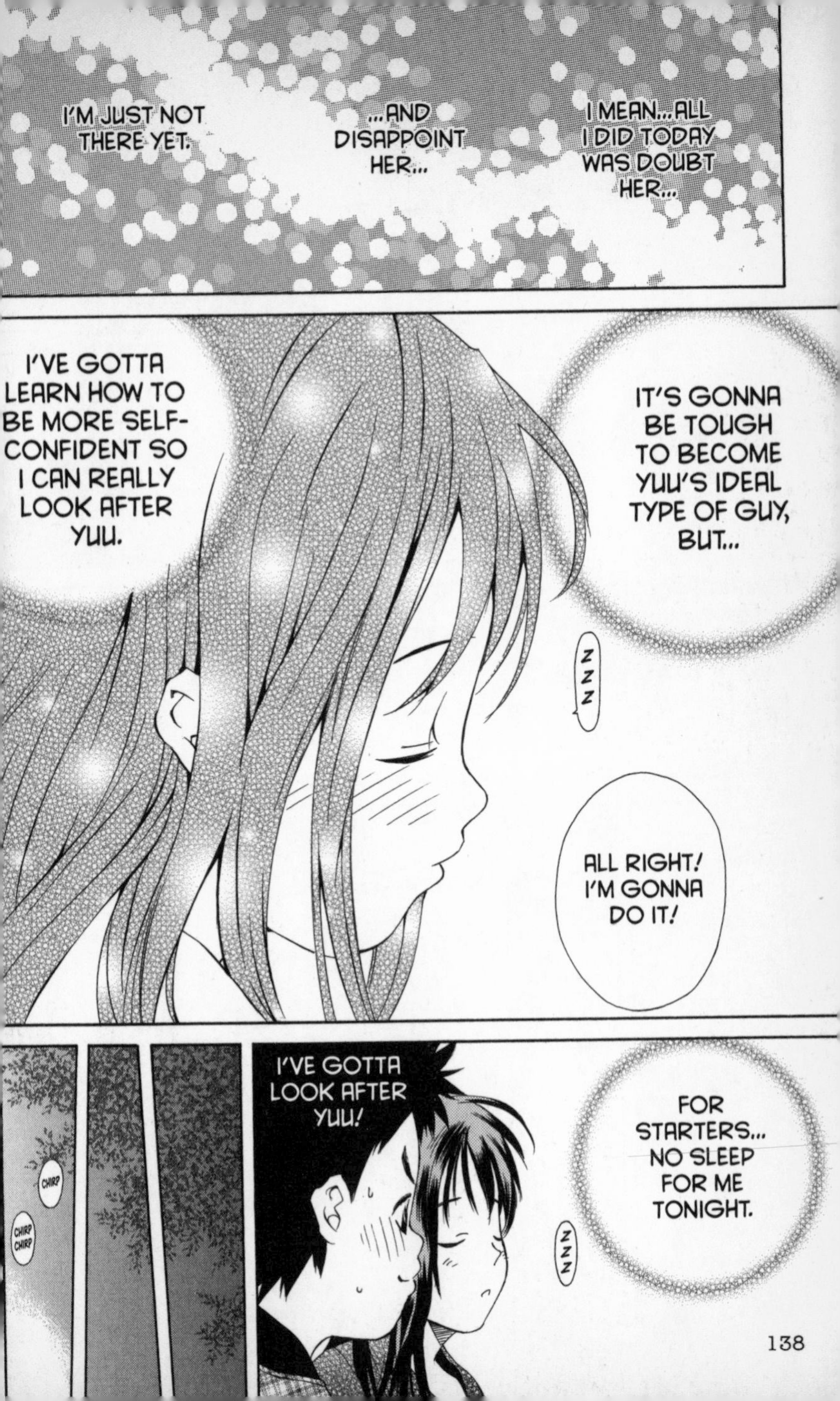
I MEAN...ALL I DID TODAY WAS DOUBT HER...
...AND DISAPPOINT HER...
I'M JUST NOT THERE YET.
IT'S GONNA BE TOUGH TO BECOME YUU'S IDEAL TYPE OF GUY, BUT...
I'VE GOTTA LEARN HOW TO BE MORE SELF-CONFIDENT SO I CAN REALLY LOOK AFTER YUU.
ZZZ
ALL RIGHT! I'M GONNA DO IT!
FOR STARTERS... NO SLEEP FOR ME TONIGHT.
I'VE GOTTA LOOK AFTER YUU!
ZZZ
CHIRP
CHIRP CHIRP

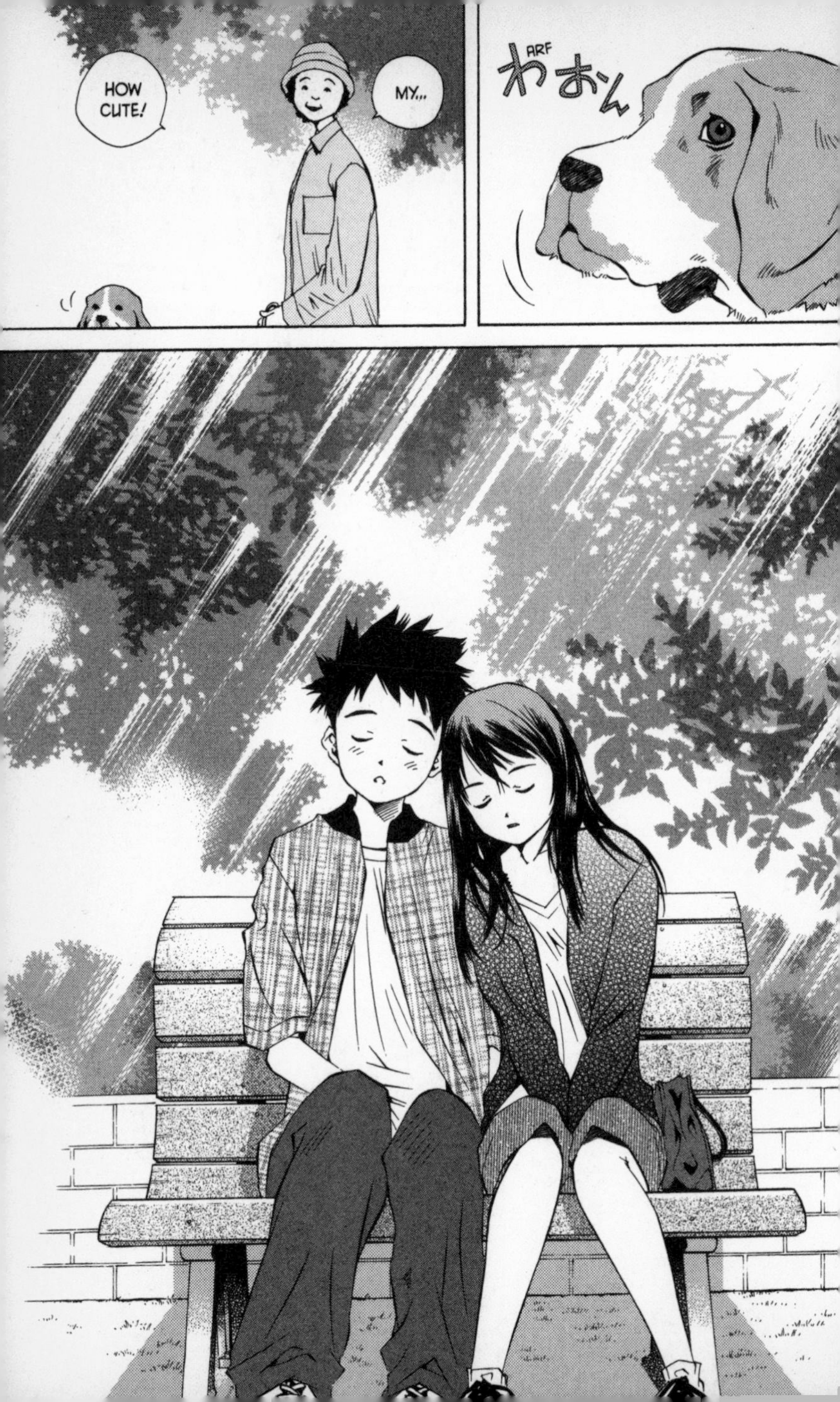
ARF
わおん
MY...
HOW CUTE!

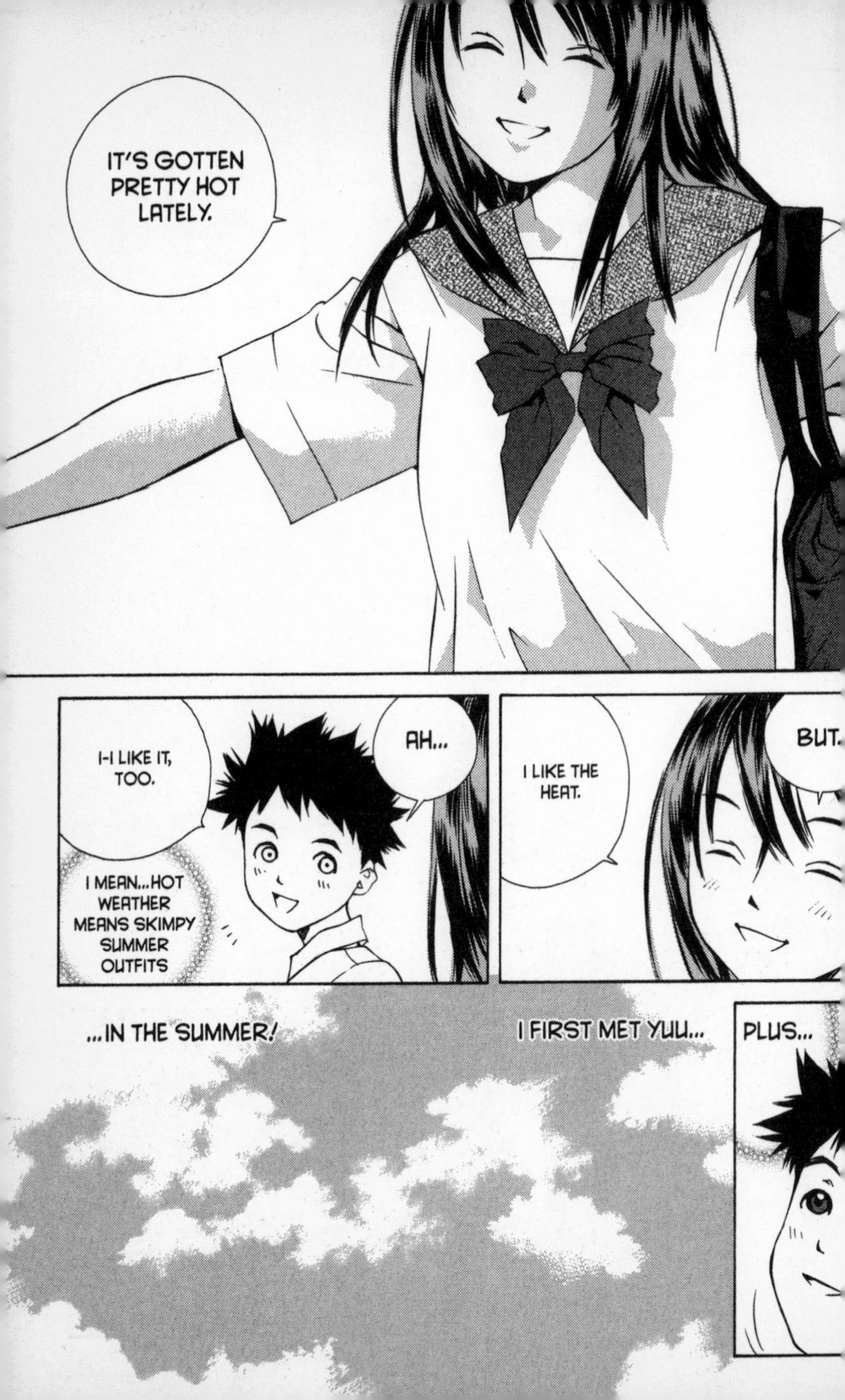
IT'S GOTTEN PRETTY HOT LATELY.
BUT.
I LIKE THE HEAT.
AH...
I-I LIKE IT, TOO.
I MEAN...HOT WEATHER MEANS SKIMPY SUMMER OUTFITS
PLUS...
I FIRST MET YUU...
...IN THE SUMMER!

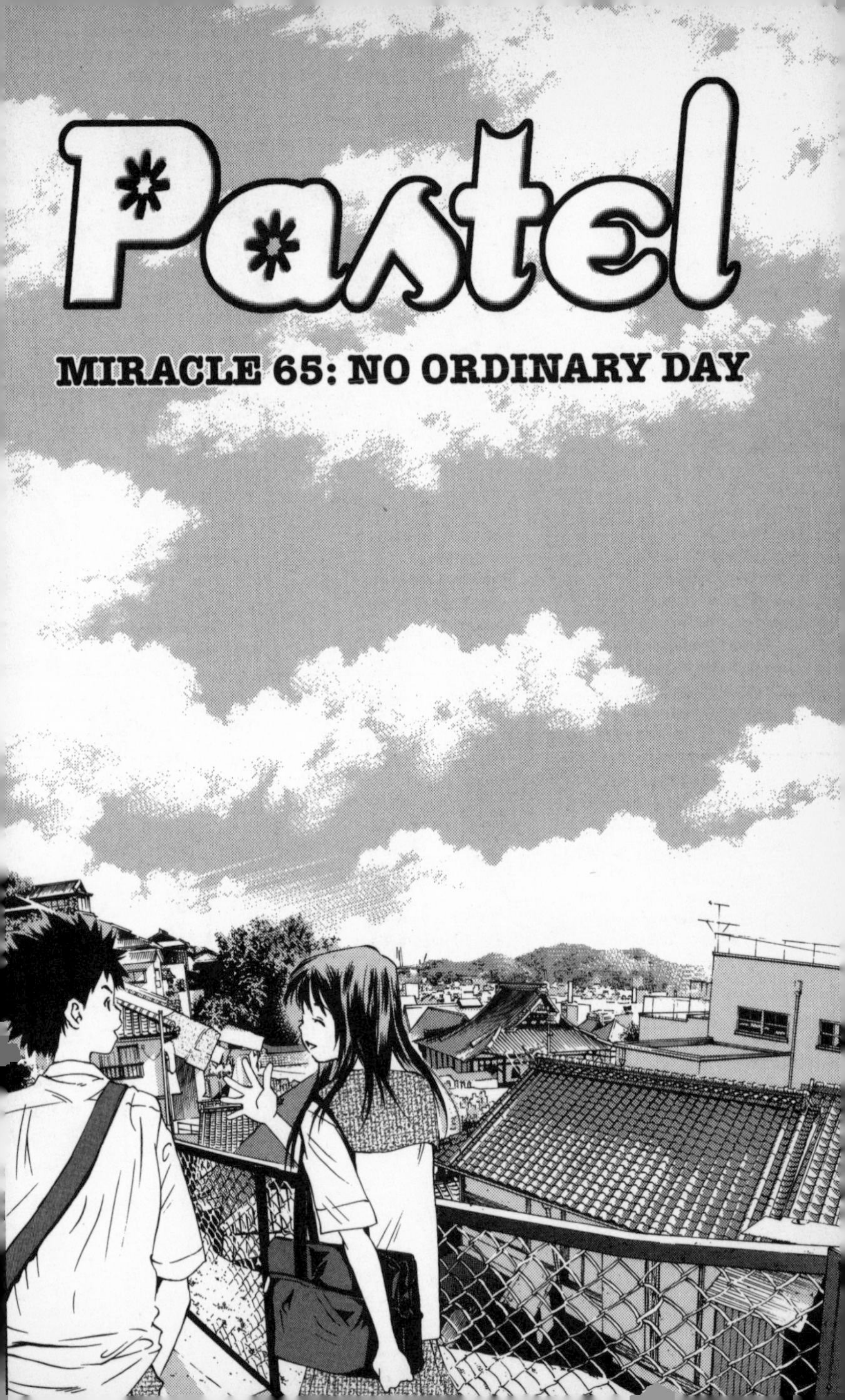
Pastel
MIRACLE 65: NO ORDINARY DAY

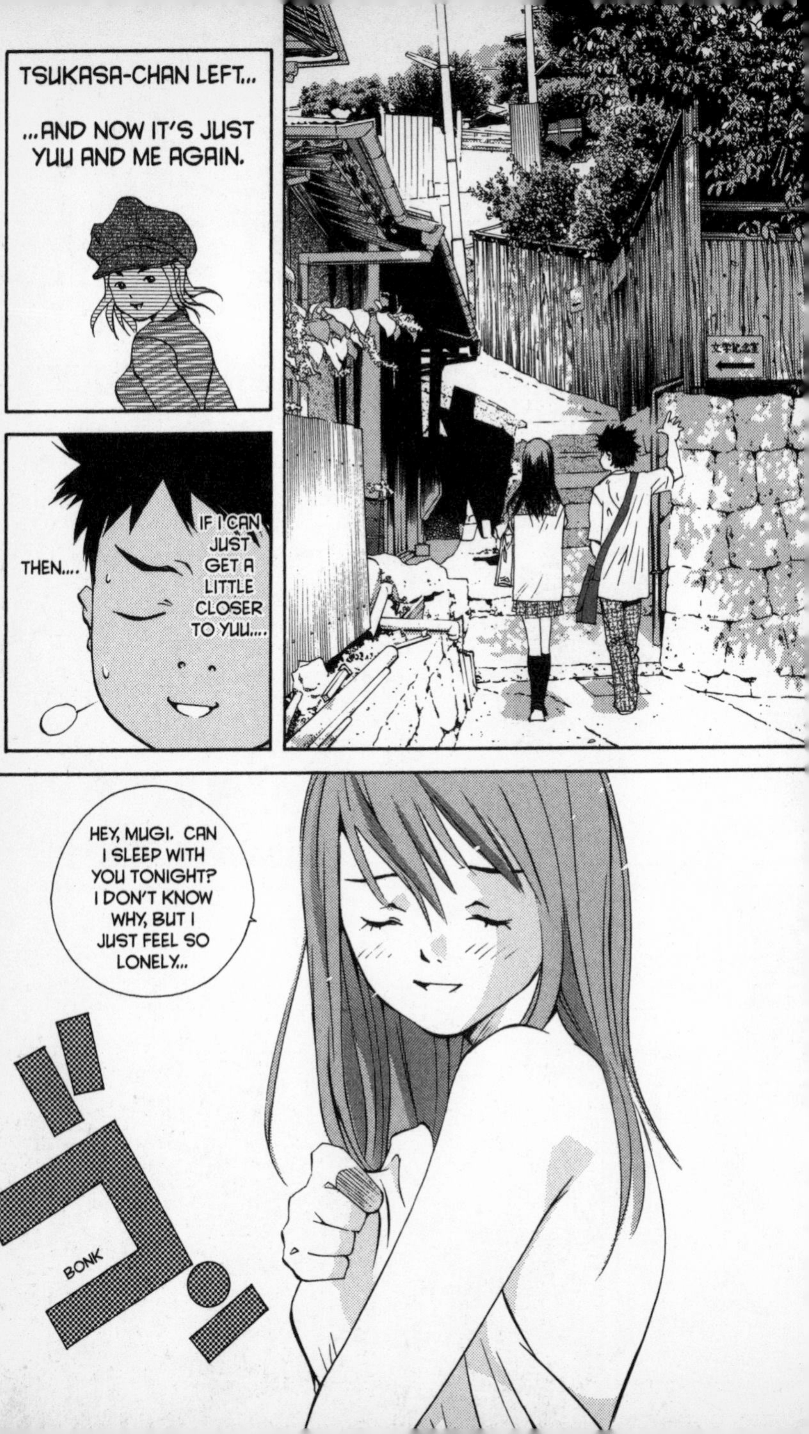
TSUKASA-CHAN LEFT...
...AND NOW IT'S JUST YUU AND ME AGAIN.
IF I CAN JUST GET A LITTLE CLOSER TO YUU....
THEN....
HEY, MUGI. CAN I SLEEP WITH YOU TONIGHT? I DON'T KNOW WHY, BUT I JUST FEEL SO LONELY...
BONK

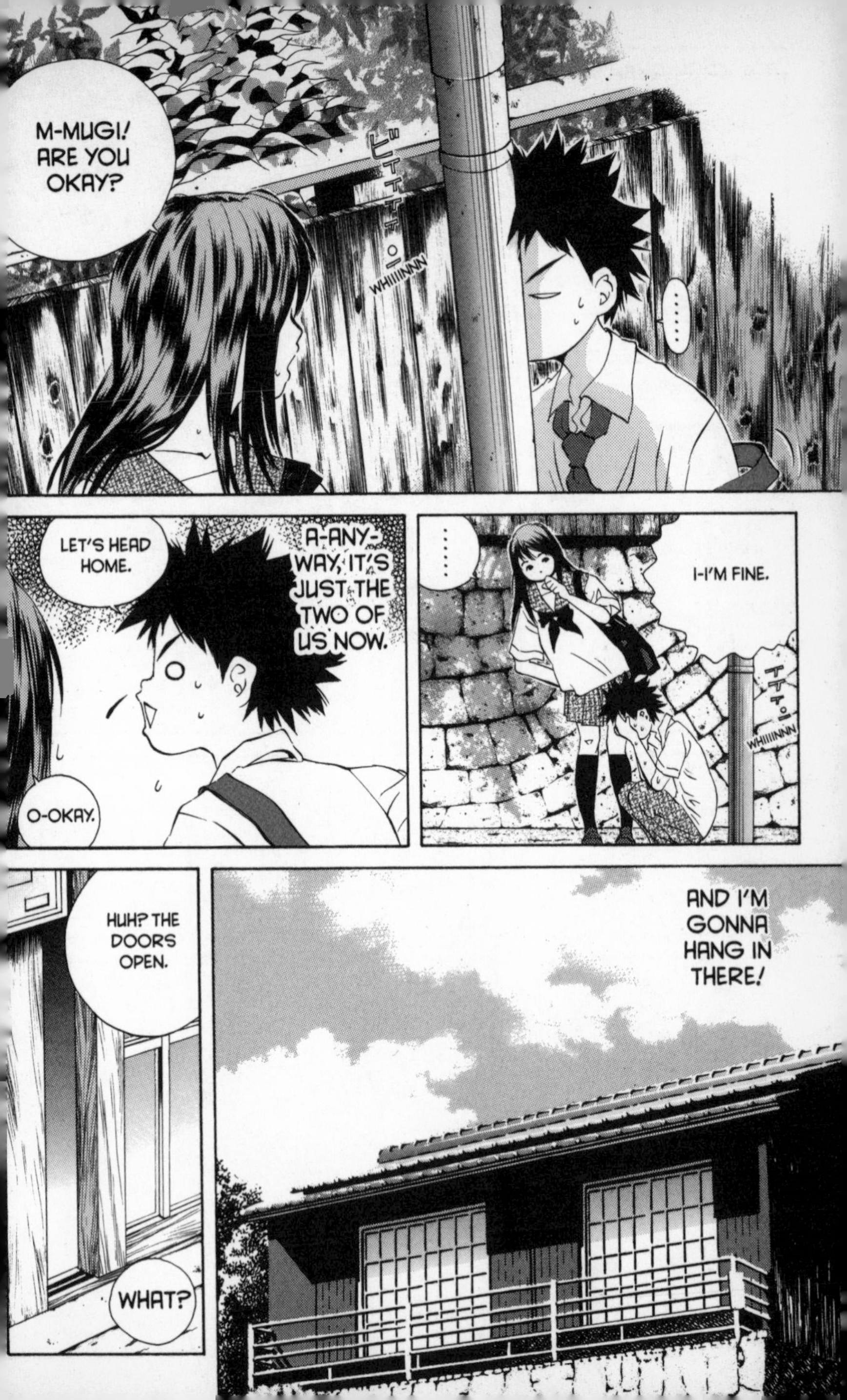
M-MUGI! ARE YOU OKAY?
WHIIIINNN
......
......
I-I'M FINE.
WHIIIINNN
A-ANY-WAY, IT'S JUST THE TWO OF US NOW.
LET'S HEAD HOME.
O-OKAY.
AND I'M GONNA HANG IN THERE!
HUH? THE DOORS OPEN.
WHAT?

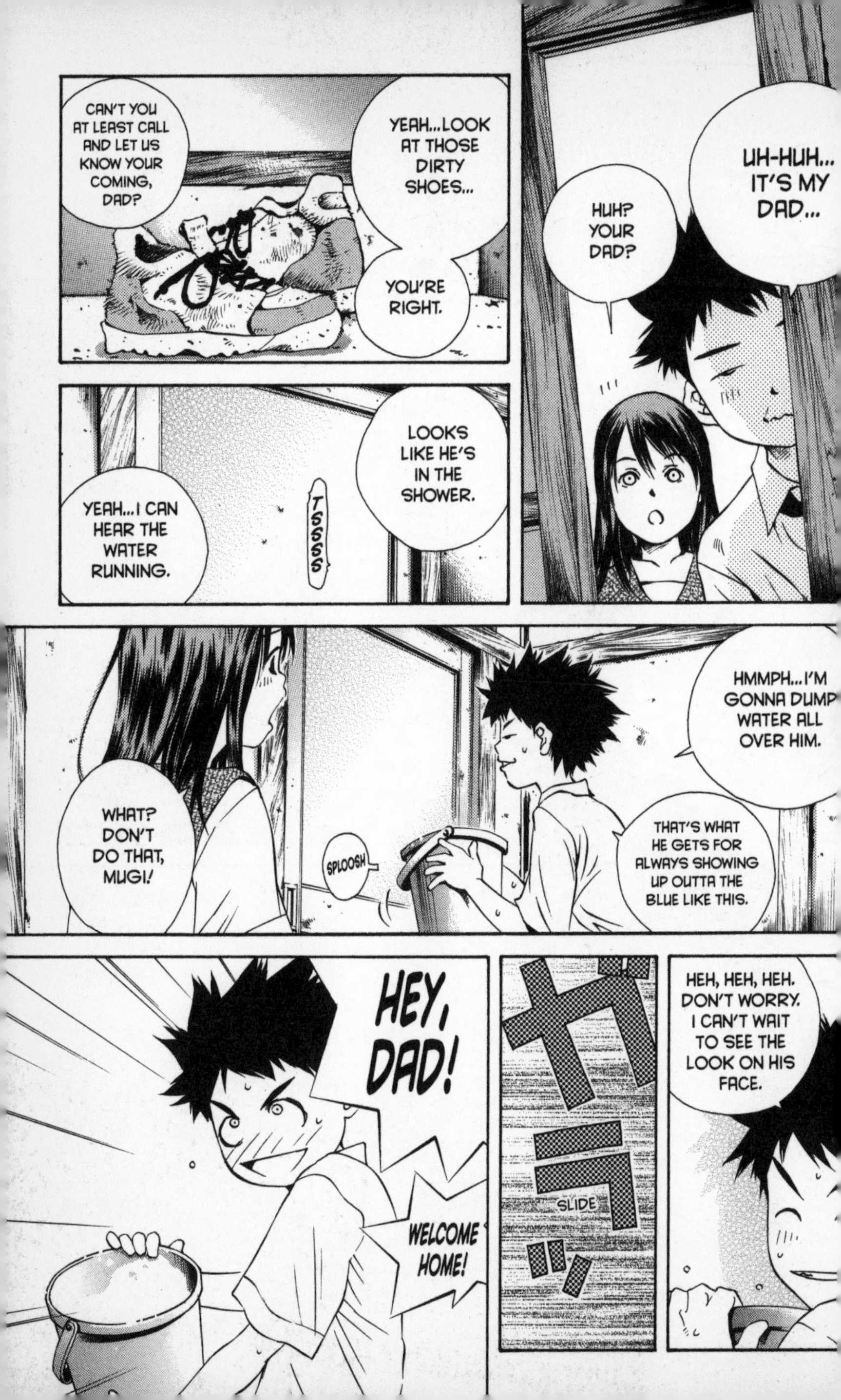
UH-HUH... IT'S MY DAD...
HUH? YOUR DAD?
YEAH...LOOK AT THOSE DIRTY SHOES...
YOU'RE RIGHT.
CAN'T YOU AT LEAST CALL AND LET US KNOW YOUR COMING, DAD?
LOOKS LIKE HE'S IN THE SHOWER.
TSSSSS
YEAH...I CAN HEAR THE WATER RUNNING.
HMMPH...I'M GONNA DUMP WATER ALL OVER HIM.
THAT'S WHAT HE GETS FOR ALWAYS SHOWING UP OUTTA THE BLUE LIKE THIS.
SPLOOSH
WHAT? DON'T DO THAT, MUGI!
HEH, HEH, HEH. DON'T WORRY. I CAN'T WAIT TO SEE THE LOOK ON HIS FACE.
SLIDE
HEY, DAD!
WELCOME HOME!

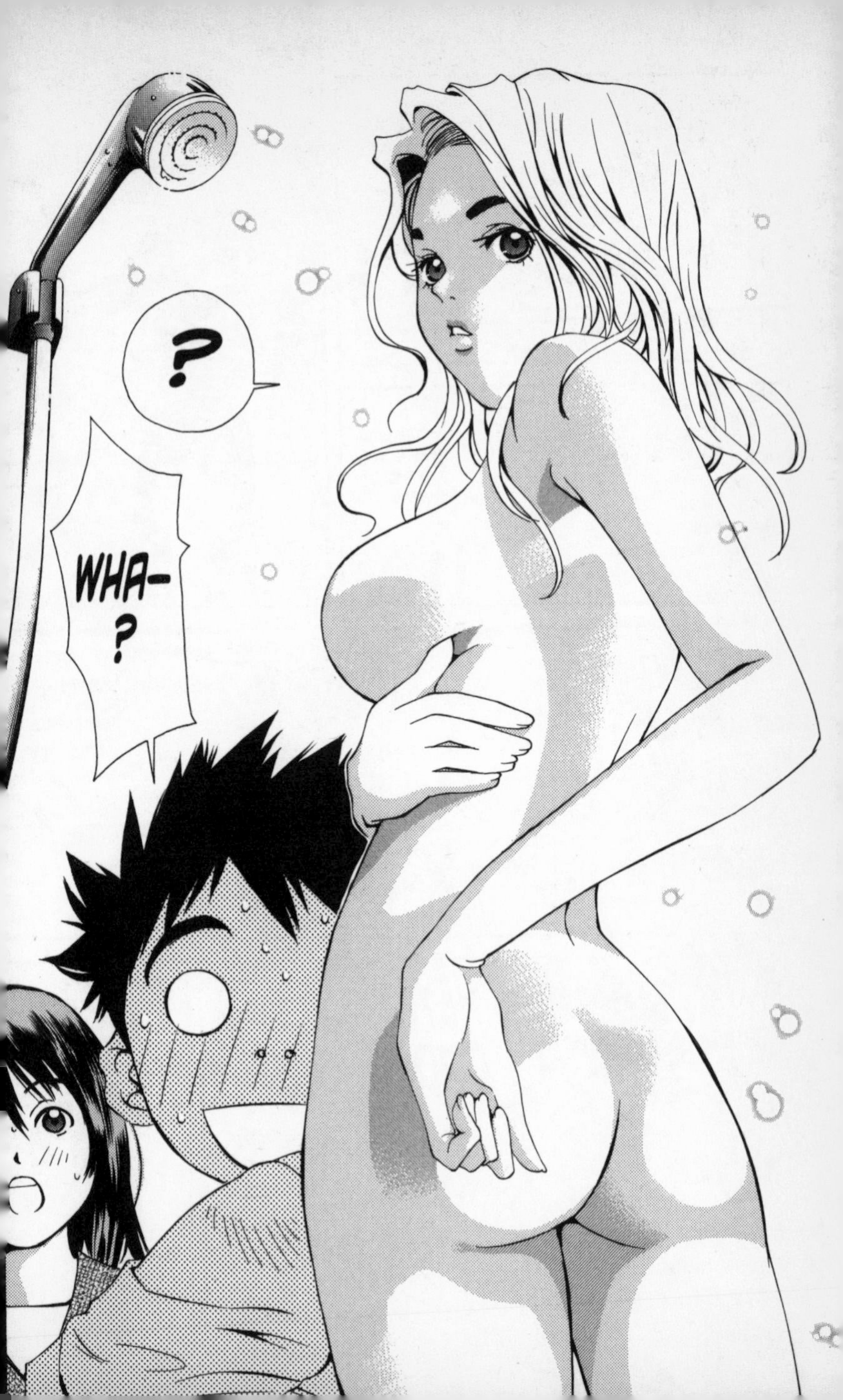
?
WHA-?

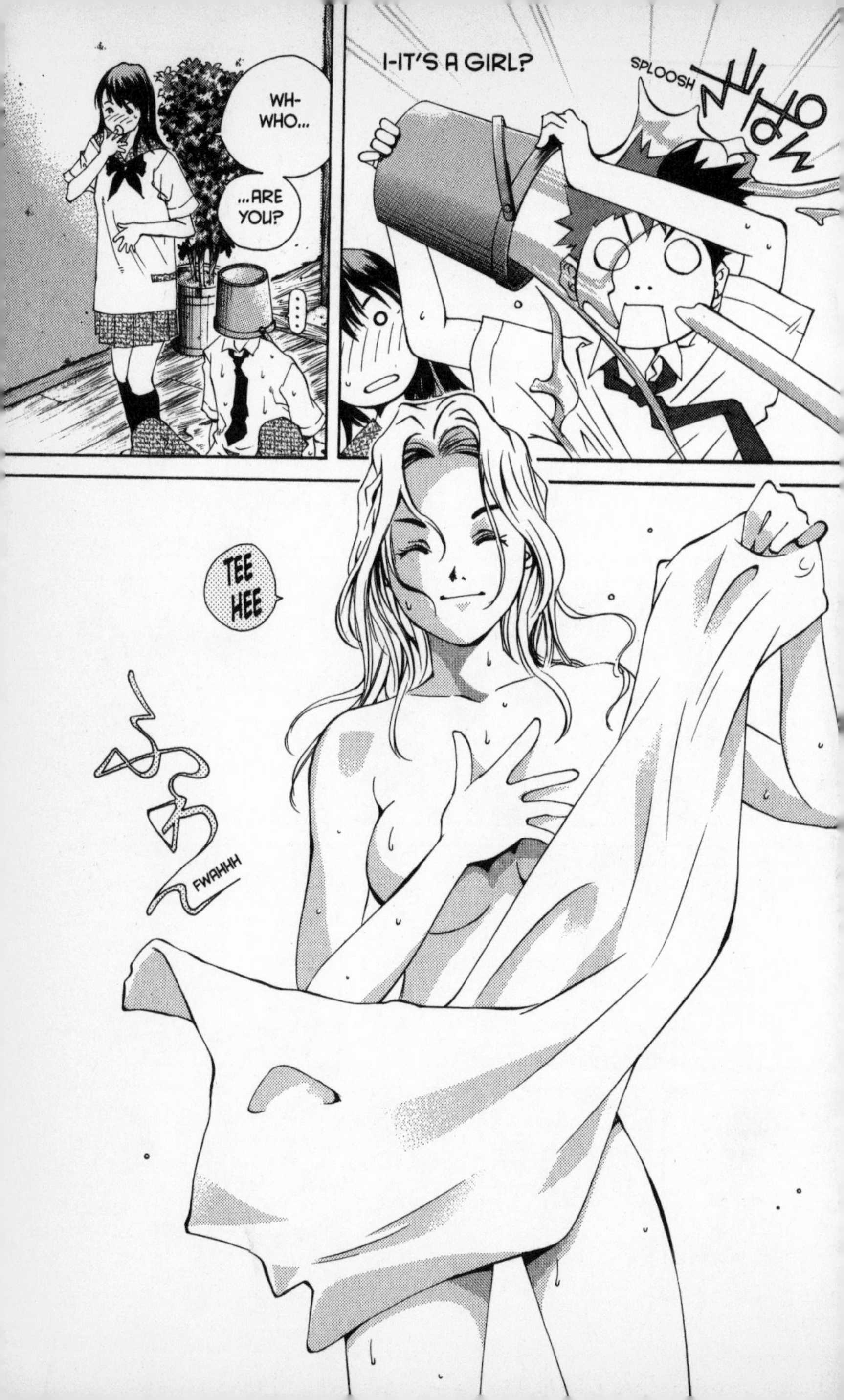
SPLOOSH
I-IT'S A GIRL?
WH-WHO...
...ARE YOU?
...
TEE HEE
FWAHHH

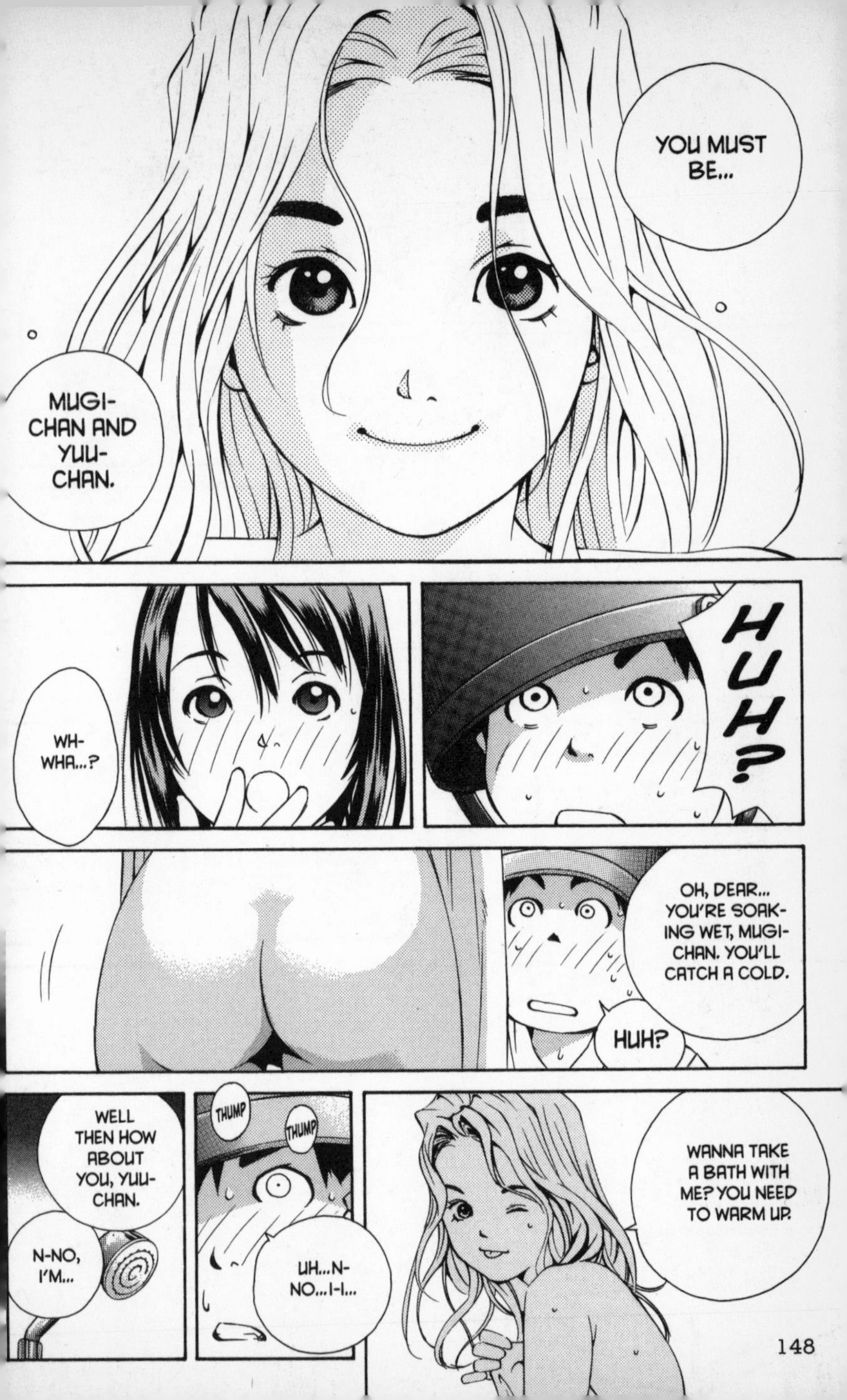
YOU MUST BE...
MUGI-CHAN AND YUU-CHAN.
HUH?
WH-WHA...?
OH, DEAR... YOU'RE SOAKING WET, MUGI-CHAN. YOU'LL CATCH A COLD.
HUH?
WANNA TAKE A BATH WITH ME? YOU NEED TO WARM UP.
THUMP
THUMP
UH...N-NO...I-I...
WELL THEN HOW ABOUT YOU, YUU-CHAN.
N-NO, I'M...

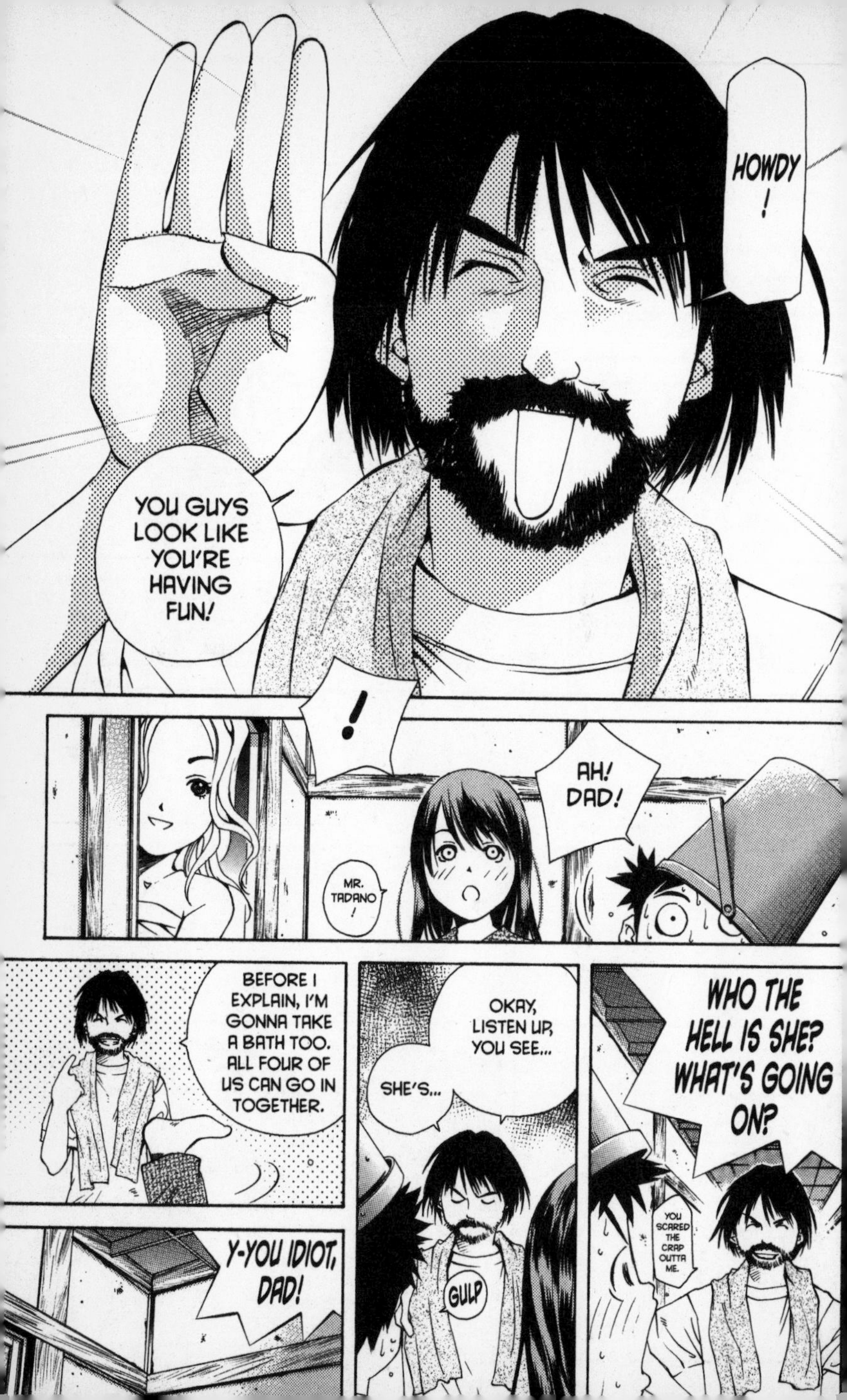
HOWDY!
YOU GUYS LOOK LIKE YOU'RE HAVING FUN!
!
AH! DAD!
MR. TADANO!
WHO THE HELL IS SHE? WHAT'S GOING ON?
YOU SCARED THE CRAP OUTTA ME.
OKAY, LISTEN UP, YOU SEE...
SHE'S...
GULP
BEFORE I EXPLAIN, I'M GONNA TAKE A BATH TOO. ALL FOUR OF US CAN GO IN TOGETHER.
Y-YOU IDIOT, DAD!

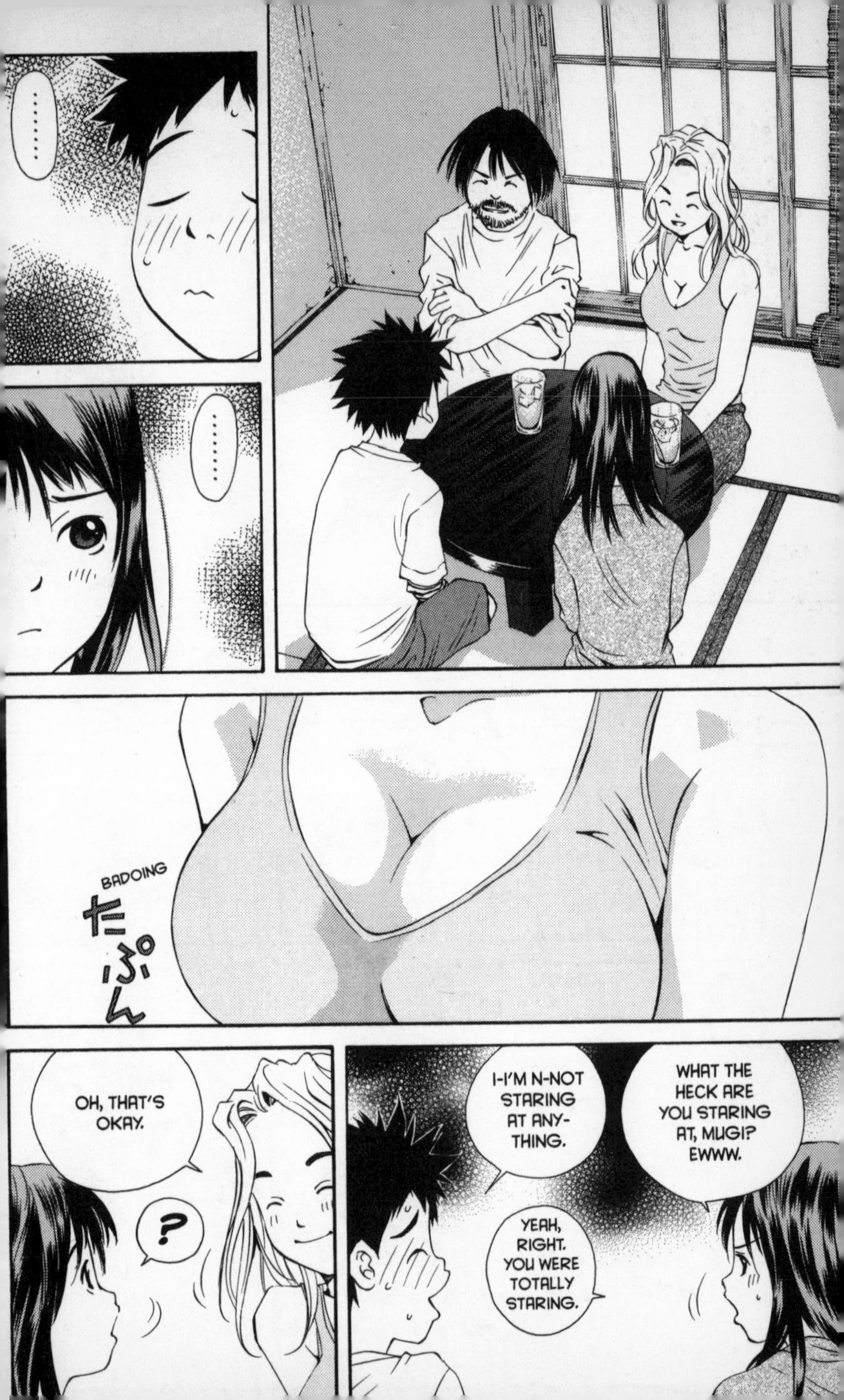
......
......
BADOING
たぷん
WHAT THE HECK ARE YOU STARING AT, MUGI? EWWW.
I-I'M N-NOT STARING AT ANYTHING.
YEAH, RIGHT. YOU WERE TOTALLY STARING.
OH, THAT'S OKAY.
?

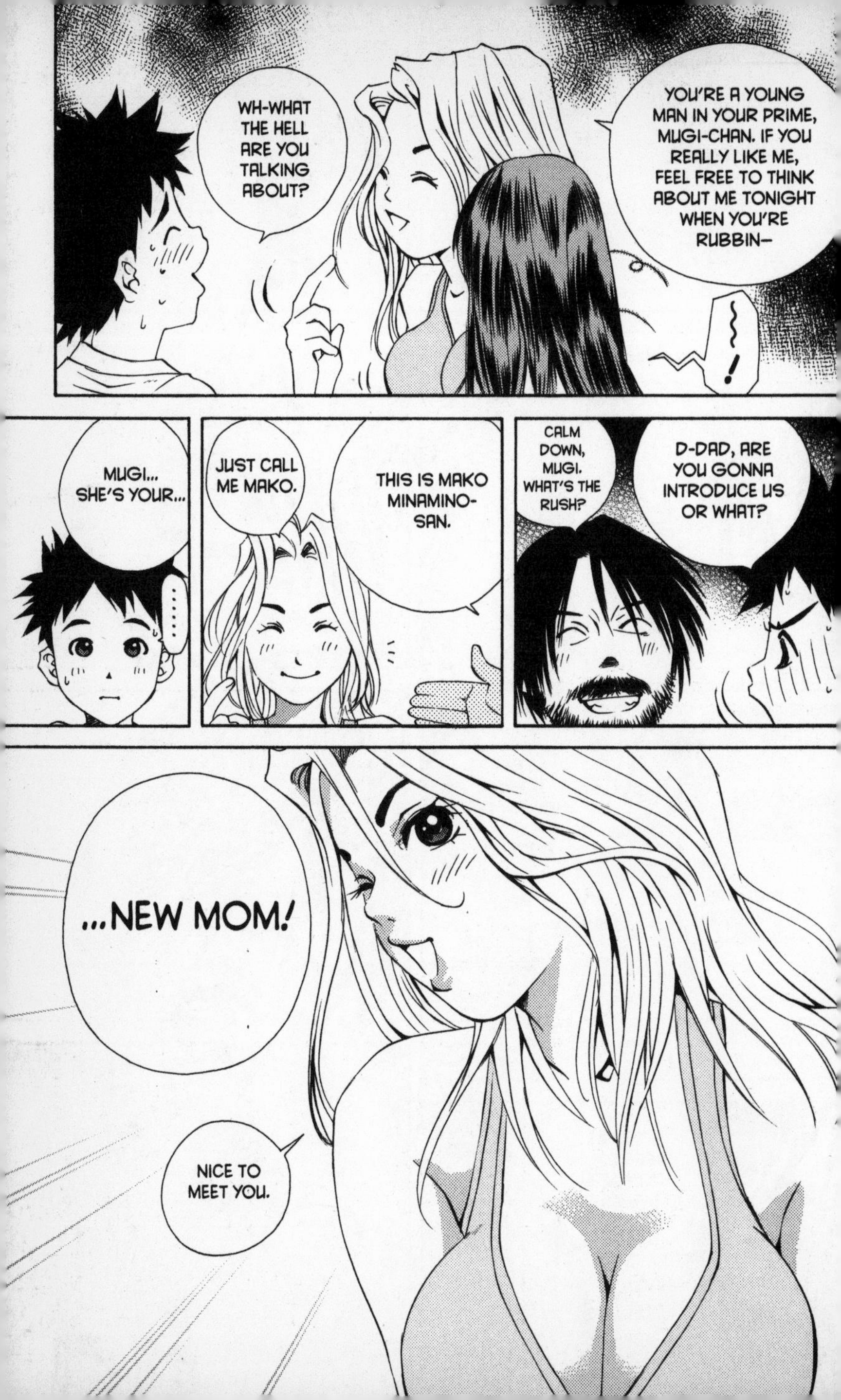
YOU'RE A YOUNG MAN IN YOUR PRIME, MUGI-CHAN. IF YOU REALLY LIKE ME, FEEL FREE TO THINK ABOUT ME TONIGHT WHEN YOU'RE RUBBIN—
~!
WH-WHAT THE HELL ARE YOU TALKING ABOUT?
D-DAD, ARE YOU GONNA INTRODUCE US OR WHAT?
CALM DOWN, MUGI. WHAT'S THE RUSH?
THIS IS MAKO MINAMINO-SAN.
JUST CALL ME MAKO.
MUGI... SHE'S YOUR...
......
...NEW MOM!
NICE TO MEET YOU.

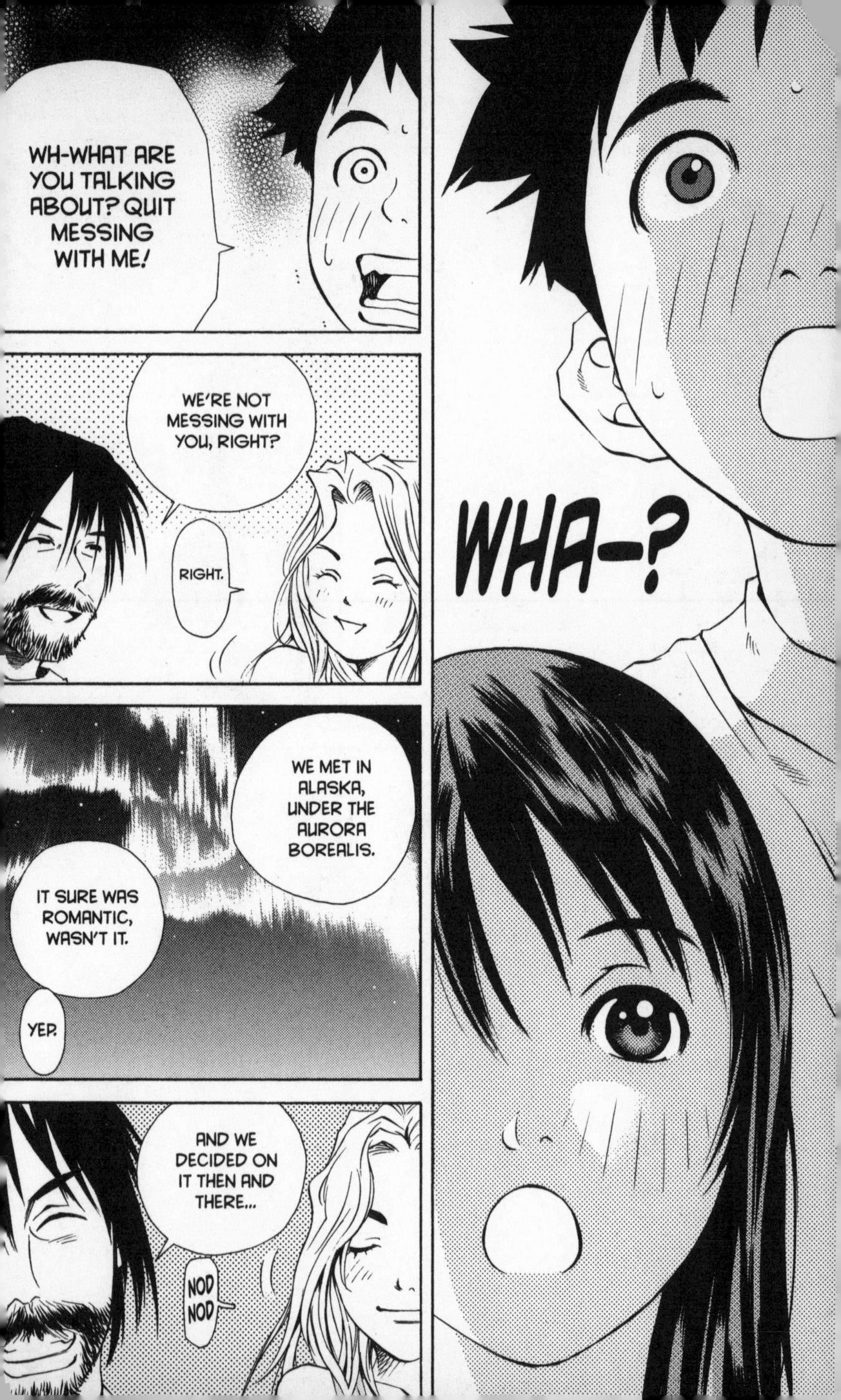
WHA-?
WH-WHAT ARE YOU TALKING ABOUT? QUIT MESSING WITH ME!
WE'RE NOT MESSING WITH YOU, RIGHT?
RIGHT.
WE MET IN ALASKA, UNDER THE AURORA BOREALIS.
IT SURE WAS ROMANTIC, WASN'T IT.
YEP.
AND WE DECIDED ON IT THEN AND THERE...
NOD NOD

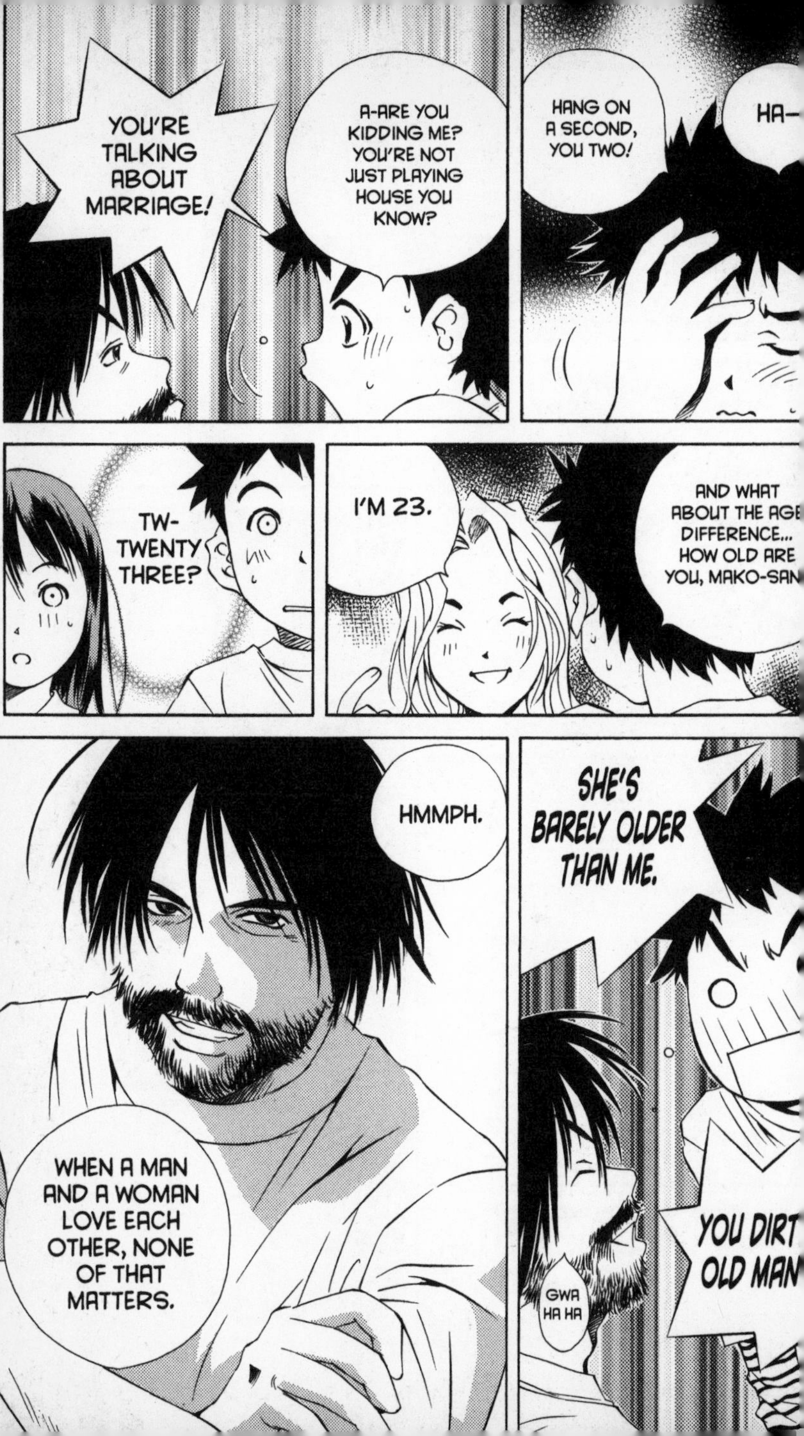
HA—
HANG ON A SECOND, YOU TWO!
A-ARE YOU KIDDING ME? YOU'RE NOT JUST PLAYING HOUSE YOU KNOW?
YOU'RE TALKING ABOUT MARRIAGE!
AND WHAT ABOUT THE AGE DIFFERENCE... HOW OLD ARE YOU, MAKO-SAN
I'M 23.
TW- TWENTY THREE?
SHE'S BARELY OLDER THAN ME.
YOU DIRT OLD MAN
GWA HA HA
HMMPH.
WHEN A MAN AND A WOMAN LOVE EACH OTHER, NONE OF THAT MATTERS.

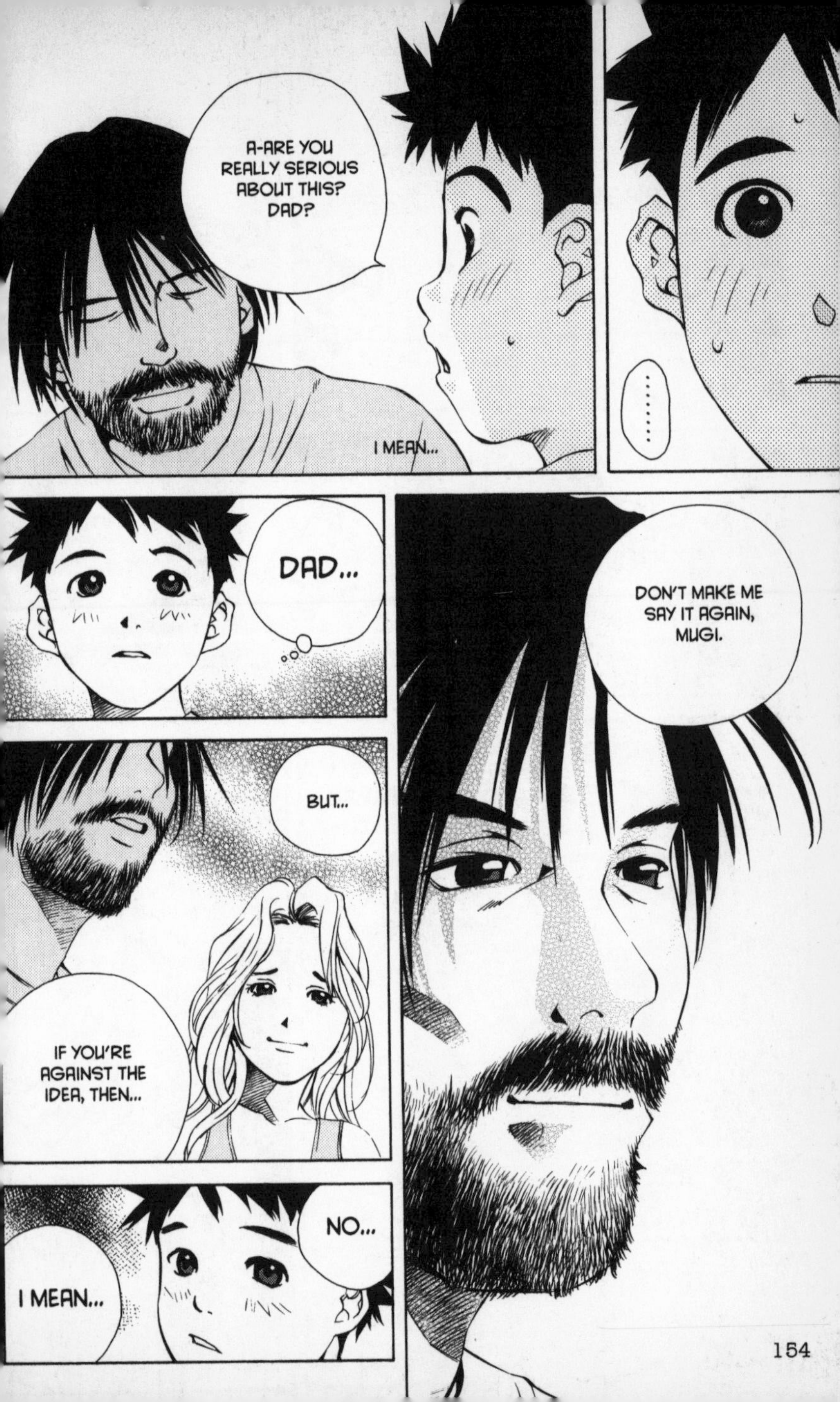
......
A-ARE YOU REALLY SERIOUS ABOUT THIS? DAD?
I MEAN...
DON'T MAKE ME SAY IT AGAIN, MUGI.
DAD...
BUT...
IF YOU'RE AGAINST THE IDEA, THEN...
NO...
I MEAN...

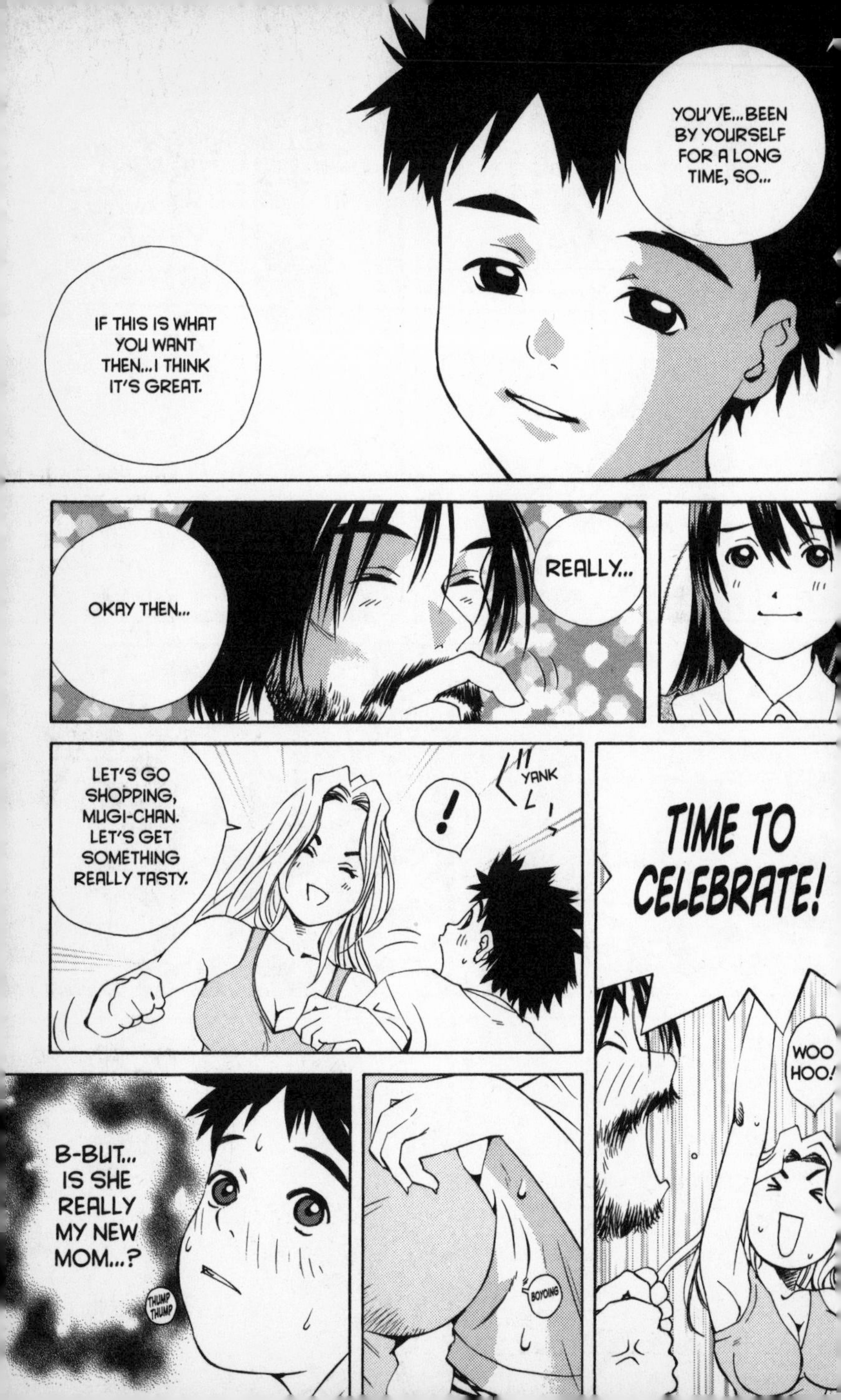
YOU'VE...BEEN BY YOURSELF FOR A LONG TIME, SO...
IF THIS IS WHAT YOU WANT THEN...I THINK IT'S GREAT.
REALLY...
OKAY THEN...
TIME TO CELEBRATE!
WOO HOO!
YANK
!
LET'S GO SHOPPING, MUGI-CHAN. LET'S GET SOMETHING REALLY TASTY.
BOYOING
B-BUT... IS SHE REALLY MY NEW MOM...?
THUMP THUMP

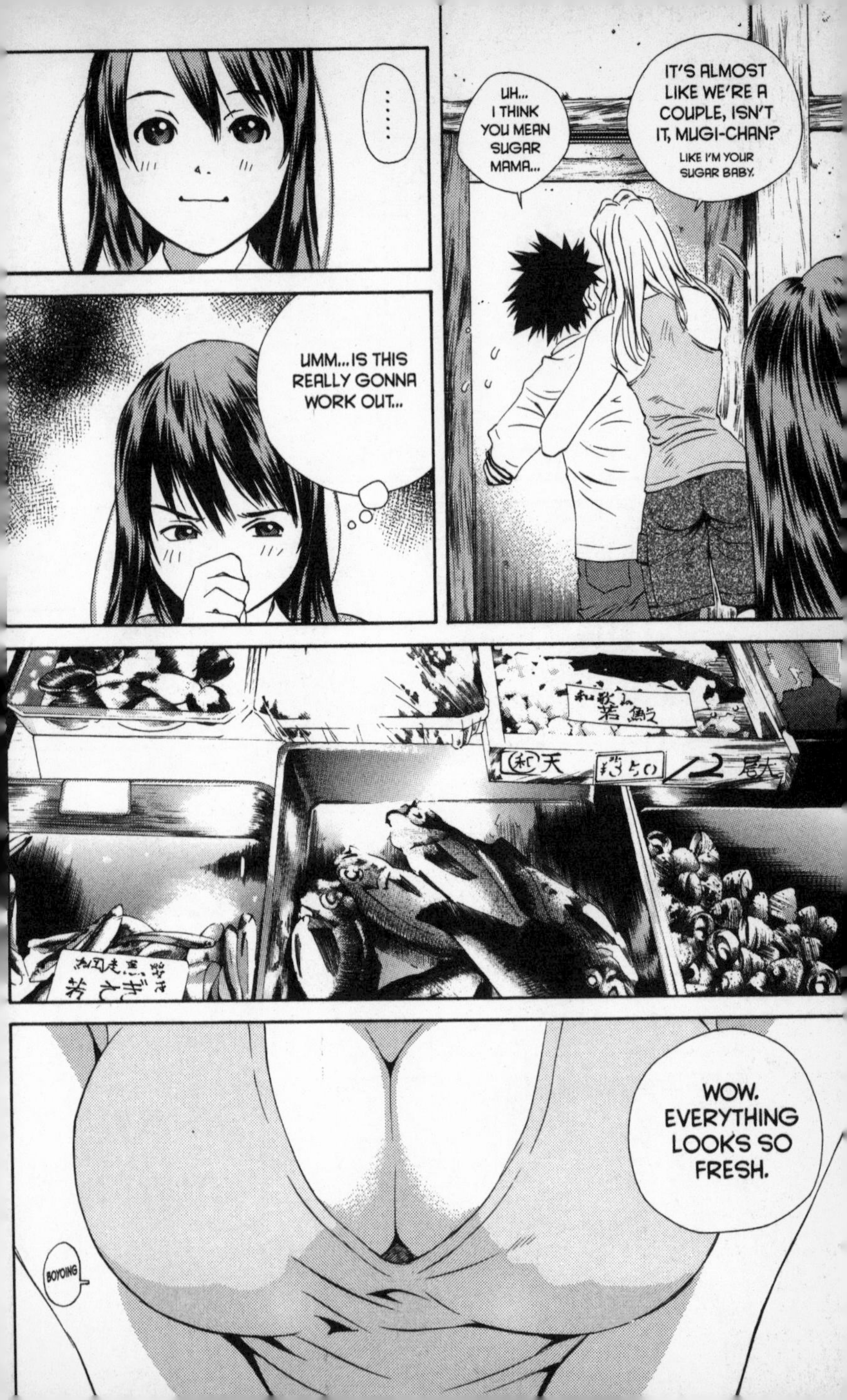
IT'S ALMOST LIKE WE'RE A COUPLE, ISN'T IT, MUGI-CHAN?
LIKE I'M YOUR SUGAR BABY.
UH... I THINK YOU MEAN SUGAR MAMA...
......
UMM...IS THIS REALLY GONNA WORK OUT...
WOW. EVERYTHING LOOKS SO FRESH.
BOYOING

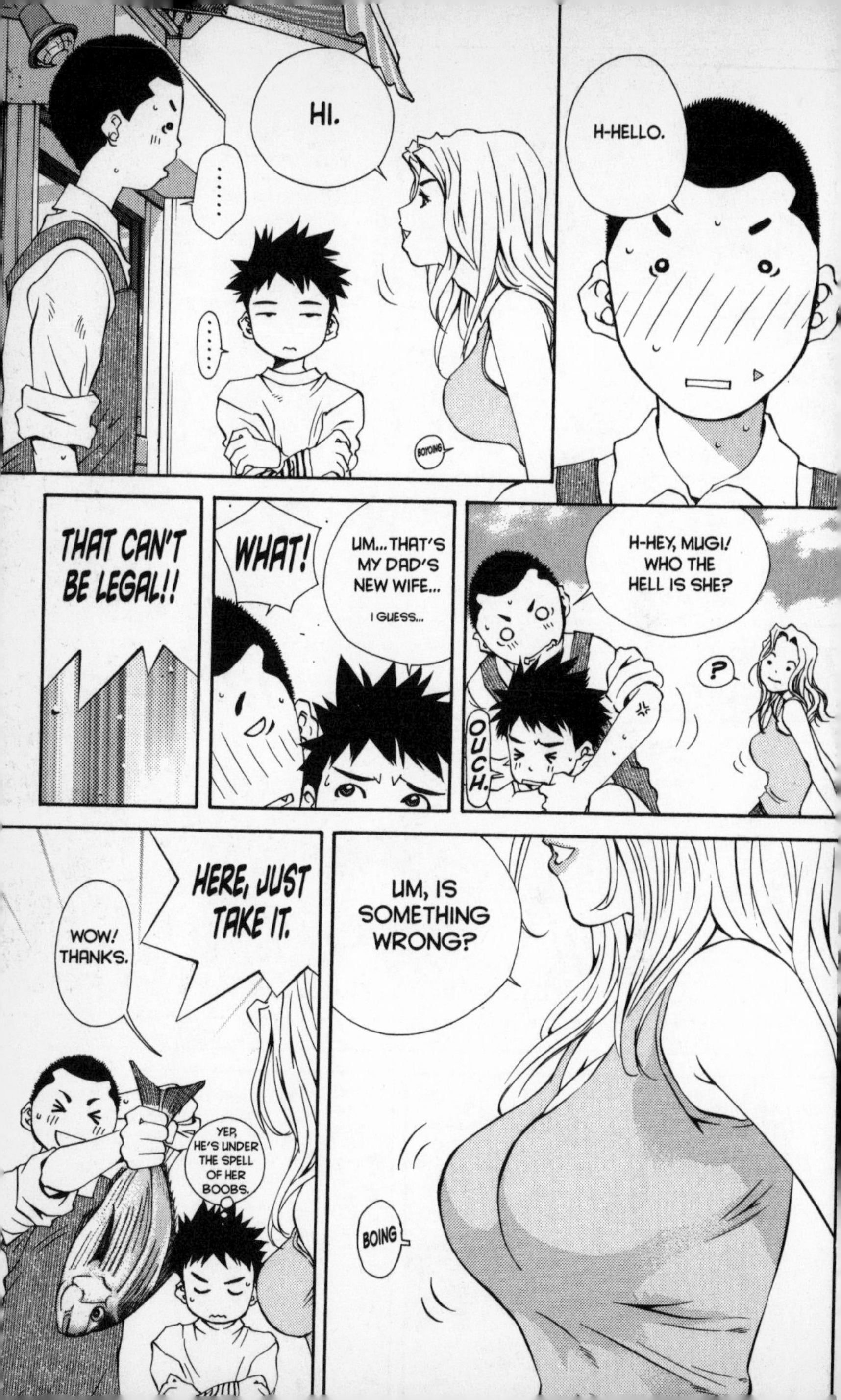
H-HELLO.
HI.
......
......
BOYOING
H-HEY, MUGI! WHO THE HELL IS SHE?
?
OUCH.
UM...THAT'S MY DAD'S NEW WIFE...
I GUESS...
WHAT!
THAT CAN'T BE LEGAL!!
UM, IS SOMETHING WRONG?
BOING
HERE, JUST TAKE IT.
WOW! THANKS.
YEP, HE'S UNDER THE SPELL OF HER BOOBS.

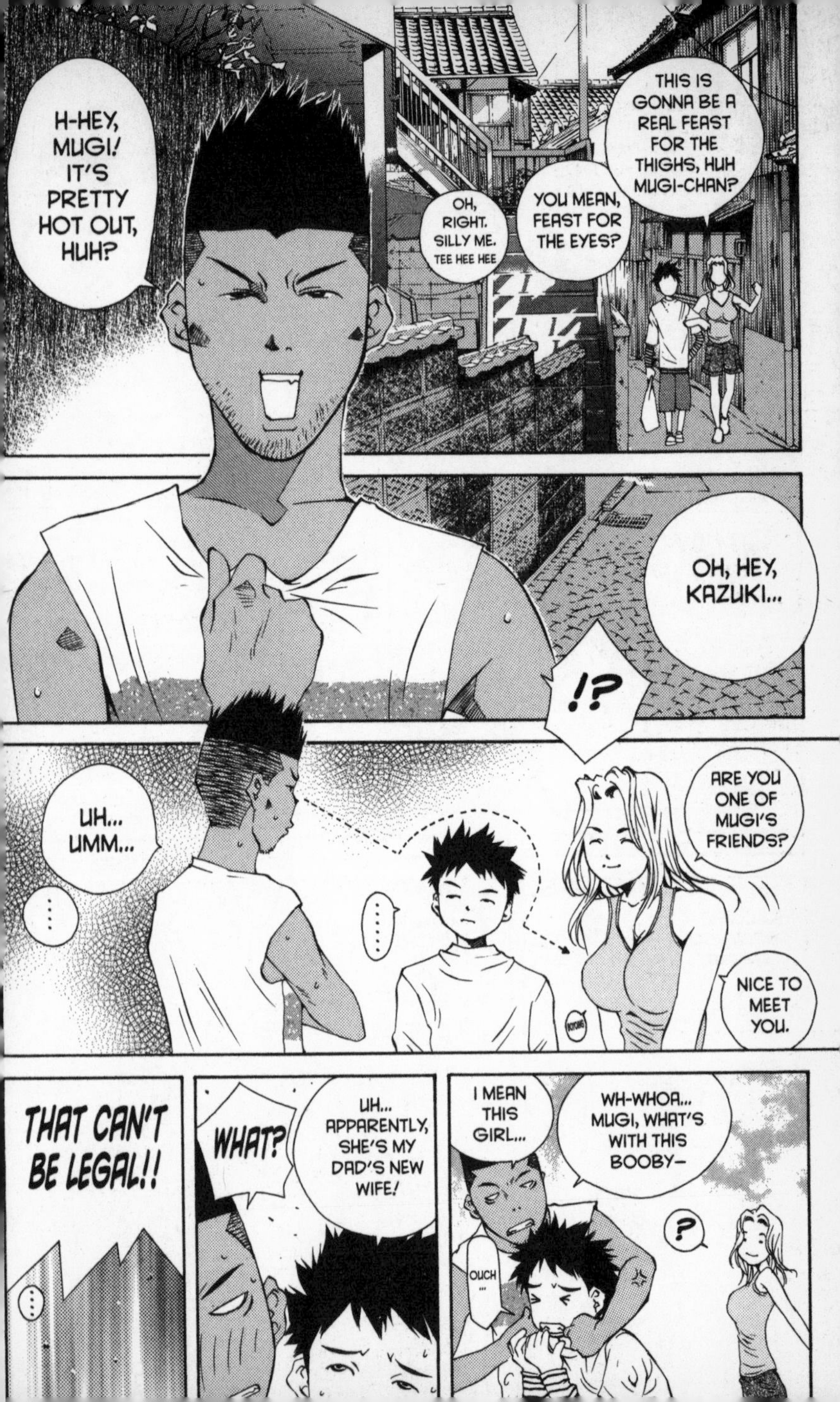

THIS IS GONNA BE A REAL FEAST FOR THE THIGHS, HUH MUGI-CHAN?
YOU MEAN, FEAST FOR THE EYES?
OH, RIGHT. SILLY ME. TEE HEE HEE
H-HEY, MUGI! IT'S PRETTY HOT OUT, HUH?
OH, HEY, KAZUKI...
!?
ARE YOU ONE OF MUGI'S FRIENDS?
NICE TO MEET YOU.
......
UH... UMM...
...
WH-WHOA... MUGI, WHAT'S WITH THIS BOOBY—
I MEAN THIS GIRL...
?
OUCH ...
UH... APPARENTLY, SHE'S MY DAD'S NEW WIFE!
WHAT?
THAT CAN'T BE LEGAL!!
...

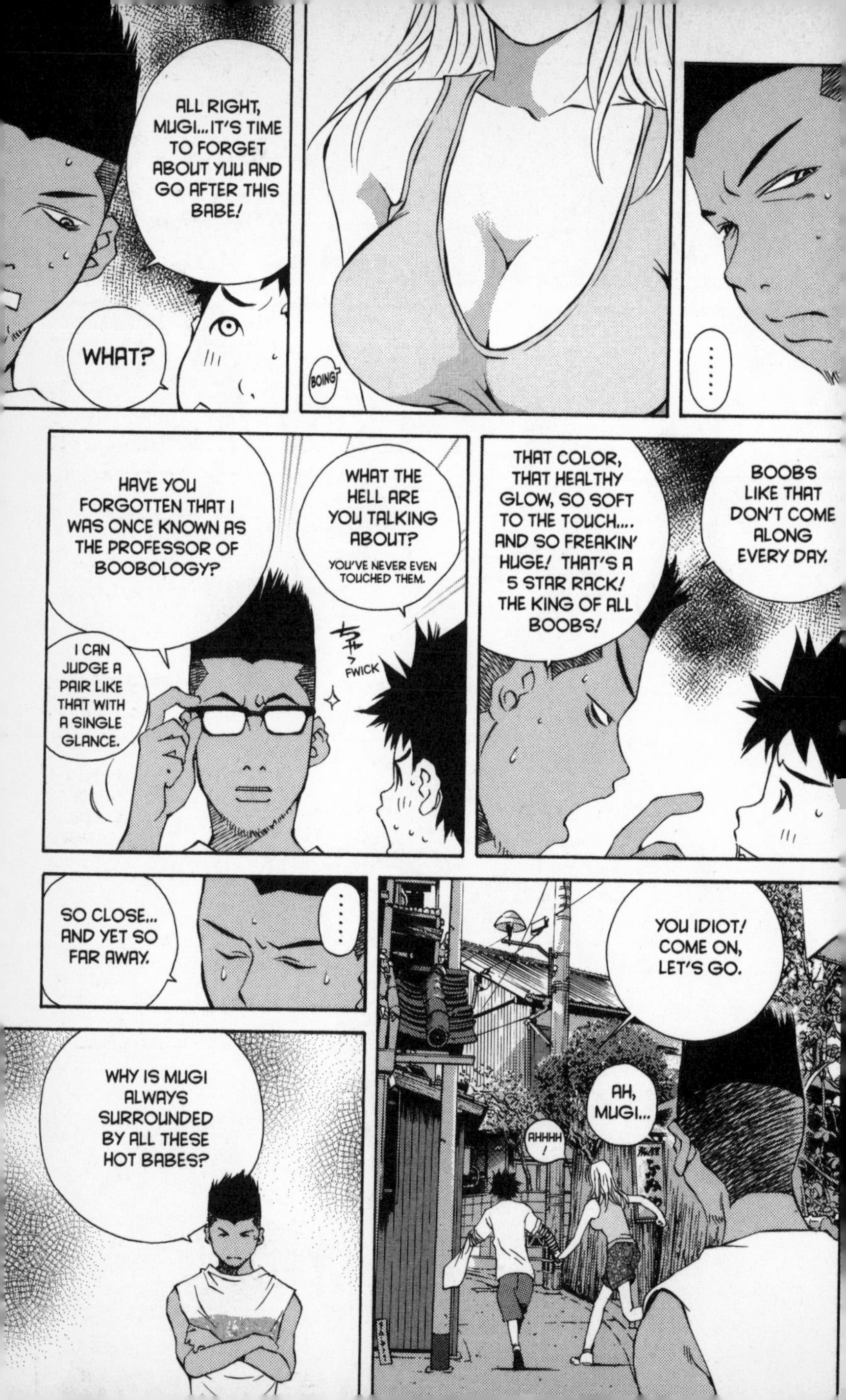
……
BOING
ALL RIGHT, MUGI...IT'S TIME TO FORGET ABOUT YUU AND GO AFTER THIS BABE!
WHAT?
BOOBS LIKE THAT DON'T COME ALONG EVERY DAY.
THAT COLOR, THAT HEALTHY GLOW, SO SOFT TO THE TOUCH.... AND SO FREAKIN' HUGE! THAT'S A 5 STAR RACK! THE KING OF ALL BOOBS!
WHAT THE HELL ARE YOU TALKING ABOUT?
YOU'VE NEVER EVEN TOUCHED THEM.
HAVE YOU FORGOTTEN THAT I WAS ONCE KNOWN AS THE PROFESSOR OF BOOBOLOGY?
FWICK
I CAN JUDGE A PAIR LIKE THAT WITH A SINGLE GLANCE.
YOU IDIOT! COME ON, LET'S GO.
AH, MUGI...
AHHHH!
……
SO CLOSE... AND YET SO FAR AWAY.
WHY IS MUGI ALWAYS SURROUNDED BY ALL THESE HOT BABES?

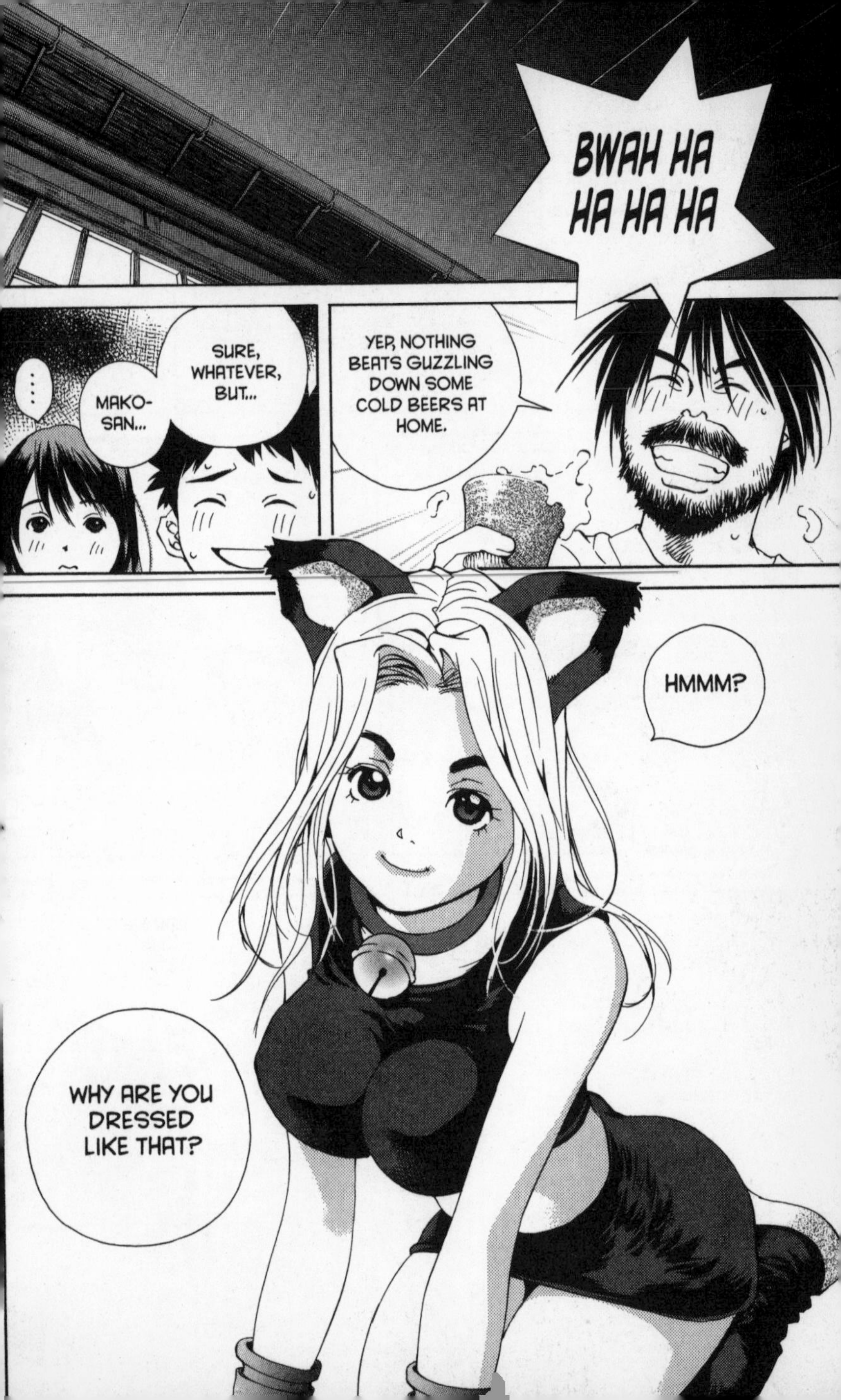
BWAH HA HA HA HA
YEP, NOTHING BEATS GUZZLING DOWN SOME COLD BEERS AT HOME.
SURE, WHATEVER, BUT...
MAKO-SAN...
....
HMMM?
WHY ARE YOU DRESSED LIKE THAT?

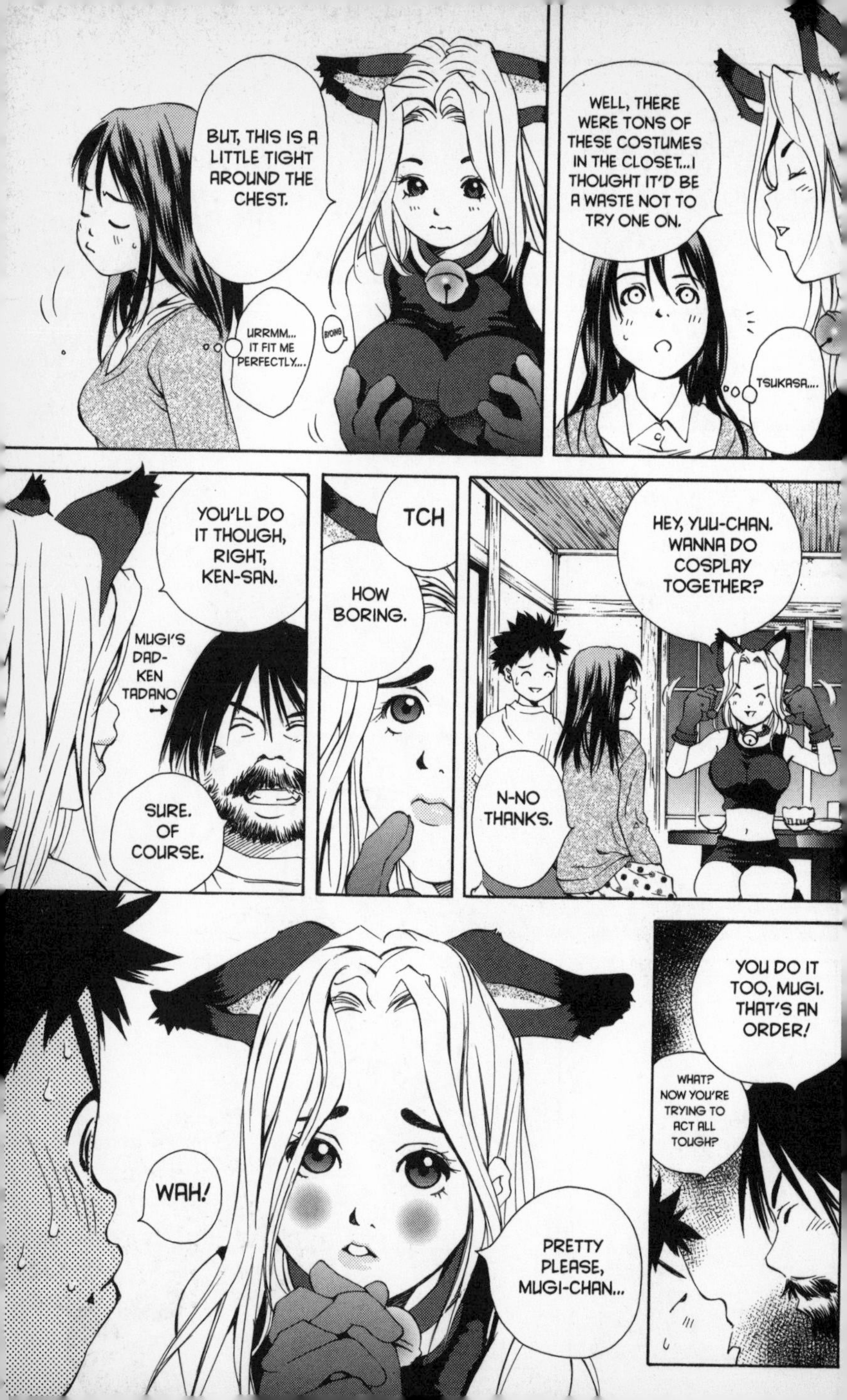
WELL, THERE WERE TONS OF THESE COSTUMES IN THE CLOSET...I THOUGHT IT'D BE A WASTE NOT TO TRY ONE ON.
TSUKASA....
BUT, THIS IS A LITTLE TIGHT AROUND THE CHEST.
BYOING
URRMM... IT FIT ME PERFECTLY....
HEY, YUU-CHAN. WANNA DO COSPLAY TOGETHER?
N-NO THANKS.
TCH
HOW BORING.
YOU'LL DO IT THOUGH, RIGHT, KEN-SAN.
MUGI'S DAD- KEN TADANO →
SURE. OF COURSE.
YOU DO IT TOO, MUGI. THAT'S AN ORDER!
WHAT? NOW YOU'RE TRYING TO ACT ALL TOUGH?
PRETTY PLEASE, MUGI-CHAN...
WAH!

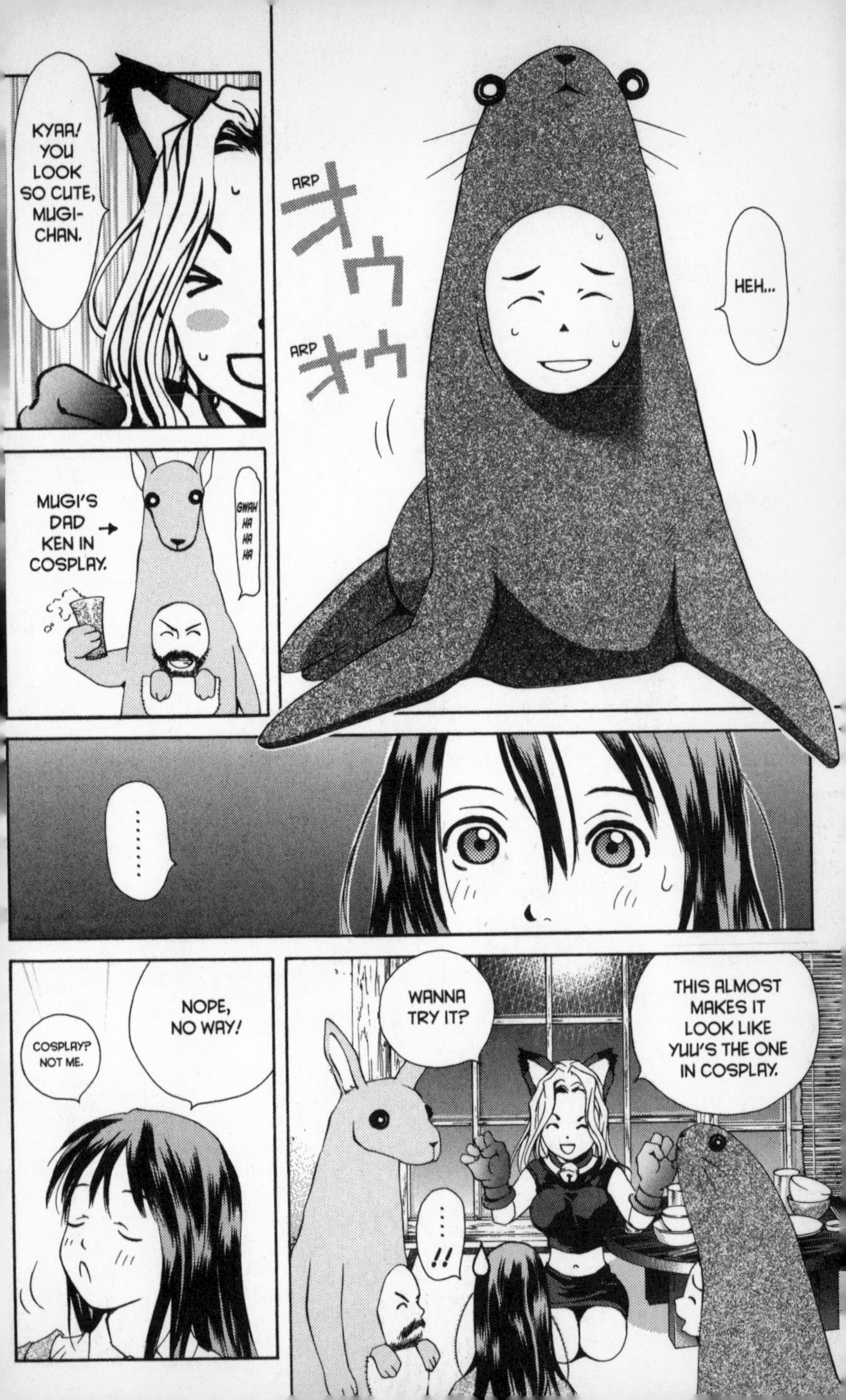
HEH...
ARP オウ
ARP オウ
KYAA! YOU LOOK SO CUTE, MUGI-CHAN.
GWAH HA HA HA
MUGI'S DAD KEN IN COSPLAY.
......
THIS ALMOST MAKES IT LOOK LIKE YUU'S THE ONE IN COSPLAY.
WANNA TRY IT?
.....
!!
NOPE, NO WAY!
COSPLAY? NOT ME.

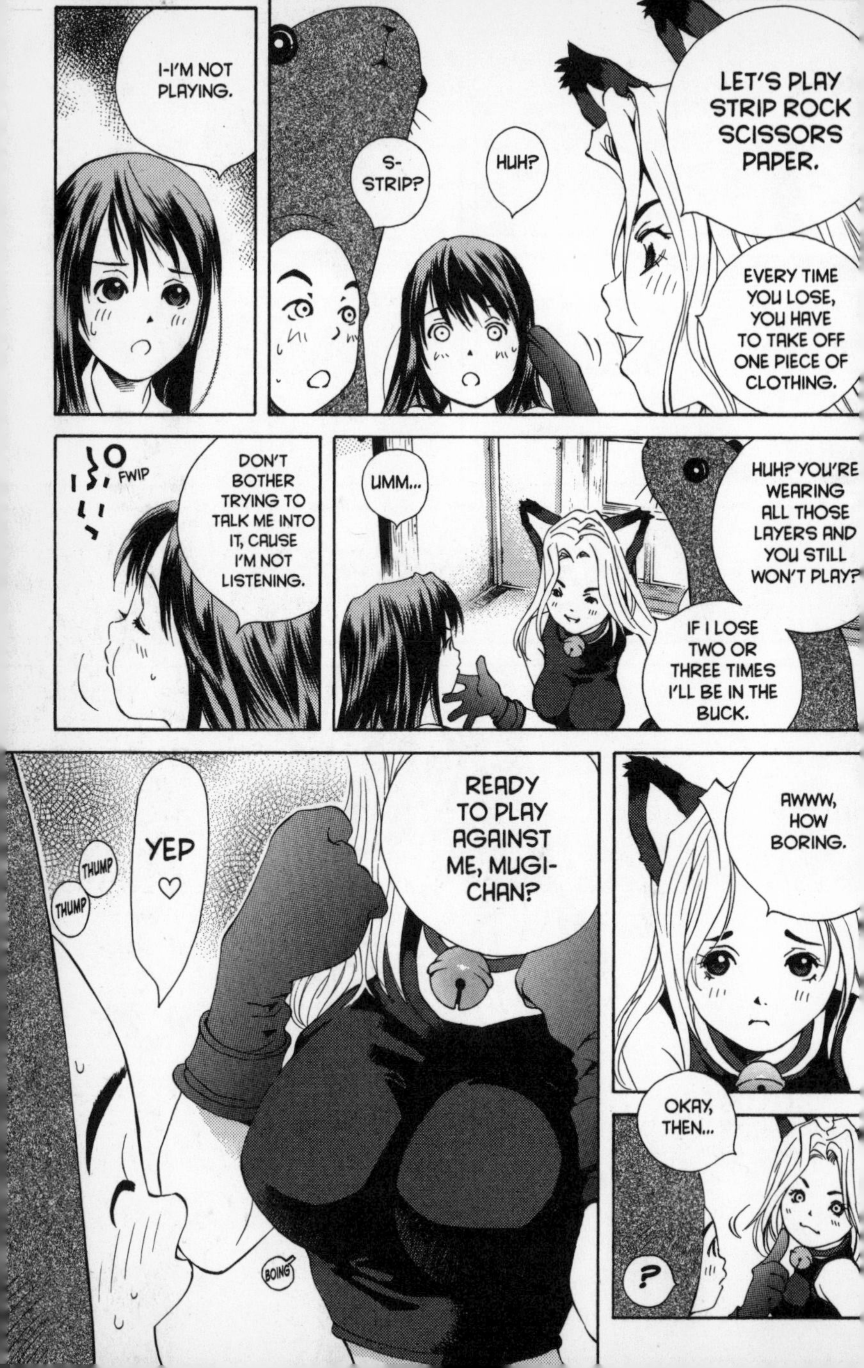
LET'S PLAY STRIP ROCK SCISSORS PAPER.
EVERY TIME YOU LOSE, YOU HAVE TO TAKE OFF ONE PIECE OF CLOTHING.
HUH?
S- STRIP?
I-I'M NOT PLAYING.
HUH? YOU'RE WEARING ALL THOSE LAYERS AND YOU STILL WON'T PLAY?
UMM...
IF I LOSE TWO OR THREE TIMES I'LL BE IN THE BUCK.
DON'T BOTHER TRYING TO TALK ME INTO IT, CAUSE I'M NOT LISTENING.
FWIP
AWWW, HOW BORING.
OKAY, THEN...
?
READY TO PLAY AGAINST ME, MUGI-CHAN?
YEP ♡
THUMP
THUMP
BOING

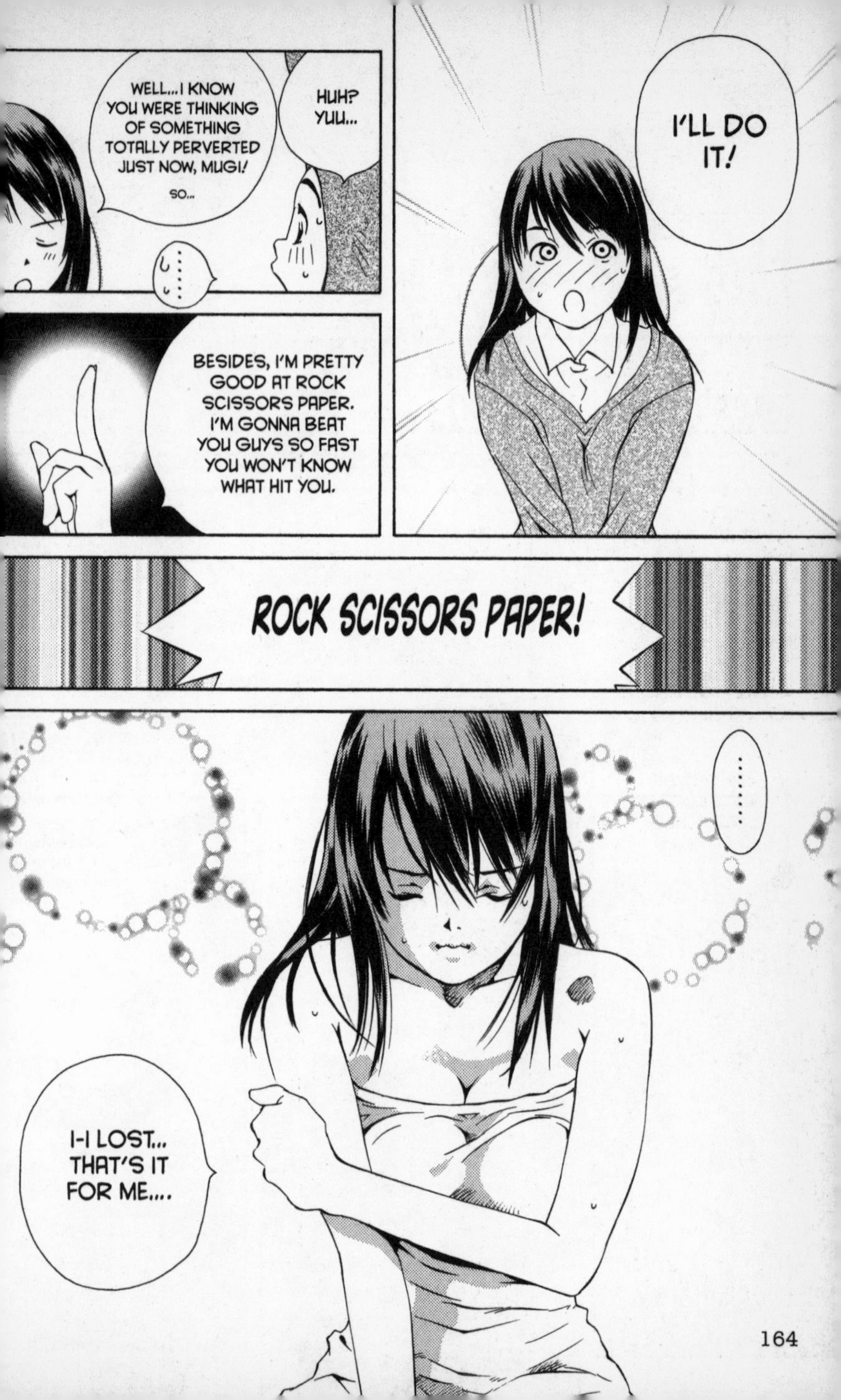

I'LL DO IT!
HUH? YUU...
WELL...I KNOW YOU WERE THINKING OF SOMETHING TOTALLY PERVERTED JUST NOW, MUGI!
SO...
......
BESIDES, I'M PRETTY GOOD AT ROCK SCISSORS PAPER. I'M GONNA BEAT YOU GUYS SO FAST YOU WON'T KNOW WHAT HIT YOU.
ROCK SCISSORS PAPER!
....
I-I LOST... THAT'S IT FOR ME....

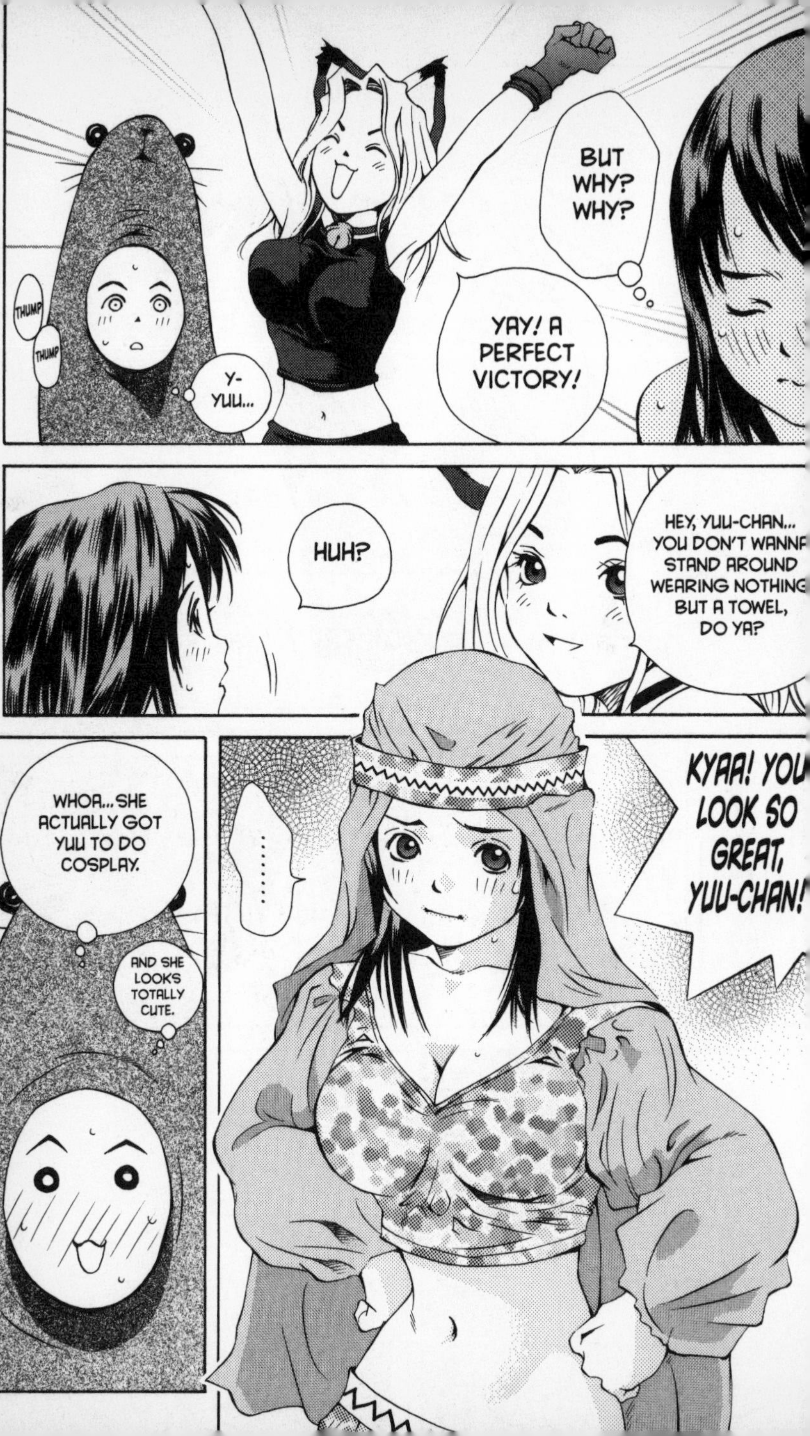
BUT WHY? WHY?
YAY! A PERFECT VICTORY!
Y- YUU...
THUMP
THUMP
HEY, YUU-CHAN... YOU DON'T WANNA STAND AROUND WEARING NOTHING BUT A TOWEL, DO YA?
HUH?
KYAA! YOU LOOK SO GREAT, YUU-CHAN!
......
WHOA... SHE ACTUALLY GOT YUU TO DO COSPLAY.
AND SHE LOOKS TOTALLY CUTE.

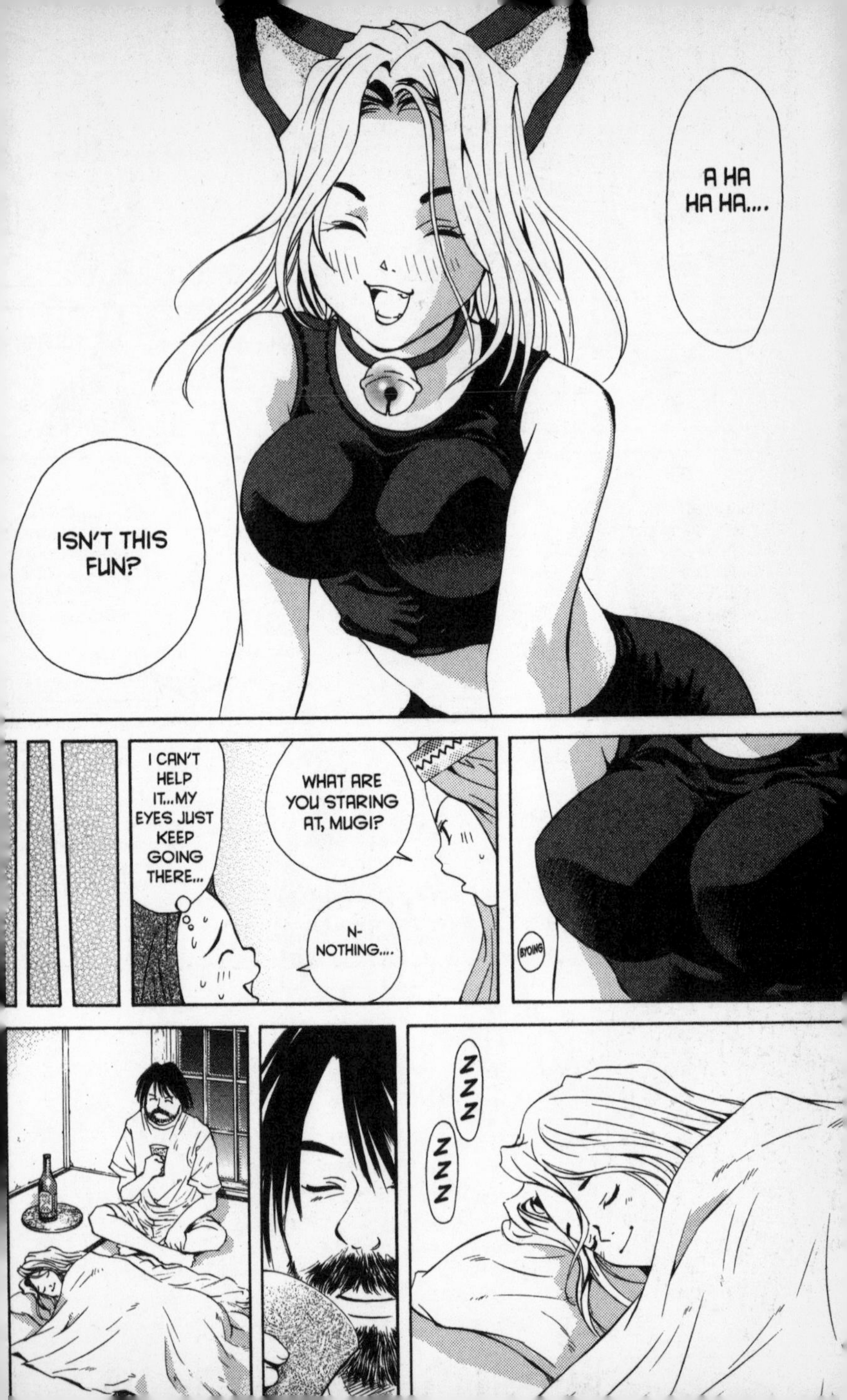
A HA HA HA HA....
ISN'T THIS FUN?
BYOING
WHAT ARE YOU STARING AT, MUGI?
I CAN'T HELP IT...MY EYES JUST KEEP GOING THERE...
N-NOTHING....
NNN
NNN

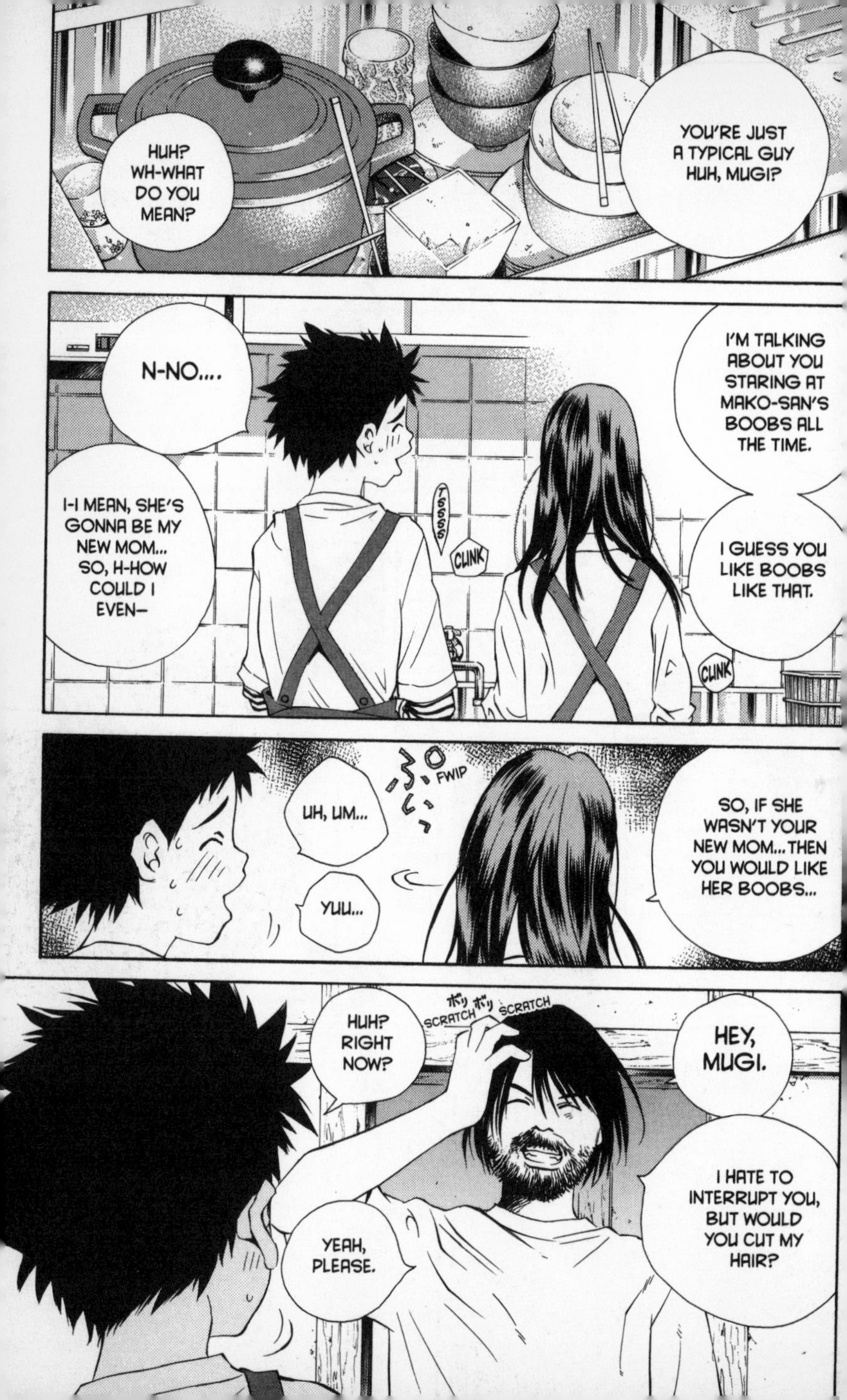
YOU'RE JUST A TYPICAL GUY HUH, MUGI?
HUH? WH-WHAT DO YOU MEAN?
I'M TALKING ABOUT YOU STARING AT MAKO-SAN'S BOOBS ALL THE TIME.
I GUESS YOU LIKE BOOBS LIKE THAT.
CLINK
CLINK
TSSSS
N-NO....
I-I MEAN, SHE'S GONNA BE MY NEW MOM... SO, H-HOW COULD I EVEN–
SO, IF SHE WASN'T YOUR NEW MOM...THEN YOU WOULD LIKE HER BOOBS...
FWIP
UH, UM...
YUU...
HEY, MUGI.
I HATE TO INTERRUPT YOU, BUT WOULD YOU CUT MY HAIR?
SCRATCH
SCRATCH
HUH? RIGHT NOW?
YEAH, PLEASE.

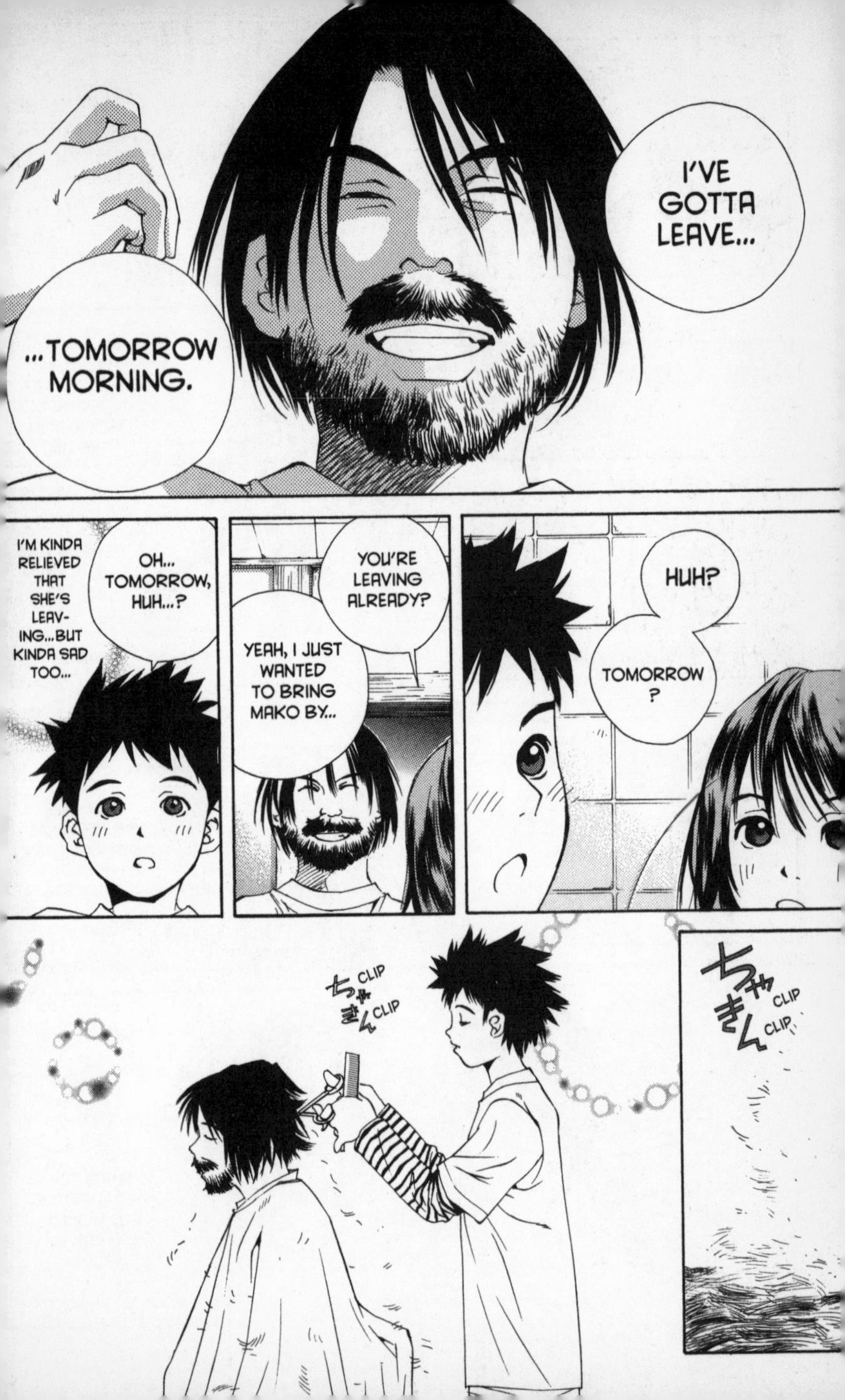
I'VE GOTTA LEAVE...
...TOMORROW MORNING.
HUH?
TOMORROW ?
YOU'RE LEAVING ALREADY?
YEAH, I JUST WANTED TO BRING MAKO BY...
OH... TOMORROW, HUH...?
I'M KINDA RELIEVED THAT SHE'S LEAV-ING...BUT KINDA SAD TOO...
ちゃきん CLIP CLIP
ちゃきん CLIP CLIP

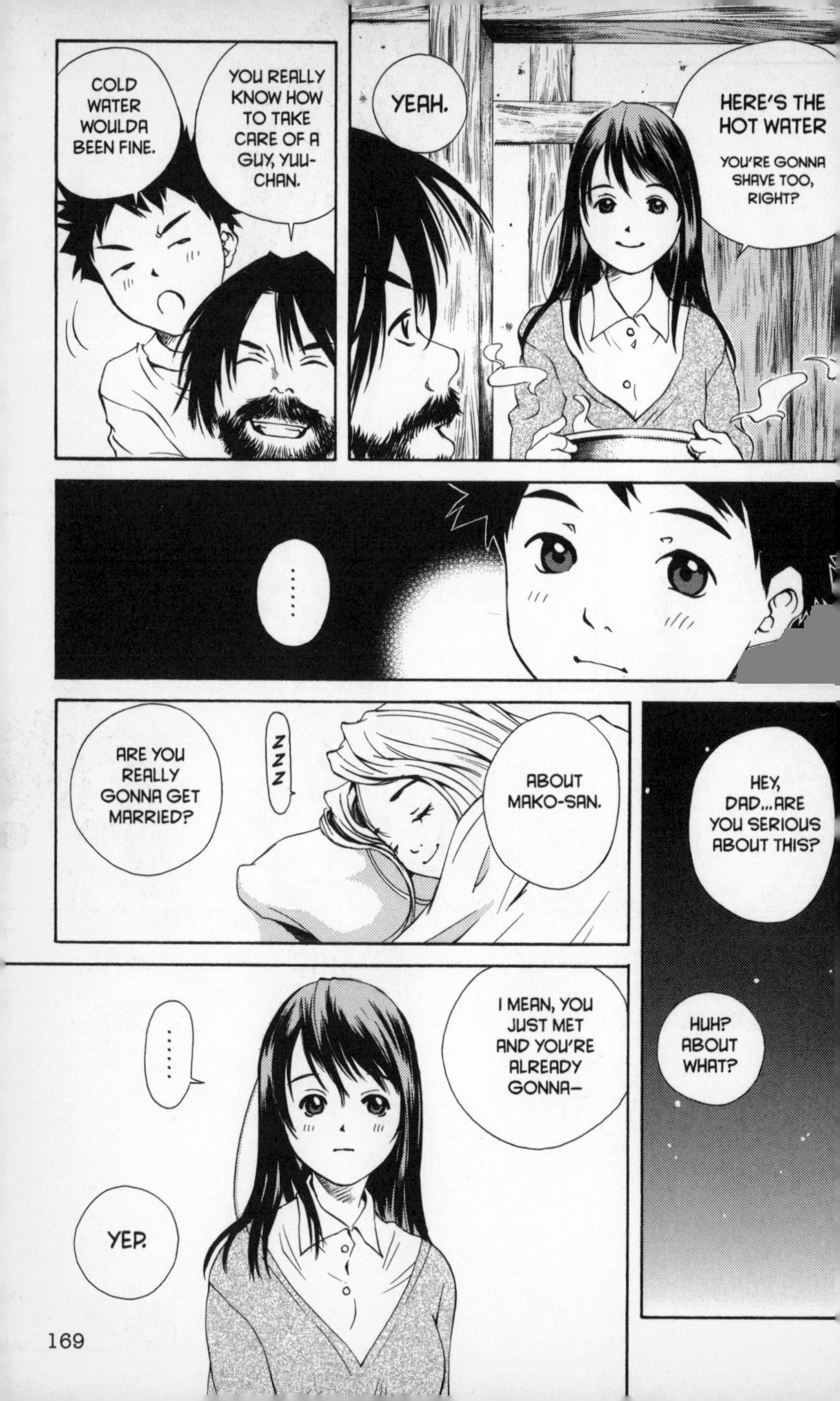
HERE'S THE HOT WATER
YOU'RE GONNA SHAVE TOO, RIGHT?
YEAH.
YOU REALLY KNOW HOW TO TAKE CARE OF A GUY, YUU-CHAN.
COLD WATER WOULDA BEEN FINE.
……
HEY, DAD...ARE YOU SERIOUS ABOUT THIS?
HUH? ABOUT WHAT?
ABOUT MAKO-SAN.
ZZZ
ARE YOU REALLY GONNA GET MARRIED?
I MEAN, YOU JUST MET AND YOU'RE ALREADY GONNA–
……
YEP.

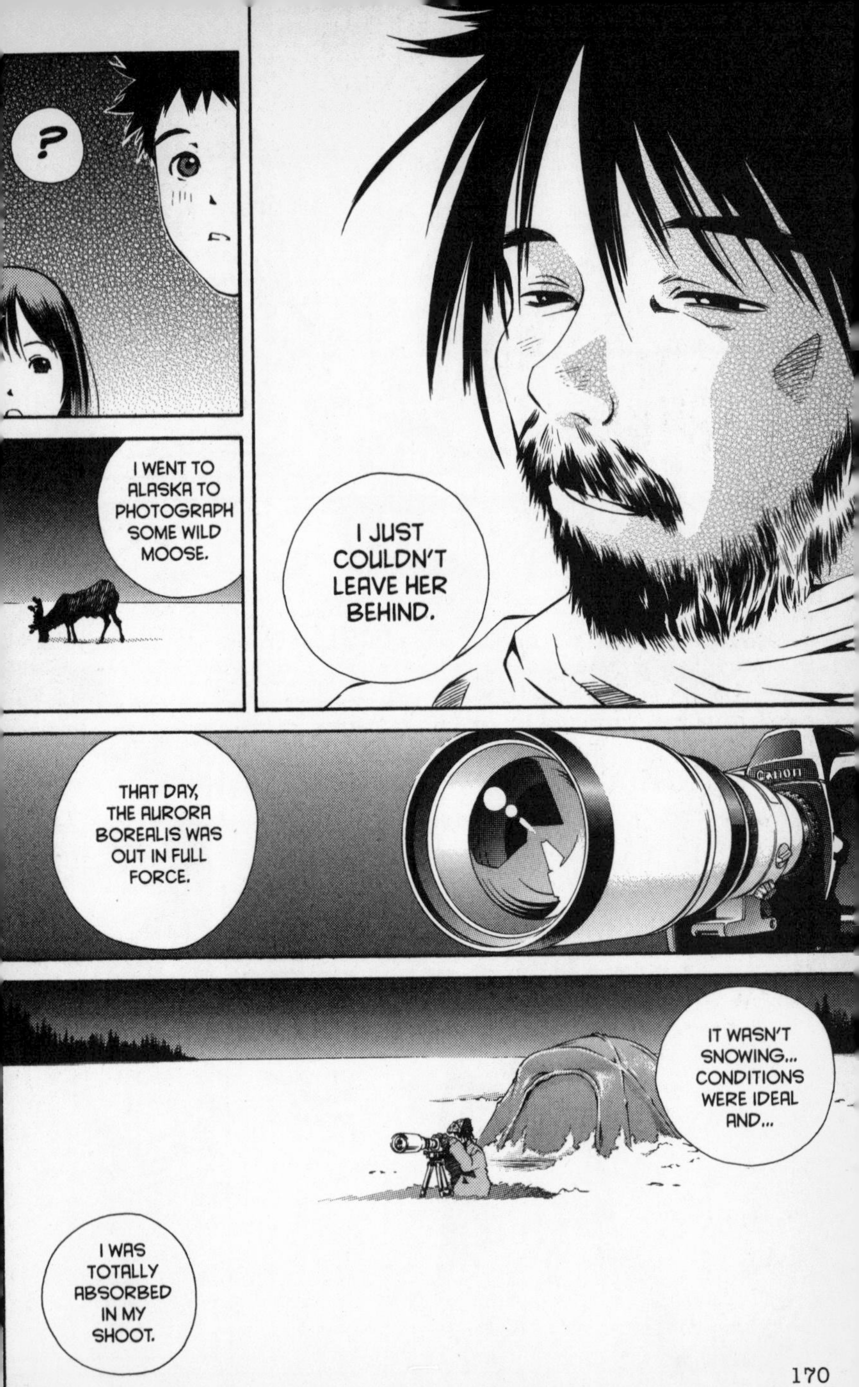
I JUST COULDN'T LEAVE HER BEHIND.
?
I WENT TO ALASKA TO PHOTOGRAPH SOME WILD MOOSE.
THAT DAY, THE AURORA BOREALIS WAS OUT IN FULL FORCE.
IT WASN'T SNOWING... CONDITIONS WERE IDEAL AND...
I WAS TOTALLY ABSORBED IN MY SHOOT.

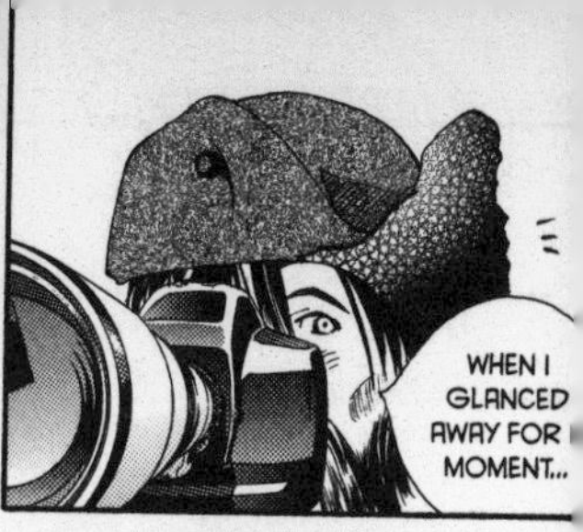
WHEN I GLANCED AWAY FOR MOMENT...
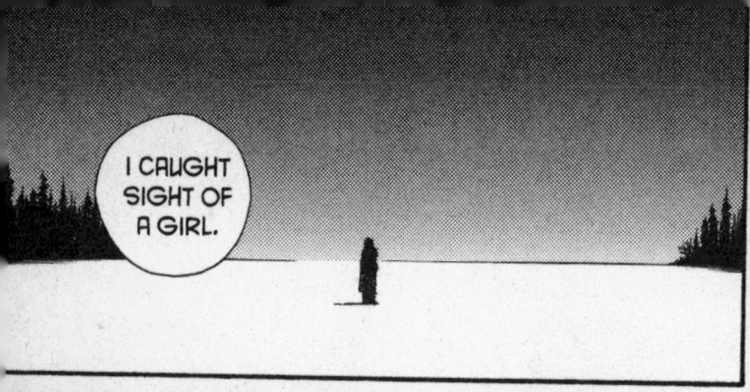
I CAUGHT SIGHT OF A GIRL.
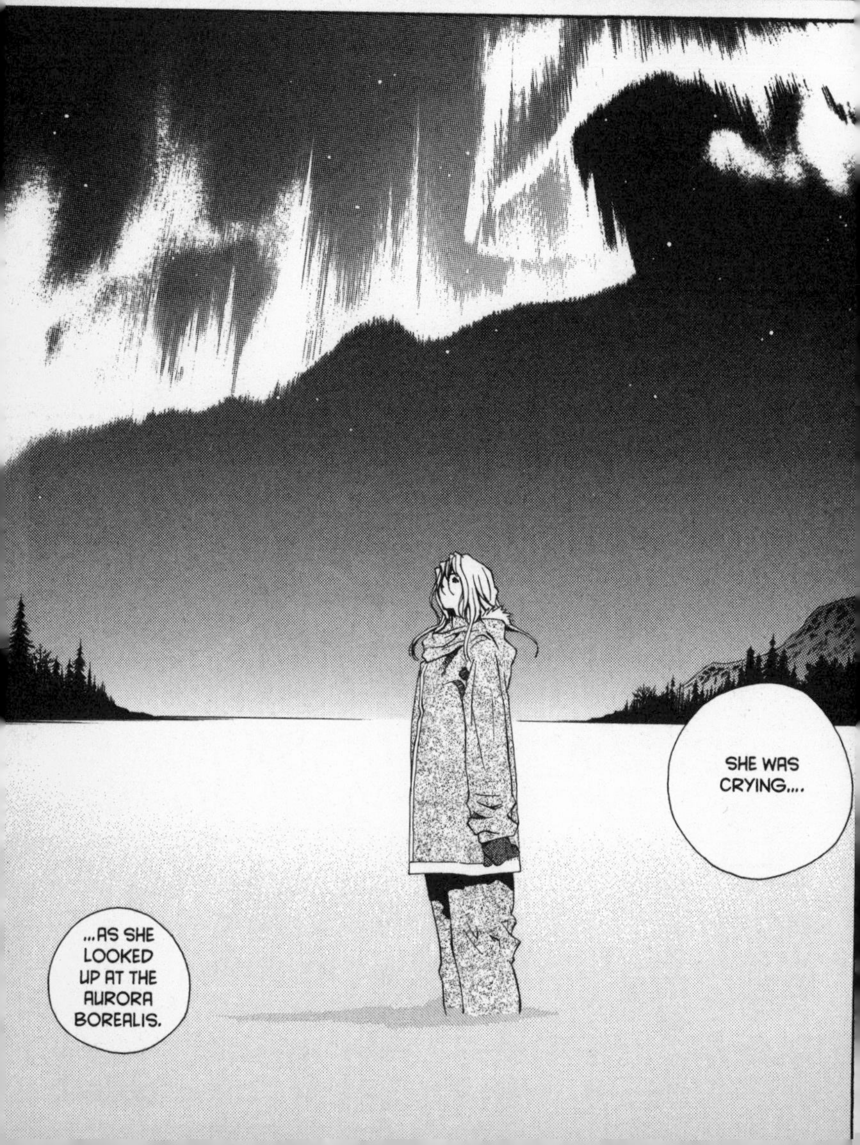
SHE WAS CRYING....
...AS SHE LOOKED UP AT THE AURORA BOREALIS.

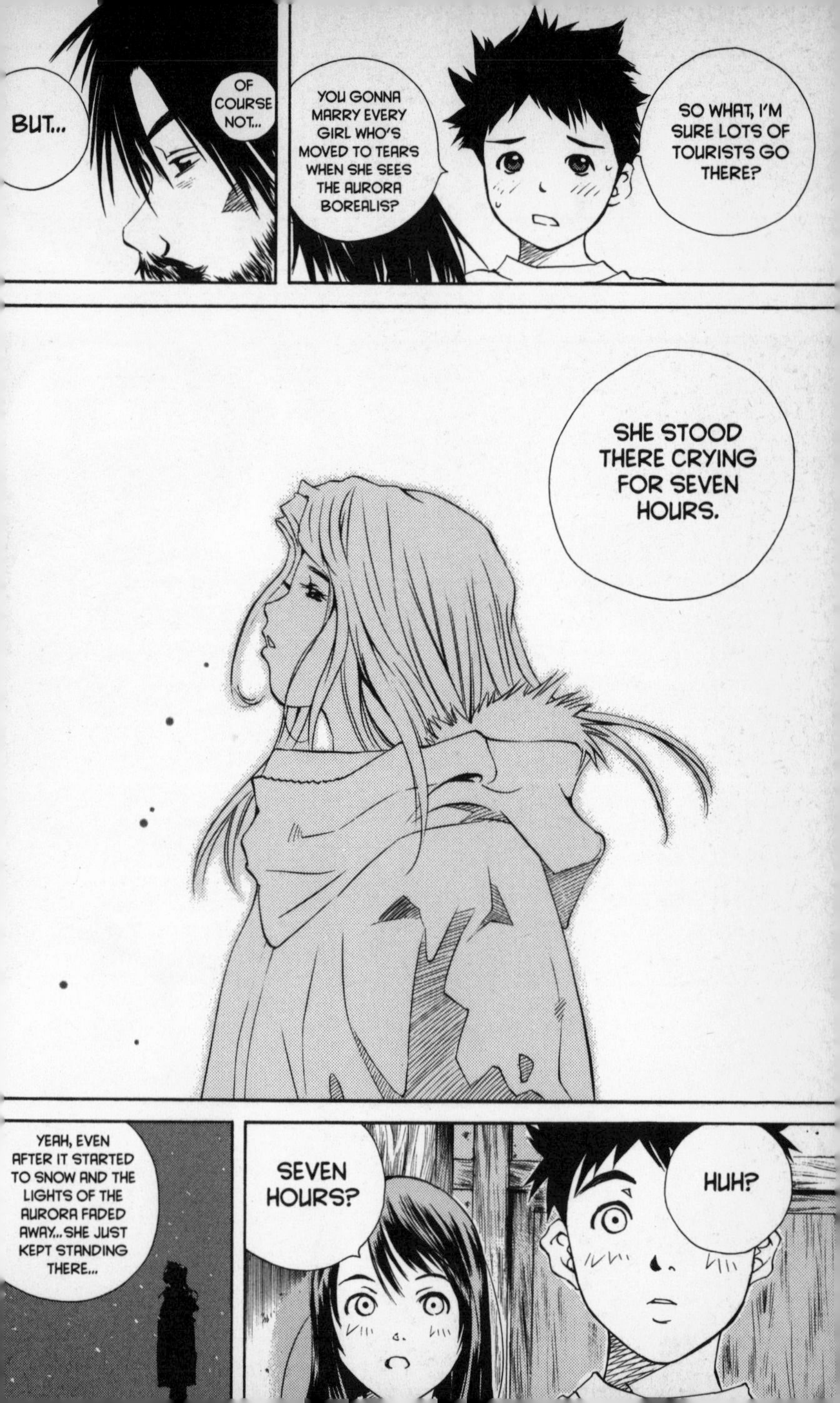
SO WHAT, I'M SURE LOTS OF TOURISTS GO THERE?
YOU GONNA MARRY EVERY GIRL WHO'S MOVED TO TEARS WHEN SHE SEES THE AURORA BOREALIS?
OF COURSE NOT...
BUT...
SHE STOOD THERE CRYING FOR SEVEN HOURS.
HUH?
SEVEN HOURS?
YEAH, EVEN AFTER IT STARTED TO SNOW AND THE LIGHTS OF THE AURORA FADED AWAY...SHE JUST KEPT STANDING THERE...

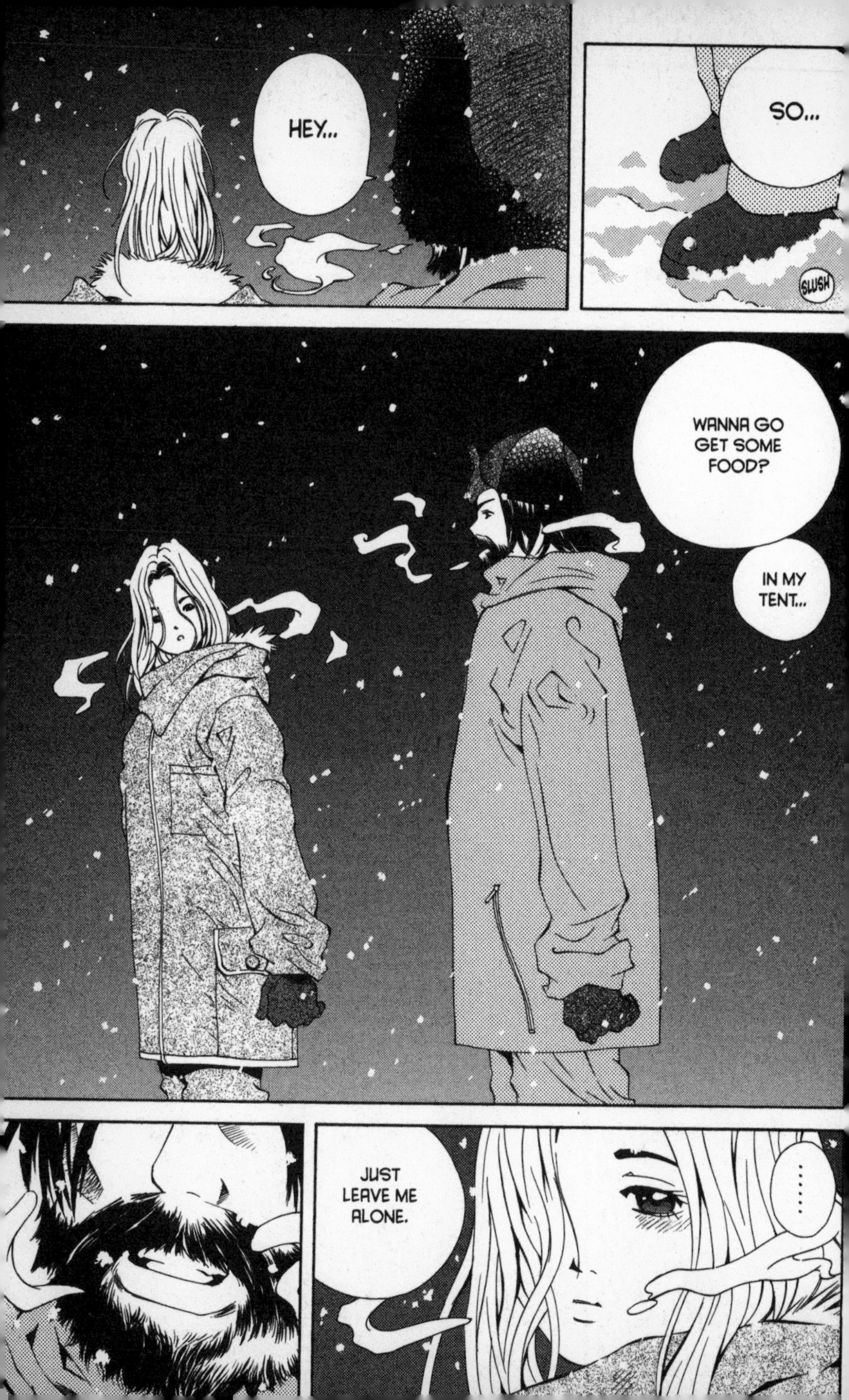
SO...
SLUSH
HEY...
WANNA GO GET SOME FOOD?
IN MY TENT...
......
JUST LEAVE ME ALONE.

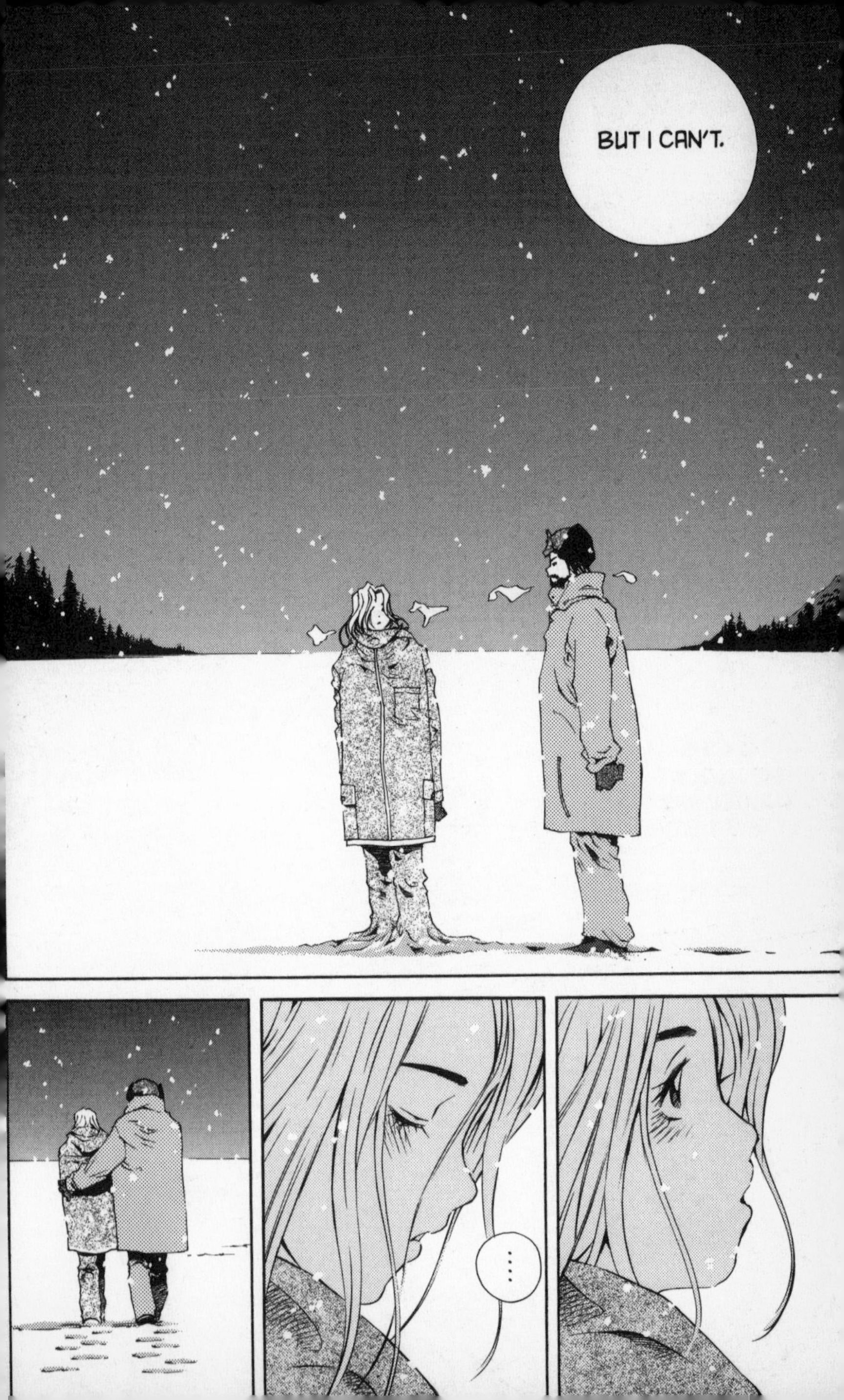
BUT I CAN'T.
....

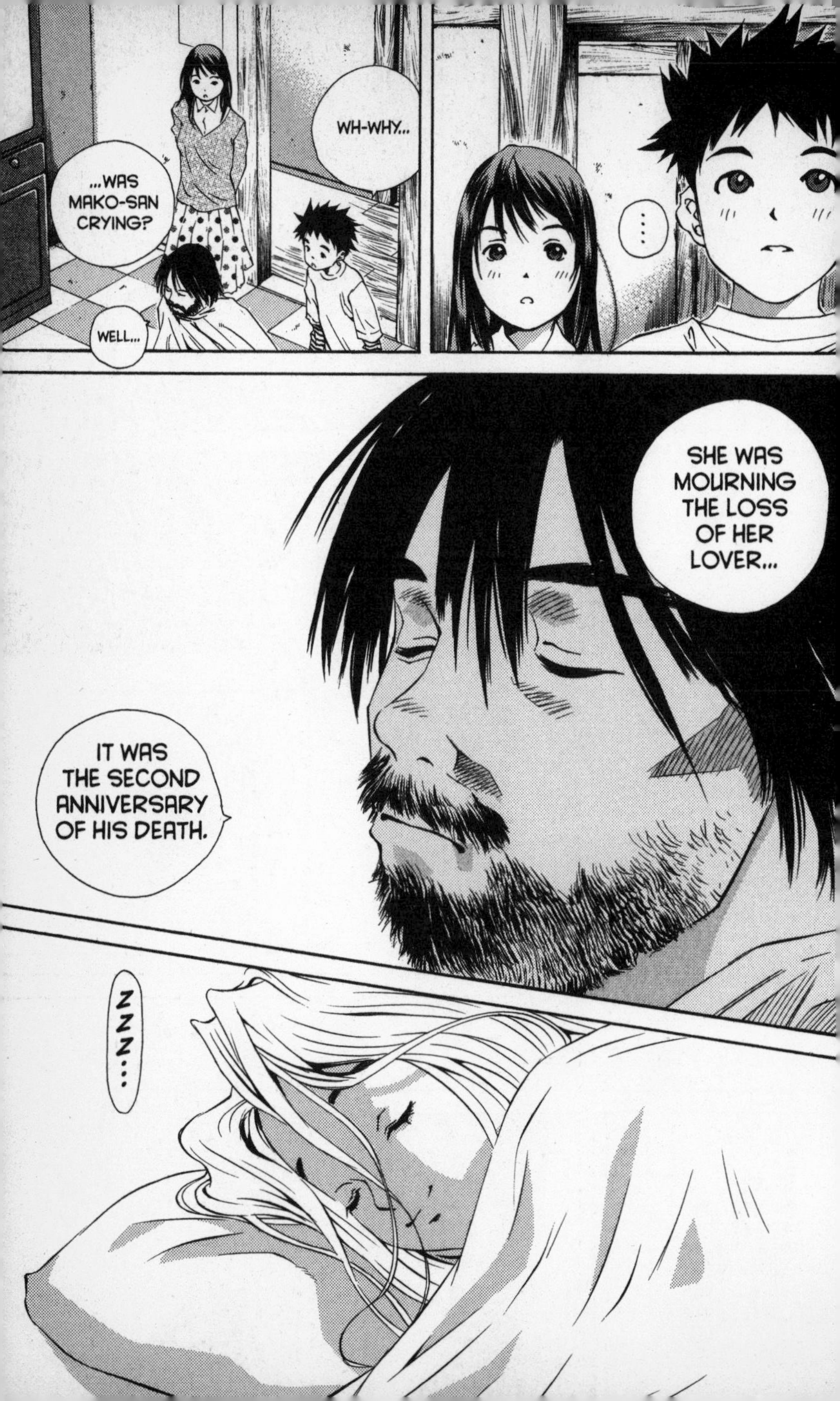
.....
WH-WHY...
...WAS MAKO-SAN CRYING?
WELL...
SHE WAS MOURNING THE LOSS OF HER LOVER...
IT WAS THE SECOND ANNIVERSARY OF HIS DEATH.
ZZZ...

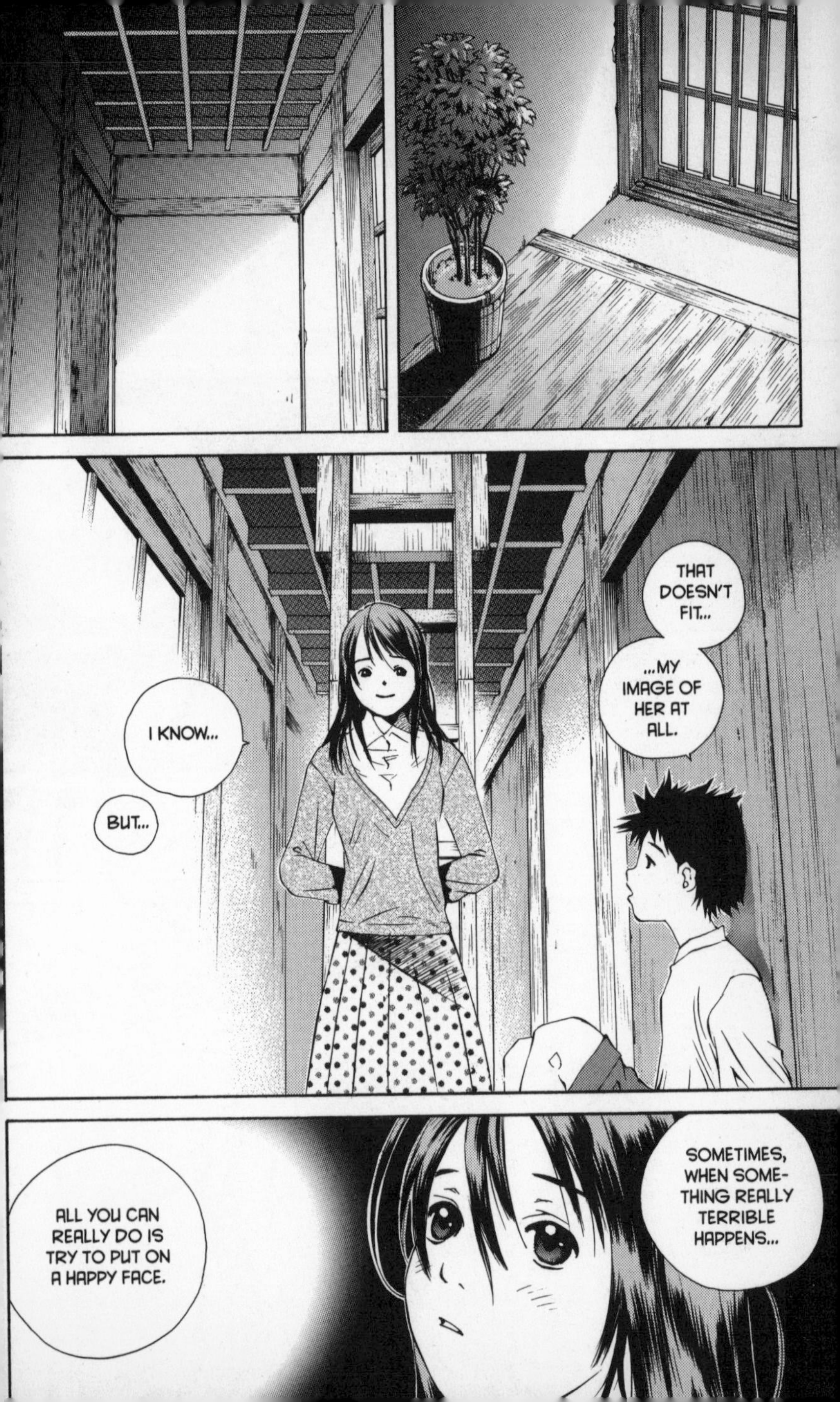
THAT DOESN'T FIT...
...MY IMAGE OF HER AT ALL.
I KNOW...
BUT...
SOMETIMES, WHEN SOME-THING REALLY TERRIBLE HAPPENS...
ALL YOU CAN REALLY DO IS TRY TO PUT ON A HAPPY FACE.

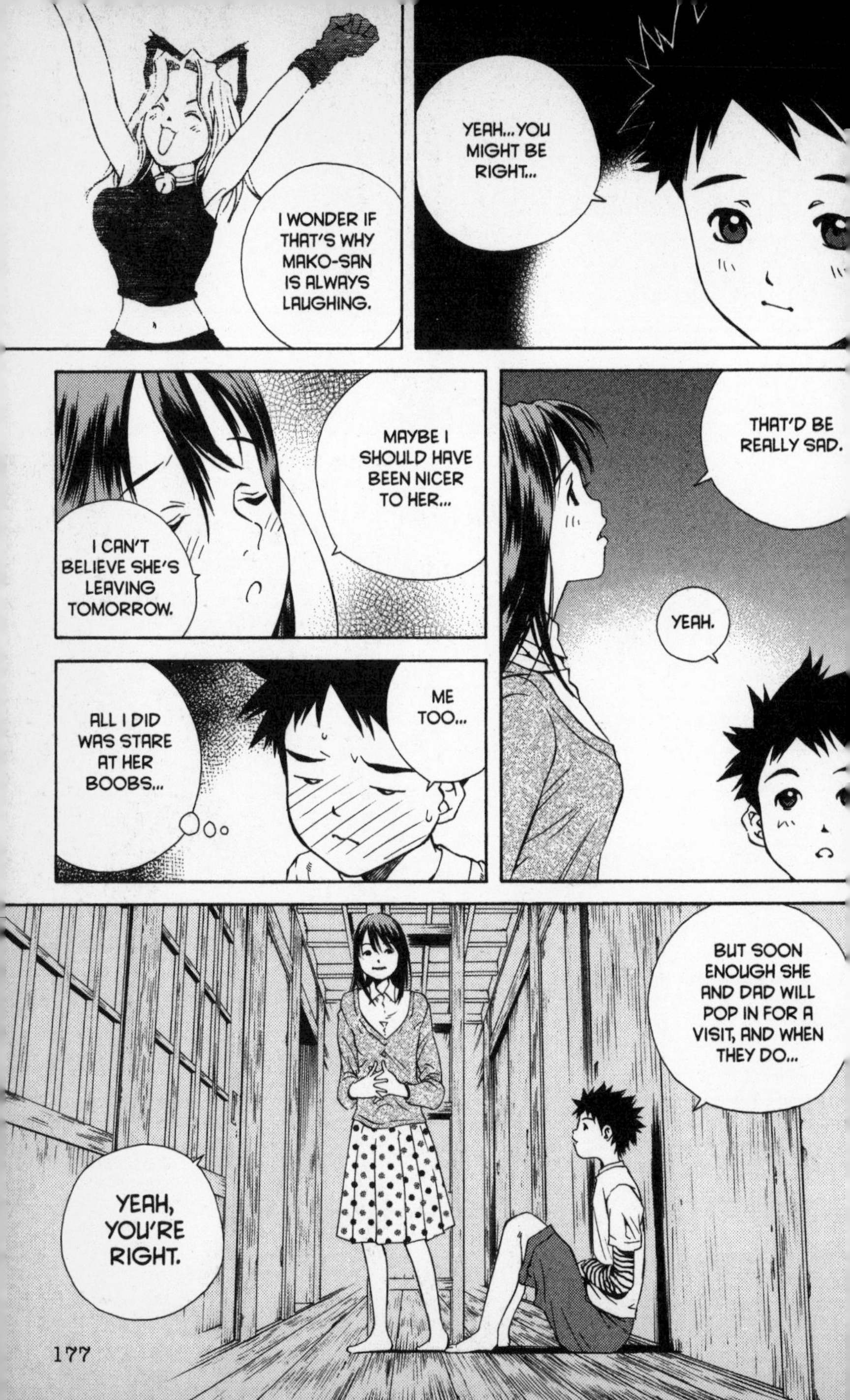
YEAH...YOU MIGHT BE RIGHT...
I WONDER IF THAT'S WHY MAKO-SAN IS ALWAYS LAUGHING.
THAT'D BE REALLY SAD.
YEAH.
MAYBE I SHOULD HAVE BEEN NICER TO HER...
I CAN'T BELIEVE SHE'S LEAVING TOMORROW.
ME TOO...
ALL I DID WAS STARE AT HER BOOBS...
BUT SOON ENOUGH SHE AND DAD WILL POP IN FOR A VISIT, AND WHEN THEY DO...
YEAH, YOU'RE RIGHT.

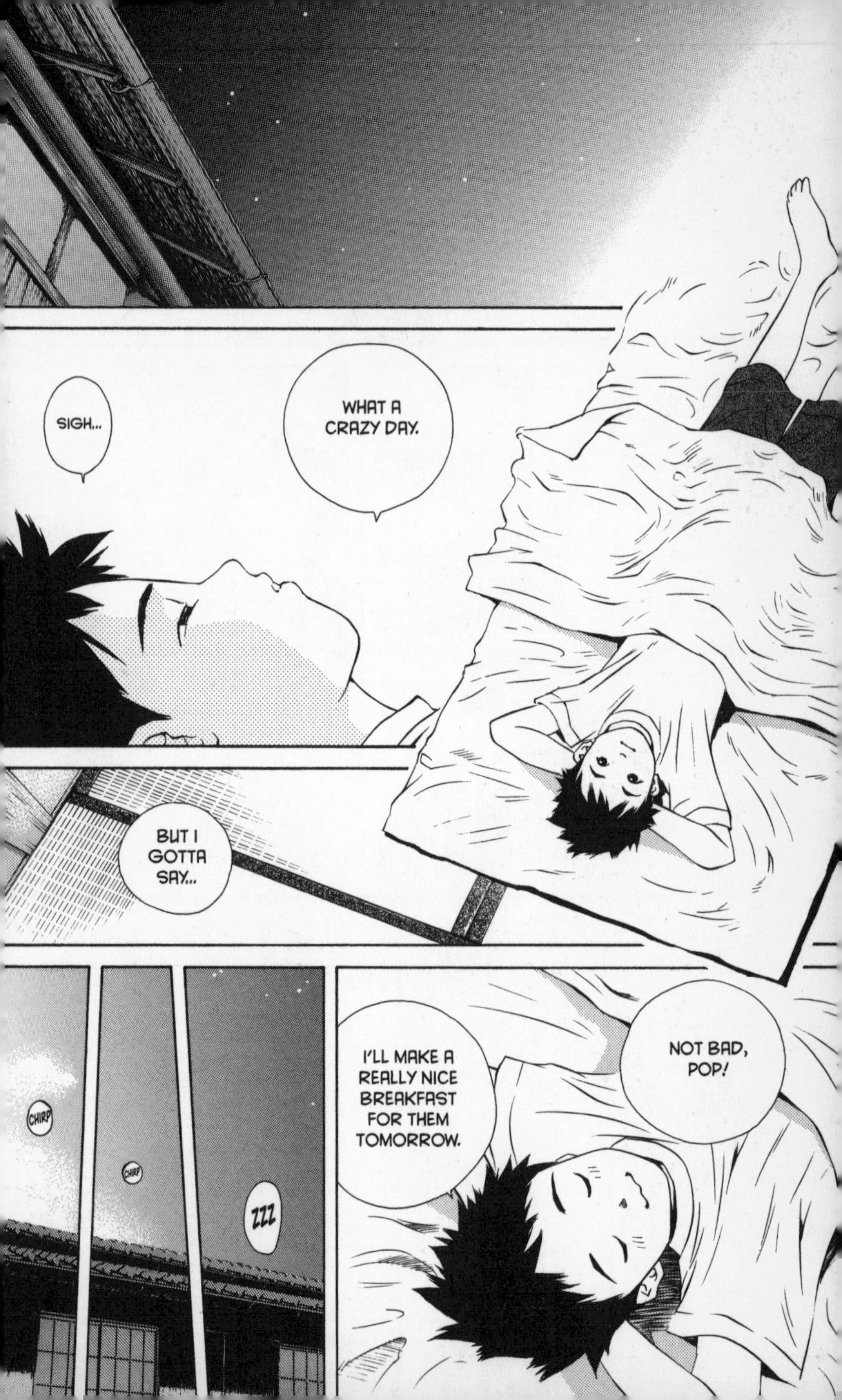
WHAT A CRAZY DAY.
SIGH...
BUT I GOTTA SAY...
NOT BAD, POP!
I'LL MAKE A REALLY NICE BREAKFAST FOR THEM TOMORROW.
CHIRP
CHIRP
ZZZ

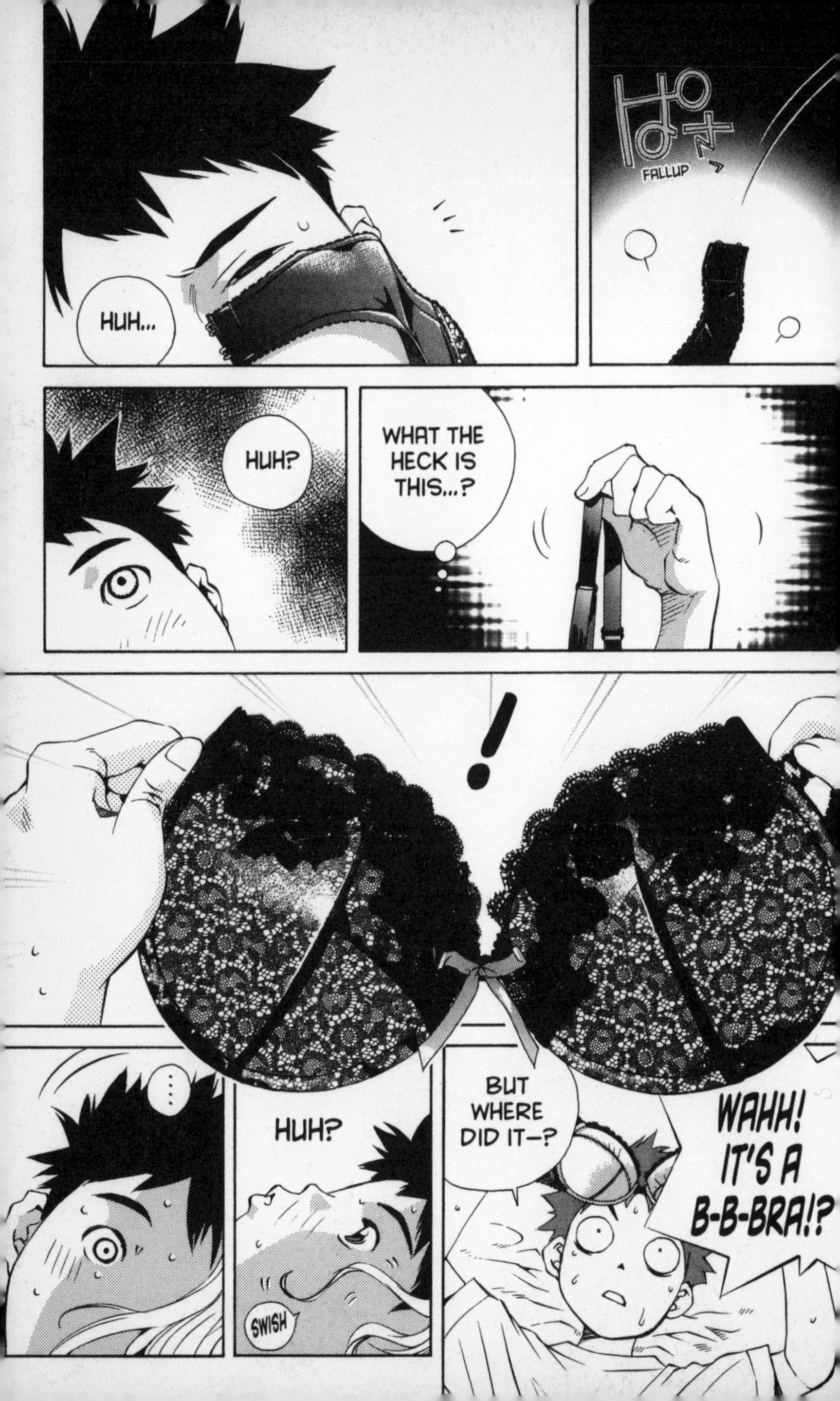
ぱさ
FALLUP
HUH...
WHAT THE HECK IS THIS...?
HUH?
!
WAHH! IT'S A B-B-BRA!?
BUT WHERE DID IT—?
HUH?
SWISH
....

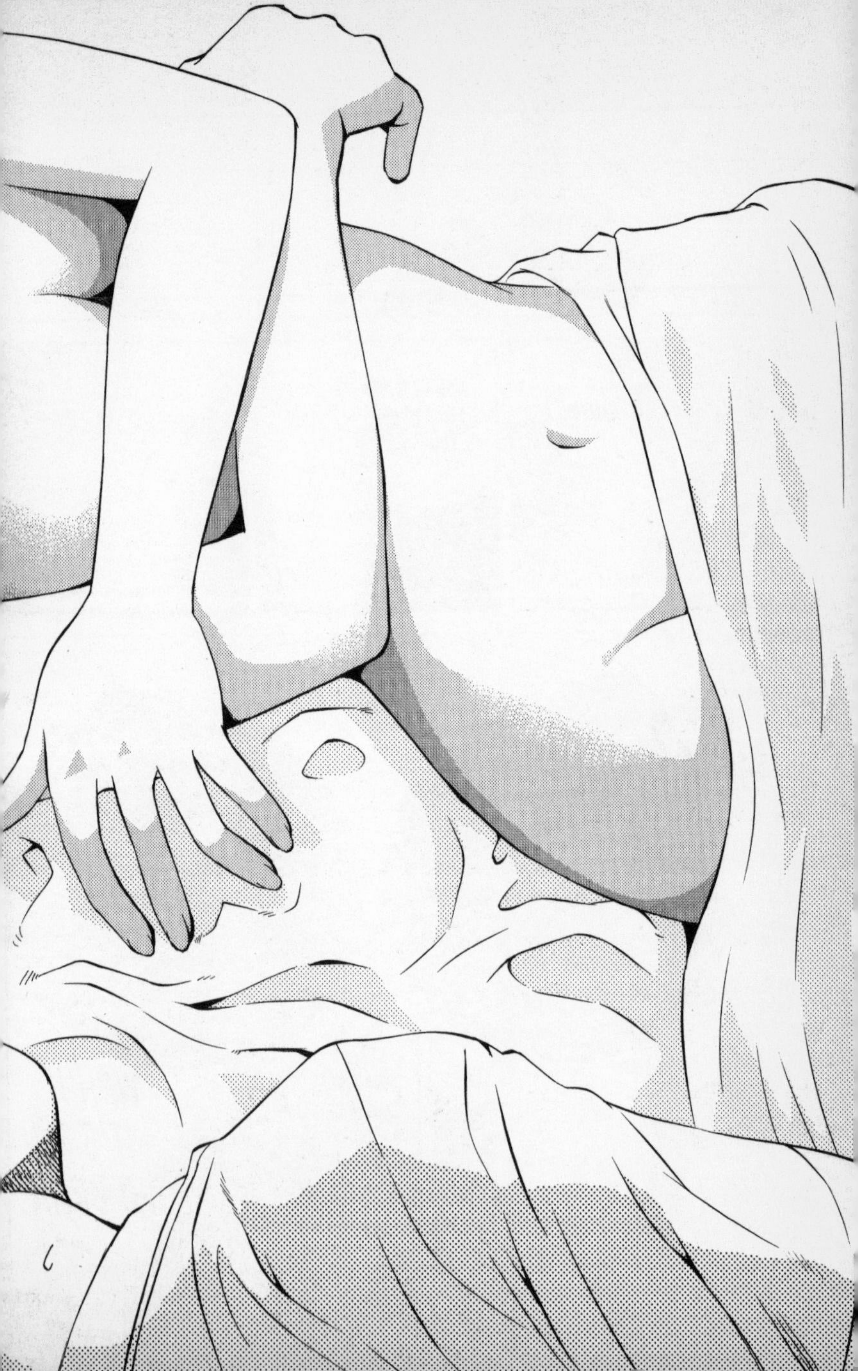

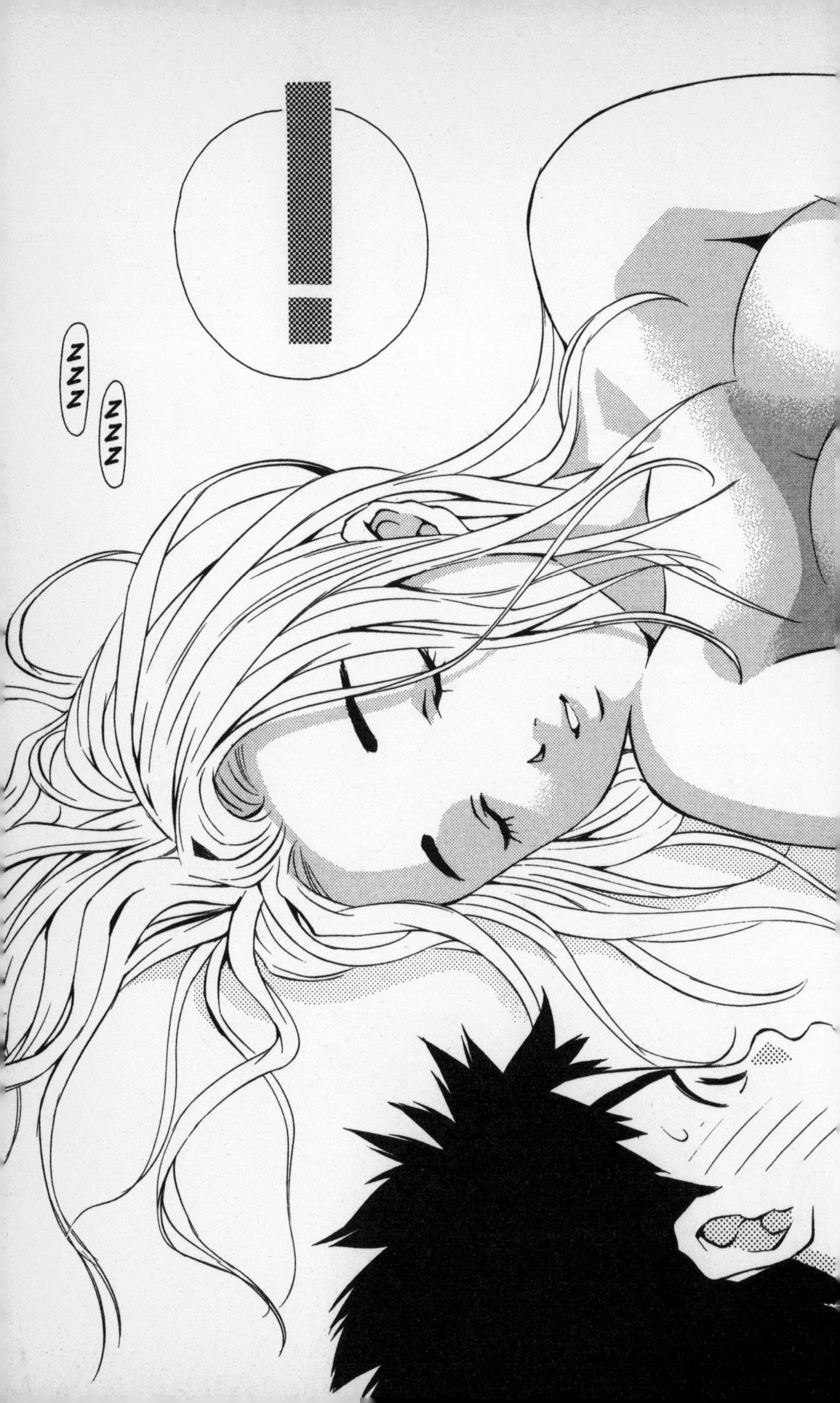
!
NNN
NNN

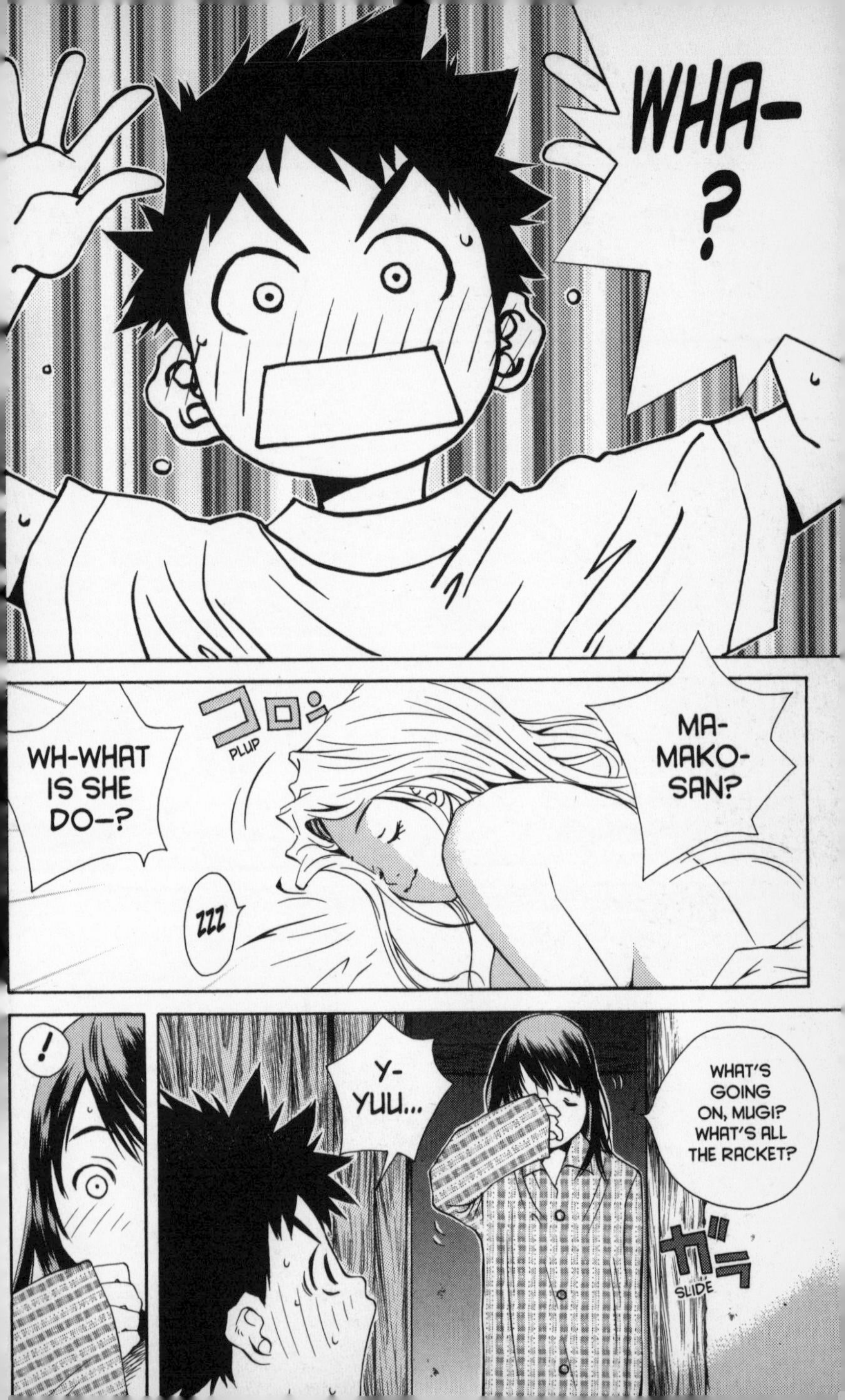

WHA-?
MA-MAKO-SAN?
PLUP
WH-WHAT IS SHE DO-?
ZZZ
WHAT'S GOING ON, MUGI? WHAT'S ALL THE RACKET?
SLIDE
Y-YUU...
!

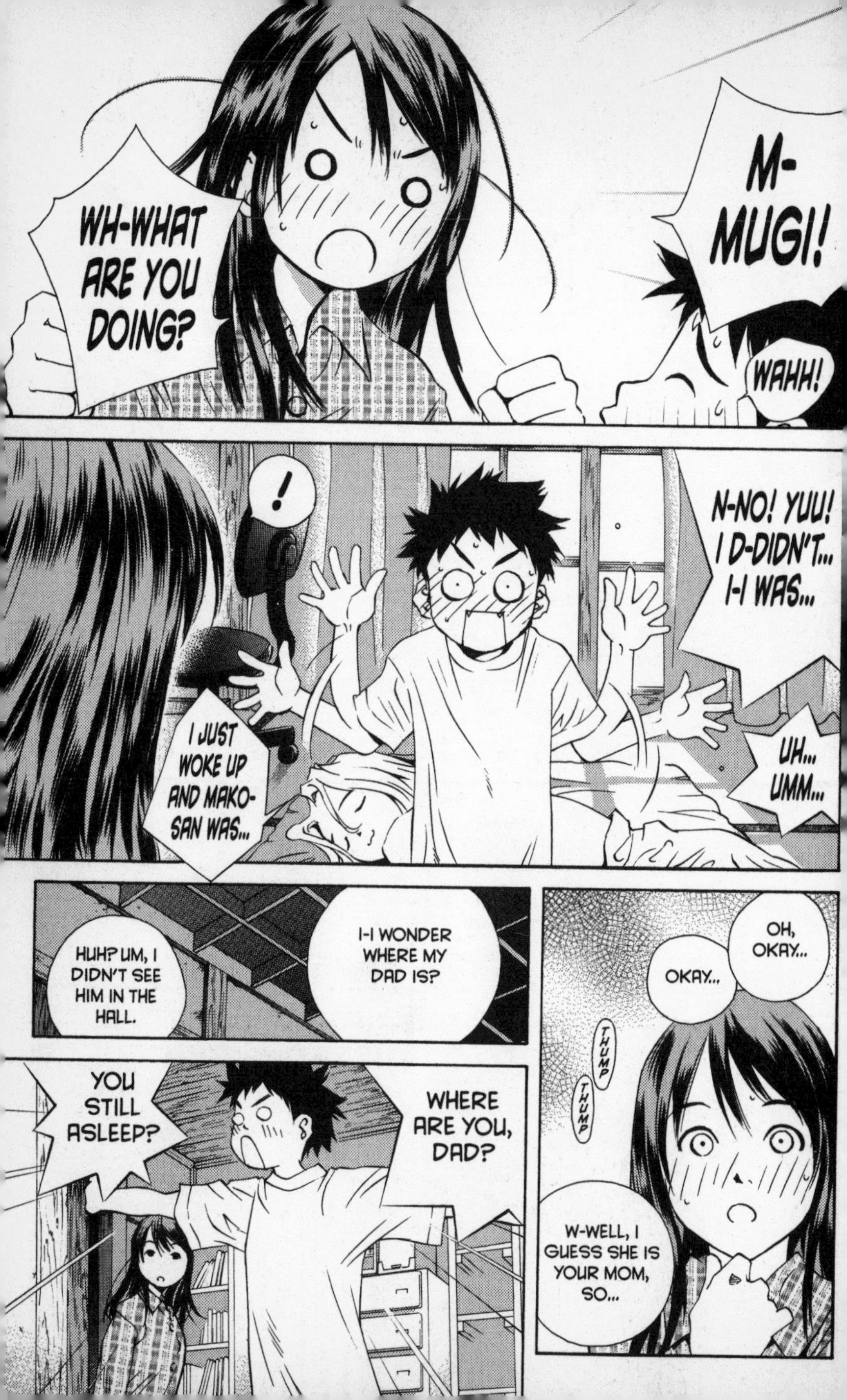
M-MUGI!
WH-WHAT ARE YOU DOING?
WAHH!
N-NO! YUU! I D-DIDN'T... I-I WAS...
!
UH... UMM...
I JUST WOKE UP AND MAKO-SAN WAS...
OH, OKAY...
OKAY...
THUMP
THUMP
W-WELL, I GUESS SHE IS YOUR MOM, SO...
I-I WONDER WHERE MY DAD IS?
HUH? UM, I DIDN'T SEE HIM IN THE HALL.
WHERE ARE YOU, DAD?
YOU STILL ASLEEP?

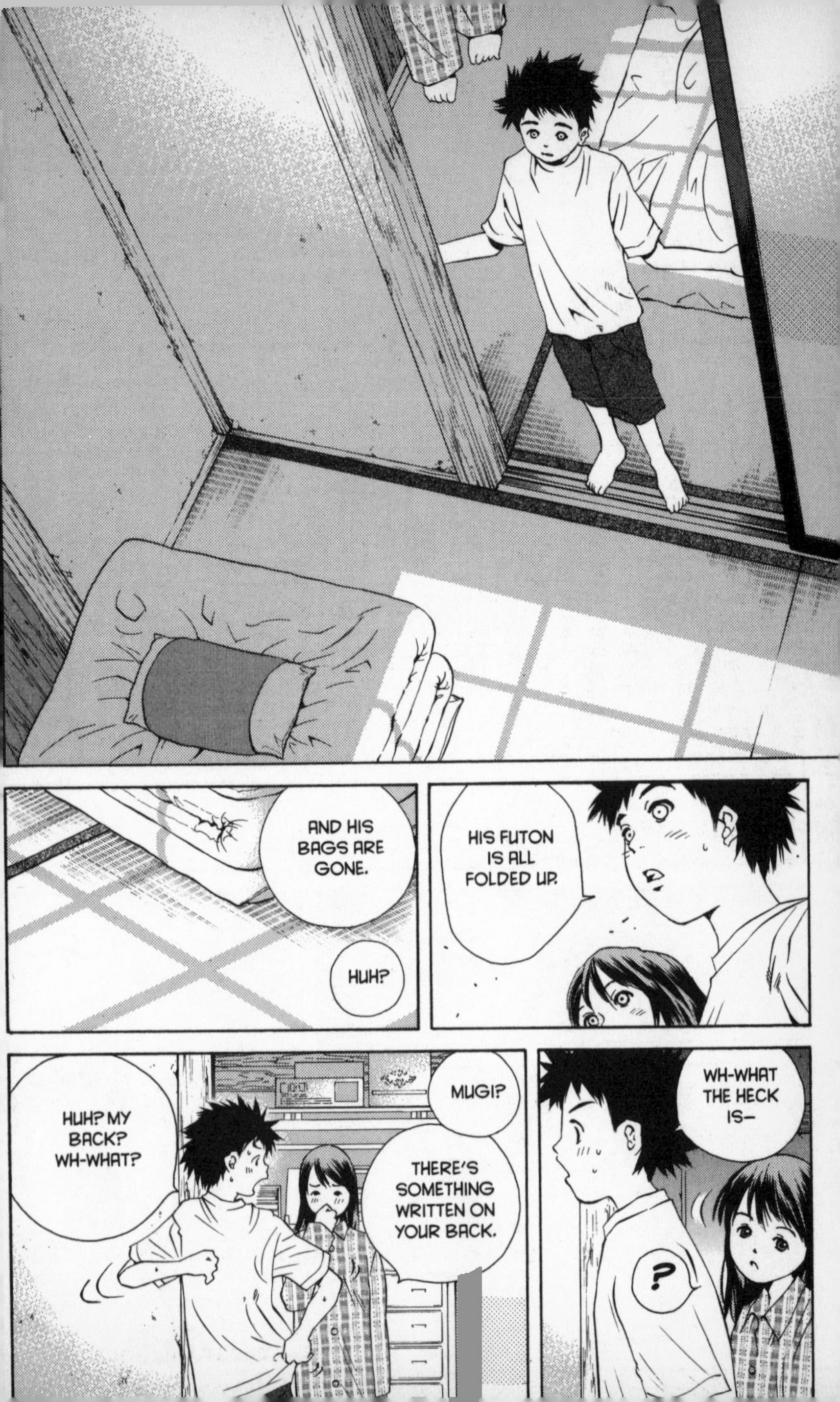
HIS FUTON IS ALL FOLDED UP.
AND HIS BAGS ARE GONE.
HUH?
WH-WHAT THE HECK IS—
?
MUGI?
THERE'S SOMETHING WRITTEN ON YOUR BACK.
HUH? MY BACK? WH-WHAT?

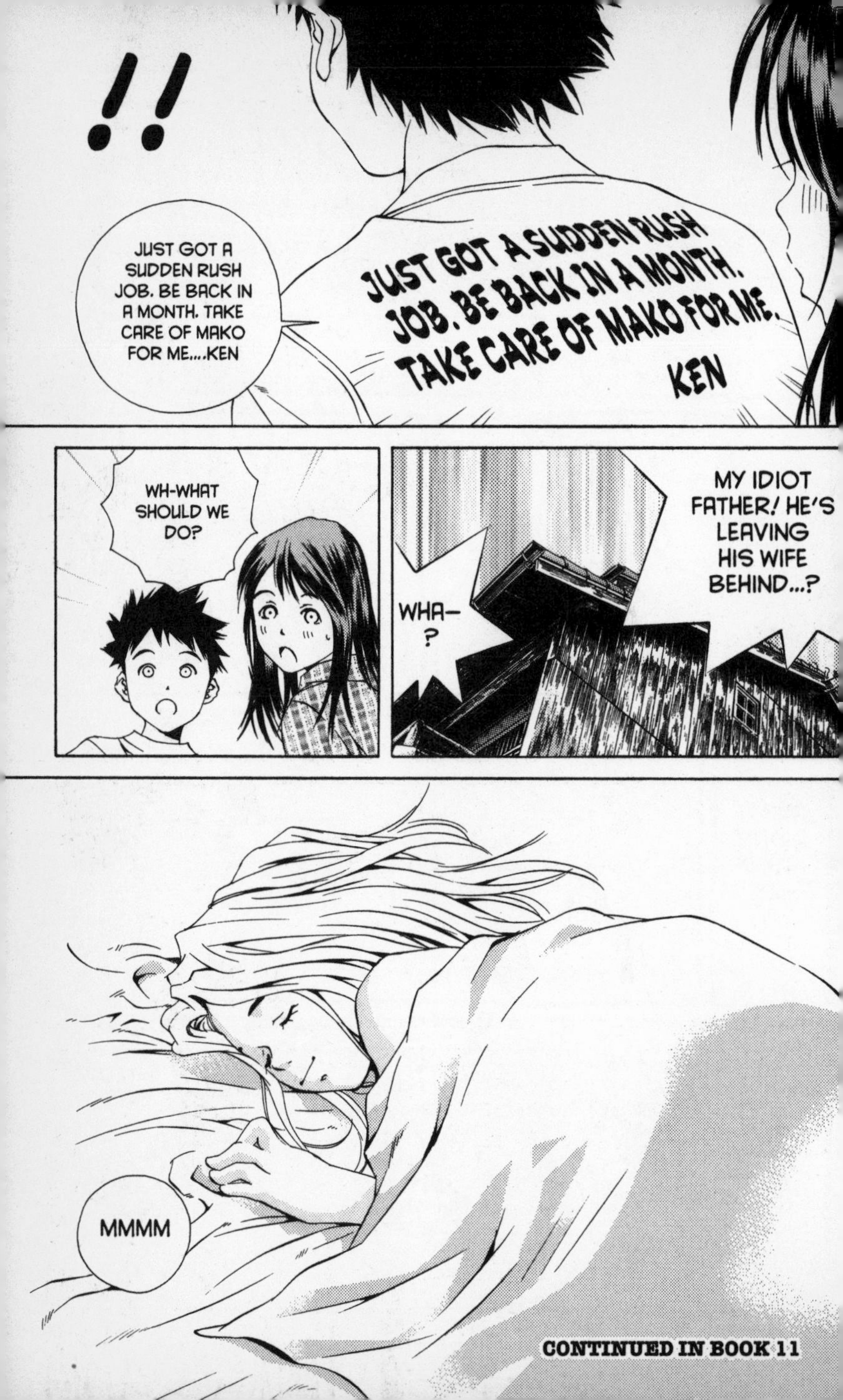
!!
JUST GOT A SUDDEN RUSH JOB. BE BACK IN A MONTH. TAKE CARE OF MAKO FOR ME. KEN
JUST GOT A SUDDEN RUSH JOB. BE BACK IN A MONTH. TAKE CARE OF MAKO FOR ME....KEN
MY IDIOT FATHER! HE'S LEAVING HIS WIFE BEHIND...?
WHA- ?
WH-WHAT SHOULD WE DO?
MMMM

CONTINUED IN BOOK 11

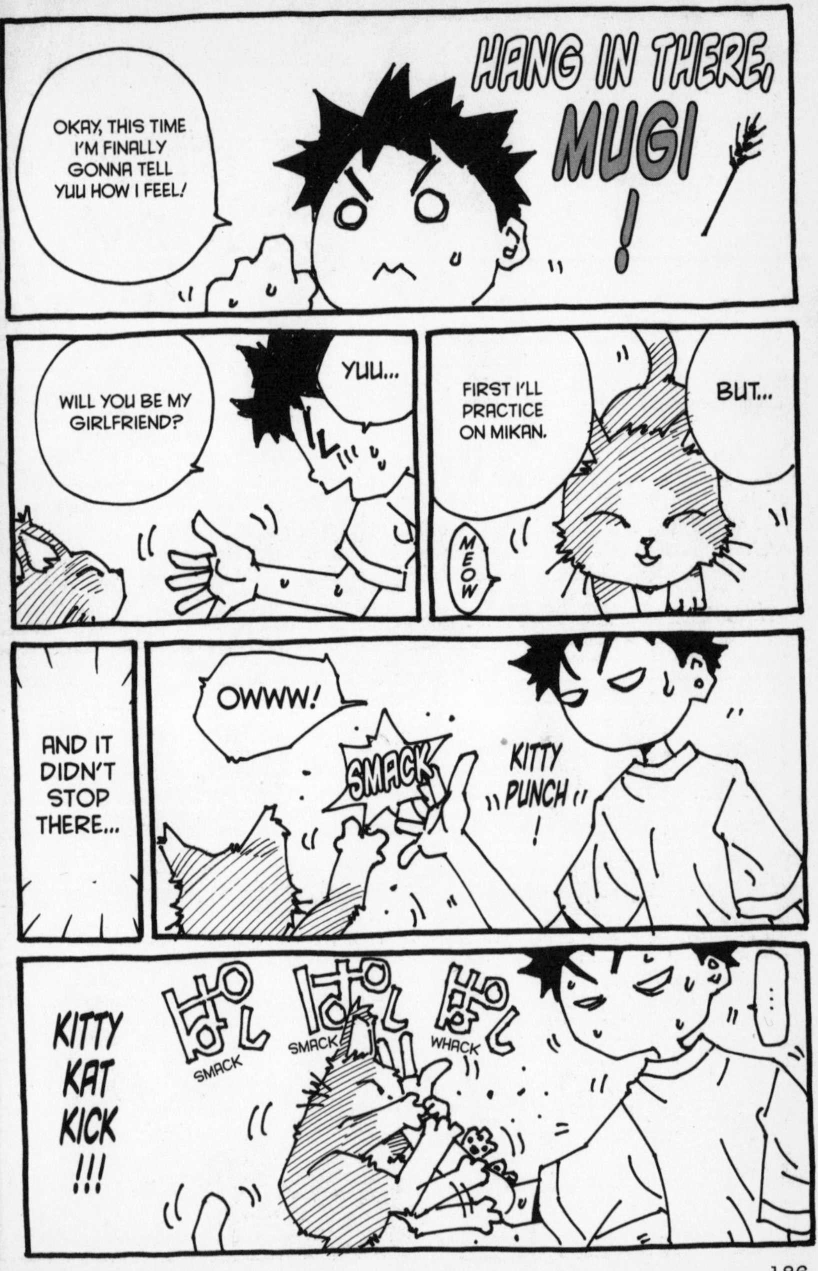
HANG IN THERE, MUGI!
OKAY, THIS TIME I'M FINALLY GONNA TELL YUU HOW I FEEL!
BUT...
FIRST I'LL PRACTICE ON MIKAN.
MEOW
YUU...
WILL YOU BE MY GIRLFRIEND?
KITTY PUNCH!
SMACK
OWWW!
AND IT DIDN'T STOP THERE...
...
WHACK
SMACK
SMACK
KITTY KAT KICK!!!

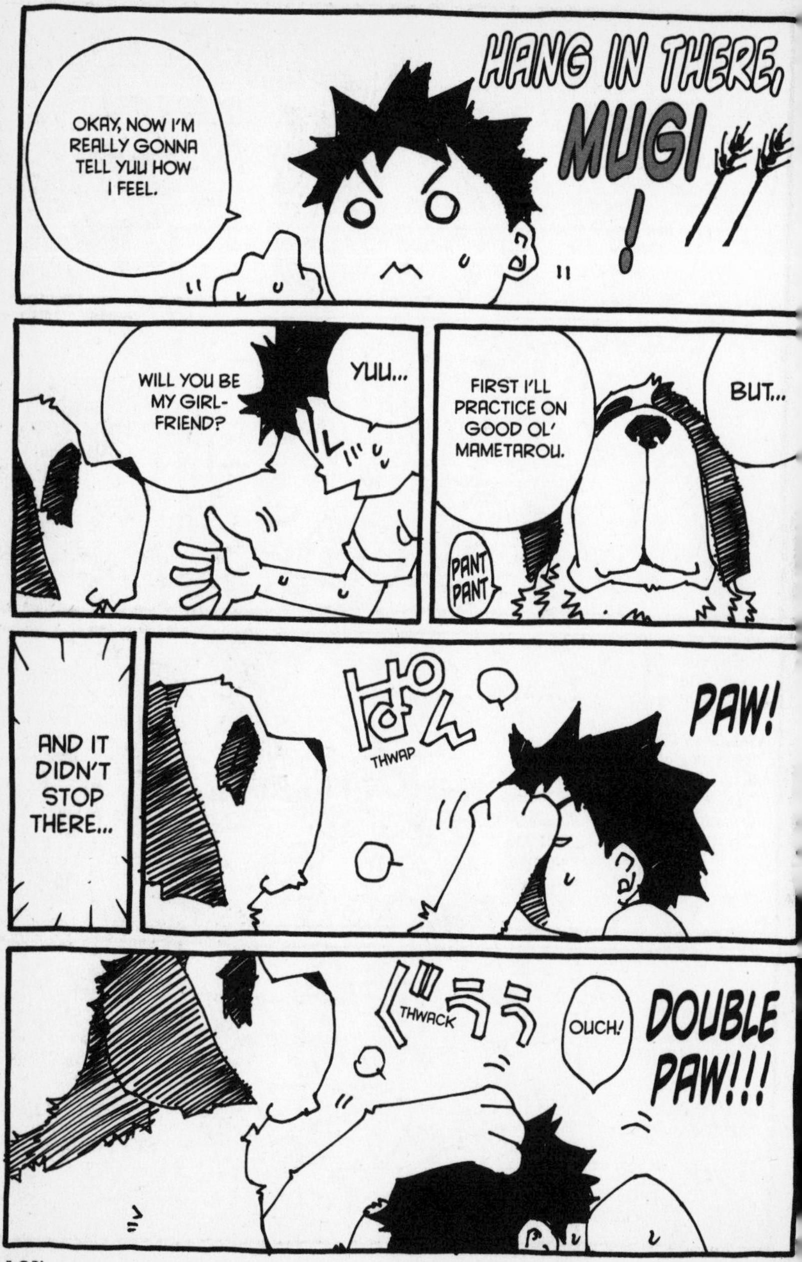
HANG IN THERE, MUGI!
OKAY, NOW I'M REALLY GONNA TELL YUU HOW I FEEL.
BUT...
FIRST I'LL PRACTICE ON GOOD OL' MAMETAROU.
PANT PANT
YUU...
WILL YOU BE MY GIRL-FRIEND?
PAW!
ぱん
THWAP
AND IT DIDN'T STOP THERE...
DOUBLE PAW!!!
OUCH!
ぐうう
THWACK

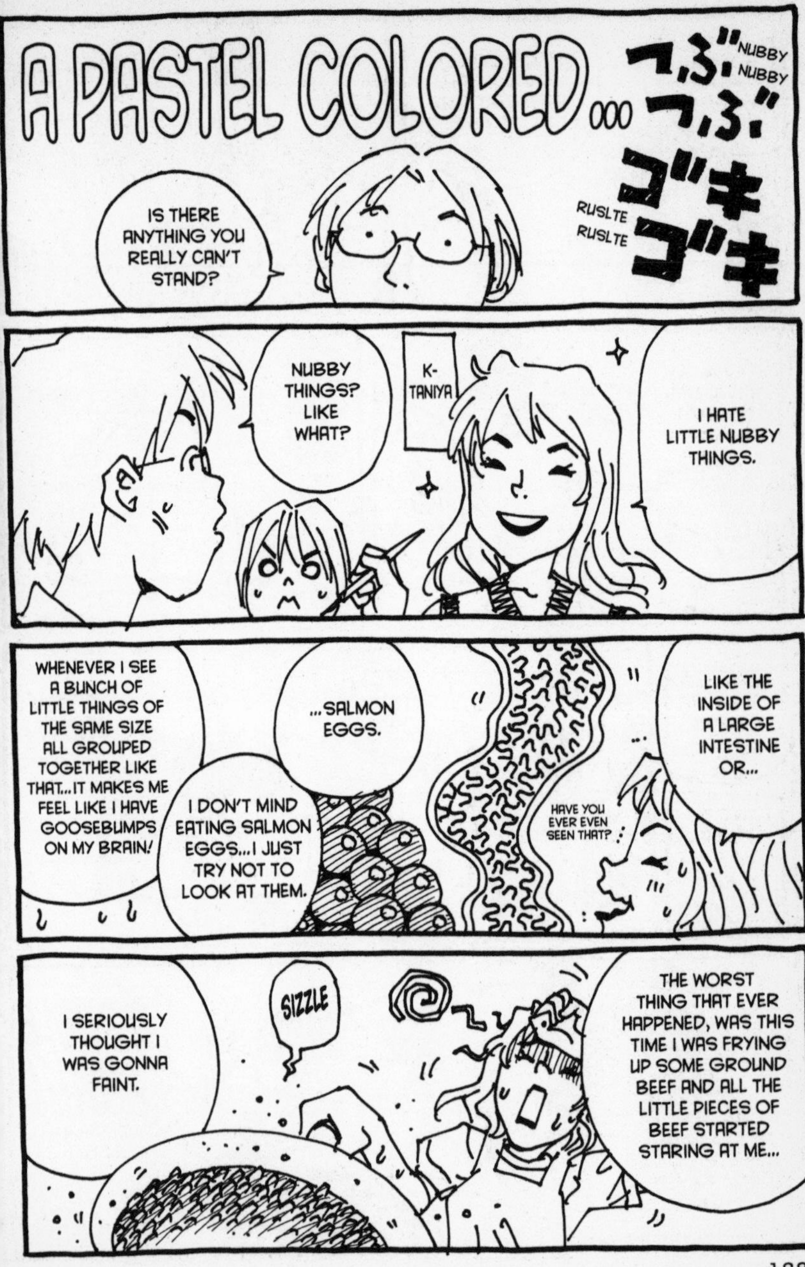
つぶつぶ NUBBY NUBBY
A PASTEL COLORED...
ゴキゴキ RUSLTE RUSLTE
IS THERE ANYTHING YOU REALLY CAN'T STAND?
I HATE LITTLE NUBBY THINGS.
K-TANIYA
NUBBY THINGS? LIKE WHAT?
LIKE THE INSIDE OF A LARGE INTESTINE OR...
HAVE YOU EVER EVEN SEEN THAT?
...SALMON EGGS.
WHENEVER I SEE A BUNCH OF LITTLE THINGS OF THE SAME SIZE ALL GROUPED TOGETHER LIKE THAT...IT MAKES ME FEEL LIKE I HAVE GOOSEBUMPS ON MY BRAIN!
I DON'T MIND EATING SALMON EGGS...I JUST TRY NOT TO LOOK AT THEM.
THE WORST THING THAT EVER HAPPENED, WAS THIS TIME I WAS FRYING UP SOME GROUND BEEF AND ALL THE LITTLE PIECES OF BEEF STARTED STARING AT ME...
SIZZLE
I SERIOUSLY THOUGHT I WAS GONNA FAINT.

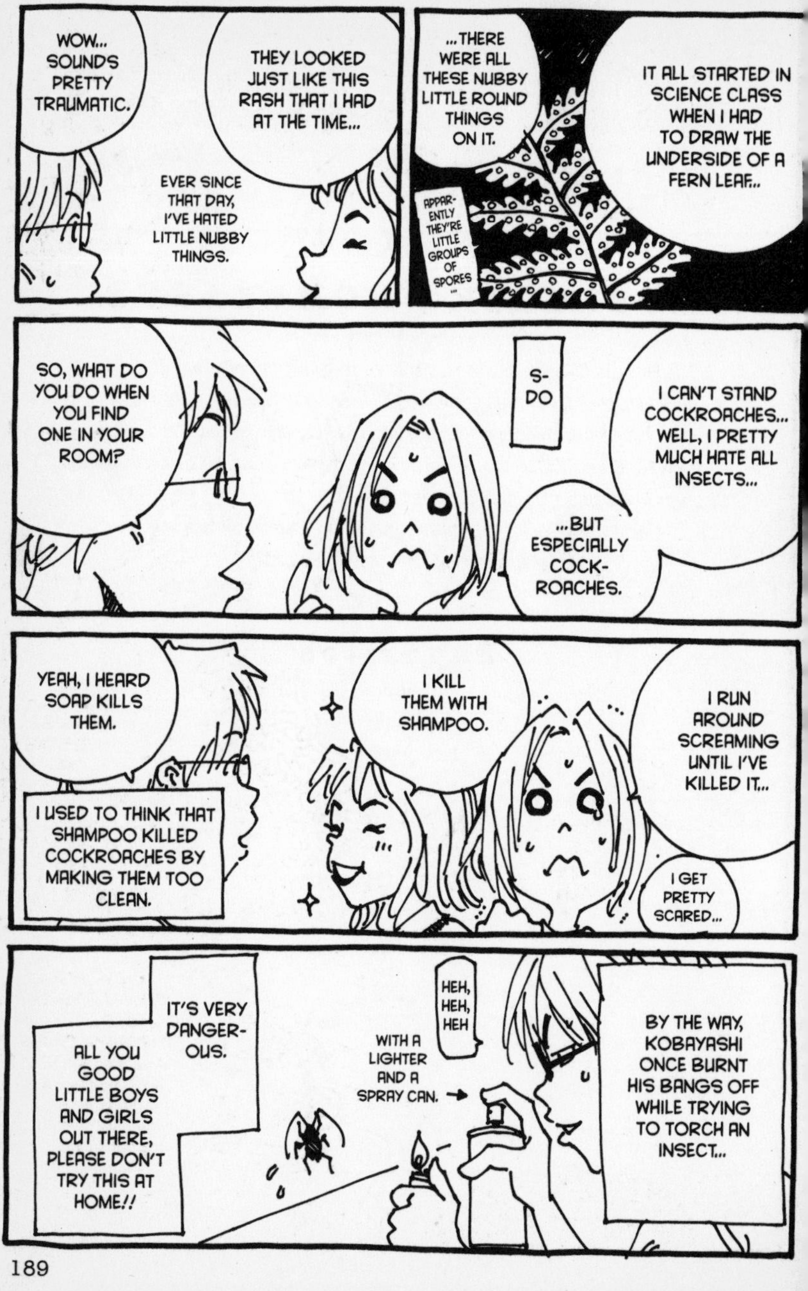
IT ALL STARTED IN SCIENCE CLASS WHEN I HAD TO DRAW THE UNDERSIDE OF A FERN LEAF...
...THERE WERE ALL THESE NUBBY LITTLE ROUND THINGS ON IT.
APPARENTLY THEY'RE LITTLE GROUPS OF SPORES...
THEY LOOKED JUST LIKE THIS RASH THAT I HAD AT THE TIME...
EVER SINCE THAT DAY, I'VE HATED LITTLE NUBBY THINGS.
WOW... SOUNDS PRETTY TRAUMATIC.
I CAN'T STAND COCKROACHES... WELL, I PRETTY MUCH HATE ALL INSECTS...
...BUT ESPECIALLY COCK-ROACHES.
S-DO
SO, WHAT DO YOU DO WHEN YOU FIND ONE IN YOUR ROOM?
I RUN AROUND SCREAMING UNTIL I'VE KILLED IT...
I GET PRETTY SCARED...
I KILL THEM WITH SHAMPOO.
YEAH, I HEARD SOAP KILLS THEM.
I USED TO THINK THAT SHAMPOO KILLED COCKROACHES BY MAKING THEM TOO CLEAN.
BY THE WAY, KOBAYASHI ONCE BURNT HIS BANGS OFF WHILE TRYING TO TORCH AN INSECT...
HEH, HEH, HEH
WITH A LIGHTER AND A SPRAY CAN.
IT'S VERY DANGER-OUS.
ALL YOU GOOD LITTLE BOYS AND GIRLS OUT THERE, PLEASE DON'T TRY THIS AT HOME!!

TOSHIHIKO KOBAYASHI

Born in Mihara city in Hiroshima. Birthday is February 25.
In 1995, *Half Coat* was serialized in *Magazine Special* from No. 1
to No. 11. After the serial publication of *Parallel* in *Magazine Special*
from No.8 in 2000 to No. 1 in 2002, *Pastel* was serialized in *Weekly
Shonen Magazine* from the 32nd issue in 2002 to the 33rd issue in 2003.
And now *Pastel* has been running as a serial ever since
Magazine Special No. 10 in 2003.

Favorites
Fruit
Sleeping
Hot green tea

Dislikes
Being scolded
Excessive expectations
Cigarette smoke

Translation Notes

Japanese is a tricky language for most Westerners, and translation is often more art than science. For your edification and reading pleasure, here are notes on some of the places where we could have gone in a different direction in our translation of the work, or where a Japanese cultural reference is used.

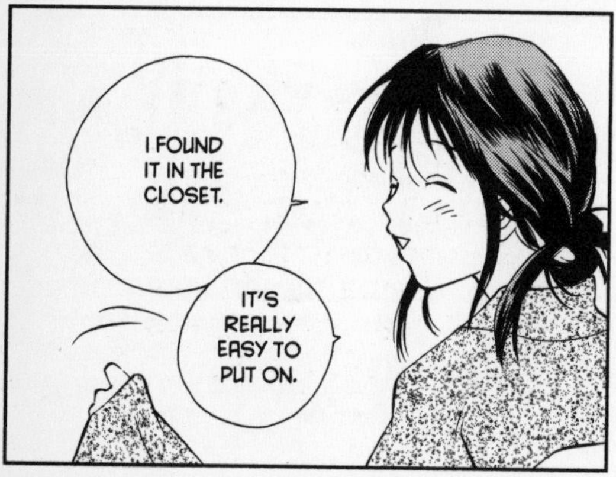
I FOUND IT IN THE CLOSET.
IT'S REALLY EASY TO PUT ON.

"Easy kimono," page 25

Kimonos are notoriously hard to put on, and there is even a field of study devoted to putting on a kimono called *kitsuke*. Wearing a proper kimono often requires hiring a *kitsuke* professional to help out.

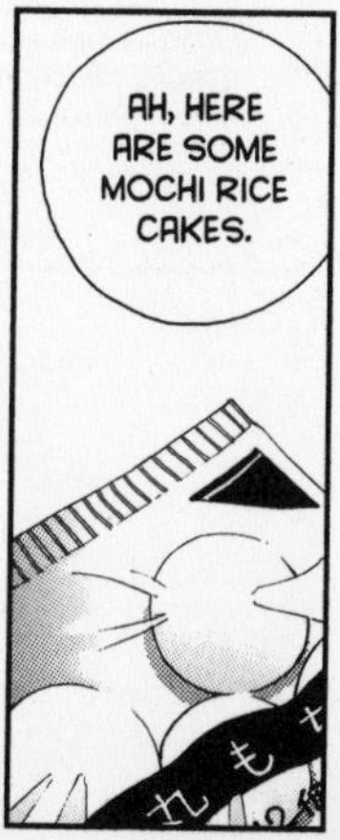
AH, HERE ARE SOME MOCHI RICE CAKES.

Mochi, page 38

Mochi are dense balls or squares made of mashed rice.

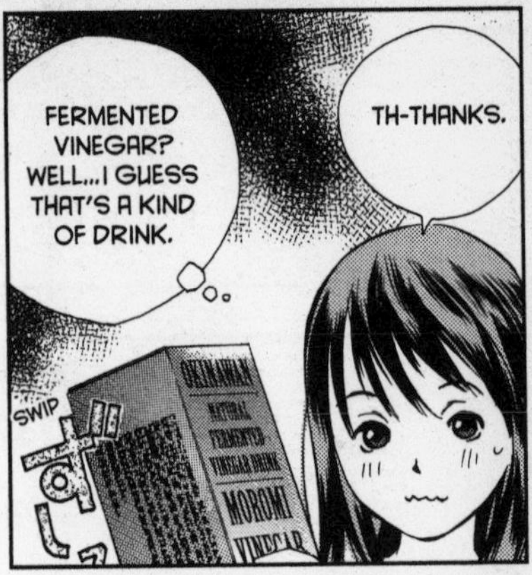
TH-THANKS.
FERMENTED VINEGAR? WELL...I GUESS THAT'S A KIND OF DRINK.
OKINAWAN
MOROMI
SWIP

Drinking vinegar, page 53

Moromi vinegar is a non-alcoholic fermented vinegar drink from Okinawa. It is said to have numerous health benefits. (This statement is not authorized by the FDA.)

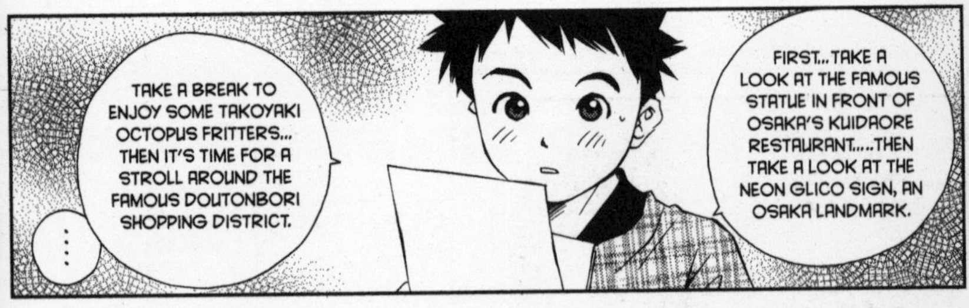
FIRST...TAKE A LOOK AT THE FAMOUS STATUE IN FRONT OF OSAKA'S KUIDAORE RESTAURANT.....THEN TAKE A LOOK AT THE NEON GLICO SIGN, AN OSAKA LANDMARK.
TAKE A BREAK TO ENJOY SOME TAKOYAKI OCTOPUS FRITTERS... THEN IT'S TIME FOR A STROLL AROUND THE FAMOUS DOUTONBORI SHOPPING DISTRICT.
....

Kuidaore, page 98

Osaka is known as a great culinary city. The restaurant Kuidaore, which literally means "eat til you collapse," is famous for the huge statue of its mascot character standing outside.

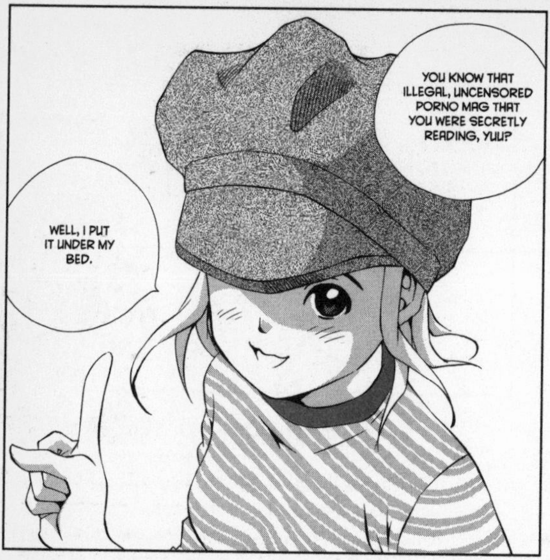
YOU KNOW THAT ILLEGAL, UNCENSORED PORNO MAG THAT YOU WERE SECRETLY READING, YUU?
WELL, I PUT IT UNDER MY BED.

Uncensored porn, page 101

In Japan, it's illegal for pornographic magazines and videos to show genitalia. All the naughty bits are blurred out. It's also illegal to bring any uncensored porn into the country, so do it at your own risk.

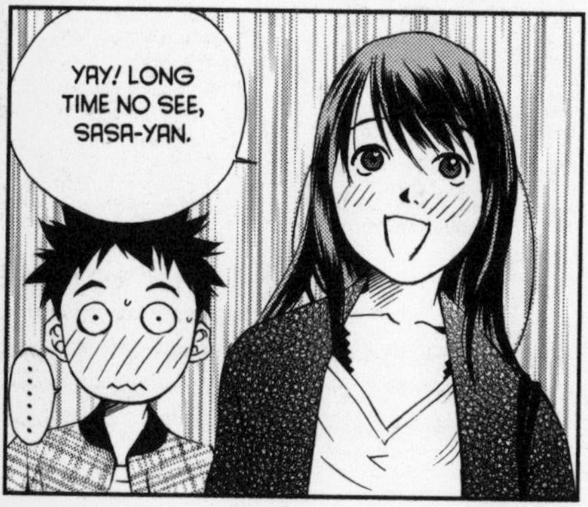
YAY! LONG TIME NO SEE, SASA-YAN.
......

Sasa-yan, page 106

The suffix *–yan* is sometimes added to a person's name (or an abbreviation of their name) to create a cute nickname.

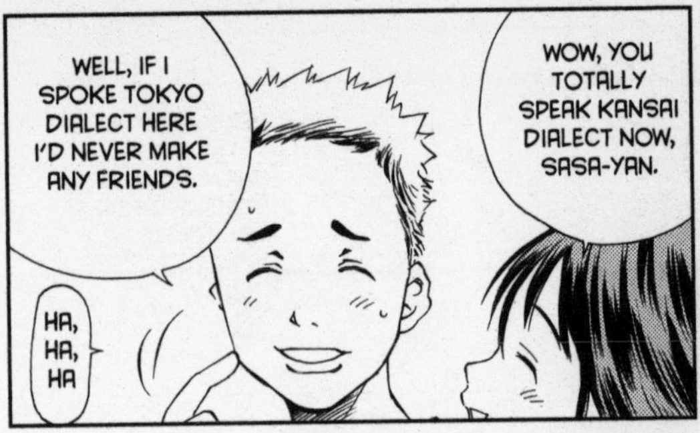
WOW, YOU TOTALLY SPEAK KANSAI DIALECT NOW, SASA-YAN.
WELL, IF I SPOKE TOKYO DIALECT HERE I'D NEVER MAKE ANY FRIENDS.
HA, HA, HA

Kansai-ben, page 109

Kansai-ben is the dialect in the Kansai region of Japan that includes Kobe, Kyoto, and Osaka. Kansai dialect is often thought of as somewhat brash and informal. Almost all stand-up comic duos speak in Kansai dialect.

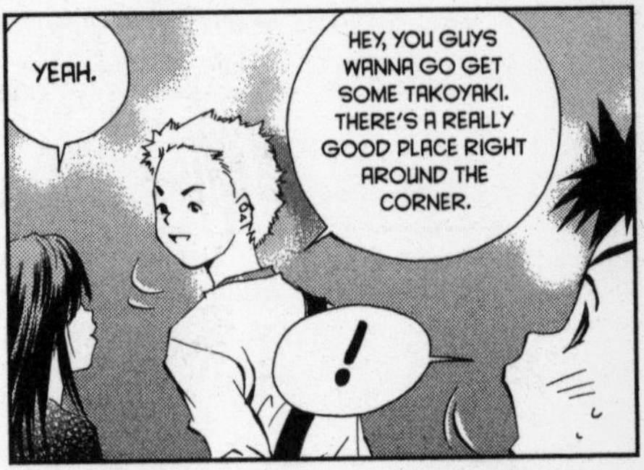
HEY, YOU GUYS WANNA GO GET SOME TAKOYAKI. THERE'S A REALLY GOOD PLACE RIGHT AROUND THE CORNER.
YEAH.
!

Takoyaki, page 110

Takoyaki, a popular snack food, are small, round octopus fritters. Although they are popular all over Japan, Osaka is particularly famous for its *takoyaki*.

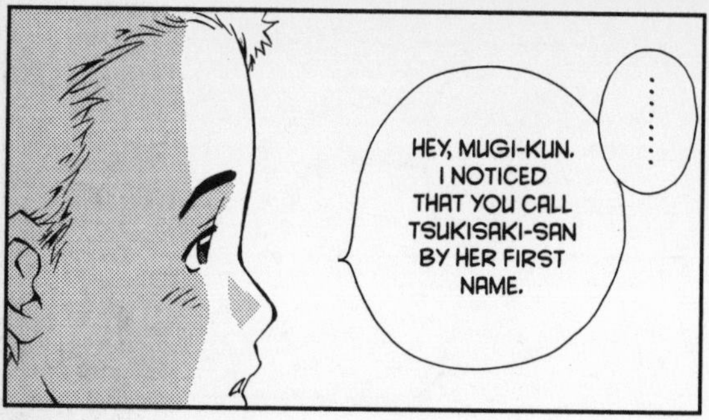
......
HEY, MUGI-KUN. I NOTICED THAT YOU CALL TSUKISAKI-SAN BY HER FIRST NAME.

Yuu, page 121

In Japan, calling someone by first name only shows a significant level of familiarity.

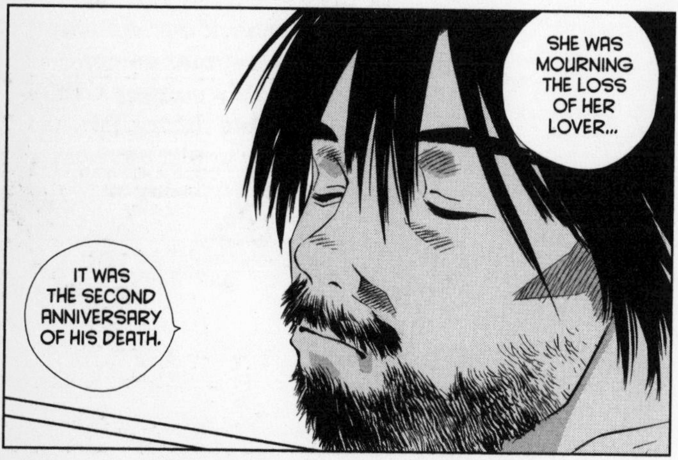
SHE WAS MOURNING THE LOSS OF HER LOVER...
IT WAS THE SECOND ANNIVERSARY OF HIS DEATH.

Sankaiki, page 175

Traditionally, the Japanese pay special tribute to their deceased loved ones on the second and seventh anniversaries of their deaths. These days are called *sankaiki* and *shicikaiki* respectively.

Preview of volume 11

We're pleased to present you a preview from volume 11. Please check our website (www.delreymanga.com) to see when this volume will be available in English. For now you'll have to make do with Japanese!

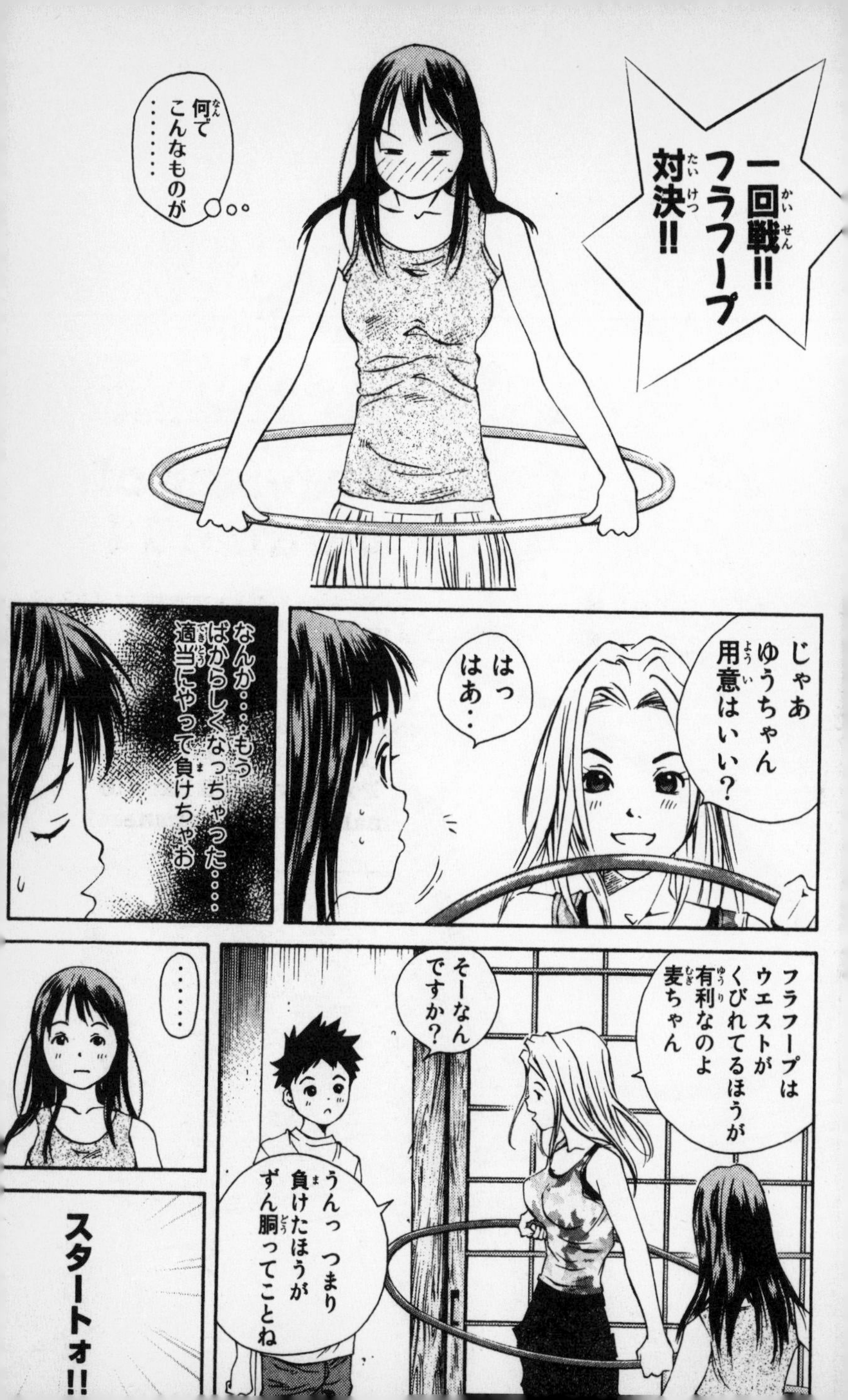

一回戦!! フラフープ対決!!
何でこんなものが・・・・・・・・
じゃあ ゆうちゃん 用意はいい?
はっ はあ・・
なんか……もう ばからしくなっちゃった…… 適当にやって負けちゃお
フラフープは ウエストが くびれてるほうが 有利なのよ 麦ちゃん
そーなん ですか?
うんっ つまり 負けたほうが ずん胴ってことね
……
スタートォ!!

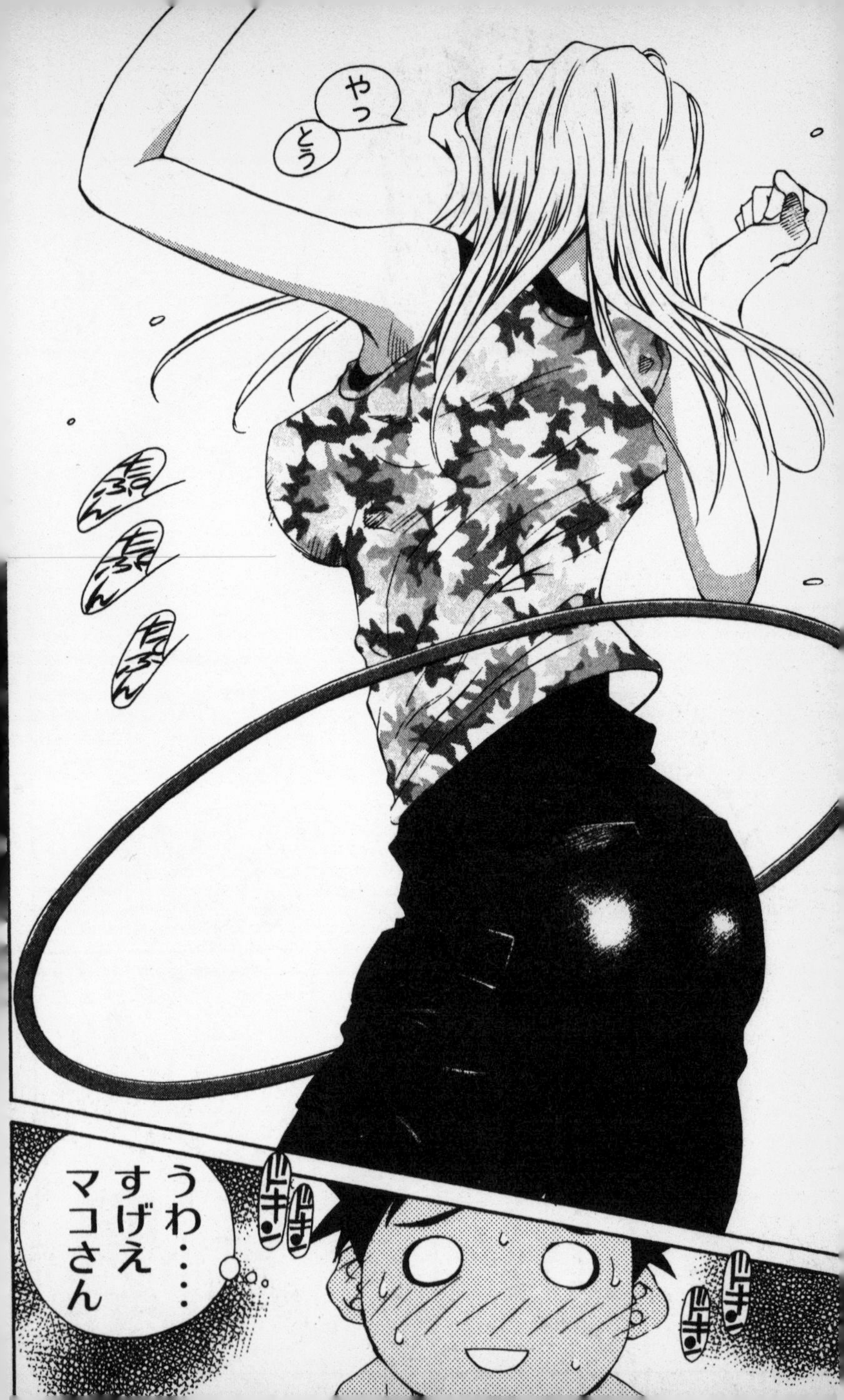
やっ
とう
うわ・・・すげえマコさん

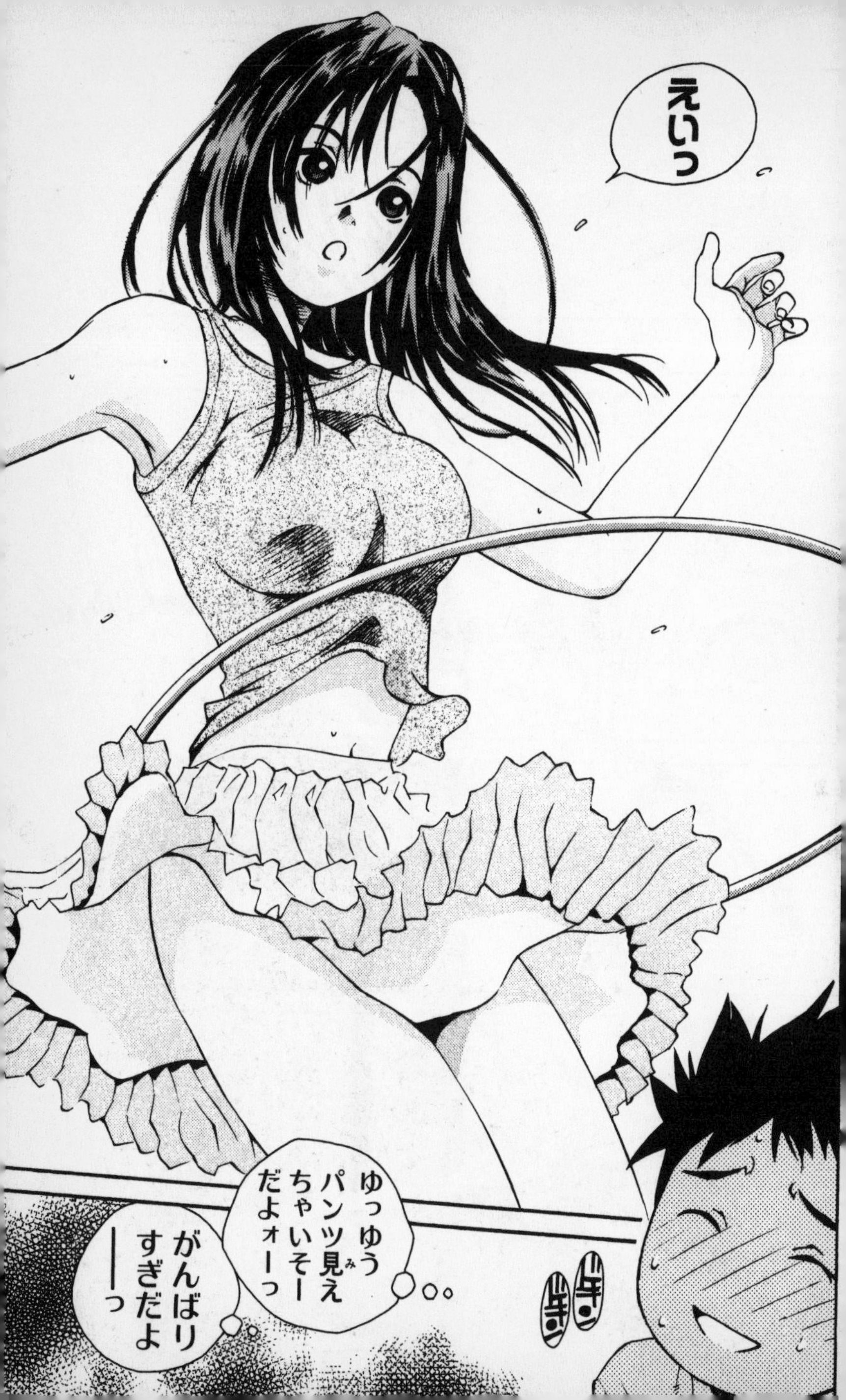
えいっ
ゆっゆうパンツ見えちゃいそーだよォーっ
がんばりすぎだよ——っ

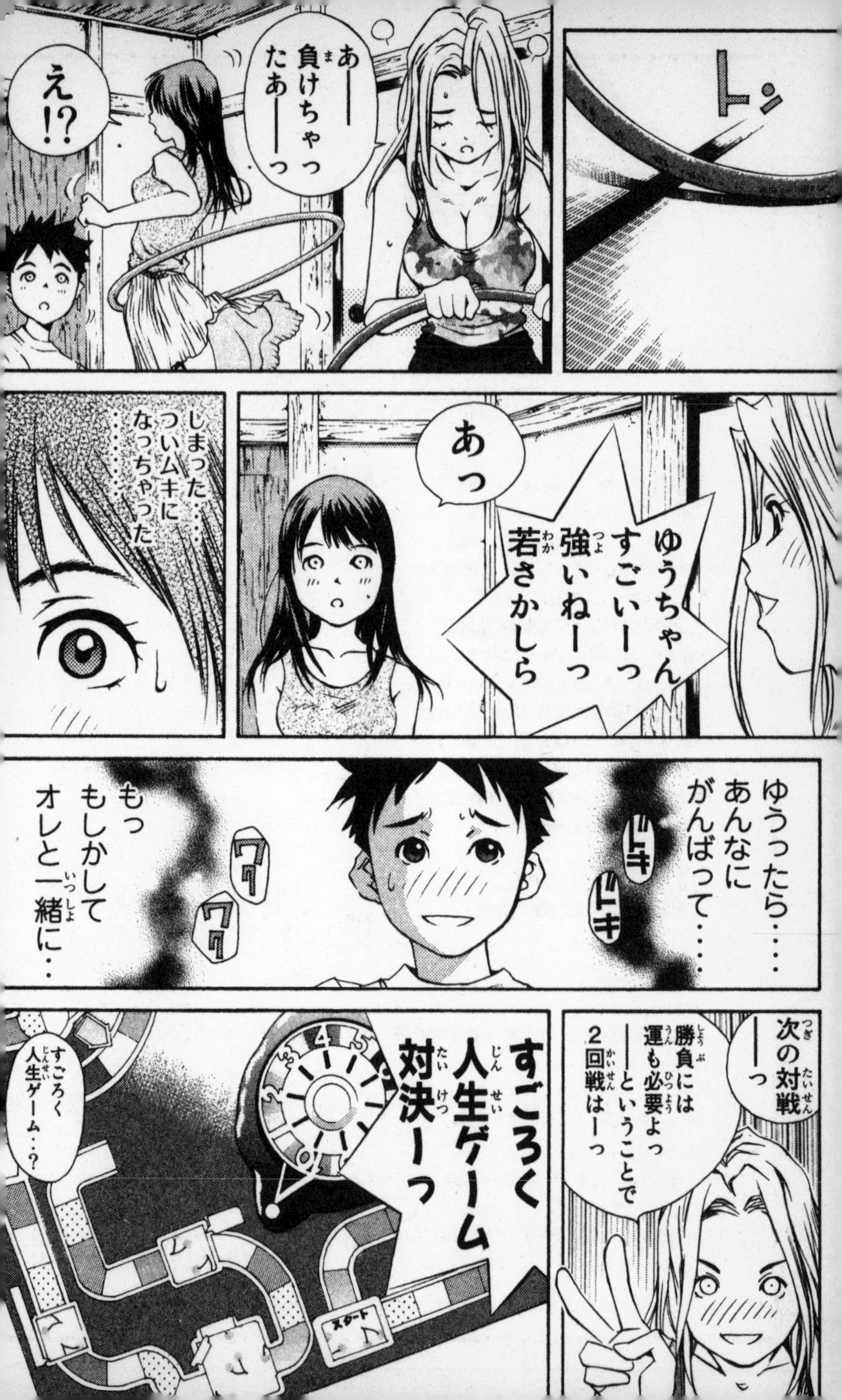
トン
あーー負けちゃったあーーっ
え!?
ゆうちゃんすごいーっ強いねーっ若さかしら
あっ
しまった……ついムキになっちゃった……
ゆうったら……あんなにがんばって……
ドキ
ドキ
ワク
ワク
もっもしかしてオレと一緒に…
次の対戦ーーっ
勝負には運も必要よっ ーーということで2回戦はーっ
すごろく人生ゲーム対決ーっ
すごろく人生ゲーム…?
スタート

Psycho Busters

MANGA BY AKINARI NAO
STORY BY YUYA AOKI

PSYCHIC TEENS ON THE RUN!

Psycho Busters
I
Manga by
Akinari Nao
Story by
Yuya Aoki,
the creator of
Get Backers

Out of the blue, a beautiful girl asks Kakeru to run away with her. This could be any boy's dream come true, but there's something strange afoot.

It turns out that this girl is on the run from a shadowy government organization intent on using her psychic abilities for its own nefarious ends. But why does she need Kakeru's help? Could it be that he has secret powers, too?

- **Story by Yuya Aoki, creator of *Get Backers***

Special extras in each volume! Read them all!

VISIT WWW.DELREYMANGA.COM TO:
- Read sample pages
- View release date calendars for upcoming volumes
- Sign up for Del Rey's free manga e-newsletter
- Find out the latest about new Del Rey Manga series

RATING T AGES 13+

DEL REY DEL REY MANGA デルレイ
The Otaku's Choice™

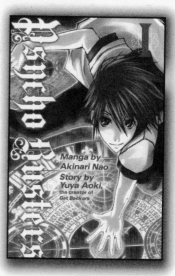

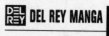

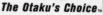

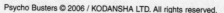

TOMARE!

STOP!

YOU'RE GOING THE WRONG WAY!

MANGA IS A COMPLETELY DIFFERENT TYPE OF READING EXPERIENCE.

TO START AT THE BEGINNING, GO TO THE END!

THAT'S RIGHT!

AUTHENTIC MANGA IS READ THE TRADITIONAL JAPANESE WAY—FROM RIGHT TO LEFT. EXACTLY THE *OPPOSITE* OF HOW AMERICAN BOOKS ARE READ. IT'S EASY TO FOLLOW: JUST GO TO THE OTHER END OF THE BOOK, AND READ EACH PAGE —AND EACH PANEL—FROM RIGHT SIDE TO LEFT SIDE, STARTING AT THE TOP RIGHT. NOW YOU'RE EXPERIENCING MANGA AS IT WAS MEANT TO BE.